There are forty-one problematic play texts, variously classified as 'bad quartos' or 'memorial reconstructions', from Shakespeare's time. Textual criticism of these quartos has been fraught with assumption and contradiction. Laurie Maguire examines all the texts in detail. She deconstructs the theories of W. W. Greg and his followers, scrutinising the methods by which critics diagnose texts as 'bad', and examines the historical evidence for the concept of memorial reconstruction (compilation from the recollection of actors or spectators).

A valuable feature of the study is the accompanying contextual information, including fresh analysis of the New Bibliographers, the rise of English studies, Renaissance oral culture, and textual problems in non-suspect texts.

The assembly of textual information about all forty-one suspect texts in easily accessible tabular form makes the book an essential reference work. The result is a study which covers a vast textual subject without sacrificing detail.

Shakespearean suspect texts

Shakespearean suspect texts

The 'bad' quartos and their contexts

LAURIE E. MAGUIRE

Associate Professor, University of Ottawa

CAMBRIDGE
UNIVERSITY PRESS

Published by the Press Syndicate of the University of Cambridge
The Pitt Building, Trumpington Street, Cambridge CB2 IRP
40 West 20th Street, New York, NY 10011-4211, USA
10 Stamford Road, Oakleigh, Melbourne 3166, Australia

First published 1996

Printed and bound in Great Britain by
Woolnough Bookbinding Ltd, Irthlingborough, Northamptonshire

A catalogue record for this book is available from the British Library

Library of Congress cataloguing in publication data
Maguire, Laurie E.
    Shakespearean suspect texts : the 'bad' quartos and their contexts
  / Laurie E. Maguire.
        p.   cm.
    Includes bibliographical references.
    ISBN 0 521 47364 0 (hc)
    1. Shakespeare, William, 1564-1616 – Criticism, Textual.
    2. Shakespeare, William, 1564-1616 – Bibliography – Quartos.
    I. Title.
    PR3071.M28   1996
    822.3'3-dc20   95-6177 CIP
    ISBN 0 521 47364 0 hardback

SE

[T]here is nothing either good or bad, but thinking makes it so

F *Hamlet* (TLN 1295–6)

Contents

Part Two

Acknowledgements

I have received generous help from many individuals and institutions during the preparation of this book; it is a pleasure to acknowledge my indebtedness and convey my thanks.

David Carlson read an entire draft at an early stage and provided copious and perspicacious comments, as did Thomas L. Berger and George Walton Williams. Irena R. Makaryk provided equally helpful feedback on a late version of chapter 2. Paul Werstine showed me how to be sceptical, and shaped chapters 2, 3, and 8 through his published papers and personal comments. Harold Jenkins shared with me his memories of Greg and McKerrow and his different perspective on the material I discuss in chapters 2 and 3. Elizabeth Joy Greg, Lady Newsam, was equally generous in sharing with me her memories and memorabilia of her father. Elizabeth M. Brennan first fanned my interest in matters Elizabethan and textual. Richard Proudfoot put his encyclopaedic knowledge at my disposal throughout the project and came to my aid frequently and at short notice.

Matt Proser and the Marlowe Society of America gave me the opportunity to present material on *The Massacre at Paris* at the MLA Convention in 1989. Diana Greenway and Laetitia Yeandle helped me work through Collier-related problems with the *Massacre at Paris* MS leaf, as did Janet Ing Freeman. I am indebted to Arthur Freeman and Janet Ing Freeman for the opportunity to consult Greg's annotated copy of Chambers's *The Elizabethan Stage* in their private collection. Arnold Hunt kindly lent me his photocopies of Greg's correspondence from the National Library of Scotland. Rosalind King engaged regularly in helpful discussion of textual and theatrical matters. Thomas Pettitt introduced me to ballad studies, and Eric Rasmussen responded to a plea for information at a crucial moment, as did David Staines, Jeremy Maule and Brian Vickers. Michael Warren and Herbert Weil provided initial encouragement for the project, and Kathleen

Irace sent me her then unpublished work on *Reforming the 'Bad' Quartos*. Both Michael Warren and Kathleen Irace provided astute comments on the first draft of the manuscript; I am grateful to them for their careful readings.

David Burke, Jimmy Gardiner, David Snodin, Donald Sumpter, and John Wilders responded helpfully to my inquiries about the BBC Television Shakespeare series. Paul Marcus gave freely of his time to discuss his RSC production of *The Massacre at Paris*. My indefatigable research assistant, Gwendolyn Guth, collated BBC Television films and texts, checked all the tables and contributed to several of them; Laura Denker provided invaluable eleventh-hour assistance.

My debts to libraries and librarians are numerous. Much of the book was researched and written in the Senate House Library of the University of London during 1992–3; the marvellous resources of the Senate House Periodicals Room enabled me to read all of Greg's publications quickly and chronologically. The staff of all the libraries whose collections I have used have been unfailingly helpful and courteous, so it is misleading to single out a few for special mention. However, Susan Brock of the Shakespeare Institute Library, and Colin Shrimpton of the Estates Office at Alnwick Castle were unstinting of time and expertise over a period of years. David McKitterick of Trinity College Library, Cambridge provided much assistance throughout my sojourn in Cambridge. The staff of the British Library Students' Room and North Library, the BBC Written Archives Centre, Lambeth Palace Library, the Bodleian Library, the Stratford-on-Avon Record Office, the Shakespeare Centre Library and Archives (Stratford-on-Avon), the Institute of Historical Research of the University of London, the Library of University College London, Newcastle upon Tyne University Library, the Folger Shakespeare Library, the National Library of Canada, the University of Ottawa Library, and Carleton University Library have helped lighten my labours in their reading rooms. I am grateful to Martin Secker and Warburg Ltd for permission to quote from 'The Marcellus Version' by Roy Fuller.

Early stages of this work were made possible by grants from the University of Ottawa University Research Fund and Faculty of Arts Research Fund; however, the project could never have been completed in its present form without a Stipendiary Release award from the Social Sciences and Humanities Research Council of Canada which released me from teaching duties in 1992–3. I am grateful to SSHRC for such timely support.

Friends and colleagues have been unstinting of time and patience throughout this project: Thomas Berger, Dympna Callaghan, David Carlson, Donald Childs, Frances Dolan, Lynn Hulse, Richard Proudfoot, and Rebecca Whiting offered much support and advice. My expression of appreciation can be but meagre recompense.

Quotations

Unless otherwise indicated, quotations from Renaissance plays have been taken from Malone Society Reprints (referred to by TLN), or Tudor Facsimile Texts, Scolar Press Facsimiles, and STC Microfilms (referred to by signature). All modern-spelling quotations from Shakespeare come from the Riverside Shakespeare, ed. G. Blakemore Evans. Quotations from Marlowe and from Beaumont and Fletcher come from the editions by Fredson Bowers (unless otherwise indicated), and quotations from Webster come from the New Mermaids volumes of individual plays edited by Elizabeth M. Brennan. Where modern editions of other non-Shakespearean texts have been used, the editor is indicated in the notes. In all quotations of dramatic dialogue I have expanded and capitalised speech prefixes and followed them with a colon.

Abbreviations

The following abbreviations are used throughout:

ELH	*Journal of English Literary History*
ELR	*English Literary Renaissance*
JEGP	*Journal of English and Germanic Philology*
Library	*The Library*
MLA	Modern Languages Association of America
MLN	*Modern Language Notes*
MLQ	*Modern Language Quarterly*
MLR	*Modern Language Review*
Mod. Phil.	*Modern Philology*
MaRDiE	*Medieval and Renaissance Drama in England*
MSR	Malone Society Reprint
N & Q	*Notes and Queries*
NLH	*New Literary History*
PBA	*Proceedings of the British Academy*
PBSA	*Proceedings of the Bibliographical Society of America*
PMLA	*Publications of the Modern Language Association*
PQ	*Philological Quarterly*
RD	*Renaissance Drama*
RES	*Review of English Studies*
RP	*Renaissance Papers*
SAA	Shakespeare Association of America
SB	*Studies in Bibliography*
SEL	*Studies in English Literature*
SN	*Shakespeare Newsletter*
SP	*Studies in Philology*
SQ	*Shakespeare Quarterly*
TLS	*Times Literary Supplement*
UTQ	*University of Toronto Quarterly*

The following abbreviations of play titles are used in chapter 5 and in the tables in chapter 8.

A&C	Antony and Cleopatra
Arden	Arden of Feversham
BBA	The Blind Beggar of Alexandria
1 Cont	1 Contention
Death	The Death of Robert, Earl of Huntingdon
DrF	Dr Faustus
Ed1	Edward 1
Ed2	Edward 2
FB	Friar Bacon and Friar Bungay
FV	The Famous Victories of Henry 5
Ham	Hamlet
1H4	1 Henry 4
2H4	2 Henry 4
H5	Henry 5
2H6	2 Henry 6
3H6	3 Henry 6
1 Hier	1 Hieronimo
HDM	An Humorous Day's Mirth
1 IfYou	1 If You Know Not Me, You Know Nobody
JB	John of Bordeaux
JC	Julius Caesar
JM	The Jew of Malta
KKHM	A Knack to Know an Honest Man
KKK	A Knack to Know A Knave
MP	The Massacre at Paris
MT	The Maid's Tragedy
MDE	The Merry Devil of Edmonton
MWW	The Merry Wives of Windsor
OF	Orlando Furioso
OWT	The Old Wife's Tale
Phil	Philaster
R3	Richard 3
R&J	Romeo and Juliet
ST	The Spanish Tragedy

STW   *Sir Thomas Wyatt*
TTR3 *The True Tragedy of Richard 3*
TTRDY *The True Tragedy of Richard Duke of York*
WT   *The Winter's Tale*
YT   *A Yorkshire Tragedy*

Part One

1 | Introduction

> [I]f scholars were misguided in their assessments of the two original printed texts of *King Lear* – if . . . these are not two *relatively corrupted* texts of a pure (but now lost) original, but two *relatively reliable* texts of two different versions of the play (as we now think) – then our general methods for dealing with such texts [are] called into serious question.
>
> Jerome McGann[1]

In the fifteen-year period 1594–1609, versions of eighteen recently performed Shakespearean plays reached print in inexpensive quarto or octavo editions. From the beginning of the Shakespeare editorial tradition in the eighteenth century, editors and textual critics have been particularly perplexed by five of these playtexts: Q1 *Romeo and Juliet* (1597), Q1 *Henry 5* (1600), Q1 *The Merry Wives of Windsor* (1602), Q1 *Hamlet* (1603), Q1 *Pericles* (1609).

This perplexity was caused by the suspicion that the London play-reading public was being offered a product very different from that given the London play-going public (even though all of these texts advertised recent performance on their title-pages).[2] Certain unusual features in these first editions (imperfect metre, blunt dialogue, and allegedly jejune depiction of characters and development of situations) were deemed incompatible with composition by a proficient commercial playwright and performance by a leading company. Furthermore, these five early playtexts were all suspiciously brief (particularly in comparison with subsequent quarto versions released during Shakespeare's lifetime, and with the Folio collection of Shakespeare's works prepared by his theatre colleagues, Heminge and Condell, after his death).[3]

Comparison of these first editions with the later versions revealed much textual reordering/disordering of phrasing, the earlier text being considered the poorer; in some instances these first editions provided totally different action; and, most significantly, in all instances their text had been rejected by Heminge and Condell as copy for their Folio collection. Following a suggestion by A. W. Pollard in 1909, modern critics came to agree that Heminge and Condell had these five playtexts in mind (and possibly others; see below) when, in an address '*To the great Variety of Readers*', prefaced to the First Folio, they inveighed against the 'frauds and stealthes of iniurious impostors' who had deceived the book-buying public with 'stolne, and surreptitious copies'. Heminge and Condell invite the prospective buyer to ignore these playtexts, all of which have been replaced in the Folio with texts which are 'perfect of their limbes'.[4]

Pollard's analysis of Heminge and Condell's rhetoric was (and still is) considered of the greatest importance in that it solved one of textual studies' besetting problems: to which texts were Heminge and Condell referring as 'stolne, and surreptitious'? To clarify matters Pollard christened the five perplexing quarto texts 'bad', thus differentiating them from the 'good' quartos (whose texts Heminge and Condell printed in the Folio without substantial change).[5] In 1910 W. W. Greg subjected one of Pollard's 'bad' quartos, that of *The Merry Wives of Windsor* (1602), to close analysis, and offered an explanation for the text's poor quality and evident abbreviation. The quarto, he suggested, could have been concocted from memory principally by the actor who had played the part of 'mine Host'.[6] Greg's suggestion provides the foundation for the phenomenon we now know as 'memorial reconstruction' or 'reporting'.

Refined and adapted over the years by Greg and his successors, the constituent elements of memorial reconstruction are as follows: actors deprived of the playbook of a text they had performed in London;[7] actors on tour in the provinces, probably during the plague periods during which the London authorities enforced closure of the city's theatres; provincial audiences with less theatrical stamina and cruder artistic palates requiring shorter plays and more comic turns; actors' inaccurate memories producing a nonetheless actable text in which accidental memorial omission and deliberate abridgement coexist with gratuitous memorial expansion of comic lines and situations designed to please the less sophisticated; and adaptation to enable the company to perform with the reduced numbers thought to typify touring companies. Although the text was reconstructed to provide a playbook for performance, the actors evidently did not object to profiting further from their mental effort, and so sold the text to a stationer when they returned to the Capital. Individually or together, these details feature in the introductions to most recent scholarly editions of Shakespeare plays which exist in a 'bad' text, and the scenario, unconvincing as it may sound when its salient features are listed thus bluntly, has become a *sine qua non* of textual studies. As recently as 1982, Harold Jenkins could describe the identification of memorial reconstruction as 'one of the achievements of twentieth-century textual scholarship'.[8]

Pollard's group of five 'bad' texts, listed above, was later supplemented by Q1 *The Taming of A Shrew* (1594), Q1 *1 Contention* (1594), and O1 *Richard Duke of York* (1595). Despite the variant titles, and the sometimes marked verbal and structural divergences from the putative originals, these texts were held to be 'bad' versions of Shakespeare's *The Taming of the Shrew*, *2 Henry 6*, and *3 Henry 6*. To this group of eight texts was then added Q1 *Richard 3* (1597) and Q1 *King Lear* (1608), although, since these quartos were verbally closer to their counterparts in the First Folio than were those in the group of eight, they were sometimes classified as 'doubtful' (i.e. potentially 'bad' but not incontrovertibly so). Nonetheless, the view that memorial reconstruction also lay behind these two texts received substantial support. The higher level of accuracy in these texts was explained by a number of postulates: group reconstruction; supplementation from shorthand; better memory or greater familiarity with the original on the part of the reporter(s).

The concept of memorial reconstruction was thus applied to an extraordinarily heterogeneous collection of texts, from the verbally sound and dramatically sophisticated *Richard Duke of York* and *Richard 3*, to the short and staccato *Pericles* and *The Merry Wives of Windsor*. These texts, although grouped together as 'bad', actually had little in common beyond their exclusion from the First Folio. Nonetheless memorial reconstruction was adopted as a blanket classification for these ten Shakespearean texts, ossifying Greg's original tentative suggestion into textual orthodoxy.[9]

There are, however, several weak spots in the theory of memorial reconstruction as formulated by Greg and adopted by most of his successors. The first is its reliance on unproven and sometimes illogical assumptions. The largest assumption – that memorially reconstructed texts must have been made for the purposes of performance – has proved the most durable. It was 1990 before Paul Werstine first queried it, and in 1994 Janette Dillon objected to an unproven symbiosis: she argued that it was only the theory that actors were responsible for memorial reconstruction that had led to the hypothesis that memorial reconstructions were made for performance.[10]

To this performance hypothesis is added the scenario of provincial performance.[11] Greg acknowledges that his scenario depends not only on touring in the provinces but on prolonged touring (time being required for progressive adaptation of the playing text);[12] but, as E. K. Chambers pointed out in 1924, there is no evidence that drama was specially adapted or shortened for touring purposes, nor is there evidence that provincial audiences required shorter or bawdier plays. These hypotheses may indeed prevail but, in the absence of firm evidence, it seems unwise to found a theory on them.[13] Elizabethan drama did not replace medieval drama overnight but grew up alongside it; there are records of mystery cycles being performed in provincial towns as late as the 1570s and 1580s. It is hard to believe that local tradesmen could perform and watch these marathon medieval sequences with their theological and moral profundity (familiar though this was) yet be unable to tolerate sixteen lines of Juliet's lyric utterance. Indeed, towns such as York and Coventry were affluent textile centres and their culture may have been relatively sophisticated. We simply do not know as much as we would like about provincial aesthetic standards.

The second problem with Greg's argument paradoxically accounts for its popularity. The theory is capacious, being able to explain almost any textual problem. Thus: the text deteriorates towards the end? – the reporter's memory was flagging, or the character he played was dead and offstage. The text is consistently good? – it is a group reconstruction. One part is exceptionally good? – the reporter played that character, or perhaps a copy of his written part was available. Staging requirements are simple? – that indicates provincial auspices. The play is short? – that also indicates provincial auspices. The text is good? – the reporter was conscientious, his memory good. The text is bad? – the reporter only had a minor role. The action varies significantly from the later printed version? – it is a report of a revised version. Conveniently, the concept of memorial reconstruction can be expanded (and allied unobtrusively with other concepts) to explain textual, social, dramatic, economic, and demographic issues; like Lavache's 'O Lord sir', it serves fit to answer all questions. But, as Greg remarked in another context, 'an hypothesis which can explain anything is as useless as one which can explain nothing'.[14]

The enthusiasm with which the theory of memorial reconstruction was accepted can best be understood in relation to earlier theories held to account for suspect texts. Eighteenth- and nineteenth-century editors had explained these texts as 1) source plays, 2) rough drafts by the young Shakespeare, 3) reports made in longhand by a thief in the audience, 4) reports made in shorthand by a thief in the audience, or 5) a combination of the above. The objections which were subsequently advanced to refute these five theories can be briefly summarised.

The evidently close relationship between the pairs of Q/F texts means that if, as theory 1 advocates, the earlier version served as source, there existed a dramatist with Shakespeare's ability in plotting, gift for character-isation, and interest in poetical experimentation who has left no other trace of his work. This is either unfortunate, or, as critics came to realise, improb-able. Theory 2 presents Shakespeare 'in the workshop', where G. I. Duthie, among others, objected to the notion of a Shakespeare who graduated very rapidly from 'quite miserable ineptitude in his early days to complete per-fection within comparatively few years'.[15] The view contained in theory 3 is supported by external testimonies to the frequent presence of table-books in playhouses. This theory involves the complicating factor of theft – someone trying to acquire a text without the company's knowledge (the motive behind the acquisition being open to various interpretations) – and the objections to this were two-fold: a scribe with pencil (or pen) and paper would surely be an obvious presence in the playhouse; and, if this method of play reproduction were a threat to the players, it is hard to see why (since the suspect texts appeared over a number of years) they did not employ someone within the theatre to be alert to potential offenders – a textual bouncer, pledging (in the manner of Horatio): 'If he steale ought the whil'st this Play is Playing, / And scape detecting, I will pay the Theft' (*Hamlet* TLN 1940–1). Theory 4, being a variant of theory 3, invites the same objec-tions, added to which not one of the shorthand systems before 1602 was known to be capable of reproducing a play, and none in the decade before or after was intended to.

Enter, then, memorial reconstruction, a theory which has two attractions: it is economic, allowing us to dispense with source plays, shorthand, longhand note-taking, revision, or any combination of the above; and it is versatile, being able to explain almost any textual problem (even if, as we have seen, it sometimes requires supplementation from other theories).

Sustained challenges to the concept and application of memorial reconstruction first came with re-examination of Q1 *King Lear*. In 1976 Michael Warren presented an analysis of *King Lear* at the International Shakespeare Congress in Washington. Focusing on the differences between Edgar and Albany in Q and F, differences which 'go beyond those which may be expected when two texts descend in corrupted form from a common original', he concluded that 'a substantial and consistent recasting of certain aspects of the play has taken place'.[16] In other words both texts were written by Shakespeare, both are 'good'; F *King Lear* is a Shakespearean text representing the author's second thoughts after composition and production of the equally Shakespearean Q *King Lear*. Steven Urkowitz argued in a similar manner in 1980 in *Shakespeare's Revision of King Lear* (the title serves as summary), and over the next three years Michael Warren and Gary Taylor edited *The Division of the Kingdoms*, a collection of twelve essays committed to the exploration of Q and F *King Lear* as alternative texts.

As the 1980s progressed, the challenge to memorial reconstruction widened. Hibbard and Werstine investigated the question of revision in relation to *Hamlet*, and Taylor applied it to *Henry 5*.[17] In a series of papers Urkowitz expressed doubts about memorial reconstruction as a viable explanation for Q1 *1 Contention*, O1 *Richard Duke of York*, Q1 *Romeo and Juliet*, Q1 *Richard 3*, Q1 *The Merry Wives of Windsor*, and Q1 *Hamlet*, championing instead the notion of Shakespearean revision in all of these plays. Randall McLeod queried the validity of the distinction drawn by Pollard between 'good' and 'bad' quartos, and his denial of the usefulness of these terms received support from Scott McMillin in two separate studies of casting.[18] This flurry of textual inquiry challenged the twentieth century's most deeply rooted beliefs and cherished assumptions about 'bad' quartos.

Whether or not one acknowledges revision as a replacement paradigm for memorial reconstruction,[19] it is obvious that this diagnostic *volte face* on *King Lear* has dealt a severe blow to the linked concepts of 'bad' quartos and memorial reconstruction. If Q *King Lear* is indeed a *bona fide* authorial text rather than a corrupt memorial derivative, how had we misdiagnosed it for so long?[20] How could the 'evidence' for memorial reconstruction suddenly become 'evidence' for revision? Does the phenomenon of memorial reconstruction exist? If so, what constitutes reliable evidence for it? Current theories invoking revision do not simply question our conclusions; they undermine our methods. And if our methods were faulty in classifying Q *King Lear* as 'memorial', why should we retain this diagnosis for the other Shakespearean playtexts on the blacklist of memorial reconstructions? What need ten be memorial, or five? What need one? Furthermore, how many non-Shakespearean playtexts had been similarly misdiagnosed?

These are the questions which lie behind the present study. Starting from a position of interrogative scepticism, my aim is to chart the topography of an area which is riddled with problems from ignorance at one end to false assurance at the other, with confusion occupying the middle ground.

This confusion has as its origin the following: 1) our criteria for diagnosing the textual effects of faulty memory in playtexts are unmethodical; 2) our understanding of how Elizabethan memory operated and what it aimed to achieve is hypothetical; 3) our textual context is negligible; and 4) our terminology is casual. The detailed analysis in the ensuing chapters will demonstrate that this four-fold claim is not exaggerated. The discussion in this introduction illustrates but the heart of the confusion.

The first two categories, diagnostic criteria and understanding of the *modus operandi* of Elizabethan memory, can be considered together. Traditional attempts to diagnose ('prove') the influence of faulty memory in a playtext typically rely on a heterogeneous collection of textual quiddities. Consider the following four approaches, not one of which doubts that we know what characterises a reported text, yet all of which place different emphases on a miscellaneous range of evidence.

A. S. Cairncross tells us that Q1 *1 Contention* 'has all the recognized features of . . . a report – abbreviation, transposition of material, the use of synonyms, recollections external and internal; with inferior metre, and verse wrongly divided as prose'.[21] Brian Gibbons finds in Q1 *Romeo and Juliet* 'anticipations, recollections, transpositions, paraphrases, summaries, repetitions and omissions of words, phrases or lines correctly presented in Q2'.[22] For H. J. Oliver, Q1 *The Taming of A Shrew* suffers from lack of literary merit, weakness in meaning, incompetent versification, slackness in diction, incompetent storytelling, superfluous stage directions. He adds: '[f]eeble repetition of words is one of the many characteristics that *A Shrew* shares with acknowledged "Bad Quartos". A further instance is the willingness to begin several successive lines with "and"'.[23] In his preface to the BBC TV Shakespeare edition of *Richard 3* John Wilders tells us that the First Quarto of the play 'seems to have been what is called a "memorial reconstruction"; in other words, it was dictated to the printer from memory by some of the actors who had taken part in it and their memories were not altogether accurate.'[24]

The above examples indiscriminately combine features of process ('dictated to the printer'), origin ('actors who had taken part in it'), literary judgement ('incompetent storytelling'), and mnemonic psychology ('anticipations, recollections' and so on). They are a heterogeneous collection, rather than a meaningful hierarchy. The disadvantages of such eclecticism are best illustrated in an article by Harry R. Hoppe in which 'mislining' as a symptom of deficient memory jostles shoulders with 'repetition'.[25] Furthermore, every one of the above features mentioned by Cairncross, Gibbons, and Oliver, can, individually, be paralleled in playtexts which are not considered by critics to be memorially reconstructed. When does incompetent versification, or lack of literary merit, or transposition, or dictation suggest memorial reconstruction rather than a hack writer, or collaborative authorship, or a revising playwright, or an overworked scribe, to name but a few of the possibilities? Where is the dividing line?

This diagnostic double-standard was inadvertently revealed by Greg in an analysis of Chapman's 'negligence or oversight' in *A Humorous Day's Mirth* (1599). Of one fifteen-line speech Greg commented:

> The conceit may not be wholly to our taste, but the writing is characteristic enough and not lacking in vigour. It is plain however from the *repetitions* and the *breakdown of grammar* and *metre* that the passage cannot have been meant to stand as it now appears. Exactly by what process of *revision* and *interlineation* it reached its present chaotic state it is impossible to say. [my emphasis][26]

Here Greg uses repetitions and broken-down grammar and verse to support a hypothesis of revision and interlining; elsewhere (in *Two*

Elizabethan Stage Abridgements, for example), he uses the same evidence to support a hypothesis of memorial reconstruction. Greg serendipitously calls attention to our dilemma: the difficulty of finding features which are *exclusively* indicative of memorial reconstruction.

Judging from the studies of 'bad' texts to date it seems that the diagnostic criterion is accumulation: the more examples from the features cited above by Cairncross *et al.* that the 'bad' text has, the more likely it is to be memorially reconstructed. This incremental technique might be of some use if it did not accord all putative indications of faulty memory equal value: one descriptive stage direction equals one mangled verse line, and one repeated word equals one transposition. But surely some indications are more equal than others? Surely some hierarchy ought to prevail?

This lack of diagnostic rigour is evident in early studies by Greg, Hoppe, and Kirschbaum (all of which include some non-Shakespearean 'bad' texts). Kirschbaum's otherwise useful 'Census of Bad Quartos' made no attempt to analyse the procedure for identifying memorially reconstructed texts, relying instead on a miscellany of textual infelicities, and impressionistic statements like the following:

> Having completed an exhaustive examination of the extant *Pericles*, I can report that all the various kinds of corruption found in it have their parallel in other bad versions.

> There are in Q [*A Knack to Know an Honest Man*] certain characteristics of bad quartos in general which definitely admit it into the category of such texts. I cannot go into the matter at present. The apparent corruption of the following lines should be evidence enough: [quotation of lines 159–68].

> *George a Greene* . . . is clearly as 'maimed and deformed' a report as *Orlando Furioso*. The following lines cannot conceivably be as the author wrote them [quotation of lines 543–82].[27]

Hoppe's work depends on circular reasoning: other plays contain features typical of memorial reconstruction (e.g. *The Blind Beggar of Alexandria*, *John of Bordeaux*, *The Old Wife's Tale*); Q1 *Romeo and Juliet* shares many of these features; *ergo* Q1 *Romeo and Juliet* is a memorial reconstruction. Kathleen Irace's computer-assisted study is a more precise variant of the old methodology, which assumes the text under examination to be a report, identifies the reporter, and thereby confirms that the text is reported.[28] Methods of detecting memorially reconstructed texts have not changed significantly during this century.

Clearly a greater understanding of the operation of memory, particularly Elizabethan memory, and the potential textual effects of its malfunction, is required. (Critics regularly talk about identifying memory in 'bad' quartos, when what they mean is identifying faulty memory.) The lapses to which memory is prone need to be investigated rather than assumed, for until we know what the textual effects of faulty memory are, we will not be able to ascertain whether memorial reconstruction exists.

The third confusion, narrowness of context, clouds all studies of 'bad' texts to date. Critics concentrate primarily on the relevant Shakespearean texts with little regard to the more numerous non-Shakespearean 'bad' texts. This insularity has prevented us from placing memorial reconstruction in its wider context.

The history of memorial reconstruction is, regrettably, if inevitably, the history of Shakespearean texts. Bardolatory necessitates an exhaustive examination of Shakespearean playtexts in all their versions, and the actors and performance conditions and stationers and compositors associated with them; in addition, the Shakespearean 'bad' quartos have invited study because of the comparative exercise enabled by the existence of 'good' quartos. But if memorial reconstruction was a widespread phenomenon, plays other than Shakespeare's would surely have been affected. What is their textual condition and their companies' circumstances?

To answer these questions I had first to compile a list of all playtexts, Shakespearean and non-Shakespearean (complete play or part of play), which critics had seen reason to classify as memorial. This list contains forty-one texts which have been identified confidently, or suggested tentatively, as memorial reconstructions by the New Bibliographers and their successors. It will be helpful to relate the development of this list.

In 1909 Pollard established the category of suspect texts with five offerings: Q1 *Romeo and Juliet* (1597), Q1 *Henry 5* (1600), Q1 *The Merry Wives of Windsor* (1602), Q1 *Hamlet* (1603), and Q1 *Pericles* (1609). This group was supplemented in 1919 by Greg's addition of Greene's *Orlando Furioso* (Q 1594), and the fly-scene of *Titus Andronicus* (not printed until the

Folio of 1623). Between 1924 and 1929 Peter Alexander identified Q1 *The Taming of A Shrew* (1594), Q1 *1 Contention* (1594), and O1 *Richard Duke of York* (1595) as suspect texts. Two further Shakespearean titles were added shortly afterwards: Q1 *King Lear* (1608) in 1930 (suggested by E. K. Chambers) and Q1 *Richard 3* (1597) in 1936 (suggested by D. L. Patrick).[29]

The swelling numbers of suspect texts received a substantial boost from Kirschbaum's 'Census of Bad Quartos', published in 1938. Criticism of suspect texts, he felt, was 'largely in a state of chaos, because *no scholar . . . has ever taken the trouble to ascertain how many bad quartos there really are*'.[30] In an attempt to remedy that deficiency he added to the existing group of twelve a further ten: Marlowe's *The Massacre at Paris* (undated octavo), Peele's *Edward 1* (Q 1593), the anonymous *Fair Em* (undated Q), the anonymous *The True Tragedy of Richard 3* (Q 1594), the anonymous *A Knack to Know an Honest Man* (Q 1596), the anonymous *George a Greene* (Q 1599), Heywood's *1 If You Know Not Me You Know Nobody* (Q 1605), Chettle, Dekker, Heywood, Webster, and Smith's *Sir Thomas Wyatt* (Q 1607), the parliament scene of *Richard 2* (first published in Q4 1608), and Beaumont and Fletcher's *Philaster* (Q1 1620). In 1945 he added *The Fair Maid of Bristow* (Q 1605), and in 1946 the A-text of Marlowe's *Dr Faustus* (1604).[31] H. T. Price had, in the meantime, declared *The Famous Victories of Henry 5* (Q 1598; SR 1594) 'certainly a bad quarto, if ever there was one',[32] while G. I. Duthie added Q1 *The Maid's Tragedy* (1619), thus endorsing Kirschbaum's tentative suspicion, expressed in 1938 in a footnote.[33] In his edition of the play, William Abrams had aired the possibility of *The Merry Devil of Edmonton* (1608) being memorial.[34] This brought the total to twenty-seven.

In 1948 Hoppe built on the foundations provided by Kirschbaum, adding the anonymous MS play *John of Bordeaux* (n.d.), Peele's *The Old Wife's Tale* (Q 1595), and Chapman's *The Blind Beggar of Alexandria* (Q 1598). In 1949 Greg and Nichol Smith suggested that the additions to *The Spanish Tragedy* (first printed in the quarto of 1602) were memorially reconstructed, as were, E. A. J. Honigmann declared (in 1954), *1* and *2 Troublesome Reign* (quartos 1591) and the anonymous *Death of Robert, Earl of Huntingdon* (Q 1601).[35] In 1955 Kirschbaum added Q1 *Mucedorus* (1598).[36] At various times in subsequent years *A Knack to Know a Knave* (Q 1594), *Arden of Feversham* (Q 1592), *1 Hieronimo* (Q 1605), *A Yorkshire Tragedy* (Q 1608), *Thomas Lord Cromwell* (Q 1602), and *Jack Straw* (Q 1593) were identified as, or suspected of being, memorial reconstructions, so that by 1990 anyone wishing to embark on a comparative study of suspect texts had forty-one playtexts with which to work.[37]

With only three exceptions (the A and B texts of *Dr Faustus*, Q1 and Q2 *The Maid's Tragedy*, and Q1 and Q2 *Philaster*) the non-Shakespearean playtexts exist only in single versions: their 'bad' texts were never replaced by 'good' (or if they were, those 'good' texts have not survived).[38] The absence of a 'good' version for comparison is serendipitous. Comparisons, we do not need to be reminded, are odious; the parallel-text 'good'/'bad' investigations which characterise textual approaches to Shakespeare cause as many problems as they solve. Obviously, when any two different items are compared, one will seem inferior; textual investigators too readily construe this as 'memorial'. (The damaging effects of this are most visible in the vocabulary of parallel-text studies; in Hoppe's analysis of *Romeo and Juliet*, for example, Q1 does not simply assign speeches to different characters, it assigns them to the *wrong* characters.)

The picture changes if we concentrate on 'bad' texts, comparing 'bad' with other 'bad'. One would hesitate to suggest that Q1 *1 Contention* or Q1 *Henry 5* were memorially reconstructed if one were to read them alongside Q1 *A Knack to Know a Knave* or Q1 *The Famous Victories of Henry 5*. Badness becomes relative, and anyone intimately familiar with Marlowe's *The Massacre at Paris* or Heywood's *1 If You Know Not Me You Know Nobody* or Chettle, Dekker, Heywood, Smith, and Webster's *Sir Thomas Wyatt* will instantly realise how 'good' are the majority of Shakespeare's so called 'reported' plays. This does not necessarily mean that the Shakespeare texts are not reported, but it should prompt us to ask why their standard is so much higher. Does it tell us that the Shakespeare texts are *bona fide*, created by actors in Shakespeare's company and that the others are 'stolne and surreptitious'? Does it tell us something about the standard of line-learning in Shakespeare's company? Or does it mean that we should seek explanations other than memorial reconstruction? Gary Taylor came close to probing these issues when he stated that the reporters of Q *Henry 5* were 'unusually conscientious', but he did not expand the implications of his statement.[39]

So far I have illustrated three major confusions which affect studies of memorial reconstruction: unmethodical diagnostic criteria, insufficient understanding of Elizabethan memory, and the limited context of the field of inquiry. The fourth confusion relates to imprecise terminology.

Randall McLeod is but one of many textual scholars to have expressed dislike of Pollard's 'good'/'bad' distinction: 'The real problem with good and bad quartos is not what the words denote, but why we use terminology that has such overt and prejudicial connotations'.[40] Sidney Thomas, E. A. J. Honigmann, Scott McMillin, Paul Werstine, and Graham Holderness and Bryan Loughrey have all, at various stages, argued for the inappropriateness or the abandonment of these terms.[41] But old habits die hard, and critics acknowledge the problems inherent in the terms 'good' and 'bad', while continuing to use these adjectives regardless.

'Quarto' is also a problematic term, since it is applied inaccurately to all 'bad' texts, although *Richard Duke of York* and *The Massacre at Paris* are actually octavos, and *John of Bordeaux* exists only in manuscript. Obviously a manuscript cannot be a 'bad quarto', but it might be a memorial reconstruction, and since 'bad quarto' is synonymous with memorial reconstruction, *John of Bordeaux* might be one. (If one believes that *John of Bordeaux* is not memorially reconstructed, one is spared the terminological predicament; see chapter 8, table XVII). The situation is further confused because 'bad quarto' was not always synonymous with memorial reconstruction. Greg used the term to mean a text with problems caused through alteration by someone other than the author, since both Q1 *The Battle of Alcazar* (1594) (which he acquitted of memorial reconstruction) and Q1 *Orlando Furioso* (1594) (which he believed to be memorially reconstructed) were both designated 'bad quartos'. This is the sense in which F. P. Wilson used the term in 1942.[42] But by 1945 'bad quarto' had narrowed in meaning to 'memorial reconstruction', and Harry Hoppe could speak of 'the vexing problem of bad quartos, particularly the question of their memorial origin'.[43]

However, as Greg implied, a quarto may be defective or disordered or reworked without being memorial; what vocabulary then is left to designate plays such as Q1 *The Wit of A Woman* (1604) which is egregiously disrupted ('bad') without being memorially reconstructed? At the other extreme, a memorial reconstruction may equally produce a 'good' quarto, since in theory there should be no difference between a perfect memorial reconstruction and a scribal transcript.[44] The term 'bad quarto' evaluates quality when what is needed is a term which indicates process – the fact of memorial reconstruction not the effect. Critics, particularly in recent years, often note the effective dramaturgy of many moments in 'bad' quartos; the coexistence of 'good' and 'bad' presents, as Holderness and Loughrey point out, 'a theoretical problem of virtually theological dimensions'.[45]

Critics who use the term 'bad quarto' variously signal their unhappiness with it, by placing it in inverted commas or using majuscule B and Q, but they do not reject it. Henceforth in this study, with the exception of quotations from critics, I avoid the term 'bad quarto'. When reference to others' value judgements is unavoidable, I use the adjective 'bad'; otherwise I use the form 'suspect text' – that is, a text for which memorial reconstruction of all or part has been suspected by critics. I do not claim that the substitute term is ideal, for 'suspect' suggests transgression; however, suspects do at least have the possibility of being acquitted.

The 'prejudicial connotations' which Randall McLeod criticises in 'good' and 'bad' extend to almost all vocabulary associated with studies of suspect texts. In one paragraph William Green uses 'illegitimately', 'traitor actor', 'pirate-actor', and 'corrupt text', and A. S. Cairncross's vocabulary is consistently partisan, relying on connotative words such as 'inferior', 'mutilation', 'pirate', and 'legitimate'.[46] ('Fine word "legitimate".') The critical dice are loaded before any survey can begin because the tools of expression are unavoidably comparative and judgemental.

Furthermore, terms such as 'pirated' and 'illegitimate' are misleading in studies of suspect texts, since vocabulary which is appropriate only to stationers' activities is being used to indicate the condition of the text. Thus Brian Gibbons: '*Romeo and Juliet* Q1 is a Bad Quarto, piratical and dependent on an especially unreliable means of transmission'; Fredson Bowers: Q1 *Hamlet* is 'a memorially reconstructed pirate text'.[47] 'Piracy' relates technically to the circumstances of publication, where it means the infringement of one stationer's rights by another. Even when critics do recognise this technical application of vocabulary, they are willing to plead for an extension of meaning. Thus, F. P. Wilson states that piracy means infringement of copyright (to the Company of Stationers), but to the players it means publication without their permission.[48] Gary Taylor asks us to distinguish three kinds of piracy: the theft of a text for performance by an unauthorised company, the theft of a text by a reporter for publication, and illegal publication itself.[49]

If Shakespeare's company reconstructs a text for performance, there is nothing 'stolen', 'surreptitious' or 'piratical' about the activity. If a rival company reconstructs Shakespeare's text for performance, or an audience member does so for publication, that is a different story. But any suggestion that memorial reconstruction was ever used for illegal acquisition of texts is an assumption not easily demonstrated.

Unfortunately the field of memorial reconstruction is full of assumptions, which critics acknowledge as such, and then treat with the authority of facts. William Green's 'almost certainly' (above) is one such example. Brian Gibbons writes that 'Presumably the Bad Quarto version [of *Romeo and Juliet*] was assembled by a group who had been involved in the first authentic production and intended to perform the play, with a reduced cast, on a provincial tour.' Just two pages later, Gibbons has progressed to certainty: 'The non-Shakespearean element in this speech may be a deliberate substitution . . . by the actor concerned, obviously without Shakespeare's endorsement.'[50] The presumed statements (there are actually five presumptions operating) and the obvious are equally inferential. And if Gibbons's presumptions are correct, there is no need to describe Q1 as 'piratical', as he does on p.1.[51]

The problems which afflict studies of suspect texts should by now be apparent. Generalisations, such as the following, about suspect texts illustrate the extent of the problem:

> Whether actually 'stolne and surreptitious', as the editors of the Shakespeare First Folio of 1623 claimed in referring to such publications as *The First Part of the Contention* . . . (the 'bad quarto' of *2 Henry VI*) and *The True Tragedy of Richard Duke of York* (*3 Henry VI*), they are considerably debased versions of their 'true originall copies'.[52]

But, as we have seen, Heminge and Condell did not specify *1 Contention* or *The True Tragedy of Richard Duke of York* as being 'stolne and surreptitious'; it is their very failure to identify the texts subsumed under this collocation that has caused so much perplexity.

If the area of suspect texts proves hazardous for textual critics, it should be no surprise that non-textual specialists trip up when negotiating the area. Julia Gasper perpetuates the connection first posited by Pollard between a play's textual quality and entrance or non-entrance in the

Stationers' Register. Although this connection was exploded long ago,[53] Gasper could comment in 1990 that: 'When *Sir Thomas Wyatt* was printed in 1607, it was not registered, and this, together with the poor state of the text, suggests that it may have been pirated.'[54] In the Penguin guide to *Richard 3*, a text designed for undergraduates, C. W. R. D. Moseley offers the following:

> It has been suggested that the first Quarto, of 1597, is a 'reported' text, but this has been challenged. It is now seen to be probable that the manuscript from which it was set was a collective reconstruction – remarkably accurate – of the play from memory by most if not all the members of the company.[55]

Moseley here distinguishes reporting from memorial reconstruction, even though the two terms are synonymous (Greg first offered reporting as a term to mean 'any process of transmission which involves the memory no matter at what stage or in what manner').[56] By 'report' Moseley appears to mean a shorthand report, for he earlier tells us that '[a]n enterprising printer might commission a shorthand reporter to attend the play and take it down from the performance'. The connection between suspect texts and shorthand reports has not been a component of studies of suspect texts for many years, having been cogently disproved by G. I. Duthie in 1949.[57] But textual myths die hard.

In fact, the editors whose work I have been criticising (Cairncross, Gibbons, Oliver) have inherited problems, not created them. As we shall see, New Bibliographic approaches to suspect texts are as problematic as the suspect texts themselves.

What follows is an exercise in textual spring-cleaning, an attempt to strip away the accumulated confusions. My topic is memorial reconstruction and my focus is the forty-one suspect texts listed earlier in this chapter, but I approach both through analysis of the New Bibliographers and New Bibliographic method. As a scenario, memorial reconstruction gained influence and maintained its hegemony because of the reputation of the New Bibliographers (particularly that of Greg), and it is important that this intersection of thesis and personality be examined. In investigating the process by which suspect texts became defined and accepted as suspect, I am simply following the lead established by Werstine and others who have recently questioned New Bibliographic hegemony and the textual system that we, in the late-twentieth century, have inherited.

Throughout this book I focus on textual methodology. In my survey of the New Bibliographers, as in my studies of individual suspect texts, I am concerned not so much with conclusions about suspect texts as with the means by which those conclusions have been and may be reached. I begin in chapter 2 with an analysis of New Bibliographic aim and method, surveying the textual and critical climate at the end of the nineteenth and the beginning of the twentieth centuries, and the conditions to which the New Bibliographers were responding. Chapter 3 continues this analysis with a focus on the seminal publications of New Bibliographers on suspect texts; these publications have, of course, affected all subsequent editorial attitudes and practices. Chapter 4 considers the available external evidence for memorial reconstruction in the sixteenth century and beyond, and chapter 5 looks at the psychology and practice of memory from Homeric epic to the BBC Television Shakespeare series.

Part 2 concentrates on the individual features of suspect texts. The theory behind part 2 is explained in chapter 6. In chapter 7 I analyse all the features that have been considered symptomatic of memorial reconstruction, reaching more sceptical conclusions than did the New Bibliographers and their successors. The material throughout is based on my study of the forty-one suspect texts. The salient features of each of these suspect texts is included in chapter 8 in a tabular format which I believe retains the best of New Bibliographic method (the patient and full listing of relevant textual material) while avoiding that which is detrimental (the impetus towards interpretive narrative).[58] This chapter provides easy access to data on the forty-one suspect texts and allows rapid scrutiny of pertinent features both within and across the texts. Chapter 9, the Conclusion, concentrates on the paradigms revealed (or exposed) by the tabulated material in chapter 8.

I should make my own textual position clear. I do not deny the achievements of revision theories, which have done much to stimulate re-thinking, and have increased our textual options by returning Shakespeare's plays to the plural conditions of the theatre. Nor do I deny the existence of memorial reconstruction, for which, as we shall see, some evidence exists. Most important, I do not deny the many achievements of the New Bibliographers; the New Bibliographers were textual pioneers, charting *terra incognita*, and establishing the foundations of a new subject ('The oldest hath borne most'). It is as well to stress this here, since the rest of the book provides little opportunity to do so. The New Bibliography may be flawed, but it is not an ephemeral movement, a passing vogue. No editor or textual critic today can approach textual studies in the way that nineteenth-century editors did. In this respect the New Bibliography is a monument, a permanent and an important one. It may seem ungrateful to attack the New Bibliographers as I do in chapters 2 and 3, particularly since I depend on so many of the materials that they have provided: the Malone Society Reprints, Pollard and Redgrave's *Short Title Catalogue*, Greg's *Dramatic Documents*, and *A Bibliography of the English Printed Drama*. The greatest compliment I can pay the New Bibliographers is to acknowledge that they have given me the tools I use to challenge them.

2 | The rise of the New Bibliography

'Nature and Nature's laws lay hid in night:
God said, *Let Newton be*! and all was light.'
– It did not last: the Devil howling *Ho*!
Let Einstein be! restored the status quo.

W. W. Greg[1]

To this science of textual criticism must certainly be joined a sketch of
the historical development of the study of our language and literature,
and this not as a means of commemorating those who have been
before us, but for the purpose of criticising their methods, and
evaluating their statements.

R. B. McKerrow[2]

In his presidential address to the Bibliographical Society in 1930, W. W.
Greg reviewed the achievements of the textual colleagues with whom he
was associated 'in what will perhaps one day be recognised as a significant
critical movement'.[3] That critical movement came to be known as 'New
Bibliography' and, as represented in editorial practice and textual journals
in Britain and North America, assumed a significance and supremacy
which Greg's modest prolepsis could scarcely have envisaged. With its
emphasis on the material book rather than its literary content, and its formidable array of technical tools (to say nothing of vocabulary) for analysing
textual evidence, the New Bibliography heralded a brave new world in editorial epistemology and procedure. By analysing all aspects of textual transmission, and formulating principles for editing, Greg and his colleagues
aimed to systematise the editing of Elizabethan drama, thus delivering
Shakespeare and his readers from the inaccuracies, eclecticism, and taste of
previous editors.

The long-term influence of the New Bibliography can be seen in the apodeictic rhetoric of textual introductions to most twentieth-century scholarly editions. Its more immediate effect can be seen in the homages of contemporary reviews which praise New Bibliographic methodology as an epoch-making 'Declaration of Independence' from nineteenth-century subjective impressionism. Greg's *Principles of Emendation*, one critic wrote, represents 'the Shakespearian scholar's final sundering from the fumbling dilettanti whose muddying of the waters has delayed the finding of much treasure trove'.[4] Critics hailed the 'revolutionary marriage between bibliography and literature', the 'inspirational' reference works and the unquestionably 'final' conclusions of W. W. Greg.[5] Greg himself contributed to the paeans with a review of E. K. Chambers's *The Elizabethan Stage* in which he praises Chambers's innovative scientific approach to Elizabethan drama for leading us 'out of that fog, that bog, that mist, that jungle of textual theories based on speculations'.[6] Hitherto, Greg writes, 'with only Collier and Fleay . . . to guide us, we have been groping in a jungle or picking our way across a morass, often both at once. Now at last we know where we stand.'[7]

External validation of New Bibliography's significance as a critical movement, and of Greg's role in developing it, came in 1950 when Greg received a knighthood for his 'services to the study of English literature.' By this date Greg's status could hardly have been higher: he had authored some 10 books containing exhaustive textual surveys and over 150 articles analysing textual minutiae; he had edited 125 collections of primary materials and plays, and he was a formidable reviewer and a prolific textual correspondent.[8] Greg and the New Bibliography, with which his name was synonymous, were apparently unassailable and were to remain so for a further thirty years.

Serious challenges to New Bibliography first came in 1975 with an article by Constance B. Kuriyama, followed by articles from Michael Warren and Randall McLeod (1981), William B. Long (1985) and Paul Werstine (1987), and books by Scott McMillin (1987) and David Bradley (1992). Each of these critics analysed a specific textual problem and found the New Bibliographical approach wanting, based not on the scientific method for which the New Bibliography was renowned, but on assumption and critical prejudice.

Constance Kuriyama assessed the two texts of *Dr Faustus* (A-text 1604, B-text 1616), revealing the insubstantial basis for Greg's belief in the superiority of the the B-text: 'Greg's arguments for the priority of B consist primarily of a vast accumulation of impressions about which scenes in A (construed by Greg to be a reported text) were derived from which scenes in B.'[9] Building on Kuriyama's work, Michael Warren showed that the analyses of Greg and his followers were made with 'a conscious norm, a hypothetical Marlovian perfection, in mind'. In other words, subjective criticism preceded objective bibliography; all Greg's analysis reveals is 'the limits of Greg as interpreter rather than any difference in quality of text'.[10]

William Long's focus was the MS play *Woodstock* (BL MS Egerton 1994). Manuscript study was one of the cornerstones of the New Bibliography. In 1930 Greg had classified seventy manuscript plays in neatly identifiable groups, with author's foul papers at one end of the spectrum and dramatic playbooks (what Greg and others called promptbooks) at the other.[11] Much of the pathognomis depended on stage directions (permissive for an author, imperative for a bookkeeper, descriptive for a reporter) and on marginalia, notably those which specified props or signalled advance warnings for actors' entrances, thereby indicating the manuscript's use as a playbook. The New Bibliographers subsequently relied on Greg's classification of extant dramatic documents to deduce the kinds of manuscript copy which lay behind early printed texts. William Long scrutinised the marginalia in *Woodstock*, reaching markedly different conclusions from those of Greg.

Furthermore, Long revealed that no extant playhouse manuscript is sufficiently tidy or orderly to support Greg's category of regulated playbook. Randall McLeod had reached a similar conclusion in his survey of playbooks, both Renaissance and modern,[12] and in 1994 Long and Leslie Thomson independently discovered an annotated quarto of I.C.'s *The Two Merry Milkmaids* (1619) in the Folger Library which, although marked extensively for use as a playbook, was far from being consistent or orderly.[13] In 1987 Scott McMillin had summarised such points as follows: 'behind the most coherent stage performance lies debris of all sorts, including textual debris. Walk backstage after a good performance and you will see the debris at once, and if you want to see textual debris, ask for the original prompt copy.'[14]

McMillin's book on *Sir Thomas More* expanded an article published in 1970 in which he had approached this complex collaborative manuscript (BL MS Harley 7368) from a theatrical point of view. McMillin's work exposed the theatrical limitations of Greg's textual approach. Considering the question of why Hand E had extended scene 8 at the end of Addition IV, Greg concluded that E was writing to fill up space.[15] McMillin pointed out that dramatists do not write simply to fill up space (*pace* Stoppard's hero–playwright Henry, who declares 'It makes me nervous to see three-quarters of a page and no *writing* on it'.)[16] Dramatists lengthen scenes to extend time on stage, and extended time facilitates doubling. To Greg the play was unfinished and abandoned; to McMillin, thinking theatrically, the play was ready for rehearsal and for copying of actors' parts.[17]

David Bradley exposed a similar theatrical failing in the New Bibliography in his study of *The Battle of Alcazar*. Greg had compared this short and apparently confusing play (Q 1594) with the extant Plot (1598), and concluded that the Plot did not relate to the text of the extant Q, which was clearly a version cut down for performance. Had Greg thought theatrically, Bradley argued, he would have been able to correlate the two documents satisfactorily. Greg's main problem in understanding the casting of the Plot stems from his failure to realise that certain actors are unavailable for doubling because the characters they play are black: the villainous Moor, Muly Molocco, and his entourage are represented in traditional iconographic (and historically accurate) fashion as black, a colour–villain correlation which is reinforced allegorically by the description of the group as devils.[18] Failure to envisage dramatic action hampers Greg elsewhere, as at the end of Act 2, scene 3, where the Plot directs Muly Molocco to remain on stage. Since Q provides no soliloquy for Molocco, Greg concludes that his lines have been cut. Bradley suggested that Muly Molocco should eat the raw flesh rejected by his wife; presumably he remains on stage to do so (see lines 617–18).[19] Thus, practical theatre finds logic where logical bibliography found only corruption.

Gary Taylor had anticipated Bradley's conclusions as early as 1979. In a note on 'W. W. Greg and *The Battle of Alcazar*' he wrote, 'Greg's analysis is ... hampered by a rather poor sense of the theatre.' Taylor advocated that Greg's work on the play be 'entirely redone', and concluded presciently: 'I suspect that in the end bibliography will stand Greg's interpretation on its head.'[20]

In recent years much New Bibliographic work has indeed been 'entirely redone', and the mood of interrogative scepticism has spread. Both specific playtexts and wider methodological issues have come under scrutiny. The recent spate of editions of *Dr Faustus* which choose the A-text as copy-text over the B-text favoured by Greg is illustrative of the changing *Zeitgeist*, a change analysed by Michael Keefer in 'History and the Canon' and decisively signalled by Leah Marcus (in 'Textual Indeterminacy') and Eric Rasmussen (in 'Rehabilitating the A-Text' and *A Textual Companion to Doctor Faustus*). Steven Urkowitz and Scott McMillin exposed flaws in the work of Peter Alexander, and Peter Blayney brought unparalleled expertise as a printing historian to a subject first tackled by A. W. Pollard, the relationship between playtexts and publication history. George Walton Williams devoted a book to speech-headings, a topic earlier discussed by McKerrow. Gary Taylor challenged traditional New Bibliographic conclusions on the texts of *Henry 5*, Annabel Patterson challenged Gary Taylor, and Eric Sams challenged everyone.[21]

Theatre companies' resources and casting deployment came under careful scrutiny from Thomas L. Berger, Gerald D. Johnson, Scott McMillin, Alan Dessen, T. J. King, and Donald W. Foster. John Wasson, Sally-Beth MacLean, and William Ingram provided factual information to temper New Bibliographic narrative about the circumstances of touring, and Paul Werstine deconstructed the work of Pollard and Dover Wilson in which the touring scenario originated. Roslyn L. Knutson tackled the subject of commercial considerations in Elizabethan repertory companies. Urkowitz, E. A. J. Honigmann, Grace Ioppolo, and Berger evaluated the case for revision in several of Shakespeare's works, and Kathleen Irace modified many New Bibliographic conclusions about suspect texts.[22]

In a series of wider analyses, Marion Trousdale, Margreta de Grazia, Peter Stallybrass, and Paul Werstine highlighted the problems behind much twentieth-century textual thought, and Leah Marcus offered a historicist model for reading plural texts. In all cases New Bibliographic methodology was challenged: Hugh Grady and Gary Taylor showed that, far from being ahistorical neutral purveyors of textual truth, Greg and his associates were historically dependent scholars working in a particular intellectual framework. After eighty years the 'scriptural status' of New Bibliography (the phrase is Werstine's) was being overthrown.[23]

What follows is an investigation of the way New Bibliography's 'scriptural status' was developed and maintained. The primary focus is the career of W. W. Greg.

MEN OF SCIENCE

Greg is a convenient synecdoche for the New Bibliography, partly because of his role in defining and promoting bibliography,[24] partly because of his longevity (1875–1959) which facilitated a staggering number of publications, and partly because of the sacerdotal status accorded him by contemporaries and successors. However, two other men share the accolade for directing the course of New Bibliography: R. B. McKerrow (1872–1940), Greg's contemporary at Trinity College, Cambridge, and A. W. Pollard (1859–1944), Greg and McKerrow's mentor, and librarian in the Department of Printed Books at the British Museum. Less pioneering, but equally influential, textual practitioners are Greg and McKerrow's contemporary and friend John Dover Wilson (1881–1969), and the younger and more remote (in terms of geography as well as acquaintance) Peter Alexander (1893–1969).

Walter Wilson Greg was named after his maternal grandfather, James Wilson, founder of *The Economist* in 1843, and after the periodical's most eminent editor Walter Bagehot. It was fully expected that the young Greg would grow up to edit the family journal. However, his failure to achieve honours in Medieval and Modern Languages at Cambridge (he studied English and German at Trinity College between 1894 and 1897) prevented him from proceeding to the Moral Sciences Tripos, which included Political Economy. Greg nonetheless spent a further year reading Economics, before deciding to abandon his proposed career in journalism in favour of that of a man of letters. Since his family wealth had freed him from the necessity of earning a living, he had 'superfluous leisure' to devote to the study of medieval and Elizabethan drama.

Ronald Brunlees McKerrow was three years Greg's senior, but the two were contemporaries at Trinity College, Cambridge because of a false career start in McKerrow's life: he fulfilled his family's expectations by training as an engineer and entered the family business, Brunlees & McKerrow. Engineering was not congenial to him as a profession and, when he inherited money on his majority, he left the family business to enter Trinity in 1894 to read Political Economy. In 1895 he transferred to

Medieval and Modern Languages (English and French) where he renewed his acquaintance with Greg (the two had first met as pupils at Harrow School). The textual influence both scholars were to have owes much to their deep friendship. It was, in fact, McKerrow who directed Greg's medieval textual interests towards Elizabethan drama. In a letter to Greg, dated 9 November 1942, G. M. Trevelyan wrote 'I cannot help feeling that Shakespeare scholarship gained greatly by the fact you and McKerrow were such personal friends',[25] a point reiterated by F. P. Wilson who welcomes such academic friendship after 'the enmities of Pope and Theobald, Steevens and Malone, Collier and Dyce, Furnivall and Halliwell-Phillipps'.[26] As undergraduates Greg and McKerrow discussed plans for editing Elizabethan drama and the textual principles on which the editions were to be founded, and Greg began collecting material for a projected bibliography of Elizabethan drama (a project so ambitious that it took him sixty years to complete).

Shortly after their graduation in 1897, Greg and McKerrow made the acquaintance of A. W. Pollard. Pollard had read Greats at Oxford, where he lived on the same staircase as A. E. Housman; he took up a post at the British Museum as a librarian in 1883, soon assuming responsibility for incunabula. In 1893 he was made secretary of the newly established Bibliographical Society (founded 1892); in 1898 he met Greg when the latter became a member; and in 1900 McKerrow completed the triumvirate when he returned from a teaching post in Japan to become a regular reader at the Museum. In 1906 Greg and McKerrow founded the Malone Society, an organisation which 'grew out of a suggestion by A. W. Pollard for reprinting Elizabethan plays'.[27]

Pollard was not initially a Shakespearean scholar. Shakespearean scholarship was thrust upon him by the bibliographic peculiarities of two 'charming little fat volumes' which were brought for inspection to the British Museum in 1902 and 1906 – the 1619 Pavier quartos. In 1907 Pollard published his cautious textual conclusions – cautious so as 'to cause the minimum of disturbance to accepted views'.[28] Greg, who as F. P. Wilson reminds us 'was never reluctant to disturb accepted views', pointed out why Pollard's analysis simply would not do, and presented a more convincing solution.[29] In the meantime *obiter dicta* in Greg's essay–review of Sidney Lee's First Folio facsimile (facsimile 1902; Greg's review 1903)[30] had prompted Pollard to consider the nature of the printer's copy for the First Folio. This consideration led to Pollard's classification of quartos as 'good' or 'bad', and the authorship of *Shakespeare Folios and Quartos* (1909), a book whose importance in directing the course of twentieth-century textual criticism it is impossible to overestimate.

Pollard took a nurturing interest in the work of his young textual protégés. A patron of Greg and McKerrow, he was also an adoptive father to John Dover Wilson.[31] Pollard and Dover Wilson met in the early years of the century when the latter, an English lecturer in Finland, would spend his summer vacations researching in the British Museum. Pollard recognised and encouraged Dover Wilson's lively intuition, and their academic association developed into a close friendship (the two spent a week's vacation together every year). In 1915 their friendship was deepened by mutual grief: Pollard lost both sons in the Great War in the same year that Dover Wilson's father died. 'It seemed natural that [they] should adopt each other.'[32] Henceforth, Dover Wilson recollects, Pollard transferred to the three younger textual scholars 'what he might have concentrated on his sons'.[33]

In 1915, assuaging his grief for his sons in a punishing work schedule,. Pollard wrote *Shakespeare's Fight with the Pirates* (1920) and prepared *King Richard II: A New Quarto* (1916).[34] In the same year a young Scotsman should have graduated from Glasgow University. Peter Alexander had begun reading Mathematics and Latin at Glasgow in 1911, but interrupted his studies in 1914 to enlist as a private in the 6th Battalion Cameron Highlanders. In 1920 he completed his degree, writing an Honours dissertation on *2* and *3 Henry 6*, plays whose textual problems he continued to investigate under J. S. Smart's tutelage as a postgraduate student, and beyond.[35]

These then, are the five scholars at the heart of the New Bibliography: one patron and mentor (Pollard), two pioneers (Greg and McKerrow), and two followers (Dover Wilson and Alexander). Their close personal and academic relations can be seen in works such as Pollard's *Shakespeare Folios and Quartos*, the preface to which states 'Mr Greg and I have been fellow-hunters, communicating our results to each other at every stage, so that our respective responsibilities for them have become hopelessly entangled' (p.vi). Pollard's dedication in Greg's personal copy of the book expresses this sentiment more succinctly: 'To W. W. Greg. All here that's mine.'

A common denominator of these five scholars is an interest in scientific and mathematical exactitude, revealed most obviously in their careers as professional bibliographers.[36] Greg, McKerrow, and Alexander, in fact, had a wider academic interest in science and maths. In 1916 McKerrow bought a microscope and joined a lending library for slides of medical and other scientific materials. 'He had always been, and continued to be, specially concerned with chemistry and medicine', Greg wrote.[37] If McKerrow was not a doctor or scientist, he could at least approach English literature on medical and scientific terms. In 1901 he wrote:

> until some curious inquirer makes a thorough investigation into all the technical details of Elizabethan printing, and from this and a comparison of handwritings arrives at some definite statement of the relative probability of various misreadings and misprintings, emendation must remain in much the same state as medicine was before dissection was practised.[38]

Greg in his turn was something of a mathematician *manqué*. His textual writings frequently invoke the name of Alfred Whitehead, the co-author with Bertrand Russell of *Principia Mathematica*, a three-volume work which Greg eagerly devoured as its parts appeared.[39] Greg frequently and directly acknowledges the influence of this work on his thinking.[40] His contemporaries acknowledge their inability to understand Whitehead and their admiration of Greg for his ability to read 'difficult books, written largely in symbols'.[41] Not content with reading books in symbols, Greg also wrote one: *The Calculus of Variants* is, to the non-mathematician, a forbidding work, quasi-mathematical in appearance, although Greg expressed impatience with those who claimed they could not understand it, explaining that it was only an exercise in formal logic.[42] That mathematical thoughts were instinctive in Greg can be seen from his tendency to express textual issues in the form of an equation. Analysing Tottel's *Miscellany*, he queries the usual explanation that the printer's copy was set up in duplicate to save time: 'If p is the number of presses available and s the number of sheets in the work, time would, as a rule, only be gained in the case in which $p-2s$ is positive – a very unlikely case when the work is of any size.'[43]

In a discussion of *Orlando Furioso* Greg applies his mathematical talents to the question of the actor's roll:

If at any given point the diameter of the roll is x, the length of the corresponding lap will, of course, be πx, and if the thickness of the paper is y the length of the succeeding lap will be $\pi(x + 2y)$, assuming that the paper is perfectly tightly rolled. The next will be $\pi(x + 4y)$, the constant difference being $2\pi y$.[44]

E. K. Chambers good-humouredly mocked such mathematical predilections when, reviewing the multiple components of Greg's explanation for the text of Q *Orlando Furioso*, he wrote: 'One is, of course, tempted to improvise the quasi-mathematical theory that the probability of such an hypothesis is in inverse ratio to the square of the number of separate conjectures which it contains.'[45]

Even when his writing eschews equations, Greg's prose is imbued with a mathematical flavour. Phrases such as 'It only remains to prove that . . .' provide his favourite perorations as he proceeds to put the last piece of a bibliographic puzzle in place. When in 1932 Oxford University awarded him an honorary DLitt, Greg found the occasion particularly gratifying, not because of the tribute to his scholarship, but because he found himself 'in company with de Sitter, the Leiden mathematician, whose cosmographical theories fascinated me'.[46]

The importance of mathematical thinking to Alexander is even more obvious than it is in the case of Greg and McKerrow. A mathematician by training, Alexander enjoyed books on topics such as the square root of minus one, abhorred 'sham mathematical methods or metaphors', and professed to look forward to a retirement dealing with taxing mathematical problems. J. C. Bryce writes that:

> To those . . . who thought of literary criticism as a free-for-all [Alexander] offered the analogy with geometry or algebra. A problem susceptible of several solutions is bogus. If five critics offer five mutually exclusive interpretations of *Hamlet*, then, since it is not a bogus play, four at least are simply wrong.[47]

If Alexander shared Greg's mathematical instincts, he had in common with McKerrow a professional interest and family connection in engineering. Surprising as it may seem, this subject provided him with fodder for his English lectures when he became a lecturer and subsequently Professor of English Literature at Glasgow.[48]

As a professional bibliographer and incunabulist, technical precision was obviously part of Pollard's credentials, although his enthusiasm for the scientific pretensions of bibliography was less than Greg's: Pollard felt that Greg's concern to prove that bibliography was worthy of the name of science was 'excessive'.[49] Dover Wilson offers the revealing insight that to Pollard scholarship was 'always something of a game, which he found himself unable to take quite seriously'.[50] If this comment is true, it sheds light on the affinity between Pollard and Dover Wilson, and on the former's encouragement of the latter's 'o'er-reaching imagination'. To Dover Wilson scholarship was an 'adventure' and imaginative hypothesising his favourite pastime.[51] In the sober company of Greg and McKerrow, Dover Wilson seems something of a maverick.

Dover Wilson attributed his interest in bibliography to the attention to scientific detail which characterised his father's occupation as an engraver and lithographer for the Natural History Museum in Cambridge.[52] Notwithstanding, Dover Wilson differed from Greg and McKerrow in being keener on speculation and inference than on fact; Sir Arthur Quiller-Couch was later to warn Dover Wilson against 'too many "discoveries"'.[53] Greg described his reaction to Dover Wilson as that of a man trying to tether a hot-air balloon which was on the verge of breaking free: 'I am ever in doubt whether to let go and risk a nasty fall, or to cling desperately and be borne I know not whither.'[54] It was Dover Wilson, however, who alerted Greg to the importance of inferring the manuscript copy which lay behind a printed book.[55] Furthermore, Dover Wilson's editions of Shakespeare for Cambridge University Press were the first to embody the New Bibliographic philosophy by providing a detailed 'note on the text'. It was also one of Dover Wilson's characteristics to observe what others had not noticed, the most celebrated example being his discovery concerning Theseus' speech in *A Midsummer Night's Dream* about the lunatic, lover and poet. Dover Wilson noticed the mislineation; he further noticed that the mislineation affected the lines about the poet, from which he drew the reasonable inference that the lines on the poet were an addition. We do not need to accept all Dover Wilson's theories about revision, or his hyperboles about the beauty of Elizabethan punctuation;[56] but the tolerant and affectionate references to his imaginative flights by Greg and Pollard show the importance of Dover Wilson in this textual band of brothers.

In stressing the technical interests of these men, I do not mean to suggest that the New Bibliographers were frustrated scientists; but their scientific abilities and interests provide a convenient encapsulation of all that the New Bibliographers held most dear (in theory at least, if not entirely successfully in practice): objective analysis and hard evidence. What they wanted were facts; and facts could be established by applying principles of science to literature: observation, comparison, formal rules of procedure, analysis of materials, and logic.[57]

'Critical bibliography is the science of the material transmission of literary texts', wrote Greg;[58] its interests are not 'artistic', but are 'governed by methods of scientific enquiry'.[59] He had earlier phrased this more strongly: 'To the bibliographer the literary contents of a book is irrelevant',[60] and the reason for this irrelevance was cogently explained as follows:

> To the bibliographer every text before him, be it the work of the most benighted scribe or the most incompetent compositor or the most audacious pirate, is a 'genuine text': it is somebody's attempt to fulfil his aim. It is the business of the bibliographer to investigate the nature of these texts, to analyse and to compare them, and thereby to place in the editor's hands tools wherewith to fulfil *his* aim, whatever it may be. It is not the business of the bibliographer to determine that aim.[61]

We shall examine shortly the major manifestos of New Bibliography which define 'bibliography' and press its claim to be ranked as a science. In the meantime it suffices to note that such approaches to Elizabethan literature differed hugely from anything which had preceded. In a modest letter to the *TLS* Greg writes: 'All the bibliographers contend is that the evidence they have to offer is of a surer and less elusive character than what has usually been brought forward in the past.'[62] Here Greg understates the previous (and contemporary) literary climate, which eschewed evidence in favour of impressionism. This climate, and the debates that surrounded it, is the subject of the following section.

THE RISE OF ENGLISH STUDIES

The Chair of Greek at Cambridge University was founded in 1540, that of English in 1910. When Greg and McKerrow studied at Cambridge there was no separate School of English; English Literature came under the aegis of the School of Medieval and Modern Languages. A *parvenu* subject such as English did not qualify as a serious academic discipline (it was 1926 before one could read for a degree purely in English Literature at Cambridge). The reason for English Literature's exclusion was simple, at least in the view of a University don, J. Mayo: 'an Englishman was English all his life and did not need to be taught English'.[63] Opposing the endowment of the Chair of English, Mayo opined that such a Chair would be 'simply a Professorship of English Literature dating from the beginning of the latter half of the nineteenth century, and the effect of that would be that it would be a Professorship of English fiction, and that of a light and comic character. For that reason, he thought that the Professorship was a Professorship unworthy of the University.'[64] Such reasoning is representative of the opposition to establishing English Literature at Cambridge.

Oxford had been through a similar but more acrimonious debate in the mid-nineteenth century. This resulted in the establishment of a School of English in 1893, although it was to be 1904 before the first incumbent of a Chair created solely for English Literature took office. The history of English Literature differs at Oxford and Cambridge because of the different structures in place at each institution, but the ambiance behind each history is identical. As the rise of English as an academic subject has been fully chronicled elsewhere, I shall merely outline the salient points.[65]

The study of English, such as it was in the nineteenth century, was egregiously philological. Literature *per se* played no part. In 1878 a Chair of Anglo-Saxon was founded at Cambridge. Far from belonging to the School of Medieval and Modern Languages, as one might expect, Anglo-Saxon belonged to the School of Archaeology and Anthropology and was a contributory subject to the study of ancient Northern European civilisation. When English Literature was eventually introduced as a degree subject it did not pose a threat to any existing Chair of English: a new Chair was created solely for English Literature, and the study of philology was unaffected.

Oxford had a well-established Chair of Anglo-Saxon, founded in 1795.[66] In 1884–5 a new Chair was established, the title of which shows its progressive potential: the Merton Chair of English Language and Literature. This split-focus title represented the triumphant result of a thirty-year debate as to whether English Literature was a subject worthy of university study. That this question should ever have been broached was the result of three developments in London: the founding of the University of London, the Civil Service examination for the India Office, and the advent of university education for women.

A Chair of English Language and Literature was founded at the newly established University of London (1826; later to be known as University College); shortly afterwards a Chair of English Literature and History was founded at King's College (1831). The different subject-pairings of the titles are a measure of English Literature's uncertainty about its identity at this time. Bolstering itself through alliance with established subjects, English Literature tried to gain credibility by adopting a fact-based approach. Early examination papers from University College illustrate the superficiality of this approach:

> Give a list of Milton's poetical works. Give a list of Shakespeare's plays; dividing them into classes, and arranging them as far as you can chronologically. (1850–1, set by Arthur Clough)

> Name a few British authors who lived to be over eighty years of age, and a few who died while under thirty. (1857–8, set by David Masson)

This emphasis on fact was to account for a great deal of English Literature's initial pedagogical disrepute: English Literature all too easily became a subject which could be crammed. To Oxford and Cambridge this was a prime example of why it was unsuitable for consideration as a degree subject. The Oxbridge proponents of English Literature countered: if London University has sullied this lofty subject, surely it becomes Oxbridge to set an example, to lead the way in raising the standard of English Literature, to show how it should be taught?

The position was further complicated by the introduction in 1853 of an English Literature section in the Civil Service exam for India – an examination which would be taken by many Oxbridge students and graduates. It was embarrassing for Oxbridge that the Civil Service should be examining a subject that Oxbridge neither taught nor felt could be taught. By this time women were entering higher education: Bedford College for Women opened its doors in 1849. English Literature's importance in cultural prose-lytising and its potential as a suitably anodyne subject for 'women . . . and the second and third-rate men who . . . become schoolmasters' was becoming increasingly obvious.[67] In 1884–5, after protracted and heated debate, Oxford inaugurated its Merton Chair of English Language and Literature, and then promptly negated this progress by appointing a philologist to the post.

No-one could have felt this disappointment more keenly than John Churton Collins (1848–1908), who was frustrated on two counts: he had been Oxford's keenest advocate of English Literature as a reputable academic discipline; and he was a candidate for the new Chair.

Collins had read Greats at Balliol, graduating in 1872; thereafter he settled in London where he eked out a living as a literary journalist, university extension lecturer, and tutor for the Civil Service examinations. The punishing work schedule he set himself enabled him to edit the plays of Tourneur and Milton's *Samson Agonistes* as parerga to his regular employment.[68] Collins despised belletristic dilettantism, and was scathing in his reviews of scholarly works which he felt were inaccurate, impressionistic, or indulgent. (One such review was to cost him Swinburne's friendship, and Tennyson allegedly called him 'a louse on the locks of literature'.)[69] After his double rejection from Oxford, Collins renewed his missionary campaign to legitimise and systematise English Literature: he launched a series of journalistic attacks on Oxford, culminating in a book, *The Study of English Literature* (1891).

Much of Collins's crusade was based on common sense. He advocated more objective analysis and less subjective impressionism. He was confident that the study of English Literature could be systematised into a properly academic approach and that the establishment of a School of English was the proper way to achieve this. Above all, English Literature could be allied to the study of Greats since English authors showed themselves everywhere in debt to the classics. (In this last point Collins overstated his case. As a result scorn was poured on his entire argument.)

Collins had a powerful and eloquent opponent, Edward A. Freeman, Regius Professor of History. English Literature cannot be taught, Freeman argued: 'all the subjects of examination now in use in Oxford . . . agree in this, that all deal with facts, that in all it is possible to say of two answers to a question that one is right and the other is wrong . . . [A] study of literature . . . is largely a matter of taste.' The attempt to turn literature into fact is impractical for 'those facts are, in practice, . . . nothing better than the gossip, the chatter, about literature which is largely taking the place of literature'.[70]

'Gossip' and 'chatter' are what the opponents of English Literature felt would inevitably ensue if one separated English Literature from English Language. Literature cannot be taught without philology. What was the point, asked Freeman, in separating literature from language, if literature meant the study of important books, and not 'mere chatter about Shelley'? (It was to be a century before Margaret Atwood, substituting one Romantic poet for another, could ironically observe that 'speculation about who had syphilis when is gossip if it's about your friends, a plot element if it's about a character in a novel, and scholarship if it's about John Keats'.)[71]

Freeman advanced the final uncounterable argument: English Literature, without English Language, is simply not a sufficiently weighty subject for university study: 'we do not want, we will not say frivolous subjects, but subjects which are merely light, elegant, interesting. As subjects for examination we must have subjects in which it is possible to examine' (p.562).

This is the background to the debate which still raged over English Literature when Greg and McKerrow read English Language as part of their degree at Cambridge. The problem faced by the Oxbridge hierarchy was quite simply, in Terry Eagleton's memorable summation, how to make English Literature 'unpleasant enough to qualify as a proper academic pursuit'. (This, he continues, is 'one of the few problems associated with the study of English which have since been effectively resolved'.)[72]

If it is something unpleasant (for which read 'difficult') you are seeking, look no further than bibliography. Greg relates an anecdote which makes this very point. An Oxford professor was listening to a conversation between Greg and R. W. Chapman. 'You fellows are making literature a very difficult subject', the professor lamented. 'I think I should have done better to go on the Stock Exchange.' Greg reflects mournfully that it was 'a hard task to make the professorial horse drink at the cold springs of bibliography'.[73]

Such unpleasant, systematic rigour as New Bibliography could supply to literature was necessary, for, despite all the good intentions, literary criticism in the early twentieth century was no more analytic than it had been in the nineteenth. The first Professor of English Literature at Cambridge in 1911, Sir Arthur Quiller-Couch, is remembered by his students for the one thing the new Professor of English Literature was supposed to eschew: gossipy criticism, 'mere chatter about Shelley'.[74]

Seven years earlier, when Walter Raleigh became the first Professor of English Literature at Oxford, he was confused, unable to adapt to the expectations that accompanied this new Chair. Raleigh was a nineteenth-century man; he was interested in biographical details and 'prized what he took to be the real human presence of an author over against the boring technicalities of literary works themselves'.[75] In his book *Style* (1897) Raleigh elevates 'the personal greatness of the author to such a point that any interest in *the litter of paper documents* seems sacrilegious'.[76] It was, of course, the litter of paper documents that was of paramount importance to Greg and McKerrow.

In 1904, the same year that Raleigh took up his Chair at Oxford, A. C. Bradley legitimised interest in 'real human presence' by focusing, not on the author, but on the *dramatis personae*. Treating them as real characters, Bradley managed to avoid the 'boring technicalities of literary works' and 'the litter of paper documents' by seeming to concentrate on nothing but – a critical sleight-of-hand which was to pass as analysis for decades. He writes of Gertrude:

> The Queen was not a bad-hearted woman, not at all the woman to think little of murder. But she had a soft animal nature, and was very dull and shallow. She loved to be happy, like a sheep in the sun; and, to do her justice, it pleased her to see others happy, like more sheep in the sun. She never saw that drunkenness is disgusting till Hamlet told her so; and though she knew that he considered her marriage 'o'er-hasty' ... she was untroubled by any shame at the feelings which had led to it. It was pleasant to sit upon her throne and see smiling faces round her[.][77]

The revealing present tense ('drunkenness is disgusting') shows that literary analysis is still confused with subjective personal response.

In 1906 Churton Collins, who had offered himself as the saviour of English Literature, was crucified in print by Greg. Collins's edition of Greene had been published in 1905, the first in a projected series of editions of Old English Dramatists. In a review so vituperative that the Syndics of Cambridge University Press were reluctant to publish it, Greg pilloried Collins and his edition from every angle. Inaccuracy, contradiction, oversight, blunder, omission, ambiguity, imprecision, neglect, misunderstanding, and misinformation were all pointed out;[78] tone, expression, collation, transcription, annotation, punctuation, presentation were criticised; research methods questioned; and the whole 'Thyestean feast' led to a rallying cry which, in retrospect, was the manifesto of the New Bibliography:

> It may be questioned whether our knowledge of the Elizabethan drama is likely to be furthered by entrusting the editing of important texts to gentlemen, whatever may be their literary reputation, who either do not think it necessary to examine the original editions of the works concerned, or if they do are incapable of distinguishing between the typography of the sixteenth and that of the nineteenth century... Can a text [such as this] be said to be edited ...?[79]

How Greg proposed to deal with the issues he raised in his review – issues of accuracy, typography, and editorial principles – is the focus of the next section.

DEFINING BIBLIOGRAPHICAL 'DESIDERATA'

After graduation Greg and McKerrow set about reforming the study of Elizabethan drama by building on the textual vision, and the preliminary work towards realising it, which had characterised their Cambridge years. Their *desiderata* were clearly defined: accuracy, a knowledge of typography and technical aspects of book production, and formulation of editorial principles.

Accuracy was a top priority. As early as 1903 Greg campaigned: 'The line in which our knowledge to-day enables us to do work which may itself have some finality is the construction of a reliable and scientific text.'[80] In 1926 Greg cited Pollard in reiteration of his point: 'work of permanent utility can be done by placing in the hands of students . . . such reproductions of the original textual authorities as may make constant and continuous reference to those originals themselves unnecessary'.[81] Throughout Greg's lengthy career as a book reviewer his highest praise is reserved for those who edit, transcribe, or otherwise present material accurately. Only three authors receive this accolade. The first is Alfred Nutt for *The*

Mabinogion which is a 'faithful reprint of the original edition'; the second is McKerrow who is praised for bibliographical 'detailed precision' in his edition of Nashe; the third, a little back-handedly, is F. I. Carpenter for his 'completely revised' edition of *The Life and Repentaunce of Marie Magdalene* – complete revision being 'an operation of which [the volume] stood eminently in need . . . We welcome the fact . . . as showing that the editor realises . . . the high standard of accuracy now rightly demanded in such work.'[82]

More frequent, however, are comments such as the following: 'in order to make any proper use of documents it is necessary to be able to read them and transcribe them accurately. Mr Ward can do neither.'[83] Inaccuracy was Greg's textual *bête noire* and he campaigned against it with unflagging energy. In 1904 he spelled out his position:

> [T]here have recently been published a number of editions of early plays of which the least that can be said is that they are grossly inaccurate. Now there is no question to-day as to what the standard of accuracy to be expected of such work is. . . We have consequently thought it our duty to compare such editions carefully with the originals, and to show no mercy to anything that appeared to us to be of the nature of slovenly editing.[84]

More than forty years later he was still making the same point. In a letter to the *TLS* he compared scholars who could not present their work accurately to scientists who could not handle instruments.[85]

One of the reasons for widespread inaccuracy was critics' ignorance of the techniques and terminology of book production. Advancing understanding of this topic became another major *desideratum* of Greg and McKerrow. Greg was punctilious in explaining the meaning of 'copy', 'issue', 'unique', 'sheet', and 'variorum'. 'Really, editors of old texts might take the trouble to acquaint themselves with such an elementary bibliographical convention as the indication of signatures', exclaimed Greg in 1903.[86] He fulminated against authors, university presses, and even officers of the Bibliographical Society who misunderstood, and therefore misrepresented, the conventions pertaining to V/U and v/u in roman and black-letter fonts. 'One hoped that by this time editors had learned the correct use of these letters!', Greg lamented in 1937 as he took yet another editor to task.[87]

It was clear to Greg and McKerrow that most editors and textual critics did not know what they were doing. Some scholars had entered the textual arena 'for the sole purpose apparently of displaying their own astounding ignorance' stated Greg.[88] Of one edition Greg wrote '[t]o pretend respect for the opinions of a writer who was obviously in no position to form any, is unworthy of . . . scholarship';[89] of another textual study Greg regrets that the author 'hardly realizes either the difficulty of his task or the deficiency of his own equipment';[90] of a statement in another, Greg comments that 'the only remark to be made is that it isn't true, and that the man who thought that it was so didn't know what he was talking about'.[91] Among such tart reviews the criticism of Wood's edition of Marston seems almost benign: 'This edition has at least the merit of not taking itself too seriously: it is bad, but it is not pretentious' and comfort is found in that 'it is too obviously defective to interfere with the production of the serious edition which is rather urgently needed'.[92]

If editors did not know what they were doing, this was because they had never thought seriously about editorial principles. Greg and McKerrow did. A system for dealing with all aspects of editing from choice of copy-text to emendation therefore became another priority. A system would make English literature in general, and editing in particular, more accurate, more professional, more scientific. The name of the system, which would embrace accuracy, understanding of book production, and editorial theory, was bibliography. And bibliography, that ambitious and sustained project of syntagmatic ratiocination, would revolutionise the study of English literature by banishing sciolism, impressionism, and ignorance.

Greg made several detailed attempts to define this fledgling topic. It suffered, as he realised, from its name.[93] He had frequently to explain that bibliography was not the compiling of bibliographies. If you classify the colours of sweet peas the result is a florist's catalogue; if you arrange them according to genetic origin you have a Mendelian approach.[94] That is the difference between bibliographies and bibliography.

For Greg bibliography comprised three branches: Elements of Bibliography, Systematic Bibliography, and Critical Bibliography. Elements of Bibliography – where 'elements' means the 'prerequisites of all further study' – covered the history of book production, whether printed or manuscript;[95] Systematic Bibliography comprised the 'description and classification of books according to some guiding principle'; and Critical Bibliography included 'what is commonly meant by Textual Criticism. It is, apart from the subject and language of his author, all that an editor requires for his work: a sort of calculus of the textual tradition.'[96] Together they permitted a taxonomic tidying of Elizabethan literature, the introduction of 'order and logic into what was a mere chaos'.[97]

Greg was anxious to promote bibliography's objective factual nature by classifying it as a science. Bibliography is, he says, 'a science by which we co-ordinate facts and trace the operation of constant causes'; it revolves round 'a rigorous method for the investigation and interpretation of fresh evidence'; it is not simply 'a descriptive science' (except in as much as all sciences are); it is 'an inductive rather than a deductive science, with some analogy to biology';[98] it has been claimed as 'an exact science',[99] although it is not yet 'a satisfactory science' because it is 'a science which has not yet been reduced to rule'. In the course of his career Greg compared bibliography to science some ninety-five times; these remarks are mostly concentrated in public lectures where the rhetorical impact could be appreciated to the full. For example, in his address to the Bibliographical Society in 1912, 'What is Bibliography?', from which all but two of the above quotations are taken, Greg uses the nominal or adjectival form of 'science' twenty-eight times.

If bibliography is a textual 'science', it follows that editions can be 'scientific': for '[i]s not exactitude the aim of every science?'[100] Hence Quinn's edition of *The Fair Maid of Bristow* is the 'worst attempt at a scientific edition of an English play';[101] Clarendon Press must not sponsor editions like Boas's Kyd if it 'wishes a reputation for scientific scholarship';[102] Leon Kellner's work on emendations could only approach 'a scientific method' if the author had surveyed the territory exhaustively.[103] Greg pays tribute to McKerrow as the man who 'probably did more than any man to place the editing of English literature upon a scientific basis',[104] referring clearly to McKerrow's *Prolegomena*, the first systematic evaluation of editorial procedure.

The year 1906 saw three related developments: the founding of the English Association, a professional organisation for teachers of English Literature; the separation of English Literature from Language at Oxford; and the founding of the Malone Society. Bibliography and pedagogy were advancing together. Shortly after came New Bibliography's first major triumph. Greg's study of the title-pages of what we now call the 'Pavier Quartos' (dated 1600, 1608, 1619) showed that certain typographical features and devices were not in use at the two earlier dates. Furthermore, all ten plays shared the same stock of mixed paper. These technical observations involved 'a draft upon the bank of coincidence which that valuable institution cannot be in reason expected to honour' and led to the conclusion that the differently dated quartos were all printed in 1619.[105] The year of this technical triumph was 1908, the same year in which the humiliated champion of a systematic approach to literature, the editor who had 'determined to spare no pains to make . . . the text [of Greene] . . . a final one', John Churton Collins, drowned in suspicious circumstances.[106]

CONTRADICTIONS

From this time the New Bibliography increased in strength, popularity, and influence. Its appeal, Gary Taylor explains, was that it offered 'the promise of science and the promise of finality'.[107] If we want to distinguish a foul paper from a fair copy, the New Bibliographers will tell us how. If we want to distinguish a compositorial error from an authorial oversight, the New Bibliographers will tell us how. If we want to distinguish those printed plays set from authorial manuscript from those which are not, the New Bibliographers will tell us how. They will tell us how authorial stage directions differ from those made by the bookkeeper, and tell us the difference in theatrical tastes between provincial audiences and those of the Capital. What the New Bibliographers offered was a do-it-yourself detective kit for Elizabethan drama.

This at least is how we have perceived their work. In fact the conclusions of the New Bibliography are not as unequivocal as posterity presents, although the rhetoric in which those conclusions are expressed, as we shall see, often is. As a result the New Bibliography sends out mixed signals.

Greg was aware of the discrepancy between his vision of bibliography and the reality of the achievement during the sixty years in which he practised and developed the subject. He is at pains to stress the number of occasions on which he is unable to reconcile the facts or offer demonstrable proof. His conclusions about the date of Ben Jonson's *The Sad Shepherd*

are not, it is true, very satisfactory in themselves, and will be no doubt
distasteful to lovers of the neat, categorical style of text-book
information; but investigations such as the present one are not
without their value, even when the results are merely negative. One of
the most objectionable features of modern criticism is the persistent
tendency to deck out vague conjecture in the garb of ascertained
fact.[108]

Practising what he preaches, Greg concludes his analysis of the
conflict between Abel Jeffes and Edward White over *The Spanish Tragedy*
with the salutary recognition that 'the results are indeed matter of inference, however legitimate and plausible, and should not be confused with
ascertained fact'.[109] Considering the differences between the scribal copy of
Bonduca (copied from foul papers) and the Folio (printed from the playbook) he concludes 'the evidence . . . incline[s] me to the view that Fletcher
prepared his own fair copy, but I should hesitate to say that the evidence
amounts to proof'.[110]

Similar caution is evident in the frequent admission that Greg does
not fully endorse all the conclusions he draws. As often as he states that Q
King Lear was taken down by shorthand he warns 'I have no great liking for
this hypothesis: I only advance it as a possible, and not too fantastic, way of
reconciling conflicting evidence.'[111] In the preface to *The Editorial Problem
in Shakespeare* Greg stresses 'the provisional character of the conclusions
presented . . ., the tentative nature of all opinions expressed'.[112] He repeats
this caution in his parallel-text edition of *Dr Faustus*: 'were some miracu-
lous revelation to prove all my guesses true nobody would be more surprised
than myself'.[113] In a correspondence in the *TLS* as to whether *Sir Thomas
More* was ever acted he states 'I am in no manner wedded to the opinion
expressed in my edition of the play, and shall be perfectly prepared to alter it
upon reason shown';[114] in his evaluation of the nature and function of playhouse Plots he admits 'I know how slender is the evidence on which [my
account] rests, and if any denying spirit objects that it is fanciful I shall not
demur';[115] and, with a twinkle, he stresses that his charitable explanation of
J. O. Halliwell's perverse statements about a manuscript of *The Trial of
Treasure* is only 'a possible explanation' and 'if anyone chooses to maintain a
view more discreditable to Halliwell it is not for the librarian of T.C.C.

[Trinity College, Cambridge] to defend him'.[116] (Halliwell is, of course, infamous for purloining seventeen volumes of manuscripts from Trinity College Library when he was a student.) Bibliography it seems can only take us so far: 'I am more than ever persuaded of the danger of relying exclusively on any one approach, whether external or internal, to literary problems.'[117]

As Greg's career advances such *caveat*s are voiced more frequently (and more wistfully). In 1933 he acknowledges that 'even bibliography is not yet able to answer all questions'.[118] Ten years later he endorses Madeleine Doran's 'well-considered estimate of the limitations and possible uncertainties of "bibliographical" and other "material" evidence'.[119] While in theory he optimistically espoused Bradshaw's bibliographic advice – 'arrange your facts rigorously and get them plainly before you, and let them *speak for themselves*, which they will always do',[120] his practical, 'material' work often frustrates that optimism. Examining an inscription by George Thomason on a seventeenth-century title-page, Greg arranges his facts rigorously, gets them plainly before him, but is forced to conclude 'Those are the facts, and they do not make sense.'[121]

Much of what we now perceive as demonstrable New Bibliographic 'fact' was questioned by Greg at some stage, or admitted as a possibility only with the proviso that more contextual research was required. We cannot assume, he says, that descriptive stage directions 'imply a text taken down at a performance';[122] it would be a mistake to assume that 'a good deal of untidiness' was not tolerated in promptbooks';[123] authors may 'never have produced a definitive text for us to recover';[124] the suggestion that suspect texts originate in plague-year provincial performances is not convincing: it is 'the desire to find a formula that will cover all cases [that] has led to a rather uncritical insistence on this factor'.[125] Allison Gaw's theory that actors' names in printed texts reveal underlying authorial manuscript (the author writing with the actors of a specific company in mind) is empirically countered by Greg for 'in every instance in which an actor's name appears in a manuscript play it is written in a different hand from the text, or at any rate in a different ink and style, showing it to be a later addition and not part of the original composition'.[126] Greg's experience inclines him to caution.

Greg's caution stems from his awareness that his research is but the first step in a process which others must continue: 'the whole question [of descriptive stage directions] badly needs studying in relation, not to *a priori* expectation, but to the actual evidence of the Books themselves, and meanwhile the more we are able to suspend judgement perhaps the better'.[127] *Two Elizabethan Stage Abridgements* is only the beginning of inevitably 'difficult and laborious investigations' into the question of shortened texts, and 'it is very desirable [that a survey] should one day be undertaken'.[128] *Dramatic Documents from the Elizabethan Stage* offers but a preliminary study of playbooks; Greg hopes that this survey will make less confusing and difficult 'than it must inevitably be the task of the detailed investigators who I trust will follow up the trail'.[129] New Bibliography was thus exploratory and experimental, not absolute and conclusive.

Nowhere is the preliminary nature of New Bibliography more evident than in the modest titles of McKerrow's publications. 'Note', 'Suggestion', 'Introduction', 'Prolegomena', acknowledge the tentative first steps in a long inquiry. 'It is in the hope of discovering whether my suggestion is a new one, and, if it is, of obtaining the opinion of others upon it, that I have put together this admittedly incomplete note', McKerrow says of a genuinely modest proposal that has become a cornerstone of textual thought.[130] In a sceptical review of *Shakespeare's Hand in the Play of 'Sir Thomas More'* McKerrow gave cautious praise to the 'most interesting beginning' of New Bibliography and its investigative method which would, he believed, 'be fruitful of results beyond our present imagining'. He continued: 'And yet we must remember that it is but a beginning and that new tools may need careful trial. I confess that in reading these chapters I have at times felt, even more than how much has been done, how much remains to do.'[131]

The following year McKerrow founded the *Review of English Studies*, the pages of which he utilised to train the next generation in the textual tools which would enable it to extend and improve the work of New Bibliography's founders. Muriel St Clare Byrne was commissioned to write on 'Elizabethan Handwriting for Beginners' (1925), and A. W. Reed on using resources in London (1926); McKerrow himself contributed a sequel to St Clare Byrne's article, dealing with capital letters in Elizabethan handwriting (1927); and Dorothy Meads was commissioned to provide a guide to using local record offices (1928).[132] In 1927 McKerrow's 'Notes on Bibliographical Evidence for Literary Students and Editors of English

Works of the Sixteenth and Seventeenth Centuries' (1914) was published in expanded form as *An Introduction to Bibliography for Literary Students*. The New Bibliographic project was not only exploratory and experimental; it was also generously and helpfully pedagogical.

If we do not perceive New Bibliography as such, it is because we have read the hopes of New Bibliography as its achievements, creating an image which is partly at odds with the reality. This is not entirely our fault. New Bibliographic writing raises false expectations, as McKerrow was the first to realise. In a letter to Alice Walker, wishing her success with Greg's *Calculus of Variants* which McKerrow had lent her, he called attention to a contradiction: 'the real trouble [with Greg's *Calculus*] is that it *looks* as if it were intended to prove something . . . where it is really meant only as a way of classifying the relationship of texts'.[133] This is an apt summary of New Bibliography: it looks as if it is intended to prove something. Although the mood of New Bibliography is simply optative, the language is confident and mathematical. Thus the scientifically deictic nature of the prose tends to override the tentative content. McKerrow, ever judicious, cautioned:

> It might, indeed, be better if in the domain of literary research the words 'proof' and 'prove' were banished altogether . . . for they can seldom be appropriate . . . Nothing can be gained, and much may be lost, by a pretence of deriving results of scientific accuracy from data which are admittedly uncertain and incomplete.[134]

Nonetheless, the scientific language remains powerful; consequently we form the impression that New Bibliography gives us proof instead of simply the steps towards it.[135]

This conflation of aim and achievement is itself the result of another conflation which complicates every stage of New Bibliography: I refer to Greg's collapsing of the term 'bibliography' with that of 'textual criticism'.[136] Bibliography is a factual and scientific subject, capable of precision and finality on most occasions. When Greg deals with purely 'material' issues his work is a delight. One need only look at items 4, 6, 8, 9, 14, 16, 27, and 30 of his *Collected Papers*, at his publications on manuscripts in the collection of Trinity College, Cambridge, at his analysis of putative Collier forgeries, of a fragment of Henslowe's *Diary*, of the hand of Lord Derby, or of Shirley's *Triumph of Peace* (this last was, in Greg's view, the most difficult bibliographical problem of his acquaintance).[137] These articles display a mind which is dexterous in handling bibliographic problems, and can advance the argument to conclusions so logical that they scarcely need to be pointed out:

> With these reproductions before him the reader should have no difficulty in forming his own conclusions, and it will be best if he proceed to do so. At the same time it may be a help to those who are perhaps less familiar than they might be with Elizabethan hands, if I direct their attention to what appear to me to be a few of the more salient points.[138]

> I said at the start that my intention was merely to submit facts, not to draw conclusions. But perhaps I may be allowed, without breach of that understanding, to add a hint as to the interpretation of the evidence.[139]

Material criticism – bibliography – is what Greg and the New Bibliographers do best.

Since in this chapter I have occasion to criticise the New Bibliographers more often than to praise them, I seize this opportunity to underline the gargantuan achievements in material criticism for which we have the New Bibliographers to thank. The area of textual studies would be much poorer (because much less well informed) without Pollard and Redgrave's *Short Title Catalogue*, Greg and Jackson's *Records of the Court of the Stationers' Company*, Greg's *A Bibliography of the English Printed Drama*, and his *Dramatic Documents from the Elizabethan Playhouse*. I know of no textual critic who does not rely heavily on the still thriving series of Malone Society Reprints. Greg's editions of *The Henslowe Papers* and *Henslowe's Diary*, notable achievements in their own right, paved the way for Foakes and Rickert's edition of the *Diary* in 1961; the valuable Shakespeare Quarto facsimiles led to Hinman's First Folio facsimile. For bibliographical (material) criticism and compilation, we are indisputably in the New Bibliographers' debt.

However, Greg expanded bibliography to include textual criticism (Critical Bibliography), although as McKerrow pointed out, the only reason for the conflation was that 'some of the principal scholars who have interested themselves in such research [textual criticism] . . . have *also* been bibliographers'.[140] Greg then divided textual criticism in two: the drudge work of collation, and 'judgements of what an author must or should have written'.[141] The one he viewed as 'mechanical', the other 'intuitional'; the one 'material', the other 'psychological'; the one 'critical', the other 'meta-critical'. Thus collation has more in common (adjectivally at least) with Greg's definition of bibliography. The judgemental side of textual criticism – the 'intuitional', 'psychological', 'metacritical' side – subsumes what we are more accustomed to call 'interpretation'.

Interpretation was not Greg's strong point. As we have seen, it was not anyone's strong point at the start of the twentieth century. In the course of his career Greg wrote only three major interpretive articles, and it is no exaggeration to say that they were all disastrous. If Bradley was literal, Greg was even more so. A play was not a fiction; it was a biographical and historical narrative which ought never to depart from logic or verisimilitude. As such it was a subject (or substitute) for bibliography.

In 1917, 1940, and 1946 Greg turned his interpretive faculties to three major works of Elizabethan drama: *Hamlet*, *King Lear*, and *Dr Faustus*. In 'Hamlet's Hallucination' Greg puzzled over the similar rhetorical styles of the Ghost and Hamlet, and concluded that the Ghost was a figment of Hamlet's imagination. This, needless to say, raised many interpretive problems elsewhere in the play, all of which Greg proceeded to rationalise in the same literal manner in which he had approached the 'problem' of the Ghost. In 'The Damnation of Faustus' Greg argued that, since Helen is a succubus, Faustus is damned from the moment he sleeps with her. Greg's argument removes the interpretive ambiguity of Act 5, transforming it, in bibliographical fashion, into a resolved problem. Limitations of space forbid my dwelling on these articles; instead I shall focus briefly on 'Time, Place, and Politics in *King Lear*'.[142]

Greg is troubled by the uncertain geography of *King Lear*, in which Dover is the only place specifically mentioned in relation to the action. He attempts to identify the play's *loci* by calculating the time taken to ride between the various ducal residences, before admitting that such calculation is impossible. The vagueness is presumably deliberate, he says, 'designed to prevent topographical difficulties impeding the rapidity of the action' (p.432).[143] This conclusion leads him to consider the related problem of chronology, a subject which responds more readily, if no more success-fully, to calculation than did geography.

Greg attempts to locate events in time, to provide a timetable for *King Lear*. He points out good-humouredly that Goneril's letter to Regan in 1.4 contains news of events which postdate the letter's inscription (p.433) but on most other occasions he is able to identify an appropriate time for an action. Thus Lear finds time to write to Regan in 1.4 while 'waiting for his horses' (p.433). Kent's quarrel with Oswald in 2.2 takes place in the ambiguous area between 'dark' and 'dawning' (lines 1, 34), but, Greg notes, by the time Kent is put in the stocks, it must be day for 'it is light enough for him to read Cordelia's letter' (p.435). This letter is unhappily the source of temporal perplexity. Kent has 'only just arrived at Gloucester's after posting hard all night, and it is difficult to understand how he can have received it [the letter] at any time after he left Albany's . . . Moreover, Cordelia . . . would of course have sent the letter to Albany's' (pp.442–3, n.). The events of 2.4 are more straightforward. Lear finds Kent in the stocks, having set out from Albany's the previous afternoon and ridden *via* Cornwall's; the company, Greg calculates, has 'journeyed comparatively slowly . . . or perhaps baited (at Cornwall's?) on the way' (p.435).

Like his critical contemporaries, Raleigh and Bradley, Greg's interpretive faculties could not separate life from art. This interpretive elision is a feature of all early-twentieth-century criticism; the early Ardens solemnly print analytic time-schemes of the action, and William Empson devotes excessive ingenuity to deducing the contents of the sibling whispers in *The Spanish Tragedy*.[144] Greg and the New Bibliographers are, in this respect, a product of their time. But New Bibliography is most idiosyncratic and most fallible when it is attempting to be interpretive: problems arise when literal interpretation is grafted on to textual logic, for the latter demands consideration as fact.[145] We see this conflation most clearly in Greg's analysis of variants in Q and F *King Lear*. Consider Kent's insult to Oswald in 2.2:

> a Taylor made thee . . . [to Cornwall] a Stone-cutter, or a Painter, could not haue made him so ill, though they had bin but two yeares oth'trade.
>
> (F TLN 1128–33)

a Tayler made thee . . . [to Cornwall] a Stone-cutter, or a Painter could
not haue made him so ill, though hee had beene but two houres at the
trade.

(Q EIV,10–14)

Given that a craftsman's apprenticeship lasted seven years, Q's reading is
the greater insult. Greg rejects it in favour of F's 'sober sense': 'Shakespeare
knows that art is long.'[146] The tell-tale present tense ('art is long'), like
Bradley's revealing 'drunkenness is disgusting', shows that we are not
dealing with detached analysis. Instead, personal moral outlook is being
passed off as textual logic. (And confidence in his personal moral outlook
encourages Greg to assert textual certainty when he might better have
rested in doubt.)

Greg has confidence in the impartiality of his interpretive sense and
frequently invokes it to support a textual decision. In the first scene of *King
Lear*, F and Q differ in the way in which Lear addresses Cordelia:

> Now our Ioy,
> Although our last and least; to whose yong loue,
> The Vines of France, and Milke of Burgundie,
> Striue to be interest.
>   (F TLN 88–91)

> but now our ioy,
> Although the last, not least in our deere loue
>   (Q B2r,13–14)

Greg believes Q to be a memorial 'perversion' of F, rather than F a revision
of Q.[147] Rejecting Madeleine Doran's argument in favour of revision, he
simply cites the above passages with the laconic challenge, 'If anybody can
see revision in this passage his conception of poetical composition must be
radically different from my own.'[148]

A brief glance at Greg's interpretation of *Hamlet*, *Dr Faustus* and *King
Lear* should be enough to shake our confidence in Greg's concept of poetic
composition. But Greg presents his interpretive predilections as if they are
bibliographically obvious facts, and so creates the impression that the issue
is not open to debate. In his review of *Dramatic Publication in England
1580–1640* Greg derides E. M. Albright for appearing to take seriously F. G.

Hubbard's suggestion that Q1 *Hamlet* represents a draft of which Q2 is a revision:

> The view that the 1603 *Hamlet* is an authoritative text is as fantastic as that which would make the 1604 *Hamlet* stolen and surreptitious. If there can be reasonable doubt on this point the sooner textual criticism shuts up shop the better.[149]

Once again we have a rhetorical appeal to taste passed off as textual inevitability.[150]

It is easy to reverse the terms of many of Greg's statements and so show them for the interpretive options which they are, rather than the textual deductions which they claim to be. For example, Greg feels that 'the idea of literary revision' has 'blinded' critics to '[t]he fact that the quarto *Richard III* contains a reported text'.[151] One might equally contend that 'the idea of reported texts has blinded critics to the fact that F *Richard III* is revised'. Or: 'we have no evidence that Shakespeare's texts were ever revised'.[152] Equally, 'we have no evidence that Shakespeare's texts were ever memorially reconstructed'. Greg analyses the variants in Q/F *King Lear* at 1.1 as follows:

> Cordelia's parting injunction to her sisters, 'Love [Q:Use] well our father', means simply: Make good your professions of love – she had yet no ground for supposing they would use the old man ill. But to an actor familiar with the sequel 'Use' would come naturally enough.[153]

And to an *editor* familiar with the sequel this explanation would come naturally enough.[154] The conclusions Greg draws are no more than interpretive possibilities; he presents them misleadingly as textual inevitabilities. In the words of H. T. Price, the New Bibliographers 'think too much of an explanation which may be true and not at all of an explanation which *must* be true'.[155] Price's distinction highlights the difference between textual criticism and bibliography, and shows why the terms cannot be synonymous. Textual criticism offers explanations which may be true; bibliography finds an explanation which must be true.

New Bibliography is least satisfactory, because least equipped, when dealing with the subject of multiple texts. Bibliography can assess variants due to corruption, because that is what it is designed to do. Present it with two readings which may possess equal validity and it cannot cope. The bibliographic mindset is trained to think in terms of good and bad, right and wrong. '[F]aced with two sheep, it is all too easy to insist that one *must* be a goat.'[156]

The origins of the New Bibliographers' attitude to revision are easy to see – and to understand – stemming as they do from attitudes to 'contamination' in post-Lachmann classical textual criticism.[157] Just as 'contamination' or transmission from mixed exemplars thwarts stemmatic analysis, so 'revision' opens the door to infinite relativism in analysis of printed transmission. As we can now see, the New Bibliographers' reluctance to contemplate revision enabled them to test to destruction the hypothesis that Shakespeare's texts could be accounted for *exclusively* by analysis of the agents and methods of transmission. This was worth doing, even if it was not their declared hope or intention; and it is this test which enabled the revision theories of recent years.[158]

Greg's desire for one original text can be seen in the conjectural reconstructions he published of *The Old Wife's Tale* in 1911 and *Dr Faustus* in 1950. This insistence on *a* or *the* (single) book probably reflects the influence of two and a half centuries of licensing by the Lord Chamberlain's Office. It may also reflect the influence of Darwinian science. Pollard was born in 1859, the year of publication of *The Origin of Species*, a coincidence of date of which he was very proud. In *Shakespeare Folios and Quartos* Pollard, like Darwin, traces his subject back to one founding original: multiple texts derived from a single authorial version.

Greg grew more tolerant of revision as a concept towards the end of his life but was still unwilling to adopt it in specific practical instances. Facing the taxing problem of variants in *Troilus and Cressida* he considered the option of revision in F, but hesitated: 'besides the more general objections there is the difficulty of deciding in which text revision is to be supposed. It is an assumption that I think the critic should avoid if possible.'[159] From this, it seems, we are to understand that because the critic cannot decide which text is 'better', s/he must put aside all thoughts of revision. Greg here faces the dilemma articulated by A. E. Housman in 1922:

> If Providence permitted two MSS to be equal, the editor would have to choose between their readings by considerations of intrinsic merit,

and in order to do that he would need to acquire intelligence and impartiality and willingness to take pains, and all sorts of things which he neither has nor wishes for; and he feels sure that God, who tempers the wind to the shorn lamb, can never have meant to lay upon his shoulders such a burden as this.[160]

The above confusions and contradictions stem from the primary problem with the New Bibliography: material analysis and textual interpretation have been subsumed under one heading. The certainty of attitude appropriate to the former has been transferred to the latter (to which it is not relevant) by enthusiastic followers of Greg and McKerrow. This has led to the impression that the New Bibliography can resolve, and has resolved, problems of textual judgement for which it is not equipped. Greg himself was aware of the problems created by the success of material criticism: 'it led in some quarters to a belief that all or nearly all textual problems could be solved by an appeal to bibliography, and that any evidence or argument that could be represented as bibliographical was impregnable'.[161] Despite Greg's clear caution, textual–bibliographical confidence continued to grow among his followers.

If the first problem with New Bibliography is one of conflation – the elision of bibliography and textual criticism – so is the second: a twentieth-century scientific approach has been superimposed on early-nineteenth-century presuppositions about authors and texts. Both conflations depend heavily on subjective response – interpretation in the first case, and blatant assumption in the second – and thus resist the neutral scientific reputation which the New Bibliography sought and acquired.

Despite all the fanfare about scientific precision and principles for editing and emending, Greg was capable of making unscientific statements like the following: 'I believe . . . that, if the general sense of educated Englishmen accepts a passage of Shakespeare as satisfactory, it is not likely to be seriously corrupt.'[162] Improbable as it may seem, this statement was made in 1925, halfway through Greg's career. Similar subjectivity informs his views elsewhere. Having painstakingly collected textual evidence, Greg is all too willing to ignore it when it offends his personal vision of the Elizabethan stage. Greg believed that the Elizabethan theatre did not allow Sunday performances; he therefore adjusted all of the Sunday entries in

Henslowe's *Diary*. Roslyn Knutson explains that there was often 'a free Saturday or Monday nearby to which he could shift the offending Sunday performance, but not always'. Nonetheless, '[t]heater historians have been curiously willing to believe Greg over Henslowe'.[163]

A similar dismissal of evidence is seen in Greg's approach to Webster's *The White Devil*. This play contains the stage direction 'Enter bed' (as do many other plays of the period). Greg acknowledges that there are similar cases, but rejects them, along with the stage direction in *The White Devil*, because 'we can hardly suppose that Webster would have tolerated such a barbarous expedient'.[164] Greg's personal *parti pris* is allowed to override the evidence. William Long provides further examples of the way in which Greg, McKerrow, and Percy Simpson, 'three of the finest as well as most knowledgeable minds in the field[,] observ[ed] evidence and then abandon[ed] it, a pattern followed by their successors'.[165] Whatever we may call this, we cannot call it science.

Many of Greg's textual decisions proceed from a desire to protect the London stage from barbarity. 'It is impossible to believe that a version such as that of the bad quarto [of *Romeo and Juliet*] was intended for performance on the London stage.'[166] Most New Bibliographic theories about suspect texts stem from this righteous dismissal; but this opinion was promulgated without any systematic inquiry or exploration of alternatives.

At the root of this assumption are two perceived anomalies: the brevity and quality of suspect texts. The question of brevity was first broached by Pollard and Dover Wilson in 1919 when, proceeding in turn on assumptions about playgoers' attitudes, they suggested that 'the groundlings of a London theatre would have had a good deal to say if, after paying for an afternoon's entertainment, they had been fobbed off with anything less'.[167] This assumption is the origin of the 'abridged rural playbook' scenario. With no consideration that the brevity of plays such as *1 Contention* and *Richard Duke of York* might have been a deliberate and *bona fide* expedient to enable a double bill,[168] or acknowledgement that plays such as *Jack Straw* (971 lines of dialogue) may have been severely abbreviated to function as inductions to another play on the same theme, or attempt to consider the reaction to short plays such as *The Old Wife's Tale*, Pollard and Dover Wilson offer, and Greg accepts, a dubious syllogism: London audiences will not accept short plays; provincial audiences will; *ergo* suspect texts are designed for, and/or result from, provincial playing.

The approach to verbal quality is equally partisan: 'Are we to assume that this state of utter textual degeneration was normal on the Elizabethan stage?'.[169] The subtext here is two-fold: an author could not have written such material, nor could an actor have spoken it in London. Greg is everywhere anxious to protect the standards and methods of professional Elizabethan performance, but, since we do not know the standards and methods of professional Elizabethan performance, Greg is merely protecting his own assumptions. This results in some extraordinary contradictions.

Actors who are textually responsible in London abandon their standards as soon as they are north of Finsbury Fields, where they intentionally vulgarise the language of a play.[170] These same textually responsible actors, however, are not responsible enough to learn their new lines for the revised ending of *Merry Wives of Windsor*, so resentful are they 'at the interference which threw extra work on their shoulders' that they 'introduced bits of gag containing sly allusions to forbidden matter'.[171] Nor do they pay attention to scansion, about which actors and audiences 'probably cared little', although they are sufficiently conservative to insist on the hierarchically appropriate ending of Q *King Lear* which Albany rather than Edgar concludes 'by right' as the highest ranked character.[172]

Such contradictory assumptions are most visible in Greg's attempts to deal with variants in *King Lear*. Problems arise initially because Greg cannot approve Madeleine Doran's picture of a Shakespeare who revised *King Lear*: '[t]hat [Shakespeare] evolved the seemingly inevitable expression of passage after passage' by 'fumbling after his expression, and even after his meaning . . . is hard to believe'.[173] Greg therefore rejects the question of revision, even though his monumental collection of manuscripts meant that he was all too familiar with authorial palimpsest and second thought. Such empirical evidence is blithely dismissed: '[t]he . . . revised type is probably not found in Shakespeare's plays, though it is well known elsewhere'.[174] Shakespeare strikes gold at once, his expression is 'seemingly inevitable', and although localised second thoughts are permissible, such as the addition to Theseus' speech about the lunatic, the lover, and the poet, the negative attitude to revision is seen in Pollard's surprise that 'in this case [Shakespeare] seems to have been better inspired in his second thoughts than in his first'.[175] Here we see how the new 'scientific' method of textual criticism has not shed the old romantic notion of the author as creative genius. The new is simply superimposed on the old, and the uneasy fit is bound to lead to problems.

For example Greg notes Kirschbaum's observation that the characterisation of Edmund is 'more aggressive' in Q than F *King Lear*.[176] Since Greg has denied himself the option of revision, he assigns the change to an actor: '[i]t seems much more likely that the actor of Edmund was of the robustious sort, who breaks in where he is not wanted and steals the speeches of others'.[177] Elsewhere, however, the cast of *King Lear* behaves more responsibly: the actors assign speeches to 'the wrong character' but thoughtfully modify them to suit.[178] Nevertheless the actors' overall textual carelessness results in indifferent variants which the shorthand reporter, a more conscientious individual, reproduces correctly. (Just how it is to be demonstrated that the shorthand reporter is correct and not the actors, Greg does not say.) In thus postulating careless and error-ridden performance Greg is condemning the very stage he elsewhere tries to protect with the scenario of suspect texts for provincial tours.

Collectively the *King Lear* variants might suggest revision. However, Greg must dismiss such a possibility because, as the suggestions of Doran on *King Lear* and Hubbard on Q1 *Hamlet* remind us, issues such as revision are essentially interpretive not bibliographic. This brings us back to the dialectic between bibliography and textual criticism. But it also introduces a new issue – the problem of how to apply bibliography to drama.

Bibliography is book-oriented, as Greg's favourite term for the subject, 'Bücherkunde', shows.[179] But plays are not books, except as an afterthought: in the epistle 'To the Reader' which prefaces *The Malcontent* (1604) Marston regrets that '*Scænes invented, meerely to be spoken, should be inforcively published to be read*' (A2r). Rather than be caught wrong-footed by applying material rules to an immaterial art form, Greg redefines Elizabethan drama. Shakespeare, he says, must always have written with one eye on publication; that is why his plays are so long. The material text is therefore more important than the immaterial performance.

This prestigidatory logic allows the New Bibliographers to be blatantly anti-theatrical, thus continuing a tradition which had dominated the nineteenth century and whose beginnings are clearly visible in Charles Lamb's famous pronouncement that *King Lear* cannot be acted.[180] Dramatic stage directions, Greg tells us, are 'sometimes impossible for a serious edition', citing as an example the 'Enter the ghost in his nightgown' of the 1603 *Hamlet*. It is not clear what he means by 'impossible for a serious edition', but the intention is obviously to make the text represent a 'book' rather than a 'play'. Thus, original stage directions are to be relegated to notes, and the editor should insert in the text whatever normalised direction is necessary to 'the understanding of the piece'. The would-be editor is reminded that 'No merely theatrical [directions] need be admitted – it is a matter of no literary interest whatever whether a noise is made by a 'Pewter' pot or a tin kettle'.[181]

The conflict is between the '*merely* theatrical' (my italics) and the 'literary'. The New Bibliography will transform the former into the latter. Greg's interpretation of *King Lear* shows one way in which this may be done. When Greg tells us that Kent received Cordelia's letter at dawn, since there was sufficient light for him to read, we see that Greg is thinking more of a realistic novel than the daylight Elizabethan stage.[182] In editorial matters we are told that reported texts are 'of small textual value'.[183] They are characterised as 'acting versions', even though 'good' quarto and folio texts are acting versions too; New Bibliography thus subtly presents 'good' texts as 'literature' and suspect texts as 'plays'.[184] The theatrical conditions inferred to lie behind reported texts do not illuminate the play, they 'contaminate' it; other printed material is scrutinised anxiously for the 'stigmas of a prompt-book',[185] the noun 'stigma' revealing the wound to the deity when authorial copy is annotated or adapted. However, reported texts have their uses in reinforcing the view of Shakespeare as book-author, not dramatist. In one of his most extraordinary speculations Greg suggests that Shakespeare welcomed the publication of the 'perverted' and 'merely theatrical' Q1 *Hamlet* because it forced him to release the legitimate *literary* text, Q2.[186]

Wherever one looks, New Bibliography thus strains against science. Greg is at times aware of this. He chastises McKerrow for 'groping after some more or less mechanical rule',[187] feeling that the fallible judgement of an editor will nonetheless 'bring us closer to what the author wrote than the enforcement of an arbitrary rule'.[188] An editor is 'wise to back his own judgement – not, of course, his personal preference, but a judgement of which he can give a reasoned account – rather than seek refuge in the rigour of a mechanical rule'.[189] Elsewhere Greg comes to the blunt recognition that 'what our judgement really implies is the rather conceited belief that the author did in fact write what we should like to think he had written'.[190]

But despite such clear-sighted realisation, there is an undercurrent feeling that what 'we' should like to think the author had written is conveniently what he did write. The New Bibliography finds the evidence it needs (and in this it differs from no other branch of literary analysis). In 1909 Pollard first advanced a thesis that he was to develop in *Shakespeare's Fight with the Pirates* – the belief that underneath some Shakespearean printed quartos lay Shakespeare's manuscripts. This twentieth-century deduction catered to the Romantic imagination, offering the opportunity to see Shakespeare at work. Pollard's thesis was hampered only by the fact that no manuscripts of Shakespeare survive. Conveniently (and convincingly) in 1916 Sir Edward Maunde-Thompson resurrected the case for Hand D in part of *Sir Thomas More* being Shakespeare's.[191] Greg recognises the cause-and-effect sequence operating here but presents it as providential ratification of the New Bibliography rather than an example of wish-fulfilment. Maunde-Thompson's discovery is 'one of those almost unbelievable pieces of good fortune which sometimes seem to set the approbation of providence upon an undertaking'.[192]

Greg identified in himself a 'missionary fanaticism' for bibliography.[193] The vocabulary of epiphany characterises both Greg's writing and responses to it: he has shed light on darkness, he has delivered us from the wilderness, chaos has turned to order, Greg's conclusions are final.[194] Despite such paeans from the next generation of textual critics, Greg continued to revise and challenge the earlier conclusions of himself and his contemporaries. His personal copies of letters, offprints, and books, authored by himself and others, are annotated with marginalia which record new factual details, register queries, delete errors, and attest to Greg's unflagging textual and personal energy. Remarks such as 'fanciful', 'rot', 'rubbish', 'conjectural', 'tosh', 'so they say', 'this surely cannot be!', 'no', 'guess work', and 'I find this great rubbish' are typical of his marginal additions. The fanaticism for bibliography continued unabated, revising old ground and interrogating new. On the day of his death Greg worked in his study till late, before passing away in his sleep.

I am aware of the conflation in the above account. I have talked about Greg as if there were one Greg when in fact there are many. There is Greg the captious and acerbic book-reviewer; Greg the gifted material critic; Greg the literal interpreter; Greg the careful editor; Greg the intuitive palaeographer. There is Greg the agelast and Greg the ironic humorist. And there is young Greg, mature Greg, and old Greg, all of whom think differently about the same problem.

However, although his conclusions may differ, the mindset is consistent: the dream of textual certainty. We see this in the wistful reviews of Fredson Bowers's work at the end of his career no less than in the frequent invocations of science at the beginning. In his review of On Editing Shakespeare in 1956 Greg confessed: 'I find the present book rather depressing, for it suggests that the essential foundations for a critical edition of Shakespeare are more remote than one had allowed oneself to hope.'[195] Three years later Greg observed the 'dwindling confidence' in Bowers's volumes of Dekker and mused: 'Is it that our hopes of being able to infer from the features of a printed text the nature of the manuscript that served as copy are fated to vanish like a dream?'.[196] This was Greg's last publication: he died in the year that he posed this question, leaving the query a rhetorical one.

The hyperbolic claims made for the New Bibliography override the wistful uncertainty of Greg's rhetorical question. The next section situates the New Bibliography historically, and considers the reasons for the enthusiastic response to it.

LOCAL HABITATIONS

Greg did not appear to recognise of New Bibliography what he recognised about politics, that one must have 'sufficient detachment to recognise that complete detachment is impossible'.[197] Much of the New Bibliography is not for all time, but for an age. What to Greg were timeless, factual verities appear now as personal predilections rooted in considerations of class and nation. Sentimental, late-Victorian, land-owning imperialism influences much New Bibliographic analysis, leading to conclusions which are as outmoded as the historical circumstances which created them.

Greg came from a wealthy family. His childhood was spent travelling with his mother in Europe, tutored by private governesses, and although he was expected to follow a career in financial journalism, there was never any question of his needing to earn a living. When he married, he was able to spend several months on honeymoon and resign his post as librarian at Trinity to attend to the added responsibilities of family life. (His wife, a first cousin, was similarly financially privileged.) In a letter to *The Economist* in 1916 Greg signed himself M.I.R.C. (Member of the Idle Rich Class).

F. W. Bateson relates this social background to Greg's textual attitudes. One of the most marked contradictions in Greg's writings is his criticism of McKerrow for too-slavish fidelity to mechanical editorial rules, while advocating himself (in (1951) 'The Rationale of Copy-Text') that an editor must adopt an author's later corrections or revisions, even if the editor has textual reasons for preferring an earlier reading. 'The author, that is to say, must be allowed, literally, the last word.'[198] Bateson views this procedure as 'textual philistinism' and suggests that it may be 'ultimately social in its origin':

> Greg was a rich man. Now the possession of wealth naturally encourages an undue interest in property and with it a special if unconscious sympathy with other property-holders. Greg's editorial assumption would seem to have been that the *Masque of Gipsies* [whose textual variants Greg discusses in 'The Rationale'] was the private property of Ben Jonson and that as such he was entitled to do what he liked with it, right or wrong.[199]

As a result of Greg's argument in 'The Rationale of Copy-Text' editors are forced into adopting a misjudged correction that 'no reasonable critic would prefer'.[200]

It is only recently that editors have concluded that authors may not always know what is best for their own property, that their rejections and replacements may be aesthetically mistimed or misjudged, and in a spirit of editorial socialism have redistributed the balance of property. Russell Jackson's edition of *The Importance of Being Earnest* 'defies the author's final decision' at 1.539–40, where the famous balanced syntax of 'To lose one parent may be regarded as a misfortune – to lose *both* seems like carelessness' was changed by Wilde to read simply 'that seems like carelessness'. In restoring the deleted line Jackson shows that editors may sometimes have a better sense than authors of what is good for their texts. D. H. Lawrence admitted as much when his autograph manuscript of *Sons and Lovers* was ruthlessly edited for publication. 'You did the pruning jolly well, and I am grateful', Lawrence wrote to his editor. 'I wish I were not so profuse – or prolix.'[201] Jackson's editorial decision does not liberate us from Manichean 'good'/'bad' territory and New Bibliographic subjective response. But Jackson's decision acknowledges what the New Bibliographers did not – that editions are works of interpretation.[202]

Greg's attitude to textual authority is also influenced by British Imperialism. Shakespeare may own his text; but Britain owns Shakespeare. As a result, Greg *et al.* are innately better qualified than Germans or Americans to decide on textual problems. I have already quoted Greg's breathtaking announcement that 'if the general sense of educated Englishmen accepts a passage of Shakespeare as satisfactory, it is not likely to be seriously corrupt'. Although such a statement (not dissimilar to Samuel Johnson's faith in the 'common reader') reasonably assumes a continuity of educational (and therefore linguistic) theory from the sixteenth to the twentieth century, it nonetheless warns that foreigners and foreign education systems are ill-equipped to deal with Elizabethan textual problems. Greg begins the section which contains this statement with: 'Nothing is farther from my wish than to "warn off" foreigners from Shakespearian criticism' (the gentleman doth protest too much?), a disingenuous denial which allows him to proceed to the brutal 'but'.[203]

Hints of textual xenophobia appear frequently:

> It is greatly to be regretted, ... that the editors of *Beiträge*, ... should stand sponsors, and, as it were, affix their *imprimatur* to the second-rate hack-work which it is the tendency of the system of dissertations to foster in German universities.[204]

> It is really a pity that scholars on the other side of the Atlantic should waste their time and energies in editing perfectly worthless copies of extant and accessible texts.[205]

> I have no particular objection to the spelling 'Love's Labors Lost' ... but the evidence clearly indicates 'Labour's' (or if you will 'Labor's'), which is the form generally recognised, at least in this country.[206]

> I regret that the Library of Congress notation for American libraries should be used in an English-printed book.[207]

Such attitudes to textual proprietorship have deep roots. In the 1830s the debate about how to organise a library catalogue for the British Museum degenerated into a conflict between nations, with Collier (a Museum reader but an Englishman) claiming superiority over Panizzi (Keeper of Printed Books but an Italian).

Greg's patriotic and proprietorial attitude towards Shakespeare is paradoxically predictable and surprising given that Shakespeare study first began seriously in Germany. From the end of the eighteenth century A. W. von Schlegel, Ludwig Tieck, Karl Lachmann, Tycho Mommsen, and Alexander Schmidt were both popularising and systematising the study of Shakespeare.[208] G. V. Gervinus had written the first critical book to deal with 'all' of Shakespeare, published in four volumes between 1849 and 1852, whereas Edward Dowden's *Shakspere: A Critical Study of his Mind and Art* did not appear until 1875, twelve years after the English translation of Gervinus. Although Greg studied German and travelled in Germany, the achievements of German scholarship are conspicuously absent from his writing.

This omission relates to a larger omission, for the effect of German scholarship had been to spur Frederick J. Furnivall (who had studied chemistry and mathematics) and Frederick Fleay (a mathematician, a man of 'fact and calculation') to use scientific principles to analyse the Shakespeare canon and to professionalise scholarship. In 1857 Furnivall founded the Philological Society, and, in 1873, the New Shakspere Society (a successor to the defunct Shakespeare Society founded earlier by John Payne Collier). Introducing the New Shakspere Society Furnivall explained the impetus for the organisation and Fleay explained the method. Here is Furnivall:

> It is a disgrace to England that while Germany can boast of a
> Shakspere Society which has gathered into itself all its country's
> choicest scholars, England is now without such a Society.[209]

and here is Fleay:

> our analysis, which has hitherto been qualitative, must become
> quantitative; we must cease to be empirical, and become scientific . . .
> If you cannot weigh, measure, number your results, however you may
> be convinced yourself, you must not hope to convince others, or claim
> the position of an investigator; you are merely a guesser.[210]

There is a striking sense of *déjà vu* in reading Fleay's statement after the Greg/McKerrow *desiderata* of the early part of this chapter. The New Bibliographers are curiously silent on the achievements of their German forerunners and on the aims and methods of their British predecessors, even as they appropriate the latter's scientific rhetoric. Pre- and post-war tensions clearly explain the former silence, but the latter has a more complicated history to which I can only gesture here.[211]

The work of the nineteenth-century British scholars, Fleay, Furnivall, Collier, Dyce, and Halliwell (later Halliwell-Phillipps), was unfortunately marked by considerable academic disagreement and personal dissension, to say nothing of theft and fraud. Furthermore, these scholars lived during a period of cultural transition, the paradigm shift of industrialisation which revered 'science, technology, and bureaucratic rationality' on the one hand, but reacted against it on the other.[212] Even more crucial, nineteenth-century textual criticism and its 'scientific' tests promoted disintegration – the identification of hands other than the Bard's in the Shakespeare canon – a heretical conclusion unpalatable to those who revered Shakespeare as a dramatic deity. The fusion between science and humanism was never resolved and disintegration fell into disrepute.

Fifty years later the New Bibliographers trod the same terrain. Their success was due to their friendship, their integrity, their collaborative and supportive work, and their agreement on methods and (with minor modifications) results, all of which had, as Grady points out, eluded the disintegrators. In reworking the textual territory, the New Bibliographers ignored that in their predecessors which they now chose to adopt (the scientific aims of the disintegrators, the comprehensive investigations of the Germans) while reviling that which they rejected (eclecticism, carelessness). Earlier English aims and German achievements were conveniently erased by ideological amnesia.

When Greg does mete out praise to foreign scholars, he manages to turn it into a backhanded compliment through geographic qualification. Thus T. W. Baldwin's *The Organization and Personnel of the Shakespearean Company* is hailed as 'one of the ablest contributions to theatrical history *that have reached us from America*' (my emphasis).[213] In 1955 Greg was accused of anti-American bias in his review of Kökeritz's facsimile of the First Folio.[214] Greg hotly denied this charge, and R. C. Bald defended him by contending that American reviews of Kökeritz had been as hostile as Greg's.[215] (It is a matter of some interest that Greg never visited the USA, relying on correspondents to provide bibliographic details of books in American collections.) But a strain of xenophobia in textual matters undeniably runs through Greg's writings, and undercuts the alleged scientific neutrality of New Bibliography.

This imperialist ethos also leads to an egregiously bardolatrous approach which is applied retrospectively to editors such as Heminge and Condell. Perhaps the reason *Pericles* was not included in the First Folio, Greg solemnly pronounces, is that since it was 'only in part Shakespeare's, it was not thought worth retrieving'.[216]

Greg's author-centred approach stems not just from imperialist attitudes but from Victorian religious piety and sentimental family values. His refusal to believe in Sunday performance on the Elizabethan stage may well owe something to Victorian respect for the sabbath, and his belief in the authority of the B-text of *Dr Faustus* is based not just on his hypothetical concept of a Marlowe who does not indulge in low comedy, but on a Marlowe who shares Greg's religious attitudes. As Michael Keefer has shown, Greg repeatedly views the readings of the B-text as 'correct' because Greg agrees with their theologically orthodox implications: 'The hermeneutical circle is thus closed: the assumption that the play is an unproblematically orthodox Christian document shapes the textual analysis by which the B text is authenticated; the B text in turn validates interpretations of the play as orthodox.'[217] Keefer wryly points out the folly of assuming that 'theological orthodoxy can be used – in this of all plays – as a textual criterion'.[218]

The relationship between an author-centred approach and Victorian sentiment is most clearly demonstrated in Greg's analysis of the Plot of 2 *Seven Deadly Sins*. As Scott McMillin succinctly shows, Greg ignores the evidence of the Plot's twenty named actors in favour of hypotheses which connect three 'appealing figure[s] of authority': Tarlton the Author (of a play on the same subject as the Plot), Alleyn the Owner (of theatrical documents analogous to the Plot), and James Burbage the Father (of an actor–son not mentioned in the Plot).[219] In the face of the extant evidence, Greg's ingenious narrative about the Plot is predicated on the hypothesis that, after the row which severed the connection between Alleyn's

Admiral's Company and James Burbage in May 1591, 'Richard Burbage, who seems to have been acting with the company at his father's theater, would not have deserted his father and followed the company after the row. Fathers and sons do not split up under pressure . . . [and so] the Plot must be dated prior to May 1591.'[220]

McMillin airs the possibility that a promising teenage actor, son of a notoriously irascible father, might be more interested in indulging his thespian ambitions by following the leading actor of the day than by demonstrating family loyalty. 'I am, of course, saying more than I know about Richard's ambitions, but Greg and Chambers were assuming more than they knew about his family devotion. On neither view should theater history be built.'[221]

Greg frequently works by gut-reaction and sentimentality. Such unscientific approaches can be seen in the impressionistic hyperbole of his analyses of literature *qua* literature:

> [Arthurian literature] . . . as an artistic saga, as an expression of the passion most deep, the utterest loyalty, the purest ideals of humanity, is not only unsurpassed but unapproached, I mean that it is the greatest history that the world has yet produced.[222]

The Edwardian nostalgia for a lost rural past in *Pastoral Poetry and Pastoral Drama* (1906) is similarly cloying:

> It was for his [Theocritus'] own solace, forgetful for a moment of the intrigues of court life and the uncertain sunshine of princes, that he wrote his Sicilian idyls. For him, as at a magic touch, the walls of the heated city melted like a mirage into the sands of the salt lagoon, and he wandered once more amid the green woods and pastures of Trinacria, the noonday sun tempered by the shade of the chestnuts and the babbling of the brook, and by the cool airs that glide down from the white cliffs of Aetna.[223]

Greg has not shed the indulgent impressionism which characterised English studies in the nineteenth century. The reviewer in *The Speaker* (4 August 1906) confessed that 'we prefer the sobriety of Mr Greg's accustomed [bibliographic] manner'. These extracts come from early publications (and Greg viewed his book on *Pastoral* as his least satisfactory work) but, as we have seen, the 'sobriety' of Greg's textual analyses sometimes conceals rather than banishes the flagrant anti-factual approach which underpins his narrative.

If historical location accounts for many of the New Bibliography's contradictions, it also accounts for the widespread enthusiasm with which the New Bibliography was greeted. Much of New Bibliography's appeal comes from the narrative charm of the chase. New Bibliography is an academic detective story in which textual sleuths follow stationers and compositors, identify type and press-corrections, and triumphantly distinguish the 'good' from the 'bad' (Pollard was born in 1859, the same year as Arthur Conan Doyle).[224] Greg presents his material with the delight in factual revelation which characterises Sherlock Holmes: 'our chain of inquiry is now complete' is a regular conclusion, and phrases such as 'in the course of an hour or so I had solved the puzzle' are common in his writing.[225] Greg refers to 'the critical detective' to whom his work is addressed,[226] and he concludes his analysis of *The Escapes of Jupiter* by drawing attention to new problems 'because, to the detective mind, it is pleasant to ponder over bibliographical and literary puzzles'.[227] Peter Alexander's British Academy lecture on the seemingly uninspiring topic of punctuation was presented with all the verve and excitement of a detective story: a problem is posed in the first page which Alexander refuses to solve until the last.[228]

Greg admits to a love for the fiction of Dorothy L. Sayers.[229] In another comment, whose relevance is less immediately obvious, he pays tribute to John Livingston Lowes's weighty book, *The Road to Xanadu* (1927). Lowes's subject is Coleridge. His aim is to identify Coleridge's reading and the processes of narrative recall in his poetry, by identifying and reading all the sources (in their entirety) quoted by Coleridge (in fragments) in his Notebooks. It is a gargantuan investigation, and Lowes presents his case with undisguised analogies to detective work. He frequently 'summon[s] the Notebook . . . to the witness-stand' as evidence (p.35), and tells of 'the joy of the chase' he had in researching the book (p.viii). The book presents facts, not preconceived notions ('if the conclusions are faulty, the facts are there by which they may be tested'; p.4), but he is aware that this collection of facts is still a narrative: 'what Conan Doyle would call "The Adventure of the Water-Snakes"' (p.49). A review in the *Herald Tribune* praised the book for its 'brilliant detective work', and J. B. Priestley hailed it as 'the greatest work of literary detection'.[230] One can see why this book had such appeal for the bibliographic detective W. W. Greg.

In an essay on the history of detective fiction, Dorothy L. Sayers, citing E. M. Wong, explains how the detective-story could not flourish until systems of collecting evidence and presenting proof had become professionally systematised.[231] As long as criminal procedure was based on prejudice, gut-reaction, arrest, and torture, there could be no detective genre. With the development of the police force, and public understanding of what constituted reliable and scientific evidence, came the rise of the detective story. A similar symbiosis is evident in New Bibliographic writing. As subjective responses to texts and authors became tempered by vocabulary tests, surveys of metrical habits, collation, classification, so a climate conducive to Greg and McKerrow's 'scientific' approach was created. When these men cross-examined the world of Elizabethan drama the public trusted them to do so fairly and exhaustively. The symbiosis of detective fiction and textual investigation is as visible in detective writing as it is in bibliographic writing: several detective stories depend for their resolution on the unravelling of textual puzzles.[232]

A reviewer of Greg's *Principles of Emendation* observed, in a perceptive analogy, that 'the future Shakespearian emendator will require . . . the intuitive and inductive powers of a Sherlock Holmes'.[233] The New Bibliographers have much in common with Sherlock Holmes. Holmes can 'distinguish at a glance the ash of any known brand either of cigar or tobacco', a subject on which he happens to have written a monograph; he regularly complains that 'the temptation to form premature theories upon insufficient data is the bane of our profession'; and he is complimented by Watson for bringing detection 'as near an exact science as it ever will be brought in this world'. Holmes can not only recognise a newspaper typographically, but will remark that it is 'stuck with gum rather than paste and that the scissors used had short blades'.[234] This is the New Bibliographic *desideratum* to a T.

It is, of course, the detective language of New Bibliography which creates the misleading appearance of textual certainty. Mysteries exist to be solved. And when W. J. Lawrence titles articles 'The Mystery of the *Hamlet* First Quarto' and 'The Secret of the Bad Quartos' or when Pollard writes on 'Elizabethan Spelling as a Literary and Bibliographic Clue' and

Muriel St Clare Byrne offers 'Anthony Munday's Spelling as a Literary Clue', one is led to believe that the case is closed.[235] In 1982 Harold Jenkins described QI *Hamlet* in criminological fashion: 'if you come across a mutilated corpse you don't deny a murder because nobody has reported one'.[236] But New Bibliographic methods of detecting memorially reconstructed texts were no more scientific, and New Bibliographic writings about those texts no more conclusive, than the writings on non-suspect texts mentioned in this chapter.

Methodological problems were pointed out by several of Greg's contemporaries; however, the romantic and hyperbolic paeans of praise to the new 'science' – '"a Darien peak in Shakespearean discovery" showing "a whole new ocean of exploration undreamt of"'[237] – overshadowed the infrequent but cogent challenges. In 1919, 1927, and 1937, respectively, W. J. Lawrence, E. M. Albright and H. T. Price attacked the credos, methods, and rhetoric of the New Bibliography. Their arguments are the focus of the next section.

CONTEMPORARY CHALLENGES

Lawrence was first into the ring responding directly to the sequence of articles in the *TLS* in which Pollard and Dover Wilson introduced what Lawrence dubbed the 'abridged rural prompt-book' theory. Lawrence scorns Pollard and Dover Wilson's theory that plays were abridged for provincial performance, exposing it as 'a double-barrelled postulate confidently advanced as a well-recognized axiom'.[238] Lawrence's criticism is no less valid today: nothing has been added in the intervening years to support Pollard and Dover Wilson's assumption which, as Paul Werstine has cogently demonstrated, remains no more than an assumption.[239] Even Greg, responding in the *TLS* the same month, acknowledged that the touring-text suggestion 'may have been too readily accepted'.[240] In 1924 E. K. Chambers observed that there is nothing to show 'that the conditions of provincial performance or the tastes of provincial audiences entailed shorter plays than were customary in London. There is not much evidence one way or the other.'[241] However such *caveats* did not prevent Greg from relying on the abridged rural playbook scenario for the rest of his career or from accepting the theories of others who did. Lawrence's logic thus fell on stony ground.

E. M. Albright's criticisms were more sustained. In a lengthy and wide-ranging survey of *Elizabethan Dramatic Publication 1580–1640* (1927) Albright raised a number of pertinent questions which struck at the heart of New Bibliographic methodology. The New Bibliographers had adopted a method of identifying the reporter(s) in allegedly reported texts. By charting the fluctuating quality of the play, and calculating which roles could be doubled, the New Bibliographers drew conclusions such as: the reporter of Q1 *Hamlet* played Marcellus, Voltemand, and Lucianus.[242] Albright suggests that it would surely be a matter of some interest to the company to identify the culprit–reporter; and if we can identify him from the quality of the roles he allegedly played, surely the company, who knew the roles each actor played, could do the same?

Albright further asks why Greg's traitor–actor in *The Merry Wives of Windsor*, the Host, who presumably had a manuscript copy of his part, should prefer to misremember his role rather than simply copy it out.[243] And why, she wonders, must memory always operate in the direction of *mis*-remembering? (p.304). Albright also objects to the multiple hypotheses which support Greg's primary hypothesis that Q1 *Merry Wives* is reported:

> Mr Greg assumes that the pirate actor 'learned his part imperfectly
> and very probably by ear, substituting passable makeshift if he forgot
> the actual words.' With this much allowance it is exceedingly difficult
> to check on such a theory.[244]

Throughout her book Albright adopts an interrogative stance. She finds revision and adaptation to be more frequent activities in Elizabethan drama than the New Bibliographers acknowledge. She queries the credo that says actors' names for speech prefixes in printed texts indicate underlying authorial copy: might not a shorthand reporter find it easier to remember the name of an actor rather than that of the character he played? And she points out that analysis of the derivation of playtexts still proceeds more by speculation than by proof.[245]

Greg wrote a lengthy and rebarbative review of Albright's book in *The Review of English Studies*. He took issue with her view that dramatic alteration and revision was 'an almost universal practice'. He expressed surprise that the traitor–actor theory ('for which she apparently holds me mainly responsible') should become such a *bête noire*. He also queried her naive assumption that scientific certainty was possible in the realm of textual studies: 'Does she look for the certainty of deductive logic in the world of concrete fact? A theory is only an hypothesis in which we believe, and all history no less than all science is founded on such.'[246] Albright defended herself in the next issue with a long and highly spirited reply, to which Greg responded penitently. In what may be an excessive display of *politesse*, Greg commented that 'the last thing I should do would be to blame her for . . . rejecting my theory of *The Merry Wives* – which is, indeed, very likely mistaken'.[247] However, as we shall see shortly, Albright's questions and Greg's *volte face* did nothing to alter the public image of New Bibliography as scientific, and of memorial reconstruction as the solution to suspect texts.

In 1937 H. T. Price provided the first retrospective of New Bibliographic methodology. His primary focus was the presentation of New Bibliography as a science. Science, he contends, investigates and establishes the surrounding contexts of a problem, and this the New Bibliography resoundingly fails to do.

> [N]o adherent of the bibliographical school has ever thought it necessary to put a clue to the proof by applying it to the whole of Elizabethan drama. As a matter of fact, no effort is made to determine whether the clue 'applies' at all.[248]

Price had been anticipated in this complaint by no less a figure than McKerrow. McKerrow felt that in the field of textual criticism

> there still is much that we must take on trust. We feel at times a lack of what in another science would be termed control experiments; indeed, we are somewhat in the position of an analyst uncertain of the purity of his reagents. It is not enough to know that wherever A occurs we find B unless we also know that when A does not occur B also is absent.[249]

Price developed McKerrow's point. The New Bibliographic school 'is inclined to guess and not to bother about getting up the facts' (p.161). Since the whole of the relevant field is not covered, the samples of the New Bibliographic school are 'not representative' (p.163); and New Bibliographic terminology is inaccurate. In support of this last point Price cites the error of calling a printer a pirate simply for printing material he has bought. 'In

Elizabethan times, a pirate was a man who infringed on another publisher's rights, not one who printed a book without the author's permission' (p.164). (Price's correction seems to have fallen on deaf ears for, as chapter 1 shows, this terminological inaccuracy still persists.)

Price's final objection comprises two distinctions which are as pertinent today as they were in 1937:

> The explanations offered are often ingenious and may seem to fit the particular case to which they are applied. Scholars think too much of an explanation which may be true and not at all of an explanation which *must* be true. It rarely occurs to scholars that their business is not so much to find explanations for special cases, as to discover the explanation which fits all the cases of the same sort. This is a truism in the natural sciences; let us hope we can make it a truism in the science of textual criticism.
>
> (p.167)

Price's distinction between an explanation which fits special cases and one which fits all cases of the same sort is one which Greg had himself acknowledged. In 1923 Greg prefaced his study of *Alcazar and Orlando* with the *caveat* that 'all the cases of the same sort' needed to be considered. This warning did not prevent Greg and others from accepting *Orlando Furioso* as a paradigm of memorial reconstruction even though Greg had specifically disclaimed paradigmatic status for the play.[250]

Price began his article by saying that it was time 'to question the methods by which [New Bibliography had] been progressing and to see how far we stand upon firm ground' (p.151). The conclusion he reached was that the ground on which New Bibliography stood was less firm than generally believed. Nowhere is the fragile foundation of New Bibliography more evident than in the series of seminal publications on suspect texts. Greg pioneered this field with his work on *The Merry Wives of Windsor* and *Orlando Furioso*, but the contributions of Kirschbaum, Hoppe and others are no less important. This work is the focus of chapter 3, to which we now turn.

3 | Memorial reconstruction and its discontents

A theory is only an hypothesis in which we believe, and all history no less than all science is founded on such. The important question is what reason we have for believing it.

W. W. Greg[1]

It is not every-one's business to let himself be convinced.

Alexander Schmidt[2]

The response to the New Bibliography was enthusiastic. New Bibliography's 'scientific method' represented 'a long-overdue revolt against the sterile warfare of theory-mongers, and cleared the air with an invigorating breeze of good sense';[3] it gave 'Shakespearean scholarship a new confidence, infusing into it a new spirit of optimism';[4] the result was 'that the history of literature will have to be largely re-written'.[5] A specific focus of praise was the identification of suspect texts as memorial reconstructions by actors. 'The establishment of the *Orlando* class of "bad" Quartos is the most important development . . . in the study of pirated dramatic texts'; 'the chief achievement of the Greg school of . . . scientific bibliography [is] the distinction between "good" and "bad" quartos'.[6]

Theories of memorial reconstruction did not begin with the New Bibliographers. The use of memory in reporting playtexts had been suggested by editors of Shakespeare from the nineteenth century. In 1842 and 1843, respectively, Collier attributed Q1 *Romeo and Juliet* and Q1 *Hamlet* to shorthand notes, supplemented by the compiler's memory, or by assistance from an 'inferior writer'.[7] Fourteen years later Tycho Mommsen developed Collier's combination package: Q1 *Romeo and Juliet* and Q1 *Hamlet* were produced from an actor's memorial and illegible notes of 'a sketch of the original play' combined with later and independent expansion of those notes by 'a bad poet, most probably "a bookseller's hack"'.[8] In 1888 P. A. Daniel added abridgement to the scenario. Q1 *The Merry Wives of Windsor*

> was first shortened for stage representation: to the performance the literary hack, employed by the stationer to obtain a copy, resorted with his note-book. Perhaps he managed to take down some portions of the dialogue pretty accurately in short-hand, or obtained them by the assistance of some of the people connected with the theatre; but for the larger portion of the play it seems evident he must have relied on his notes and memory only, and have clothed with his own words the bare ideas which he had stolen.[9]

New Bibliography's contribution was to refine this scenario by reducing the amount of ancillary involvement (the literary hack, the commissioning stationer, the shorthand note-taker were invoked only *in extremis*) and by increasing the involvement of an actor or actors. Whereas before we had memorial reconstruction by diverse agents for the purposes of publication, now we had memorial reconstruction by actors for performance.

GREG AND 'THE MERRY WIVES OF WINDSOR'[10]

It was Greg who was responsible for popularising this notion of memorial reconstruction. In 1910 he published a type-facsimile of the 'despised' quarto of *The Merry Wives of Windsor* (1602),[11] a project which led him to consider 'the perplexing but fundamental problem of the relationship of the two extant versions of the play [Q 1602, F 1623]' (p.xv). 'The most cursory examination of the [Q *Merry Wives*] text shows that there is everywhere gross corruption, constant mutilation, meaningless inversion and clumsy transposition', Greg wrote; '[t]he playhouse thief reveals himself in every scene, corrupting, mutilating, rewriting' (pp. xxvi–xxvii).

In an attempt to identify this thief Greg adopted Daniel's suggestion that 'the reporter may have enjoyed the personal assistance of some of the actors' (p. xxxvii). Greg's initially cautious approach to this proposal ('*if* any actor in the *Merry Wives* played the knave after this fashion'; my emphasis) quickly proceeds to confidence: 'that mine Host had a main finger in the work I feel convinced' (p.xxxvii, xli).[12] The actor of the Host produced 'as the result of a week or two's labour with a not very ready pen, a rough reconstruction of the play, in which, naturally enough, his own part . . . was the only one rendered throughout with tolerable accuracy' (p.xliii).

I shall consider the details supporting Greg's conclusion shortly. For the moment it is necessary to look ahead to the way in which Greg vacillated about the role of memorial reconstruction in *The Merry Wives of Windsor*. In 1928 he retracted his theory, saying that it was 'very likely mistaken'.[13] Yet in 1930 E. K. Chambers declared, 'Greg has shown that in *Merry Wives* the reporter was almost certainly an actor who played the Host',[14] and in 1941 G. I. Duthie praised Greg's hypothesis, 'now widely accepted, that . . . [the actor of the Host] wrote down the entire Quarto text from memory'.[15] In 1942 Greg modified his original proposal: 'there are difficulties . . . Perhaps it would be safer to assume an independent reporter relying generally on mine Host's assistance.'[16] Notwithstanding, in 1948 Harry Hoppe wrote: '[Greg's] study . . . led him to the conclusion that the quarto must have been a memorial reconstruction by an actor who had participated in the comedy, the player of the Host of the Garter Inn.'[17] The fact that Greg had subsequently changed his mind was acknowledged by Hoppe only in a footnote. Greg's hesitant and rejected proposal had become a certainty; the resultant orthodoxy of memorial reconstruction is thus itself a memorial reconstruction.[18]

By 1953, however, Greg had changed ground again, moving closer to his original position in a paragraph in a book review which appears to take the popularity of his theory as an indication that the theory is correct.[19] However, he omits to consider the way in which enthusiasts of his theory of memorial reconstruction had distorted it. Chambers, Duthie, Hoppe *et al.* had streamlined the memorial scenario in *Merry Wives*, consequently claiming more for memorial reconstruction than Greg ever did. In 1965 William Green could declare confidently and simply that '[t]he pirate was most certainly "a hired man" who played the Host in the original Lord Chamberlain's Men productions of the play'.[20]

This is, in fact, an oversimplification of Greg's theory of memorial reconstruction. In his introduction to *The Merry Wives of Windsor* Greg presents a complex scenario involving over a dozen stages. 1) Shakespeare writes *The Merry Wives of Windsor* 'substantially as we know it', but with greater prominence accorded the plot in which the Host is cozened of his horses. 2) Minor cuts are made for performance. 3) It becomes necessary to remove the horse-stealing plot, and the task of altering the play is entrusted to another playwright in the Chamberlain's Men; Act 5 is totally recast and two alternative endings supplied (for public and Court performance). 'These alterations were clumsily applied to the stage version' (p.xlii). 4) The actors are lazy and do not learn the new dialogue properly. 5) Furthermore, resentful of the extra work, the actors deliberately introduce allusions to excised material. 6) The Chamberlain's Men are in disgrace because of topical scandal attached to the original version of the play (William Brooke, seventh Baron Cobham, the then Lord Chamberlain, was offended by Ford's disguise as a character named Brook), and they exile themselves from London. 7) The 'hired man' who played the Host remains in the Capital. 8) An 'unscrupulous stationer' suborns the hired man–Host to recreate the play. 9) In the first place the Host had learned his part imperfectly and by ear. 10) The Host possibly dictates the play to someone in the stationer's office. 11) The Company further alters the original play, changing Ford's alias of Master Brook to Master Broom. 12) Later, Shakespeare revises the phrasing of the earlier scenes, but leaves the 'patchwork of the closing portion' untouched while nonetheless pulling 'a wry face' over it. 13) After Shakespeare's death, in preparation for the First Folio of 1623, this playhouse copy was 'prepared for press with such care as the circumstances seemed to demand' (pp.xlii–xliii).

Greg's narrative depends on a sequence of interrelated procedures: collaboration, revision, aural learning, political exile, and thespian sloth.[21] As Werstine was the first to realise, memorial reconstruction alone (*pace* Kirschbaum, Duthie, Hoppe) is not sufficient to explain the state of the quarto text.[22] It is curious that it is memorial reconstruction which caught the critical imagination when clearly the narrative depends less on memorial reconstruction than on revision (which Greg elsewhere frequently eschews).[23]

There are three further problems in Greg's analysis of *Merry Wives*. The first concerns his attitude to parallel texts. In a procedure which we shall see repeated in his study of the parallel-text portions of *Orlando Furioso*, Greg exaggerates the difficulties of the 'bad' text and plays down the problems of the 'good'. The 'good' Folio *Merry Wives*, Greg tells us, has problems with its time scheme (p.xix), conveys the Mompellgart story 'by hints and innuendoes' (p.xx), and suffers from 'clumsy repetition' and 'inferior writing' in Act 5 (p. xxi). Restricted, however, by the antithetical mindset of the New Bibliography, Greg is forced to characterise one text as 'good' (F), the other 'bad' (Q), despite his acknowledgement many pages later that neither text represents the play as Shakespeare wrote it (p.xliv).[24]

The second problem concerns the conflicting attitudes with which Greg approaches the alleged reporter. Greg uses the same textual phenomenon – omission – in different ways to characterise the reporter as both careful and careless, dramatically intelligent yet too unintelligent to be responsible for one omission which must, therefore, be attributed to a reviser.

In scene 4 we meet the careful reporter: since it would have been difficult for him to remember Fenton's portion of the scene, he may have conscientiously 'preferred to omit it' (p.63). In scenes 1, 5, and 6 we meet the careless reporter, with omissions blamed on his negligence. In scene 9, and the absent F 4.1, we see omission due to a reviser and a reporter. Sometimes, however, omissions and compressions attributable to the reporter show the same dramatic intelligence as elsewhere characterises the reviser (scene 13, p.80); however, the intelligence of the reporter does not extend to understanding lines (p.71). Either Greg's reporter is confused, or Greg is.

The third problem relates to the reason for identifying the reporter. It was 'the very unusual accuracy with which the part of mine Host is reported' (p.xxxvii) that led Greg to identify the actor of the Host as the reporter (as almost all subsequent editions of the play remind us). However, Greg went on to argue that other portions of the text also exhibited a close correspondence between Q and F, 'closer, indeed, than that of some of the Host scenes' (p.xl). These portions involve the part of Falstaff. Greg rejects Falstaff as a possible reporter because of the fluctuating verbal quality of his scenes. The Host's scenes, he says, are significantly consistent. But this significance comes from Greg's manipulation of the figures: '*if we omit two scenes which are open to suspicion*, his part is faithfully reproduced' (p.xl; my emphasis). By such manipulation Greg is able to proceed from hypothesis to fact. Indeed, we can witness the move within a single sentence: 'The rapid succession of short scenes *would* be difficult to remember accurately, and the reporter *was* moreover growing very tired of his task' (p.xxxi; my emphasis).

This third problem, reporter identification, was recognised by both Leo Kirschbaum and William Bracy. Both pointed out the anomaly of the

Host giving his lines to Shallow in 3.1. (Q D3r,14, 16–17; F TLN 1225–6) and to Dr Caius in 2.3. (Q D2r,6–10; F TLN 1131–5). Surely, they reasoned, an actor–reporter would know which lines were spoken by his own character?[25] Bracy also points out that the Host's role, a key structural part of the plot, afforded little scope for abridgement; he thus counters Greg's belief that the relative prominence of the Host's part is due to its being well remembered.[26]

Q and F *The Merry Wives of Windsor* present complex textual problems. Greg was aware of this, and his textual commentary is judicious in pointing out irreconcilables. Unfortunately, the veridical detail of the commentary is overshadowed by the speculative narrative of the introduction which necessarily elides the difficulties. Since the line-by-line commentary comes after the text, and the coherent story of the introduction precedes it, the introduction is accorded greater prominence. Duthie hails Greg's conclusions about the text of Q *Merry Wives* as 'one of the two main foundation-stones of the present-day study of "bad" Quartos which have been securely laid by Dr Greg.'[27] But, as Paul Werstine has suggested (in 'Narratives'), this foundation-stone is not as secure as Duthie believed.

GREG AND 'TWO ELIZABETHAN STAGE ABRIDGEMENTS'

Greg's second foundation-stone was *Two Elizabethan Stage Abridgements* (1923), an exhaustive textual analysis of two short quartos, Peele's *The Battle of Alcazar* (Q 1594) and Greene's *Orlando Furioso* (Q 1594). The problems in the transmission of these texts had preoccupied Greg since 1906, the year in which he had prepared both plays for the Malone Society.[28] In this year also he reviewed John Churton Collins's edition of *The Plays and Poems of Robert Greene*. In his review Greg offered three alternative textual options which might explain Q *Orlando Furioso*:

> (1) that Q is a mutilated and surreptitious version; (2) that Q represents an abridged playhouse version made for some special object, as maintained by Mr Fleay, and (3) that the MS. represents a revised and expanded version made when the play was revived by Strange's men in 1592.

Greg concluded this section of his review by regretting that Collins provided no discussion of 'this interesting problem'.[29]

This 'interesting problem' was discussed by Greg in an article in 1919; he subsequently developed this article into the 373 pages of *Two Elizabethan Stage Abridgements*.[30] Both *The Battle of Alcazar* and *Orlando Furioso* were, Greg concluded, 'bad' quartos, by which he appears to mean a text which 'does not contain the full version of the play either as written by the author or as usually acted on the London stage'.[31] *The Battle of Alcazar* represents 'the normal form of shortening . . . the adaptation having been made in the manner which on general grounds one would expect' (*2ESA*, p.4), while *Orlando Furioso* represents a memorial reconstruction by actors of a text which incorporates reductions (of cast, length, poetry, and *gravitas*) and expansion (of comic clowning) to suit the theatrical taste of provincial audiences (*2ESA*, pp.133–4).

In the years since the Malone Society's inception in 1906 Greg had prepared, or overseen the preparation of, no less than fourteen plays with textual unorthodoxies sufficient to merit the adjective 'bad' in the sense quoted in the paragraph above. These plays are: Peele's *The Battle of Alcazar*, 1594 (1906); Greene's *Orlando Furioso*, 1594 (1906); Drayton and Munday's *Sir John Oldcastle*, 1600 (1908); the anonymous *Locrine*, 1595 (1908); Peele's *The Old Wife's Tale*, 1595 (1909); the anonymous *Selimus*, 1594 (1909); the anonymous *A Knack to Know an Honest Man*, 1596 (1910); the collaborative and revised manuscript *Sir Thomas More*, (1911); [Greene's?] *George a Greene*, 1599 (1911); Peele's *Edward I*, 1593 (1911); Peele's *David and Bethsabe*, 1599 (1913); the anonymous *A Larum for London*, 1602 (1913); the anonymous *The Wit of A Woman*, 1604 (1913); and Greene's *James 4*, 1598 (1921). Greg consequently had wide experience of texts with various degrees of 'badness'.

The two he chose for analysis, *The Battle of Alcazar* and *Orlando Furioso*, were not typical of '"Bad" Quartos Outside Shakespeare' for both plays had a semi-parallel text. An Admiral's Men's Plot of *The Battle of Alcazar* (c.1598?) provided a check for sequence of action and entrances of characters in the quarto of 1594; and the actor's Part for Orlando (designated A, since it belonged to, and was corrected by, Edward Alleyn, for whom it was probably prepared) provided a parallel for 531 lines of the 1613-line quarto of *Orlando Furioso* (1594). Greg specifically selected these two texts because of their parallel theatrical documents; these documents prove 'that neither printed text can be regarded as at all an adequate representative of the playhouse copy' (*2ESA*, p.2).

Orlando Furioso, Greg tells us, is a 'bad' quarto, the result of memorial reconstruction. However, this is not the only 'bad' text of this play. The parallel 'good' text, the Alleyn MS of Orlando's Part, is, paradoxically, also 'bad'. Thus Greg finds thirty-five passages in A that are suspect; A and Q sometimes agree in 'what is seemingly an impossible reading' (*2ESA*, p.267); furthermore, the extra-metrical inductions and exclamations found in Q sometimes appear in A where 'it is difficult to accept them as original' (*2ESA*, p.267). In at least one place Q actually offers 'a better arrangement than A' (*2ESA*, p.294).

Comments such as the following are frequent in Greg's commentary: 'A 80. . . is probably due to corruption' (*2ESA*, p.203); '[t]he passage as it stands in A is really obscure' (636, *2ESA*, p.217); '[Q] at least makes sense of a sort, which A . . . does not appear to do' (664, *2ESA*, p.220); '[t]he conceit in A is hard to follow and the text is not above suspicion' (1052–3, *2ESA*, p.231); 'it will not do to press this nonsense' (A 229, *2ESA*, p.233); '[t]his passage, as it stands in A, is certainly involved and, strictly speaking, senseless' (623–7, *2ESA*, p.216); 'A . . . to which it is difficult to attach any meaning' (1269, *2ESA*, p.239).

Thus, in reading Greg's conclusions about the 'badness' of Q, we must not forget the corresponding 'bad' areas of A, and Greg admits that the evidence he has assembled is 'not only very complicated, but . . . contradictory' (*2ESA*, p. 349). It is important to stress this, since we remember Greg's conclusions about Q *Orlando Furioso* more readily than we recall the details of his arguments.

The cumulative details of Greg's analysis of Q *Orlando Furioso* are nonetheless forceful in advancing the case for memorial reconstruction. However, their force comes mainly from negative analogy with Greg's conclusions about *The Battle of Alcazar*: since *Alcazar* represents 'normal' abridgement and *Orlando* does not, Greg reasons, *Orlando* must be a memorial reconstruction.

The Battell of Alcazar, fought in Barbarie betweene Sebastian King of Portugall, and Abdelmelec King of Morocco. With the death of Captaine Stukeley dramatises recent tragic history. On 4 August 1578 over 200,000 were killed, and the Portugese royal household extinguished, in a battle at El Ksar Kibir (Alcazar) in Morocco. The disputants were Abdilmelec, rightful King of Morocco, and his usurping nephew, Muly Molocco (the latter supported by the chivalric Sebastian, King of Portugal, and a group of Englishmen led by the valiant blusterer Captain Thomas Stukeley).

It is generally agreed that the 1591-line quarto text of *Alcazar* shows signs of revision. Greg sees reduction of cast as the motive behind the revisions. For example, in scene 2 the Moor and his son enter in a chariot, but the stage direction does not provide for the Moor's wife, Calipolis, who is addressed eight lines later: 'Madame, gold is the glue, sinewes, and strength of war' (221). 'This scene affords some of the clearest evidence of revision in the Quarto' writes Greg; Calipolis has clearly been cut for reasons of casting (*2ESA*, pp.104–5). One might argue, however, that Calipolis is a later addition to the scene – a view which has, moreover, textual evidence to support it. The extra-metrical apostrophe in line 221 suggests that 'Madame' may be an insertion rather than a careless relic. In addition, as David Bradley points out, the elaborate explanatory direction for Calipolis' later entrance at line 510 ('*Enter the Moore, with Calipolis his wife*') indicates that this entry was originally intended as her first appearance, and the earlier appearance is an afterthought.[32]

Greg's belief in adaptation by a later playhouse official stems from the mixture of italic and roman stage directions in the text which, Greg maintained, must reflect the bipartite nature of the copy. Greg seeks a system which must operate across the whole text. (It is, of course, precarious to attribute a coherent system to the Elizabethans, who were happy to mix corrected and uncorrected sheets in the printing house, to use old style and new style dates in their business records, and to spell their names in varying ways.)[33] David Bradley finds an *ad hoc* system which makes sense scene by scene. He reminds us that Peele's sources contained three characters with identical names. Although these names vary *between* scenes in the quarto, they are consistent *within* scenes. Bradley sees this variation, not as a sign of a 'bad' text, but as evidence of an author careful to differentiate father from son from uncle where confusion could arise. Thus, Muly Mahamet is called Muly Mahamet except when his son (also Muly Mahamet) is present; on these occasions the father becomes 'the Moor'. When neither the Moor nor his son is present Abdilmelec's brother – Muly Mahamet Xeque – can be given the speech prefix *Muly Maha*.

Bradley's and Greg's arguments have a common denominator: both see the quarto as based on authorial foul papers. However, where for

Bradley the quarto represents self-consistent authorial foul papers (revised by the author himself to dovetail the action with the available cast), for Greg the authorial foul papers were subsequently adapted for a smaller cast in straitened circumstances. The difference of emphasis is significant.[34]

The Battle of Alcazar, Greg says, is shortened and adapted in *bona fide* fashion; *Orlando Furioso*, on the other hand, provides an example of the same processes taking place in a degenerative *mala fide* manner. However, there seems to me little difference in the textual quality of these two plays, and it is difficult to see how Greg could have differentiated *Alcazar*'s quality from that of Q *Orlando Furioso* so much as to call the latter 'bad'.

Both texts are verbally uneven; both contain garbled speeches; but both are dramatically intelligent and consistent in their own ways. (In fact, Greg says that *Orlando Furioso* is 'theatrically more consistent' than *The Battle of Alcazar* (*2ESA*, p.287)). The structure of *Orlando* is coherent, the language makes sense in a basic fashion, and the themes are developed sensitively and dexterously.[35] All of this can also be said of *The Battle of Alcazar*. The two texts do not seem very different.

In terms of 'badness' there seems little to choose between the following two extracts:

> The Bassa grosly flattered to his face,
> And Amuraths praise aduancde aboue the sound
> Vpon the plaines, the souldiers being spread,
> And that braue gard of sturdie Ianizaries,
> That Amurath to Abdilmelec gaue,
> And bad him boldly be to them as safe,
> As if he slept within a walled towne,
> Who take them to their weapons threatning reuenge.
>   (*The Battle of Alcazar* 252–9)

> Nor Tilt, nor Tournay, but my Speare and shield,
> Resounding on their Crests and sturdy Helmes
> Topt high with Plumes, like Mars his Burgonet,
> Inchasing on their Curats with my blade,
> That none so faire, as faire Angelica.
>   (*Orlando Furioso* 34–8)

Indeed, it is easier to find 'bad' passages in *The Battle of Alcazar* than in *Orlando Furioso*. Bradley comments, for example, that Mahamet's lines in *Alcazar* 'do not ordinarily make much sense'.[36] By contrast, Greg's eight examples of corrupt or suspicious passages in *Orlando* can be construed as making perfect dramatic (if not grammatical) sense.[37] Even the above quotation, which I have selected as representing the worst of *Orlando Furioso*'s 'bad' passages, can be defended if one is prepared to interpret the period after 'Angelica' as an anacoluthic interruption of the catalogue of hyperboles, leading to the effectively bathetic concluding couplet:

> But leauing these such glories as they be,
> I loue my Lord, let that suffize for me.

There is little, if anything, in Q *Orlando Furioso* that cannot be explained without recourse to memorial reconstruction. In fact, we have two alternative explanations conveniently to hand. First, graphic problems in transcription: as Chettle tells us, 'Greene's *hand was none of the best*' (a point supported by the blanks and confusions in A).[38] Secondly, abridgement: the text, as represented in the quarto, was apparently owned by the Queen's Men, a company whose plays in the 1590s, with one possible exception, all show signs of abridgement.[39] In addition, Greene's excessive and indulgent love of classical allusion would be tricky to abridge without disturbance to structure or grammar. Collectively these points would result in a text like *Orlando Furioso*. If *The Battle of Alcazar* represents 'the normal form of shortening', so does *Orlando Furioso*.

If Greg's conclusions about *Orlando Furioso* are reached *via* conclusions about *The Battle of Alcazar*, conclusions which are open to question, we find even larger problems of methodology within his analysis of *Orlando* itself. Nowhere in his study does Greg make a convincing case for concluding that Q *Orlando* is a memorial reconstruction. He twice states that Q is a 'derivative' of A (*2ESA*, pp.261–2; p.314). This may be so; but 'derivative' does not necessarily mean 'memorial'. Greg is guilty of converting a two-stage inquiry into a single process. Instead of asking 'is Q derivative of A? If so, how was it derived?', he asks 'is Q memorially derived?'. This is obviously a loaded question.

Greg's method of identifying memory in Q *Orlando* is characterised by a lack of rigour. He offers a number of features which he deems likely to have arisen in the course of reporting (e.g. extra-metrical insertions, avoid-ance of the unfamiliar, repetition) and then demonstrates their presence in Q. He does not attempt to show that these features are unequivocal 'proof' of reporting, and in certain cases he admits that other explanations are pos-sible, although his preferred explanation is reporting. Here we see Greg hampered by the 'good'/'bad' contrast imposed on him by his parallel texts. He clearly did not compare *Orlando Furioso* with other 'bad' texts of the 1590s, an omission which is all the more striking given that his alleged indices of faulty memory can be found in almost all the fourteen problem-atic texts which he had prepared or overseen for the Malone Society between 1906 and 1923.

Greg's failure to define his indices of faulty memory limits the useful-ness of his study still further. Consider, for example, the subject of repeti-tion. Greg does not explain what constitutes a significant repetition, juggling repetitions of just one word with those of a line or more. His dis-cussion of Sacrapant's 'poyson, prowesse, or anie meanes of treacherie' (323–4) as a memorial anticipation of Orgalio's 'as full of prowesse as policie' (331–2) is rendered absurd by his failure to realise how dissimilar (and therefore how unrepetitive) are these lines, and by his neglect of logical alternatives: if 'prowesse' is a repetition, compositorial eye-skip can explain the fault just as well as faulty memory.[40] Thus, the principal methodological difficulty in Greg's analysis of *Orlando Furioso* is a not inconsiderable one: failure to demonstrate that the text is memorially reconstructed.

Furthermore, as with *The Merry Wives of Windsor*, Greg acknowledges that the theory of memorial reconstruction alone is insufficient to account for idiosyncrasies in the quarto text. Greg needs to hold a scholar–acquain-tance of the printer responsible for correcting *Orlando*'s classical names and quotations; the high textual quality of the roundelays is explained by the postulate that property scrolls were available (*2ESA*, pp.350–1); the aural errors are rationalised by dictation; and a prolonged period of country touring is invoked to explain the 'gradual' adaptation of the play's comic elements. As with *The Merry Wives of Windsor* we have a multi-layered hypothesis.[41]

The individual layers of this hypothesis do not stand up to scrutiny, as E. K. Chambers noted in a searching review:

How could the company, with a shifting cast and a fluid text, have got on for so long as the hypothesis postulates without a prompt-copy, and presumably without 'parts'? . . . [T]he Queen's had had a long career, and must have held many plays, quite enough to furnish an adequate provincial repertory, without falling back on one which they could only manage with great inconvenience. Then again, Dr Greg's account of the double sale departs very far from the scandal about Greene, behind which he thinks it lies . . . it is difficult to see how the Admiral's can ever have had occasion to produce a version of *Orlando* without having recourse either to the 'book', or if that was lost, even to Alleyn's part, which was not.[42]

However, with the enthusiastic streamlining familiar to us from chapter 2, posterity has ignored the complications of Greg's multiple scenario, and presented memorial reconstruction as a catch-all.

It is Greg's textual successors who are primarily responsible for this image of memorial reconstruction. Greg himself is honest about the conditions and limitations of his argument in *Two Elizabethan Stage Abridgements*, and admits that on occasion there is 'some connexion between Q and the original play which cannot be accounted for by mere reporting of a shortened adaptation' (*2ESA*, p.344). Of the question of abridgement he writes, 'the circumstances . . . remain largely matter of speculation' (*2ESA*, p.5). He acknowledges that his theory of memorial reconstruction 'includes as an essential element prolonged touring in the country' and that without this assumption it fails (*2ESA*, p.5). What was needed, he concluded, was a systematic survey of all suspect texts.[43] Greg had no intention of undertaking this survey himself; he announced that he would leave it to 'another occasion' and 'a fresher mind' (*2ESA*, p.1).

LEO KIRSCHBAUM

Leo Kirschbaum was that fresher mind, and in 1938 he published 'A Census of Bad Quartos', listing twenty suspect texts: Marlowe's *The Massacre at Paris* (undated), *Fair Em* (undated), Peele's *Edward 1* (1593), Greene's *Orlando Furioso* (1594), *The True Tragedy of Richard 3* (1594), *1 Contention* (1594), *Richard Duke of York* (1595), *A Knack to Know an Honest Man* (1596), *Romeo and Juliet* (1597), *Richard 3* (1597), *George a Greene* (1599), *Henry 5*

(1600), *The Merry Wives of Windsor* (1602), *Hamlet* (1603), Heywood's *1 If You Know Not Me You Know Nobody* (1605), Chettle, Dekker, Smith and Webster's *Sir Thomas Wyatt* (1607), *King Lear* (1608), the Parliament scene in *Richard 2* (1608), *Pericles* (1609), and Beaumont and Fletcher's *Philaster* (1620). In 1945 he added *The Fair Maid of Bristow*, and in 1946 the A-text of *Dr Faustus* (1604): 'In all, then, there are twenty-two known bad quartos.'[44]

Kirschbaum's interest in identifying non-Shakespearean suspect texts stemmed from his dissertation, *Elizabethan and Jacobean Bad Quartos among the Stationers* (1936). In 1945 he turned his attention to Shakespeare in an attempt to iron out problems in Greg's earlier analyses of *King Lear*. Greg, it will be remembered, was adamant that *King Lear* was a reported text. He was less certain about the agent responsible for reporting it and had concluded (reluctantly) that shorthand was involved. The unusual length of the quarto then had to be explained by postulating performance at Court where the reporter 'would be more difficult to detect and also more difficult to remove'.[45] This, said Kirschbaum, was 'letting speculation run away with itself'.[46] He offered a simpler explanation: memorial reconstruction by actors.

Kirschbaum analyses Q/F variant passages in *King Lear*, offering a series of exercises in practical criticism which betray literary predilection rather than bibliographic deduction. Considering the sequence at F 1.4.49–59 Kirschbaum explains:

> [In Q t]he giving of [line] 55 to Kent [rather than to a Knight as in F] spoils *Shakespeare's intention* in this scene [my emphasis], for in F Kent's *first* action for his master is his sudden manhandling of the saucy steward at 95 to 100. This prompt and surprising defence by his new servitor affects and pleases Lear. Between his hiring by Lear at 43 and 95, Kent stays silently in the background. Then he suddenly emerges. Q spoils this by having him speak at 55.[47]

This is critically sensitive and provides a plausible account; but the same critical sensitivity can be applied in the reverse direction. Thus: Shakespeare, writing Q, gave line 55 to Kent with satisfactory effect, but later (five minutes? five weeks? five years?) saw the increased dramatic potential if Kent were to remain silent until line 95. The 'evidence' can operate in two ways.[48]

New Bibliographic studies of suspect texts protect themselves from this kind of counter-reasoning with an expansive and permissive view of what can happen in the process of memorial reconstruction. Thus Kirschbaum: 'almost anything can happen in a memorial reconstruction'; Greg: 'my own study of *Merry Wives* has led me to doubt whether any limit can be set to the possible perversion which a text may suffer at the hands of a reporter'; F. P. Wilson: 'memorial transmission may be held responsible for almost limitless perversion'; Duthie: 'no limit can be set to the amount of corruption a pirate may introduce into a reported text'.[49] Such latitude encourages literary criticism to be treated as bibliographic fact.[50]

Kirschbaum's work presents the case for memorial reconstruction by another tactic which forestalls objection: rhetorical absolutism. 'Dramatists simply don't turn the kind of text represented by *The True Tragedy* into the text of *3 Henry VI* in the 1623 Folio'; 'It is quite as impossible to believe that Shakespeare *consciously* turned *The Contention* into *2 Henry VI* as it is to believe that some one *consciously* turned *2 Henry VI* into *The Contention*.'[51] We have already encountered this tactic in the work of Greg on *King Lear*, and it recurs in Greg's study of *Dr Faustus*: 'anyone who maintains that the A-text preserves substantially the original version of the play will have to do a lot of explaining'.[52] As recently as 1992 we find the same rhetoric in a study of Q1 *Hamlet*: 'One who can believe, for example, that the Q1 text of Hamlet's "To be or not to be" soliloquy is the work of Shakespeare can believe anything.'[53]

Allied to this rhetorical denigration of alternative theories are two further denigrations – of the alleged reporter's function and of his intellectual abilities. Function first. Although several suspect texts, notably Q1 *Hamlet*, Q1 *Romeo and Juliet*, A *Dr Faustus*, and Q *The Taming of A Shrew*, show clear evidence of a second hand contributing new writing, this 'new writing' is never conceptualised as 'authorship', even when the 'reporter' is behaving suspiciously like a 'playwright'.[54] Kirschbaum tells us that in A *Dr Faustus* 4.2:

> we catch the reporter literally copying from *EFB* [*English Faust Book*], which he has opened in order to see how he could construct a scene which would omit all reference to Bruno and which would both begin and terminate the scoffing knight situation.[55]

When Shakespeare or other known authors perform such activities they are 'using sources'; when a nameless other does it, he is mindlessly 'copying'.[56]

This leads us to intellectual ability: it is curious how reporters are rarely credited with intelligence. Greg talks about the 'dull reporter' of *Henry 5*, Kirschbaum believes that the reporter of *King Lear* had a 'capable auditory memory but not a very high degree of intelligence'; Alexander tells us that '[t]he compiler of *A Shrew* while trying to follow the sub-plot of *The Shrew* gave it up as too complicated to reproduce, and fell back on love scenes'.[57] Faulty memory, however, does not automatically imply faulty intelligence.[58]

Two further general points arising from Kirschbaum's work require mention. We have already seen how Greg minimised the problems in F *The Merry Wives of Windsor* and A *Orlando Furioso* in order to create a 'good' text to compare with the perceived 'bad'. Kirschbaum follows the same procedure in his study of *Dr Faustus*. After analysing textual problems in A *Dr Faustus* Kirschbaum concludes that 'A must be a bad quarto *and that B must be a good quarto*'.[59] But the first conclusion does not lead inevitably to the second, nor does it follow that if A is not 'good' it is inevitably 'bad'.

The New Bibliographers come very close to the rhetorical sleight-of-hand used by Richard 3 when he presents 'lover' versus 'villain' as the only two character options in his opening soliloquy, or tells Lady Anne in the next scene that if she does not kill him, she must marry him. These options are not logical alternatives, just as they are not the only available alternatives. It does not follow that if A *Dr Faustus* and *The Blind Beggar of Alexandria* and *John of Bordeaux* and *The True Tragedy of Richard 3* and *The Fair Maid of Bristow* are problematic they must be 'bad', or if 'bad' must be memorial (or, for that matter, if memorial must be 'bad'). The New Bibliography's antithetical terminology leads to an antithetical mindset, both of which are hard to cast off. As Paul Werstine has pointed out, even *The Division of the Kingdoms*, which attempted to overturn New Bibliographic thinking about Q *King Lear*, simply swapped one set of New Bibliographic antimonies for another: bad versus good became foul papers versus revision.[60]

Kirschbaum's 'Census of Bad Quartos' highlights the astonishing diversity of texts grouped together under the label 'bad'. In the 1990s critics tend to agree that texts such as *The Taming of A Shrew* are remarkably different in quality (and perhaps origin) from those such as Q *Richard 3*. But it is apparent that, in the first half of this century, New Bibliographers did not know what they meant by a 'bad' text. Greg felt that *Pericles* 'nowhere approaches the worst of the other "bad" quartos, and on the whole resembles *Henry V* . . . less than it does *King Lear*'. Pollard considered *Pericles* 'a scandalously bad text', so bad that he likened it to Q1 *Romeo and Juliet*. Alfred Hart declared Q1 *Romeo and Juliet* the 'least corrupt of the bad quartos' and Greg found it as good as Q *King Lear*. *1 Contention*, which critics from Alexander onwards generally declare far superior to other suspect texts, is characterised by Hart as being, along with Q1 *Hamlet*, 'the most corrupt of the five bad quartos written mainly in verse'.[61]

This disagreement stems partly from the lack of context in New Bibliographic studies of suspect texts. Kirschbaum's method of diagnosis was impressionistic, as we saw in chapter 1. However, his census was valuable in assembling a list of suspect texts so that critics could begin to discern their similarities and differences.

HARRY R. HOPPE

In 1948 Harry Hoppe expanded the associative inquiry begun by Kirschbaum, adding the anonymous manuscript play *John of Bordeaux* (no date), Peele's *The Old Wife's Tale* (1595), and Chapman's *The Blind Beggar of Alexandria* (1598) to the list of suspect texts and resurrecting the case for *The Taming of A Shrew* (1594).[62] (Greg, reviewing the book-length study of Q1 *Romeo and Juliet* in which these additions were presented, praised Hoppe's work on other suspect texts as being of particular value.)[63]

Hoppe also systematised the method of diagnosing faulty memory which Greg had developed in *Two Elizabethan Stage Abridgements*. He arranged copious examples of alleged memorial error under orderly headings: improvisations, transpositions, anticipations, recollections, borrowings, mishearings, paraphrase. Anticipating possible objections to these categories he announced:

> Not so many years ago it might have appeared perilously close to begging the question to follow this line of argument, namely: A memorial reconstruction of a play by former actors should display certain qualities; such qualities can be pointed out in numerous plays

whose texts have been judged corrupt and can be illustrated extensively from the bad text of *Romeo and Juliet*; therefore, these plays and *Romeo and Juliet* in particular are memorial reconstructions. However . . . we now have independent evidence to bolster this reasoning.[64]

The first part of Hoppe's independent evidence comes from the Sheridan canon in which two plays were 'reconstructed largely from memory'. In fact, Alexander had already pointed out that, although memory played a part in reconstructing *The Duenna* and *The School for Scandal*, the systems responsible for both texts were more different than similar, and it would be an over-simplification to say that the texts were memorial reconstructions.[65] Hoppe's second piece of independent evidence comes from the manuscript play *John of Bordeaux* which he has identified as a memorial reconstruction because its verbal difficulties match those in other alleged suspect texts. Sadly, despite the disavowals, this kind of circular logic underpins Hoppe's book.

Hoppe's attempt to classify Greg's symptoms of faulty memory was laudable in its goal of imposing order on a large collection of heterogeneous symptoms. However, an initially promising division of evidence into 'external' and 'internal' signs was undermined by the definition of 'external' as being those signs 'which would be immediately evident to an educated person...if he had copies of the texts before him', and 'internal' as being 'those which would be manifest to him only after prolonged reading and examination'. Hoppe's discussion therefore begins with 'such relatively obvious manifestations as stage directions, palpable errors in versification, omitted scenes or lengthy passages, and attributions of speeches to wrong characters'.[66]

Hoppe is on firmer ground with the verbal features included in his 'internal' category, but he misapplies them. Thus, a lengthy list of borrowings from other plays cites only Shakespearean plays written mostly at the same time as *Romeo and Juliet*, and so introduces the possibility of common authorial vocabulary and phrasing (which Hoppe ignores). Furthermore, Hoppe's list contains analogous rather than identical borrowings. *Richard 2*'s 'And then be gone, and trouble you no more' may or may not be echoed memorially in *Romeo and Juliet*'s 'So get thee gone and trouble me no more'.[67] But if this parallel is admitted only as a possibility, it has limited value in a diagnostic check-list. Diagnosis of faulty memory must be based on substantial evidence, not on outside chance.[68]

The same criticisms apply to Hoppe's examples of repetitions ('[w]ords, phrases or passages that are used more than once'; p.128) within Q1 *Romeo and Juliet*:

> 'Tomorrow morning,' obviously wrong, recalls II.ii.173, 'What o'clock tomorrow shall I send?' and Romeo's reply, 'At the hour of nine'; and 'she shall not fail' is reminiscent of II.ii.176, 'I will not fail.'
> (p.133)

Repetition of such conventional phrasing carries little weight as evidence of anything (as we shall see in detail in chapter 7); it is nonetheless a mainstay of diagnostic studies of suspect texts by Greg, Patrick, Kirschbaum, Duthie, Hart, and Hoppe.

CONCLUSION

In 1950 Greg published what he considered his greatest work: *Marlowe's 'Doctor Faustus' 1604–1616*. This weighty study repeated the diagnostic methods and conclusions of his work on *Orlando Furioso*. (The added complication of Henslowe's *Diary* entry in 1602 recording payment to Bird and Rowley for additions to *Dr Faustus* was dealt with by dismissal: material in the 1616 B-text not present in the 1604 A-text did not represent the Bird and Rowley additions, Greg concluded.)[69]

Greg's conclusion that A *Dr Faustus* was a memorial reconstruction had been reached, independently, by Kirschbaum in an article published in 1946. It was two decades before dissent was voiced. This dissent was surprisingly ignored, perhaps because of the timid *politesse* with which it was voiced, perhaps because the dissenters were primarily literary critics. In 1964 C. L. Barber confessed:

> Almost everything I find occasion to use is in the 1604 Quarto; and I find its readings almost always superior to those of 1616. This experience inclines me to regard most of the 1604 text (with some obvious interpolations) as Marlowe's, or close to Marlowe's, whereas most of the additional matter in the 1616 version seems to me to lack imaginative and stylistic relation to the core of the play. Thus my

experience as a reader runs counter to the conclusions in favor of the 1616 Quarto which W. W. Greg arrives at from textual study and hypothesis.[70]

Four years later Robert Ornstein began his analysis with a trenchant defence of the A-text as 'more powerful and artistically compelling' than the B-text:

> Indeed, if the 1604 Quarto is, as Greg argues, a memorial reconstruction of a truncated and degraded performance version of Marlowe's play, then it is a uniquely remarkable one which reproduces the main plot with extraordinary accuracy, which restores more memorable and unmistakeably Marlovian passages than it omits, and which again and again either corrects errors in the 1616 text or offers more terse and vivid readings.[71]

Shortly afterwards, Philip Brockbank qualified his summary (and endorsement) of Greg's thinking on the texts of *Dr Faustus*: 'it is hard to see why the supposedly garbled report of the A-text should preserve so much of what we value in the play'.[72] Although they do not state it as such, what the above critics are questioning is New Bibliographic methodology.

The common denominator of all the above studies, from Greg to Hoppe, is an apparently stringent diagnostic ('scientific') methodology which nonetheless conceals a large measure of illogic. Let us briefly consider some cases in which near-identical sets of repetitions are ascribed totally different explanations.

In Q2 *Romeo and Juliet* Romeo closes Act 2, scene 2 as follows:

> The grey eyde morne smiles on the frowning night,
> Checkring the Easterne Clouds with streaks of light,
> And darknesse fleckted like a drunkard reeles,
> From forth daies pathway, made by *Tytans* wheeles.
> Hence will I to my ghostly Friers close cell,
> His helpe to craue, and my deare hap to tell.
>   (D4v,13–18)

The Friar opens the next scene with a repetition of Romeo's lines (bar the concluding couplet) with minor variations: 'Checking' for 'Checkring', 'fleckeld darknesse' for 'darknesse fleckted', 'daies path' for 'daies pathway' and '*Titans* burning wheeles' for '*Tytans* wheeles'. Until recently, the explanation has been that Q2 reflects underlying authorial manuscript copy: Shakespeare was undecided as to who should speak these lines.[73]

In *Richard Duke of York* we have a similar repetition. At CIr,30–CIv,I Warwick says,

> For strokes receiude, and manie blowes repaide,
> Hath robd my strong knit sinnews of their strength,

He repeats himself, with minor variants, on E2v,27–8:

> For manie wounds receiu'd, and manie moe repaid,
> Hath robd my strong knit sinews of their strength,

For this text, however, the explanation is memorial error. The reporter, we are told, has anticipated, misplacing Warwick's lines from E2v, where they should correctly occur (since they feature at that stage of the action in the related text, F *3 Henry 6*), on CIr–v.

The two cases are not identical (since in *Romeo and Juliet* two speakers are involved and the repetition is immediate, whereas in *Richard Duke of York* we are dealing with one speaker and repetitions separated by several hundred lines), but they are close enough to make a point. And the point is: why does one 'prove' indecisive authorial copy and the other 'prove' memorial reconstruction?

I Contention contains a related problem concerning a two-line repetition by York. On A4r,30–I York responds in soliloquy to an earlier conversation about the loss of France:

> Cold newes for me, for I had hope of *France*,
> Euen as I haue of fertill England.

On D4r,3–4 he repeats these lines identically (in a presumed aside), following Somerset's announcement that English territories in France are lost. At first glance it might seem that the earlier appearance of the line is an anticipation, for the second appearance is rhetorically integrated and better motivated. In the lead-in sequence King Henry asks 'what newes from France?', to which Somerset replies 'Cold newes my Lord'. Having heard the news, Henry supports Somerset's judgement ('Cold newes indeed'), which paves the way for York's second 'cold newes for me . . .'. Interestingly, this set of repetitions appears identically in the Folio. By the current diagnostic rules both these repetitions may be considered memorial; but one text is designated 'bad' and the other 'good'. As Hamlet reminds us, '[t]here is nothing either good or bad, but thinking makes it so'.

In this chapter I have tried to show that those who first pioneered memorial reconstruction claimed far less for it than we suppose, and that those who subsequently adopted the theory of memorial reconstruction did so without developing a sufficiently rigorous system for diagnosing it. Alan Dessen has recently stated that the claims for memorial reconstruction are 'possible but by no means proven (or perhaps provable)'.[74] This has not prevented memorial reconstruction becoming established in the popular imagination, as illustrated by James Fenton's creative characterisation of a drink-induced Marcellus,[75] or Roy Fuller's poem, 'The Marcellus Version' (*with thanks to James Fenton*), part of which reads:

> It must be twenty years ago he came
> And asked me what I remembered of the play.
> Nick Lang or Ling his name; and then a dog
> Called Sims, black-fingered printer from the City,
> Took down my words. Odd's blood, the longest sessions
> Of canting and Canary ever known!
> I'd been a quick study, quick also to forget.
> Whether the fellows knew this, who can tell?
> Or why they lit on me. There was a haste
> To be the first to sell it to the gulls
> And play it in the provinces. Quoth I:
> 'What part for me?' 'Marcellus.' 'Goblin damned!'
> 'Also the doubling in the pantomime.'
> I took the ducats for my memory
> And let them toil to Preston with the play.
> I stayed in town. Worked, yes, but rested more.[76]

Having questioned the way in which the New Bibliography has built up the theory of memorial reconstruction, our task now will be to see what evidence can be found to support it. Chapter 4 accordingly considers the external evidence for reporting.

4 | Reporting speech, reconstructing texts

of our text, / You make a wronge construction
Heywood, 1 If You Know Not Me (1605) 78–9.

EVADNE: where got you this report[?]
MELANTIUS: Where there was people[,] in euery place.
Beaumont and Fletcher, The Maid's Tragedy (1619) G4r,14–15

Up to now my investigation of memorial reconstruction has concentrated on the twentieth century and the theories offered by textual critics to explain suspect texts. I now turn my attention to the sixteenth and seventeenth centuries, to ascertain what external evidence exists for invoking memory, reconstruction, and actors, independently or together, to explain suspect texts.

As we shall see, what evidence there is supports the theory that plays could be, and were, reconstructed from memory. However, the evidence suggests that the concept of play reconstruction is not a single sequence of processes with a single objective (reconstruction from memory by actors for the purpose of performance) but a variety of processes involving different kinds of agents (auditors, actors, or other playhouse personnel), different purposes (performance, publication, private transcript), and different combinations of memory and other aids to recall (longhand notes, shorthand notes, reports of narrative outline) often supplemented by new composition.

The brevity of this chapter testifies to the paucity of external evidence. The evidence, such as it is, is nonetheless complex, drawing on a wide range of genres, periods, and cultures. My departure point is not Elizabethan drama, but its parallel in terms of popular and edifying entertainment: church sermons. This subject enables us to consider the evidence for reconstructing speech in a broader sense in the Elizabethan period. From here I turn to the Elizabethan playhouse, before moving further afield to seventeenth-century Spain and eighteenth-century England.

REPORTING SERMONS AND SPEECHES

Abundant references by congregation members and preachers attest to the prevalent phenomenon of notetaking in church. The devotional diary kept by Lady Margaret Hoby between 1599 and 1605 refers repeatedly to the accompanying sermon book (no longer extant) into which she copied notes made at the Sunday church services. The diary kept by the young Inns of Court lawyer, John Manningham, between 1602 and 1603 regularly provides accounts of sermons, with summaries and quotations ranging from four to four thousand lines. In his poem 'On Dr Donne's Death' Jasper Mayne describes how Donne's gestures could be translated into notes as meaningfully as could his words:

> Yet have I seene thee in the pulpit stand,
> Where wee might take notes, from thy looke, and hand;
> And from thy speaking action beare away
> More Sermon, then some teachers use to say.[1]

Clearly, conscientious churchgoers regularly took notes of the material they heard.[2]

In his preface to the second edition (STC 7539) of the 'Lecture on Restitution' which he delivered at the Blackfriars in 1589, the preacher Stephen Egerton writes:

> And nowe touching noting at Sermons giue me leaue . . . to tell thee what I thinke. For the thing it selfe, I dare not . . . condemne it as vnlawful, but rather commend it as expedient, if there be iudgement, memory and dexteritie of hand in the partie.
> (A4r–v)[3]

Egerton condemns notetaking for 'filthy lucre or vaine-glory' (A4v), and continues:

> my aduise is, to such as haue . . . ready hands, and conuenient places to write at Sermons, that they would vse it for their owne priuate helpe and edification[.]
> (A5v–A6r)

Egerton's advice almost certainly refers not to notes made for private devotional use, such as those taken by Lady Margaret Hoby and John Manningham, but to notes taken in shorthand to provide a text of the sermon for publication: for in the 1580s and 1590s a number of sermons reached print claiming to be reports by shorthand.

The title-page of the first edition of Egerton's 'Lecture on Restitution' (1589; STC 7538) states that the text was '*taken as it was vttered by Characterie*' (a system of shorthand), by a young reporter, A. S., who provides a preface to the edition:

> It hath bin (Christian Reader) till of late, much wished, that there
> were an ordinarie way of swift writing, whereby, Sermons and
> Lectures of godly Preachers might bee preserued ... This desire of
> manie, hath lately bene satisfied, by an Art called Characterie, which I
> hauing learned, haue put in practise, in writing sermons. ... I haue not
> missed one word; whereby, either the truth of doctrine might be
> peruerted, or the meaning of the Preacher altered. Such is the vse of
> the art, which I haue learned.
> (Aiir–v)[4]

Despite such claims to accuracy, numerous preachers lament the way in which reporting has 'mangled' their sermons. Even so the preachers are, without exception, content to allow the reported version to serve as the basis of the later revised text. The reason for this procedure is not entirely clear, but, as we shall see, it cannot be because the reported text faithfully represents the original sermon.[5]

Sermons normally lasted one hour. (John Manningham indicates that Egerton was accustomed to time his sermons with an hour-glass,[6] and in the published texts of their sermons, Robert Saunderson and Thomas Playfere provide marginal marks to indicate the material they were obliged to omit to prevent overrunning the hour's limit.) The sermons supplied by Henry Smith for his collected works each contain approximately 10,000 words, totals which far exceed those of either his reported sermons (c.4,000–6,000) or those sermons which were reported and subsequently corrected (c.6,000–7,800). If we exclude the possibility that the increased totals represent material added for publication (an unlikely possibility, since the shorter versions' 4,000–8,000 word-totals represent a painfully slow pace of delivery for a sixty-minute sermon; Saunderson's sermons, by contrast, all contain approximately 11,200 words when his cuts tailoring the sermon 'to the houre' are observed), it is clear that Elizabethan shorthand reporting was incapable of reproducing an hour-long sermon in its entirety.[7]

The reporter of Egerton's 'Lecture on Restitution' describes himself as a practitioner of 'Characterie'. Timothy Bright's *Characterie, An Art of Short, Swift, and Secret Writing* (1588) presented a complex, non-orthographic, non-cursive method of shorthand, written vertically, and based on an 'alphabet' of eighteen signs. To these signs could be attached end-signals, resulting in a total of 537 possible permutations which would indicate words. Charactery depended on the reduction of a word to its 'character'; thus 'heaven' was the root symbol for element, firmament, moon, planet, pole, sky, sun, star, and zone. 'Day' was the root element for Sunday, Monday, Tuesday (etc.), cockcrow, dawning, evening, hour, midnight, minute, morning, night, and twilight. Bright provided a table of suggested associations at the end of his book: 'because euery man by his own reache can not consider how to refer all words, thou hast in this booke an English dictionary, . . . to help such as of the[m]selues can not so dispose the[m]' (A7v). Bright also provided instructions for paraphrase and summary when Charactery could not achieve verbatim reporting, a clear admission that his system is an *aide-mémoire* rather than a means of transcription.[8]

In 1590 Peter Bales published a rival system, Brachygraphy (*The Writing Schoolmaster*, STC 1312), which seems to have been more popular than Bright's method (his book had a second edition and a sequel). However, Brachygraphy was not a significant improvement on Charactery, being a system of abbreviation rather than shorthand. It used the letters of the alphabet, to which forty-eight end-signals were attached. A letter accompanied by a dot, for example, has twelve different meanings depending on the position of the dot: d means Descend, ˙d means Day, ·d means Deceive, ·d means Dedicate, .d means Defend, and ˌd means Deprive. The opportunities for confusion when writing carelessly or in haste are obvious. Bales's system, like Bright's, depended on synonyms and antonyms, while relying heavily on the practitioner's memory for comparisons, tenses, numbers, auxiliaries, and derivatives.

In 1602 a third system was published, John Willis's *Stenography*. This method was superior to the systems of Bright and Bales in that it was a phonetic shorthand. Although its late publication appears to disqualify it from potential responsibility for the suspect texts of the 1590s, it was probably in use before 1602. In 1588 Bright was granted a royal patent which gave him a fifteen-year monopoly on teaching and publishing shorthand. Systems already in existence were not affected by the monopoly. Since Bales's and Willis's systems were published within the period of the monopoly, we must conclude that they were already known.

Both Bright and Bales were modest in their claims for the application of their systems. Bright said his system could enable practitioners to 'write Orations, or publike actions of speach, **uttered as becommeth the grauitie of such actions**, *verbatim*' (A3r; my emphasis). Bales promised verbatim reporting of sermons or speeches only if they were 'deliuered *treatablie*, as best becommeth the grauitie of the Preacher or speaker' (C1r; my emphasis). Sir George Buc's statement in *The Third Universitie of England* (1615) actually claims more for Brachygraphy than Bales ever did: those who know brachygraphy 'can readily take a Sermon, Oration, *Play*, or any long speech, as they are spoke[n], dictated, acted, & vttered in the instant' (my emphasis).[9] As we saw in chapters 2 and 3, later writers enthusiastically claim more for a system (memorial reconstruction, brachygraphy) than do its first exponents. That shorthand was used to report sermons is evident; that it was capable of doing so accurately is less likely.[10]

A seventeenth-century stationer's apprentice provides more details about shorthand and its usefulness in preparing texts of sermons, when he describes his master's methods of acquiring textual copies:

> he[,] ... observing what books sold best, ... found that factious
> Sermons, and such like things would do the business; he thereupon
> bestirs himself, and gets acquainted with most of the factious Priests
> about Town, by often hearing them and frequenting their Companies,
> and having learned to write short-hand, took notes of their Sermons,
> which he Collected together, and now and then he would get them to
> revise one of them, and print it; by this means spending much time
> and mony amongst them, he grew very intimate, and was become the
> general publisher of most of their Sermons and Controversies.[11]

Notice that, even in the seventeenth century, shorthand is only used to write sermon notes, not to make verbatim transcripts, and, as was often the case in the Elizabethan period, the preacher is prevailed upon to correct the shorthand version, not to provide the original manuscript copy.

Mention should be made here of the reports by the chronicler Edward Hall of Henry 8's speeches. In 1529 rumours about Henry's marriage had reached such heights that the King summoned his nobility and counsellors to Bridewell to tell them 'his entent and purpose'. Then, Hall writes, Henry uttered 'as nere as my witte could beare away these wordes folowyng'; 'these wordes folowyng' comprise seventy-four lines of moral considerations about marriage to a deceased brother's betrothed.[12] The vocabulary is conventional and the speech, as presented, short, and would not have presented insuperable difficulties to anyone writing in long- or shorthand.

The same can be said of Henry's last speech to Parliament, 24 December 1545, which Hall reported 'as foloweth worde for worde, as nere as I was able to report it'.[13] The 146 lines presented are theological, moral, appreciative, and hortatory, the vocabulary being the conventional language of formal manners. The sentiments are repeated and repetitive (althought the phrasing is not); the speech limits itself to three ideas (a standard oratorical device); and it is well structured and brief. (The brevity of both reports may of course reflect the limitations of Hall's reporting and not the length of the original speeches.) Although this seems a straightforward oration to report, the Secretary of State, Sir William Petre, apparently did not find it so: his report of that speech, as A. F. Pollard tells us, was written within a few hours of its delivery but never published in Henry's *Letters and Papers*, because 'Gairdner, the archivist, thought Hall the journalist's a better report than the Secretary of State's'.[14] Athough Hall does not claim that his reports are accurate (both speeches are reported 'as nere' as he was able), Gairdner's editorial decision is a high compliment to the chronicler.

REPORTING PLAYS

The reporting of sermons in church, whether in longhand or shorthand, whether for private use or public sale, whether the entire sermon or choice quotations, is attested to with some frequency. Less frequent but more varied references exist to reporting in the playhouse. Audience members, we know, took their table-books (pocket notebooks) to plays to record jests, *mots justes*, pithy quotations, and *sententiae* for later personal contemplation. In the induction to Marston's *The Malcontent* Sly tells the tireman 'I am one that hath seene this play often, & can give them [the players] intellegence for their action: I have most of the ieasts heere in my table-booke' (A3r). The prologue to Beaumont and Fletcher's *The Custom of the Country* describes how such note-taking could provide the gallant with dinner-table conversation. The players

> dare looke
> *On any man, that brings his Table-booke*
> *To write downe, what againe he may repeate*
> *At some greate Table, to deserve his meate.*

In Q1 *Hamlet* the Prince warns the players that gentlemen note the clown's jokes in their table-books.[15] In *The Scourge of Villainy* (1599; STC 17486) Satyre X Marston mocks Luscus who

> nere of ought did speake
> But when of playes or Plaiers he did treat.
> H'ath made a common-place booke out of playes,
> And speakes in print, . . .
> He writes, he railes, he iests, he courts, what not,
> And all from out his huge long scraped stock
> Of well penn'd playes.
>   (H4r,4–17)

Note-taking by individuals in the playhouse for personal use was clearly a frequent practice, acknowledged and accepted by the players.[16] It is when we narrow our focus to the evidence for reconstructing an entire drama that the scene begins to cloud. There are, as we shall see, references to this practice but they are complicated and/or ambiguous. Some invoke memory, some invoke note-taking or note-taking supplemented by memory, some invoke entirely new writing to supplement notes or memory. A glance at the strongest piece of evidence, a reference to a *form* of memorial reconstruction, will show how potentially complicated the subject of dramatic reporting may be in practice.

Robert Taylor's play *The Hog Hath Lost His Pearl* was entered in the

Stationers' Register on 23 May 1614 and published in the same year (Harbage and Schoenbaum date the composition as 1613). The play has apparently been revised: contemporary comments suggest that the content was less innocuous than that represented by the extant quarto.[17] As it stands, however, the play is a harmless burlesque, full of theatrical jokes and conscious of parodic stage effects. It is this theatrical awareness which calls attention to an otherwise innocuous reference.

The plot concerns the attempts of Haddit, a youthful gallant, to win his sweetheart from the clutches of her father, Hog, a usurer. This he does by staging an elaborate play – which Hog mistakes for a magical visitation – in Hog's bedchamber at night. Haddit employs a player to help him in his enterprise, and, in Act 1, the player comes to collect the written entertainment. Haddit is initially hesitant:

> I feare you haue learned it by heart, if you haue powdred vp my plot in your sconce, you may home sir and instruct your Poet ouer a pot of ale, the whole methode on't, but if you do so iuggle, looke too't[.]
> (166–9)

This seems to be a reference to reconstruction by memory, not of the verbal fabric of the play, but of the outline, which was then expanded by another dramatist.

It was this combination of resources which Chapman apparently had in mind in his dedicatory sonnet to the 1605 edition of *All Fools*.[18] In it Chapman explains how he aims to forestall publication of an *Ersatz* edition of the play by sanctioning publication himself:

> least by others stealth it be imprest,
> without my pasport, patcht with others wit.

The inference is that reports of plays (whether of plot, language, or both) were tidied up with new writing to make texts suitable for publication.

The conversation in *The Hog Hath Lost his Pearl* contains a further item of related interest. The player responds to Haddit's suspicion with 'Nay, I pray sir be not angry, for as I am a true stage-trotter, I meane honestly' (172–3). The *OED* does not record this compound. Outside equestrian use, however, the term 'trotter' means 'one who moves or goes about briskly and constantly', specifically (in university slang) 'a tailor's assistant who goes around for orders (*OED* 'trotter' 2).[19] A manager like Henslowe must have employed a messenger to communicate between dramatist and play-house. (Such a person must have been employed in Henslowe's dealings with Robert Daborne to chivvy the tardy dramatist, and to take his fair and foul copies back to the playhouse.) Haddit's mistrust of the player is pre-sumably based on knowledge of contemporary practice, and the player's avowal of loyalty suggests that there were stage-trotters who were not honest. This conversation complicates the conjectured transmission of suspect texts, for it suggests that memorial reconstruction was not limited to actors, nor was it as straightforward as we would like to believe. A stage-trotter would have had access to rehearsals and to the tiring-house, and if he lacked 'a little money and much discretion', as did the person who supplied an unauthorised and corrupt copy of *Gorboduc* to the printer in 1565, who knows what the result may have been?[20]

In 1608 Heywood lamented plays 'corrupt and mangled, (copied onely by the eare)',[21] a complaint he repeated less ambiguously in 1637 in a pro-logue to a revival of *1 If You Know Not Me* (a play first published in 1605 in a suspect text). Heywood blames the poor textual quality of the first edition on stenography:

> some by Stenography, drew
> The plot: put it in print: (scarce one word trew)[22]

He then explains that he has set the lame edition back on its feet. Since no extant edition contains either Heywood's original or his corrected text, we have no means of assessing the divergences between the first edition and Heywood's belated replacement. It is, however, the belatedness of Heywood's testimony that renders it less reliable than it might have been thirty years earlier. Our confidence in the statement also depends on whether it should be taken literally as a reference to the plot, for surely longhand would suffice for a scenario? In his analysis of Q1 *1 If You Know Not Me* Giordano-Orsini concludes that the text is a memorial reconstruc-tion; Heywood, he says, was mistaken in his suggestion of shorthand, or, if shorthand were used, it was supplemented by other means.[23] If Giordano-Orsini's conclusion is correct, it suggests that Heywood had no idea how his text had been constructed and was clutching at possible explanatory straws.[24] If, on the other hand, Heywood's allegation is taken at face value, we have a scenario very close to that in Chapman's statement or that in *The Hog Hath Lost his Pearl*.

I. A. Shapiro is but one of several critics from Tycho Mommsen onwards to argue that notes of a play's outline with some speeches and quotations, subsequently reworked into a new dramatic whole by another dramatist, provides the most plausible explanation for a number of suspect texts.[25] Shapiro's hypothetical scenario corresponds almost exactly to that depicted in *The Hog Hath Lost his Pearl*.

The primary difference between the evidence adduced so far and twentieth-century theories of memorial reconstruction is the suggestion of theft: Haddit's 'iuggle', the player's protestation of honesty, and Chapman's 'stealth'.[26] With the exception of Greg's analysis of *The Merry Wives of Windsor*, and a throwaway remark about Abel Jeffes's lost/destroyed edition of *The Spanish Tragedy*,[27] dishonesty and theft have not been major features in narratives of memorial reconstruction. The *raison d'être* of reconstruction is generally seen as performance, with publication very much an afterthought: 'the natural object of the exercise was not to sell them [reconstructed texts] (though they evidently were sold later) but to act them'.[28] But, in so far as their ambiguous references can be pressed, Chapman and Heywood seem to be assuming theft for publication. 'Assuming' may, however, be the operative word here: we do not know that Chapman and Heywood had any more evidence to support their assumption about publication than did the New Bibliographers to support their assumption about performance.

For reference to another scenario for suspect texts, one involving reconstruction for neither performance nor publication, we must turn to the Beaumont and Fletcher Folio (*Comedies and Tragedies*) of 1647. The stationer, Humphrey Moseley, provides a preface to the volume in which he explains his choice of textual copy (unabridged authorial texts in preference to abridged playbooks) and adds:

> When these *Comedies* and *Tragedies* were presented on the Stage, the *Actours* omitted some *Scenes* and Passages (with the *Authour's* consent) as occasion led them; and when private friends desir'd a Copy, they then (and justly too) transcribed what they *Acted*.
>
> (A4r)

Peter Blayney, who cites this passage in a discussion of suspect texts, explains that in 1647 'transcribe' meant 'only to make a copy *of*, not necessarily *from*, and Moseley isn't talking about fair copies of promptbooks'.[29] Since it is unlikely that an actor would be permitted to borrow a playbook simply to make a private copy for a friend, Blayney concludes that the actors must have copied out the text from memory of performance. Moseley, in other words, is referring to memorial reconstruction.

The scenario Moseley depicts is innocuous in intent and origin, the money the player presumably received for his efforts falling into that moral grey area known as 'perk of the job', not theft. If this memorial copy, or a copy of this copy, happened to reach a printer, it would indeed be a suspect text; but it would not be 'stolen and surreptitious' in the usual sense.

Moseley's narrative can explain the multiple layers Greg found in *The Merry Wives of Windsor*, and it can also explain the diverse quality of suspect texts where much must depend on the size of the role of the actor who receives a request for reconstruction. (M. M. Mahood has recently suggested that the suspect texts 'represent a surprising familiarity with the text on the part of the hired men'.)[30] However, it would be a mistake to assume that Moseley's scenario must supersede those of Chapman or Heywood or *The Hog Hath Lost His Pearl*. Given the extraordinary range in quality and features of suspect texts (see chapter 8) it is likely that no single scenario explains all suspect texts.

For further evidence relating to the method, agent and purpose behind suspect texts we now move further afield.

REPORTING SPANISH GOLDEN-AGE DRAMA

Lope de Vega (1562–1635), Madrid's (and Spain's) most prolific dramatist, composed about 1500 plays, of which approximately one-fifth survive. A number of these dramas were apparently reconstructed by *memoriones* (memory men). On several occasions Lope complained in print about the damage inflicted on his texts by these memory men. In 1620 he inveighed against

> the stealing of comedias by those whom the vulgar call, the one *Memorilla*, and the other *Gran Memoria*, who, with the few verses which they learn, mingle an infinity of their own barbarous lines,

whereby they earn a living, selling them to the villages and to distant theatrical managers[.][31]

In 1615 Cristobal Suarez de Figueroa described the antics of Luis Ramirez, 'a young man of remarkable memory' who could reproduce from memory 'an entire comedia on hearing it three times, without the slightest variation either in plot or verses'. On one occasion an actor on stage called attention to Ramirez's presence by performing his lines so inaccurately that the audience was moved to demand an explanation. The actor explained that he was attempting to foil any subsequent reconstruction by Ramirez by giving him a faulty text to memorise. The audience insisted that the performance be suspended until Ramirez had left the theatre.[32]

It should be noted that the first reference above provides, and the second assumes, a financial motive for reconstruction: the auditor is reconstructing a text for sale (and for personal gain). In neither case are actors involved in the reconstruction.

José Ruano de la Haza has compared the MS version of Lope's *Peribañez y el Commendador de Ocaña* with the printed version.[33] He concludes that the manuscript is a memorial reconstruction. The details of his argument have a familiar ring. The manuscript version is 573 lines shorter than the printed text's 3,131 lines. Only about 100 lines are identical or near-identical, the remainder reproducing the 'ideas, thoughts and images of the original' but in different 'vocabulary, imagery, and mode of expression' (p.7). The result is a 'more pedestrian text than Lope's original' (p.7). It tones down or omits sexual imagery, omits mythological, classical and literary allusions, errs in historical details, exaggerates, anticipates, simplifies, renders ambiguities explicit, creates one-dimensional characters, and alters plot. Notwithstanding, the manuscript's alterations result in a dramatically more effective text, making, for example, 'a more effective use of the stage-balcony than Lope does' (p.13), transposing scenes, and inserting others which increase the dramatic suspense and heighten the emotional impact (p.26). Seven new scenes, totalling 218 lines are inserted; 388 lines of Lope's play are omitted.

These omissions are deemed deliberate. Ruano believes that the *memorion* 'took down the details of the original plot . . . and . . . also tried to reproduce from memory as much as he could of the original text'; the text was then supplemented by an *autor de comedias* who 'filled in the lacunae left by the *memorion* and then adapted and modified the play with a performance and a specific audience in mind' (pp.8–9). This specific audience Ruano believes to be provincial. A provincial venue is deemed consistent with many of the alterations, for the reduced sexuality and the suppression of daring sentiments (such as the Commendador's willingness to change his position for that of his inferior) 'might have seemed offensive to the sensibilities of a rural audience' (p.9). Topical references intelligible only in Madrid, such as the reference to Italian acrobats, are omitted. What remains is emphasised, clarified, and repeated, so that the (less sophisticated) rural audience will not fail to grasp its significance.

So far this narrative, and the authorial statement which gives rise to it, overlaps in an interesting way with the details supplied by Elizabethan testimony (alleging memory supplemented by new writing) and with the scenario advanced by Greg *et al.* (postulating reconstruction for provincial performance). Ruano's article is similar in tone and attitude to much New Bibliographic writing on the same topic. The difference is that Ruano's assumptions have the contemporary and clear authority of the playwright to support them, which the assumptions of the British New Bibliographers do not.

It should be stressed that I have not subjected Lope's statements or plays, or Ruano's analysis, to the same sceptical enquiry as I did the evidence and conclusions advanced by the New Bibliographers. It would take a more competent Hispanist than myself to interrogate this material fairly and thoroughly. I include this brief summary of the Lope material for one reason: it provides independent contemporary evidence of the phenomenon of play reporting. How useful that evidence is remains to be seen.

REPORTING PLAYS (AND PROSE) IN THE EIGHTEENTH CENTURY

The next cluster of references which support memorial reconstruction is closer geographically but more distant in time. At the end of the eighteenth century two of Sheridan's plays, *The Duenna* and *The School for Scandal*, were reconstructed for provincial performance. Frustrated by authorial reluctance to publish new plays – a reluctance designed to prevent unauthorised performances such as those I am about to describe – Tate Wilkinson, manager of the Theatre Royal, York, created an acting text of *The Duenna*.

He had already seen the play performed several times.

> I locked myself up in my room, sat [*sic*] down first the jokes I
> remembered, then I laid a book of the songs before me, and with
> magazines kept the regulation of the scenes, and by the help of a
> numerous collection of obsolete Spanish plays I produced an excellent
> opera; I may say *excellent*[.][34]

The Duenna was first performed at Covent Garden in November 1775;
Wilkinson's text was performed at York early in 1777.

Two years later the cooperation of several actors facilitated the reconstruction of *The School for Scandal* for performance in Exeter. John Bernard offered to mastermind the reconstruction of the text provided the manuscript was destroyed by the theatre manager at the end of the season.

> This was agreed to, and I set about my task in the following manner. I
> had played Sir Benjamin at Bath and Charles at Richmond, and went
> on for Sir Peter one or two evenings when Edwin was indisposed; thus
> I had three parts in my possession. Dimond and Blissit (Joseph and
> Sir Oliver) transmitted theirs by post . . . Old Rowley was in the
> Company, and my wife had played both Lady Teazle and Mrs
> Candour. With these materials for a groundwork, my general
> knowledge of the play collected in rehearsing and performing in it
> above forty times, enabled me in a week to construct a comedy in five
> acts[.][35]

Peter Alexander rightly points out that these reconstructions of Sheridan resulted from two different techniques 'and the Shakespeare piracies, being more numerous, may offer much greater variety in method'.[36] Steven Urkowitz further contends that the textual quality of the reconstructions of Sheridan is markedly inferior to that of the Elizabethan suspect texts.[37] Different from the Jacobean testimonies (because the purpose of reconstruction is performance), and different from the Lope evidence (because reconstructed by theatrical personnel), and further different from both because belonging to a theatrical climate whose continuum with the Renaissance had been severed by the closing of the theatres, the Sheridan references nonetheless suggest that certain circumstances could drive theatrical personnel to recreate a text for performance.

John Bernard had the cooperation of his colleagues; he also had the good fortune to understudy the role of Sir Peter, which enabled him to add a third role to his repertory. It is sometimes contended that Elizabethan actors were unlikely to know other roles accurately in this way because understudies are a product of the long-run system, a system not in use until the Victorian period. However, Bernard, we notice, does not say that he 'understudied' Sir Peter; he says simply that he 'went on for Sir Peter', implying less that he knew the role perfectly than that he could do it. This may be a modest litotes meaning 'understudy'. Either way it refers to a practice, whether planned or *ad hoc*, to which Philip Henslowe also refers. In 1593 Henslowe's son-in-law, Edward Alleyn, was on tour with the Admiral's Men. In a letter to Alleyn, Henslowe expresses concern at the news that Alleyn has been sick. The line that concerns us is as follows: 'we hard that you weare very sycke at bathe & that *one of you' felowes weare fayne to playe you' parte for you'* (my emphasis).[38] Clearly the notion of 'understudy' was not totally foreign to Elizabethan repertory companies. There were substitutes who, if not regularly rehearsed in another role, knew something of the words and the action, and, in an emergency, could suit the one to the other.

A French anecdote from the eighteenth century returns us to the phenomenon of reconstruction by an audience member. In 1784 Thomas Holcroft and a friend tried to obtain a copy of *Le Mariage de Figaro* by attending the theatre in Paris on seven to ten consecutive evenings; on return to their lodgings they wrote, compared, and revised their versions every night 'till they had brought away the whole with perfect exactness'.[39] While this practice may add an ironic twist to the Doctor's words to Lady Macbeth's gentlewoman ('I haue too Nights watch'd with you, but can perceiue no truth in your report'; TLN 2095–6, 5.1.1–2), it is not directly transferrable to Elizabethan theatrical conditions, where ten (non-consecutive) performances often constituted an entire run. Henslowe's *Diary* shows that an auditor–thief would frequently need to wait several months to see the requisite number of performances. Still, some auditors did see the same play regularly as we find in the Induction to *The Malcontent*, where Sly boasts that he has 'seene this play often', and has all the jests in his tablebook. In *Jests to Make You Merry* (1607) Dekker refers to plays from previous seasons which 'euery punck and her squire . . . can rand out by heart they are so stale'.[40]

My last reference to reconstruction comes from a different genre of the eighteenth century, and concerns reconstruction from memory for the purpose of publication. In a letter to her sister Cassandra (11 June 1799) Jane Austen writes

> I would not let Martha read 'First Impressions' again upon any account, and am very glad that I did not leave it in your power. She is very cunning, but I saw through her design; she means to publish it from memory, and one more perusal must enable her to do it.[41]

This allusion is more problematic than initially appears. Martha (the friend Martha Lloyd, sister of Mrs James Austen) seems to be accused (proleptically) of memorially reconstructing a manuscript which she has read and therefore had in her hands as a material document. This is not as illogical as it sounds: although Martha would be able to take notes, she could presumably not make a transcript, full or partial, without arousing suspicion. Thus supplementation from memory would be required.

Austen may be using 'read' in the sense of 'hear' (i.e. attend a reading): oral presentation of novels was a family activity until at least the nineteenth century, an activity well suited to Jane Austen's dramatic dialogue. In such a case Martha would have no alternative but to reconstruct the novel memorially. However, the balance of probability is against this interpretation of 'read'. On 8 January 1799 Jane Austen wrote to Cassandra as follows: 'I do not wonder at your wanting to read "First Impressions" again, so seldom as you have gone through it, and that so long ago.'[42] Here 'read' clearly refers to the detailed contemplation of a manuscript draft, presumably with a view to providing constructive criticism.

The way in which Martha became acquainted or reacquainted with *First Impressions* is not important. What is significant is that Jane Austen accepts the phenomenon of 'unauthorised' publication of a text from memory without surprise. And if this were possible for an eighteenth-century novel, why not for a sixteenth-century play?

First Impressions, written between October 1796 and August 1797, was eventually published in 1813 as *Pride and Prejudice*. In 1797 Jane Austen's father offered *First Impressions* to the publisher Cadell, describing it as a novel 'comprising three volumes, about the length of Miss Burney's *Evelina*'. (Cadell rejected the offer without reading the manuscript.) R. W.

Chapman points out that *Pride and Prejudice* is 'not much more than three-quarters of the length of *Evelina*' but cautions 'it would be rash to build anything on this', citing evidence to show that Jane Austen inaccurately calculated the relative lengths of *Pride and Prejudice* and *Sense and Sensibility*.[43] Whatever the exact length of *First Impressions*, it is clear that Martha was proposing to memorise a considerable quantity of prose. While one regrets the absence of figures to attach to 'one more perusal' (how often has Martha read the novel? once? twice? ten times?) it is clear that even frequent perusal does not mitigate the excellence or ambition of Martha's memory.

It should be noted that, without exception, the references above are to a phenomenon we can call memorial reconstruction, not memorial reconstruction by actors as the twentieth century has come to know it. Even the references which specifically involve actors (*Hog*, Moseley) depict individuals (mis)behaving for personal gain rather than an acting company discarding the reconstructed text of a play which it no longer had occasion to perform. In other words the evidence, such as it is, is closer to Greg's scenario for *The Merry Wives of Windsor* than it is to his scenario for *Orlando Furioso*.

At this point it is necessary to ask ourselves just how gallants or putative play-reporters were positioned when writing in the playhouse. One assumes they must have been seated, for it would have been difficult to exert pressure or achieve fluency with Elizabethan writing instruments from a standing position. Paper was thick and textured, although table-books may already have been bound, thereby affording an *ad hoc* writing surface. Whether pen or pencil was used, speed would have been difficult to achieve. Pencils were coarser than their modern mass-produced descendants, and had to be sharpened regularly with a knife. A quill pen and inkwell are not the most portable of equipment (although Lord Scroop produces both from his pocket in Act 3 of *Sir John Oldcastle*). Elizabethan pockets were, however, external accessories resembling what we would call a Dorothy bag, and therefore stronger and more capacious than their modern equivalents. What is clear from the above references to sermons and table-books is that the inconvenience of contemporary writing implements was no bar to note-taking.

In seeking external testimony to support the concept of memorial reconstruction I have so far concentrated on evidence for the more general category of reconstruction, a category in which memory may or may not be involved. It is time now to focus on memory *per se*. Greg based his case for memorial reconstruction on assumptions about how memory functioned and malfunctioned. Given the paucity of research on narrative recall at the time that Greg was formulating his theory, this dependence on hypothesis was unavoidable. However, if we are to investigate memorial reconstruction fairly, the psychology of memory and its effects on textual reproduction can no longer be ignored. This topic comprises chapter 5, the last of the contextual prolegomena, after which we may turn to analysis of the suspect texts themselves.

5 | Memory

If any one faculty of our nature may be called *more* wonderful than the
rest, I do think it is memory. There seems something more speakingly
incomprehensible in the powers, the failures, the inequalities of
memory, than in any other of our intelligences. The memory is
sometimes so retentive, so serviceable, so obedient – at others, so
bewildered and so weak – and at others again, so tyrannic, so beyond
controul! – We are to be sure a miracle every way – but our powers of
recollecting and of forgetting, do seem peculiarly past finding out.

Jane Austen, *Mansfield Park* (1814) vol.II, chapter 4

ORAL CULTURE

Elizabethan England was not a 'primary oral' culture in the sense that
Homeric Greece was with its dependence on transmitting material (legal,
historical, poetic) memorially from one mind to another. Sixteenth-century
England was 'residually oral'; a society in transition, en route to becoming a
documentary society, it nonetheless had very strong roots in the oral world,
whether through habit, illiteracy, or expense of paper. *Aides-mémoire*
abounded, but they were, literally, what the noun suggests: aids to memory,
not a substitute for it. So important was memory to the culture that numerous systems existed for stretching its capacity and enhancing its accuracy. In
dealing with the subject of memorial reconstruction we must acknowledge
that actors were not the only people with trained and efficient memories.

Walter Ong has suggested that we can measure the degree of residual
orality in a chirographic culture from the emphasis accorded memory in its
education system.[1] Elizabethan England placed enormous emphasis – in
school, Inns of Court, university, and church – on the related concepts of
orality and memory. Repetition of the sermon was a regular Sunday feature

in noble households; young lawyers were trained through readings in the Great Hall and moots; the university timetable was structured around lectures and disputation, culminating in a three-day oral examination. When Ben Jonson, in the seventeenth century, explains punctuation as marks which signal pauses for breath, we see the influence of an oral rather than a print culture.

From the late 1920s onwards the work of Milman Parry (continued by Alfred Lord after Parry's early death) on Homer's *Iliad* and *Odyssey* has shed much light on the way oral societies compose and transmit poetry. Parry's achievement was the identification of the Homeric formula: flexible but stable metrical units which enabled the bard to complete a metrical line while keeping his mind free for other things such as narrative. 'The wine-dark sea', 'wily Odysseus', 'the wise one' (Nestor), 'swift-footed Achilles', 'the rosy-fingered dawn' are repeated either verbatim or with incremental variation on numerous occasions; one in eight verses of *The Iliad* 'recur at least once elsewhere in the poem'.[2] Such formulae enable the bard to improvise and vary his narrative within strict metrical limits. The poetic effect of the smaller formulaic repetitions is comfortingly stabilising; larger repetitions provide a cross-reference, as when the death of Hector is described in the same words as the death of Patroclus (whom Hector slew).

Homeric epic depends not just on verbal but on structural formulae. The challenge, the preparations for departure, the farewell – such formulaic episodes recur even when they interfere with narrative consistency. (Thus Odysseus bids a lengthy farewell to Calypso only to remain a further four days with her, preparing for departure.) Narrative consistency is a low priority for the oral poet, because he cannot motivate future episodes in the way that chirographic cultures, with the luxury of palimpsest, can. The oral poet does not aim for the kind of integration we associate with narrative; instead, his technique is dramatic, providing a series of episodic highlights.[3]

We shall examine oral formulae in closer detail in chapter 7. For the moment I wish simply to call attention to the forms in which oral–formulaic repetitions survive in Shakespearean England. Spenser's *Faerie Queene* is heavily imbued with oral patterns. The style is orally additive, connecting phrases with the conjunction 'and', in contrast to formal written prose which has the leisure and grammatical control to write in subordinate clauses. Formulaic phrases abound, serving the requirements of the metre rather than any succinct meaning (see for example 'back to turn again', 'forth he rode', 'as it then befell'); these formulae are often combined in incremental fashion (so forth he rode, as his adventure fell); and the poem is based on traditional medieval romance motifs (structural formulae) which in combination provide narrative inconsistencies.[4] The same techniques can be observed in a more controlled manner in the works of Milton; and Gascoigne, as Marion Trousdale has shown, is a 'latter-day oral poet'.[5]

The Renaissance devotion to commonplace books – collections of *sententiae*, proverbs, pithy epithets on politics, religion, morality (always, we notice, referred to as *sayings*, not writings) – is itself a residue from an oral culture. Commonplaces enable the mind to be stocked with familiarly phrased material which can be accessed quickly. The oral, Walter Ong explains, deals with the known: 'commonplace' did not become a pejorative term until the nineteenth century.[6] Today's metaphoric clichés are often yesterday's mnemonic commonplaces. Their colourful epithets show their oral origin for, quite simply, the easiest way to remember something was to think it in memorable terms. 'To hide one's light under a bushel' comes from the oral culture of Matthew; 'to bury the hatchet' is a phrase of Native American oral origin.[7]

Most proverbial commonplaces of this kind are deeply rooted in the visual, and relate to practical domestic activities: the visual and the practical is an effective mnemonic combination. 'A leap in the dark', 'an iron in the fire', 'brass with use grows bright', 'when the cat's away the mice will play' – all these phrases retain wide currency today, even though the physical domestic circumstances which first made them appropriate no longer ubiquitously apply. Members of the English Shakespeare Company who were performing seven Shakespeare history plays in repertory in 1986–9 revealed that they had more trouble accurately recalling 'colourless and nondescript lines' than 'bright images':

> John Darrell, who had to say 'Good my lord of Lancaster' in one play
> and 'My Lord of Gloucester' in another, found himself addressing
> Richard of Gloucester as 'Good my lord of Lanc–,
> Leicester–Gloucester' ('all famous cheeses', he pointed out).[8]

Drama is a paradoxical genre, in as much as it has to be written before it can become an oral medium; it might therefore be expected to have more in common with print culture. But Thomas Pettitt has recently applied his research on orality to Marlowe's drama, and has demonstrated the indebtedness of *Dr Faustus* and *The Massacre at Paris* to episodic and verbal formulae.[9] Thus in *The Massacre at Paris* the scene in which the Admiral's dead body is to be disposed of leads to a formulaic conversation between the two attendants, in which they debate the pros and cons of drowning, burning, abandonment, or hanging. A similar formulaic debate takes place in B *Dr Faustus* when Benvolio, Martino, and Frederick propose practical domestic uses for the body parts of the apparently dead Faustus (scene 13). Two intriguing examples of formulaic dramaturgy occur in scene 7 of A *Dr Faustus* which concludes with episodes in which Mephistopheles frightens the clowns with fireworks before returning to transform them into animals. (The B-text omits the firework episode.) Pettitt suggests that these two episodes represent alternative formulaic endings to the scene in question. They survive in print by accident. '[S]ince each alternative. . .is formulaic, this sequence provides a revealing instance of the utility of the dramaturgical formula in the revision. . .of dramatic performances by the process of formulaic substitution'.[10]

Formulaic episodes can be witnessed across the canon of Elizabethan literature: a servant solicits her lady's opinion about her suitors in *Two Gentlemen of Verona*, *The Merchant of Venice*, *'Tis Pity She's a Whore*; pretended lack of interest in news of a lover appears in *Two Gentlemen of Verona*, *As You Like It*; scenes in which an ale-wife or tapster is cheated feature in *Mucedorus*, *The Famous Victories*, *John of Bordeaux*; formulaic charming someone to dumbness occurs in *Dr Faustus*, *The Birth of Merlin*, and *John of Bordeaux*. Pettitt suggests that such formulaic episodes aid both the professional dramatist and the professional player. William Long, for example, in a discussion of formulaic blocking (i.e. general resemblances between 'certain kinds of scenes') acknowledges that although '[d]ifferences . . . would be wrought, . . . players would not have had to reinvent the wheel for each play'.[11]

Marion Trousdale points out that Shakespeare's plays are composed of structural and verbal repetitions which Shakespeare's dramatic skills prevent from seeming repetitive. Leontes in *The Winter's Tale* echoes lines from *Othello*; Macbeth repeats lines from *Richard 3*; the Duke of Milan describes Sylvia in *Two Gentlemen of Verona* in terms that anticipate Lear's description of Cordelia; Polonius uses lines already spoken by Pandulph in *King John*; both Othello and the Old Shepherd in *The Winter's Tale* repeat lines from *Macbeth*.[12] Repetition, as we shall see, can be both a symptom of faulty memory (as Greg maintained) and a compositional quiddity of a residually oral culture.

People in oral cultures tend to have better memories than those in chirographic or print-dependent cultures. If you live in a century when writing has not been invented, or in the Renaissance and happen to be illiterate, or in the twentieth century and happen to be blind, or in any century when writing was a prohibitively expensive luxury, an efficient memory will be your primary lifeline. Socrates relates the story of an Egyptian king's response to the invention of letters. '[T]his invention', the King said sadly, 'will produce forgetfulness.'[13]

Anecdotes abound of individuals renowned for extraordinary memorial ability, the result of innate ability or systematic practice. Keith Thomas describes the activities of a servant of John Bruen, the Jacobean Puritan, who

> could not read or write, but who had memorized scripture and could identify the book and chapter from which any sentence came. He wore a leather girdle, long enough to go around him twice, and on it he tied knots. With its aid he could repeat a complete sermon when he got home.[14]

C. V. Le Grice reminisces about evenings spent in Coleridge's rooms at Cambridge discussing the pamphlets of the day: 'Ever and anon, a pamphlet issued from the pen of Burke. There was no need of having the book before us. Coleridge had read it in the morning, and in the evening he would repeat whole pages verbatim.'[15] Julius Caesar could dictate four letters on different subjects while writing a fifth in his own hand. William of Ockham contentedly read the well-stocked library of his memory when he was in exile in Munich.[16] Fictional references to the phenomenon abound. For example, Tim Yellowhammer's tutor read him the Dunces (the writings of Duns Scotus) at Cambridge and as a result, Tim boasts, 'now I haue 'em all in my owne Pate, and can as well read 'em to others' (Middleton, *A Chaste Maid in Cheapside*, F2v).

An extreme example of excellent memory is the focus of a book by the

Russian neuropsychologist A. R. Luria. Luria presents a fascinating account of a man whom he met in the 1920s and studied for thirty years, S. V. Shereshevskii. Shereshevskii was simply unable to forget. He filed everything in his memory: sequences of digits containing over a hundred numbers, lengthy mathematical equations, foreign words, lists, nonsense vocabulary, nonsense formulae, musical notation, and images. He was able to recollect everything in its correct sequence, whether five minutes or fifteen years after first acquaintance with the material. Unable to hold down a regular job because of his inability to filter memories – quite literally, he remembered everything – he eventually made a career as a music-hall artist, performing mnemonic feats.[17]

Shereshevskii was clearly blessed (or afflicted) with extraordinary powers of cognitive recall. In most people, however, recall facility of the semantic and episodic components of declarative memory falls off sharply after the age of ten.[18] This is not a design fault in nature; until very recently the experiences and encounters of the first ten years would provide a familiar backdrop for the next sixty. Furthermore adults utilise perceptual filtering to interpret and prioritise experience; thus, eidetic recall is no longer needed in the way it is in childhood where inexperienced eyes have no choice but to take in all experiences as equal. Adult memory, however, improves with training. And oral cultures were especially interested in systems of memory training: mnemotechnics.

Many systems existed, some so complex that the practitioner could derive no benefit from them unless (as Jack Wilton protests in Nashe's *The Unfortunate Traveller*) 'hee haue a naturall memorie before'.[19] The most popular system – known to the twentieth century as the Visual Symbol System of Recall or the Locality System – was discovered by accident. The poet Simonides of Ceos (c. 500 BC) was entertaining diners at a banquet. He was summoned outside, and, during his absence, the ceiling of the banqueting-house collapsed, killing all the guests. Simonides was able to identify the bodies for the relatives because of the position they had occupied during the meal: he simply summoned up the visual memory of the banquet and with it came the seating arrangement. This memorial feat is allegedly the origin of the phrases 'in the first place', 'in the second place', used to order points in a story. Simonides' technique developed into a full-fledged system which used visual symbols such as streets (with doorways), rooms (with cupboards and windows), theatres (with doors and balconies) and grids (with numbers attached) to secrete the objects or points one wished to remember. As Cicero (heavily influenced by Simonides) explained, it is easy to find a mislaid object if you know where it is located; so with points hidden in the memory.[20]

Shereshevskii describes how every item he encountered prompted visual images. By weaving these images into a narrative he could recall sequences of objects. Thus, a mnemonic system was operative, although it was an innately automatic system, not an artificially applied one. Shereshevskii simply had very rich associative powers.[21] Shereshevskii explained how he would remember objects (numbers, words, objects in a sequence) by taking an imaginary walk from Pushkin Square to Gorky Street. He would store images, corresponding to the objects he needed to remember, at strategic points along this route. To recall them he needed only to retrace his steps, looking at the scenery around him: background wall, doorways, street lamps.[22]

Five centuries earlier Peter of Ravenna had advocated the use of living images, such as attractive women as mnemonic 'places' (adding that this system was not advisable if you hated women, or could not control yourself).[23] In his poem 'The Soul' Abraham Cowley wittily anatomises his mistress's body, storing memories in each place: 'So that thy parts become to me / A kind of *Art* of *Memory*'.[24] Shakespeare's Mercutio rejects such lovesick anatomical inventorying, not just in his famous parodic conjuring in 2.1, but in an earlier rhetorical question whose phraseology is indebted to the Visual Symbol System of recall: 'what care I / What curious eye doth quote deformities' (F *Romeo and Juliet* TLN 483–4). 'Quote' here means to 'number or mark mentally', a reference to a numerical grid system of visual memory imaging. Mary Carruthers, who cites this example, reminds us that the English verb 'quote', and its parent Latin verb 'quotare', are derived from the adjective 'quot' ('how many?'). To 'quote' means literally to 'number' a book, dividing a larger text into numbered sub-divisions. This is clearly the primary sense of the verb in *Love's Labour's Lost* TLN 750 ('His faces owne margent did coate such amazes') and in a passage in Q1 *Hamlet* (not represented in Q2 or F) which combines references to commonplace books and the Art of Memory: 'and Gentlemen quotes his ieasts downe / In their tables' (F2r–v).

Memory systems are thus encoded in the metaphors and vocabulary used by Renaissance poets and dramatists. Explicit references are made to the Art of Memory in the anonymous MS play *The Wasp*, Nashe's *Have With You to Saffron Walden*, and Marston's *The Malcontent* where Sly boasts that despite 'never [having] studied the art of memory' he can 'walke but once downe by the gold-smiths row in Cheape, take notice of the signes, and tell you them with a breath instantly' (A4v). There are fifty-five such signs, he explains, adding that he concentrates when he attends plays too.

The New Bibliographers seem not to have researched the subject of memory. Greg, Hoppe and Kirschbaum, for instance, take as evidence of memorial errors those textual problems in the suspect texts in which they are trying to diagnose memory. This is circular reasoning with a vengeance. Greg and his successors frequently proclaim their assumptions about the way memory operates and the mistakes it makes:

> [W]e can conceive well enough what many qualities of ... a reconstruction would be like. In the following pages these hypothetical qualities will be illustrated ... by examples and citations from several bad texts[.][25]

> The important fact about the quarto text [of *Richard 3*] is that all of the changes which can be expected from the theory of memorial transmission are found in large numbers. The following suppositions seem reasonable: [anticipation, recollection, transposition, substitution, omission, etc.].[26]

These suppositions may indeed be reasonable, but they remain suppositions. What is needed is an independent survey of evidence for the way declarative recall functions and the semantic errors to which it is prone. The results of this survey may then be applied to the suspect texts. This survey is the focus of the remainder of this chapter.

NARRATIVE RECALL

The first (now the classic) study of narrative recall is that made by Sir Frederic Bartlett in the 1930s.[27] Bartlett presented a subject with a prose passage, and had him recall it at intervals of days, weeks, or years. The results of a single test recall were as follows: 1) the story was considerably shortened, for much was omitted; 2) although shorter, much became more coherent. Despite distortions, there was no unrelated recall. 3) Events were omitted from the account unless they could be fitted into a familiar framework (i.e. interpretation has a significant role to play in memory).[28] 4) The story became conventional, 'shorn of its individualizing features . . . [D]escriptive passages los[t] most of what peculiarities of style and content they possess[ed], and the original phrasing [was] replaced by current, commonplace *clichés*.'[29] 5) The general replaced the specific. 6) Definite numbers and proper names were the most common items of omission. If they did not disappear, they were transformed. Furthermore, omission went 'hand in hand with an emphasizing of what is retained'. And this emphasis was 'pointed up by elaboration'.[30]

Ian M. L. Hunter tells how literal remembering (exact words) 'falls off much more rapidly than content remembering' (general sense),[31] and he provides an example directly relevant to our investigation of suspect texts when he discusses briefly the hypothetical textual effects of a schoolboy's attempt at reciting a Shakespearean sonnet learned twenty hours previously:

> He may start off well and then fumble. He may pause now and then,
> unsure how to continue. He may say some words, then stop and
> correct himself. He may omit a portion, or substitute a phrase which is
> not that of the original although close to it in meaning. He may get all
> the lines correct but in a wrong order. At one point, he may remember
> the rhythm or rhyme or general sense of what comes next but may not
> remember the exact words; and so he may hesitate, or fill in with other
> words, or come to a stop[.][32]

This example, although hypothetical, presents memory operating in favourable circumstances, when a character is recalling a short passage which he himself has intentionally learned. What would be the result if he were attempting to remember a passage of 2,500 lines, of which he knew only a portion, and had not considered his portion or the whole for some time? Brief though they are, Hunter's and Bartlett's accounts lend support to New Bibliographic assumptions.

However, the relevance of such experiments to suspect texts is decreased in one major respect. Bartlett's and Hunter's subjects (actual or hypothetical) were products of a literate and documentary age, unaccustomed to using memory as a primary storehouse or filing system. For a more pertinent analogue, we must turn to an earlier era and a different area: the subject of folk ballad transmission.

FOLK BALLADS

Folk ballads have much in common with Elizabethan drama. They are narrative, and this narrative is advanced by dialogue; they are dramatic, pictorial, structured in scenic units; and, like drama, they are also economic, because, as Thomas Pettitt explains, 'the ballad is extraordinarily selective in what it chooses to narrate, concentrating on a limited sequence of moments of tension, confrontation, climax and resolution, and generally fails to provide much narrative introduction leading up to them'.[33] Like an Elizabethan play, a ballad may involve extempore improvisation, and the ballad text, like the dramatic text, is unstable because it is under the control (or lack of it) of a live performer. The performance context of the ballad, like that of an Elizabethan play, is social, 'with a good deal of noise and disturbance interfering with the communication between singer and listener'.[34] Anyone reciting or singing a ballad would find himself in a position similar to that of an Elizabethan actor.

Folk ballads are especially useful to the investigator of suspect texts. Since folk ballads flourished in the period before literacy was widespread, their transmission history involves people who depended on memory and concentration, rather than on reading and writing.

Though far from illiterate, Mrs Brown of Falkland, a prolific and prominent Scottish ballad singer of the eighteenth century, depended on her memory. Flemming Andersen and Thomas Pettitt explain her significance:

> Born in the middle of the eighteenth century, learning her ballads as a child, and recording them, as a Church of Scotland clergyman's wife, toward the end of the century, Mrs Brown is early enough – and oral enough – to be in contact with an authentic ballad tradition, but late enough – and literate enough – for her ballads to have been preserved.[35]

'Bonny Baby Livingston', for example, was dictated to the collector Jamieson in the summer of 1800 (version *b*). Mrs Brown was unhappy with the version which she had recited to Jamieson, and shortly afterwards she sent him another version (version *a*): 'On the other page you will find the whole ballad of Bonny Baby Livingston. I found upon recollection that I had the whole story in my memory, and thought it better to write it out entire, as what I repeated to you was, I think, more imperfect.'[36]

Comparison of the two texts of 'Bonny Baby Livingston' endorses both Mrs Brown's self criticism and the judgment of F. J. Child: 'the fact seems to be that, at the time when she recited to Jamieson, she was not in good condition to remember accurately'.[37] A large number of trivial variants occur: the exclamatory 'O' which begins stanzas 2, 5, and 16 in *a* is replaced by the conjunction 'And' in the memorially 'more imperfect' *b* version. On one occasion Mrs Brown's faulty memory creates a repetition in *b*:

oer yon hich hich hill   He's carried her oer hills and muirs

   (stanza 4*b*)   (stanza 4*a*)

Synonymous words and substitute phrases abound: 'fu' o' care'(*b*) for 'filld wi care' (*a*) in stanza 5, 'This mony a year and day' (*b*) for 'This twelve month and a day' (*a*) in stanza 13. In stanza 29, *a*'s direct speech is changed to indirect in *b*. All such substitutions in *b* occur at the same place as in *a*, and, as Andersen and Pettitt point out, serve the same dramatic and narrative purpose:

And there were kids sae fair   And lasses milking there

   (stanza 5*b*)   (stanza 5*a*)

Says, I wad gie a' my flocks and herds   Says, I'd gie a' these cows and ewes
Ae smile frae thee to win.   But ae kind look to win.

   (stanza 6*b*)   (stanza 6*a*)

I've lued her lang and lued her weell   And tho I've lood her lang and sair
But her love I neer coud win;   A smile I neer coud win;
And what I canna fairly gain   Yet what I've got anse in my power
To steal I think nae sin   To keep I think nae sin

   (stanza 14*b*)   (stanza 14*a*)

More extensive variants occur. The later *a* version includes two stanzas (25 and 26) in which a boy delivers a letter to Baby Livingston's sweetheart Johnny (25) and tells him about Baby's captivity (26). The earlier *b* version reduces these eight lines to four, so that in one stanza the boy leaves, and in the next we see Johnny's reaction. To compensate for this reduction, the earlier *b* version adds a stanza to extend Johnny's reaction: whereas in *a* Johnny is given only two lines of reaction before springing into action (and the saddle), in *b* he is given six lines of lament.

The manner in which Baby writes her letter to her sweetheart in each version differs. Andersen and Pettitt analyse these differences as follows:

> The first version, in highly traditional terms, expresses her wish for 'paper, pen, and ink' (stanza 20) and a 'bonny boy' to take the message (stanza 21). In the next stanza (22) the bonny boy is duly acquired, but nothing is said of paper, pen, and ink. In the second version, however, both writing materials (stanza 20) and a bonny boy (stanza 21) are acquired, but, remarkably, Baby Livingston has expressed a wish only for the former (stanza 19). Here, clearly, in the ballad Mrs Brown was trying on each occasion to reproduce, there should be a double balance: a request for writing materials, balanced by their acquisition, interspaced with a request for a bonny boy, balanced by his acquisition. Mrs Brown has reproduced the system imperfectly, but differently, on each occasion.[38]

Similar verbal and structural variants can be observed in the two versions of the 'Lass of Roch Royal'. Several of Mrs Brown's ballads exist in variant texts, being supplied for collectors at different dates during her life.[39] Mrs Brown supplied one version to Jamieson in 1783, and another to Alexander Fraser Tyter in 1800, with 'virtually no likelihood that the second performance was interfered with by a written text of the first'.[40] Length and detail are reduced in the 1800 version: for instance, the two love-tokens (napkin and ring), introduced in two stanzas in 1783 as proof of the Lass's identity, are reduced to one stanza in 1800. Pettitt shows this to be the result of memorial anticipation – 'the second repetition setting in too early, effectively telescoping the two statements into one'.[41] Elsewhere in the text of 1800 Mrs Brown introduces new material, some of which consists of commonplaces, or else replaces one commonplace with another; and at the end of the version of 1800 Mrs Brown 'omits the mother's final false revelation, and hence the Lass's response to it, making the dismissal more abrupt'.[42]

One of the most interesting alterations for the investigator of suspect texts concerns the Lass's 'yellow hair'. In the 1783 version the Lass's brother 'kembd her yallow hair' (stanza 4, in response to her question 'wha will kemb my yallow hair' in stanza 2), and in stanza 30, when she has drowned, Love Gregor 'catchd her by the yallow hair'. In the 1800 version the details of the Lass's hair remain the same in stanzas 2 and 4; her hair is referred to again in stanza 9, when she requests entry to Love Gregor's house because 'the wind blaws thro my yellow hair'. By the time of her drowning, however, this epithet has been transferred to Love Gregor, who 'tare his yellow hair' (stanza 25), while the drowned Lass is described with the substitute phrase 'gowden was her hair' (stanza 26). As we shall see in chapter 7, repetition with transferred subject/object occurs in several suspect texts. In *The Massacre at Paris*, for instance, King Charles suffers from death symptoms which, 'whether by accident or design, are almost identical with those of the poisoned Queen-Mother of Navarre'.[43]

Folk-ballads, it seems, can provide a useful parallel for diagnosing memory in suspect texts. The samples above contain examples of anticipation, recollection, transposition, telescoping, omission, expansion, emphasis, synonymous substitution, and redundancy; all these features were assumed by the New Bibliographers to be symptoms of memory. This is encouraging. However, ballads are short, prone to more frequent performance than plays, and structurally dependent on repetitive formulae. The quantity of material they can provide for analysis of the memorial process is accordingly limited. We must continue to seek examples of the memorial process closer to the Renaissance.

COMMONPLACE BOOKS

Renaissance commonplace books may provide such examples, and one is especially relevant to the present subject. BL MS Add. 64078 was acquired by the British Library in December 1987. The MS contains a letter to an anonymous Lord (inside the front cover) in a late seventeenth-century hand, several folios (fols. 3r–11r) of Latin notes on theological and metaphysical matters, and, on the back flyleaves, fifteen extracts (63 lines) from Shakespeare's *1 Henry 4*. Slight resemblances between the hand of the notes and the hand of the Shakespeare extracts raise the possibility that the copyist in each case was the same. On folio 3r a contemporary hand has added, but at a later date, a line attributing the Latin notes to Thomas Harriot (1560–1621).[44]

It is impossible to describe a 'typical' commonplace book of the English

Renaissance, for they are as varied as the individual(s) who owned them.[45] Some consist only of a few loose leaves recording personal expenditure, poems, and drafts or copies of letters. Others are elaborately ordered and indexed compilations, such as the collections of historical and political anecdotes made by Sir Francis Fane, seventh Earl of Westmoreland. Fane subsequently made presentation transcripts, neatly arranged by geographical subject, to give his son, and later his grandsons, when they came of age.[46]

Several commonplace books contain material relating to the owner's professional affairs: legal controversies, ecclesiastical matters, affairs of state or university, exemplars for teaching. Inventories of possessions (from books to servants), lists of debts and taxes, genealogies (whether of Kings of England or the owner's family) are frequent. Sometimes one comes across epitaphs, poetic anagrams, shorthand notes, and lute tablature. Occasionally commonplace books are furnished with illustrations, either for aesthetic decoration (accompanying botanical or Biblical texts, for example) or practical purposes (such as illustrating how to construct a mousetrap). Sometimes several family members contribute to a commonplace collection, jointly or sequentially; and sometimes the book is passed down through generations and its change of ownership or content signalled by the book being reversed and inverted to create a new opening page.[47]

The most frequent contents of commonplace books are: aphorisms, apothegms, and *sententiae*, usually on moral topics, and listed under appropriate abstract headings (Abstinence, Contentment, Patience, Slander, Creation, Eternity, Repentance); posies (sentiments to be engraved on wedding-rings – for example, 'my sweet jewel, be not cruel'; 'if two consent who can prevent'); quotations, in English or in Latin, from Biblical or Classical authors; extracts from, or complete copies of poems (Shakespeare, Jonson, Sidney, Raleigh, and the contents of *The Passionate Pilgrim* being among the most popular); prayers; recipes, whether for medical or gastronomic purposes (e.g. 'A Remedie agaynst the stone in the bladder'; 'To make shortcakes'); and material relating to contemporary political events (the trial, death speech, and letters of Sir Walter Raleigh constitute the most popular topics).

Occasionally one finds lengthy dramatic extracts or complete plays. *The Comedy of July and Julian*, and several academic plays, are known only from manuscript commonplace books (Folger MSS v.a.159 and j.a.2).

Fragments of *Roxana* and *Gismond of Salerne* appear in two others (Folger MSS v.b.222 and v.a.198), and a curious volume of the c.1650s contains thirty closely written leaves of dramatic quotations from Shakespeare, Marston, Shirley, Massinger, and Chapman (Folger MS v.a.87).

The physical appearance of commonplace books varies enormously. We find everything from hastily written notes, disfigured by palimpsest and *currente calamo* corrections, to impressive presentation volumes with margins ruled in gilt and artistically decorated headings. The size can be anything from a small octavo to a large folio. Sometimes several pages are missing, presumably quarried for writing material for other purposes; at the other extreme we have the handsome printed volume published by John Day in 1572, containing 600 blank folio leaves with alphabetical headings for future commonplace book entries.[48]

British Library MS Add. 64078 is a folio volume which originally contained forty-eight leaves. At some stage thirty-four leaves were removed, and all but a fragment of the second leaf torn, leaving only the thirteen leaves which contain (now, if not then) the Harriot and the *Henry 4* material. The compiler began with the Latin notes; he (or his successor) later reversed and inverted the volume to begin again with the Shakespeare material. This Shakespeare material was written sometime between 1594 (the date ascribed to the Harriot notes) and March 1602/3 (the date of the death of Queen Elizabeth, a reference to whom is inserted in one of the extracts to provide contemporary relevance). The extracts are written hastily, with *currente calamo* alterations. The nature of the alterations suggests that the author is not making notes directly from performance or reading: he is clearly straining to remember something he has heard or read, and the probability is that he is recalling material heard at a performance (or performances) of the play.[49] (The MS's variance from all known quartos of *1 Henry 4* would require us to believe that, had our playgoer transcribed the extracts from a copy in front of him, that copy is no longer extant. *Entia non sunt multiplicanda praeter necessitatem.*)

The extracts (from the roles of Henry 4, Hal, Hotspur, Glendower, Worcester, Gadshill, the Chamberlain, and Vernon) enable us to construct a parallel text for sixty-three lines of the play. This is, of course, what critics do when comparing parallel suspect texts. The difference in this case is that we have one text in whose transmission memory almost certainly played a part.

I present the extracts in the order of dramatic chronology and I have numbered them for convenience.[50] I give first the relevant text from *1 Henry 4*, quoted from the Riverside edition. This is followed by the MS version, in which I have indicated deletions in square brackets, expansions and superior letters by italics, hypothetical readings for illegible letters in pointed brackets; I have brought superior letters down to the line. The MS was read with the help of ultra-violet light.

(1)   *1 Henry 4* 1.1.17–18
        The edge of war, like an ill-sheathed knife,
        No more shall cut his master.
                MS (fol. 47v)
        The edge of warr like an Ill sheathed <kn>yff
        no more shall cutt his master.

(2)   *1 Henry 4* 1.1.82
        Amongst a grove the very straightest plant,
                MS
        Amongst a grove *ye* very straitest pla*n*t

(3)   *1 Henry 4* 1.1.84–6
        Whilst I, by looking on the praise of him,
        See riot and dishonor stain the brow
        Of my young Harry.
                MS
        [In margin: in praise / of one / in dispraise][51]
        Dishonor staynes his brow

(4)   *1 Henry 4* 1.1.98–9
        Which makes him prune himself, and bristle up
        The crest of youth against your dignity.
                MS
        To prune hy*m*self & bristle vp
        the Crest of youth agaynst y*or* dignity.

(5)   *1 Henry 4* 1.3.1–13
        KING: My blood hath been too cold and temperate,
        Unapt to stir at these indignities,
        And you have found me, for accordingly

You tread upon my patience; but be sure
I will from henceforth rather be myself,
Mighty and to be fear'd, than my condition,
Which hath been smooth as oil, soft as young down,
And therefore lost that title of respect
Which the proud soul ne'er pays but to the proud.
WORCESTER: Our house, my sovereign liege, little deserves
The scourge of greatness too be us'd on it
And that same greatness too which our own hands
Have holp to make so portly.

    MS

[In margin: of a Tem/perat man]
<??> my bloud hath bin too cold & temp<erate>
vnapt to stirr at small indignities
& you haue found me for acordingly
you tread vppon my Patience
————————but, my conditi<on>
wch hath bin smooth [like] as oyle soft <as y n > down
hath therfore lost yt title of Respect
wch ye proud soule neare payes but to <ye> proud.

————

Our house little deserves ye scourge of greatness
of yt same greatness wch or own hands haue holp
to make so portly.

(6)   *1 Henry 4* 2.1.49–51
That's even as fair as – at hand, quoth the chamberlain; for thou
variest no more from picking of purses than giving direction doth
from laboring:

    MS

great [C< > Counsellors] ostlers & Chamberlans differ no more
from hangmen / then [as] giving direction doth from labouring.

(7)   *1 Henry 4* 2.1.79–85
GADSHILL: they pray continually to their saint, the commonwealth,
or rather, not pray to her, but prey on her, for they ride up and down
on her, and make her their boots.

CHAMBERLAIN: What, the commonwealth their boots? Will she hold out water in foul way?

GADSHILL: She will, she will, justice hath liquor'd her.

MS

He compares ye common welth to a paire of / boots wch great men ride in. he asketh whether ye common welth will / hold out water in fowle way./he aunsers, yea. Iustice hath liquord / her.

(8)   *1 Henry 4* 3.1.13–19

GLENDOWER: I cannot blame him. At my nativity
The front of heaven was full of fiery shapes
Of burning cressets, and at my birth
The frame and huge foundation of the earth
Shak'd like a coward.

HOTSPUR: Why so it would have done
At the same season if your mother's cat had
But kitten'd, though yourself had never been born.

MS

To one yt sayd at his Nativity ye Earth quakt / he aunswrd yt so it would haue don yf a Katt had euen but / Kittend, though he had neur bin born. Adds / [see extract 9 for continuation]

(9)   *1 Henry 4* 3.1.26–32

Diseased nature oftentimes breaks forth
In strange eruptions; oft the teeming earth
Is with a kind of colic pinch'd and vex'd
By the imprisoning of unruly wind
Within her womb, which, for enlargment striving,
Shakes the old beldame earth, and topples down
Steeples and moss-grown towers.

MS

Diseased Nature oftentymes breaks forth
In strange Eruptions, oft the teeming Earth
is wth a kynd of Collick pinct't & vext
by ye Imprisoning of vnruly wynd
wthin hir womb, wch for inlargement striving

[shakes] shakes *ye* old beldame Earth, & topples down
Steeples & Mossgrown Towrs:

(10)   *1 Henry 4* 3.1.132–3
mincing poetry.
'Tis like the forc'd gait of a shuffling nag.
MS (fol. 48r)
ill Poetry is like *ye* forc't gate of
<a> sufling Nagg

(11)   *1 Henry 4* 3.2.61
With shallow jesters, and rash bavin wits
     MS
<shal>low Iesters & rash bavin witts.

(12)   *1 Henry 4* 3.2.40–1
So common-hackney'd in the eyes of men,
So stale and cheap to vulgar company
     MS
<Tis?> not good for a great mann
<to> be a stale & cheap in [the Eyes]
[of men] Com*m*o*n* Compan*a*y, nor co*mm*o*n*
hagney in the Eyes of *m*en

(13)   *1 Henry 4* 3.2.50–7
And then I stole all courtesy from heaven,
And dress'd myself in such humility
That I did pluck allegiance from men's hearts,
Loud shouts and salutations from their mouths,
Even in the presence of the crowned King.
Thus did I keep my person fresh and new,
My presence, like a robe pontifical,
Ne'er seen but wond'red at,
     MS
his Prese*n*c<e?> must be like a Robe po*n*tifical
not seene but when tis wondred at
& then [*you*] he must steale Curtesy
fro*m* Heavn, & dress hy*m*self in

sutch hummillity, as he may pluck
allegiance from menns harts euen in
the presence of ye Queene wch els

(14)   *1 Henry 4* 3.2.42–5
Opinion, that did help me to the crown,
Had still kept loyal to possession,
And left me in reputeless banishment,
A fellow of no mark nor likelihood.
         MS
opinion wch must & doth [aid] oft help
one to a Crown will still keepe
loyall to posession, & [left] hold hym as a
fellow of no marke nor likelihood<e?>

(15)   MS
[In margin: bruising / armes][52]

(16)   MS
[In margin: being no / more indebt / to yeares / yen you]

(17)   *1 Henry 4* 3.2.81–3
But rather drows'd and hung their eyelids down,
Slept in his face and rend'red such aspect
As cloudy men use to their adversaries
         MS
hung yeir Ey lidds doun
slept in his face, & rendred sutch aspect
as clowdy men vse to yeir ad<versar>ies

(18)   *1 Henry 4* 3.2.124–5
Thou that art like enough, through vassal fear,
Base inclination, and the start of spleen
         MS
through feare base Inclination & ye
start of spleene

(19)   *1 Henry 4* 4.3.8–14
Do me no slander, Douglas. By my life,

And I dare well maintain it with my life,
If well-respected honor bid me on,
I hold as little counsel with weak fear
As you, my lord, or any Scot that this day lives.
Let it be seen to-morrow in the battle
Which of us fears.

    MS (fol. 47r)
(In margin: a valia*n*t/ ma*n* taxed/ of feares)
do me no slau*n*der
If well respected ho*n*or bid me on
I hold as little [Cou*n*cell] Councell w*th* weake fear
as yo*u*.
lett it be seen tomorrow in the battayle

Our theatre-goer was attracted by witticisms, *sententiae*, and choice images (habitual fodder for commonplace books), in a variety of roles. The length of several of his extracts is impressive: in extract 5 he produces eleven lines from a thirteen-line conversation in Shakespeare's original, and in extract 9 he produces seven lines verbatim from the original. Overall he has made very few errors: extracts 1, 9, and 17 are word perfect, and the remainder contain only occasional variants.

Several variants of phrasing are due to the need to turn personal dialogue into maxims suited to a commonplace collection: see, for instance, extract 10 ('ill Poetry is like' for 'mincing poetry. 'Tis like'), extract 13 ('his' for 'my', 'Queen' for 'King', and tense changes), extract 14 ('one' for 'me', and tense changes). Summaries which provide a succinct introduction to the *mots justes* are presumably deliberate additions, as in extracts 7 ('He co*m*pares y*e* com*m*on welth to a paire of boots w*ch* great me*n* ride in') and 8 ('To one y*t* sayd at his Nativity y*e* Earth quakt he aunswrd . . .'); in extract 19, omission of the vocative 'Douglas' transforms the line into a more generally applicable statement.

The remaining variants provide material relevant for analysis of memorial error.[53] Our playgoer uses synonyms – 'small indignities' for 'these indignities' (5), 'quakt' for 'Shak'd' (8), 'ill Poetry' for 'mincing poetry' (10), 'Co*m*mon Co*m*panay' for 'vulgar company' (12; the use of 'common' for 'vulgar' was doubtless influenced by the proximity of 'common hackney'd' in the original), 'aid' for 'help', an error which he realised and corrected (14). Elsewhere the playgoer couples synonyms with expansion of the original phrase: Henry 4's 'Ne'er seen but wond'red at' becomes 'not seene but when tis wondred at' (13). Extract 6 caused him considerable difficulty, perhaps because he was recasting it, and had therefore to create as well as remember.[54] He stumbled with 'Counsellors' for 'ostlers', which he corrected immediately, then followed 'then' with 'as', which he rejected before hitting on the correct gerund. Extract 12 proved equally troublesome. The playgoer transposed lines: 'stale & cheap' incorrectly precedes 'common hagney', as does 'the Eyes of men', which he telescoped with his previous phrase, before correcting it; the corrected result still includes a memorial repetition – 'Common Companay' followed by 'common hagney'. Extract 13 is disordered, beginning with two lines which should conclude the piece. This extract, whether accidentally or deliberately, omits a line (3.2.53, which simply expands on 3.2.52); omissions are also noticeable in extracts 2 and 3 (intervening lines are missing), extract 8 (where he omits Hotspur's reinforcement 'At the same season'), extract 14 (where the deleted 'left' shows that our playgoer had heard the missing line), and extract 18 (the adjective 'vassal' is omitted). Thus, our playgoer reproduces accurately for the most part, and the minor errors are of the kind which Bartlett and Hunter attribute to slips of memory.

What we cannot know, of course, is whether the errors are memorial slips of the actors or of the playgoer. Does extract 13 represent Burbage on a bad day? Are all the extracts representative of the players on an average day? Answers to these questions are not available, nor are they necessary, for we are collecting evidence of faulty memory, not trying to see where memorial variants originate. The important point to establish is that the textual variants were caused by memory. Whether the memory was a player's or a playgoer's does not matter.

The above sample is small, and its results must be interpreted accordingly, for ten-line repetitions are unlikely to appear in a collection of extracts, the longest of which is eleven lines. However, the sixty-three MS lines contain repetition, transposition, telescoping, emphatic expansion, and omission as examples of the variants memorial transmission introduces. The fact that our small sample contains five different kinds of memorial slip has an important implication for single-text diagnostic studies, for it suggests that the more verbal features a text has from the cata-logue discussed in chapter 7, the more justified are our suspicions of memo-rial transmission.

BBC SHAKESPEARE

My last category of examples is drawn from the twentieth century. One reg-ularly hears errors and additions in the theatre, of just the kind the New Bibliographers supposed an actor would make. But the errors and the improvisations are unquantifiable because they depend on random recogni-tion: what theatre-goer collates the text with performance? Furthermore, unless the performance is recorded, the errors cannot be checked by another to prove that their origin is the actor's faulty memory and not the auditor's faulty hearing.

In 1974–5 Philip Gaskell overcame both these obstacles. He tape-recorded a performace of Stoppard's *Travesties*, and collated this performance version (P) with both the original script (S) and the revised publication version (R). Although Gaskell was more concerned to trace the genesis of dramatic scripts ('the textual bibliographer may ask . . . what *is* the text of this or any other play?') than the effects of memory, his collation of P and S revealed that the actors introduced verbal alterations that affect 'the detailed texture of the play rather than its larger structure' – transpositions, rhetorical interjections, and colloquialisms – 'in order to ease their delivery'.[55]

The filming of Shakespeare's plays by the BBC has since made it easier for critics to collate P and S versions of Shakespeare texts. Moreover, a study of memorial errors in the BBC Shakespeare can be checked by anyone who wishes to do so.

In 1979 the BBC began filming Shakespeare's plays for television. The rehearsal period for each play was six weeks, and, because of the pressures of finance and time which filming imposes, only the most serious errors could be corrected by reshooting. As David Snodin, the script editor, explains, 'when a scene can be recorded only three or four times at the most, the version that is finally chosen for transmission has to be the best in terms of performance rather than absolute textual correctness'.[56]

BBC Publications issued a playtext to accompany each film. The edition used as the basis for each film was the Alexander Text, but the published version conveniently marked the director's cuts and other departures from

Alexander in the margin. In other words the BBC provided a control: critics interested in memorial error can collate the BBC text as published with the text as performed. (To verify that the variants recorded below were indeed memorial errors and not later script changes or post-production edits, I checked the material against the BBC's 'text as transmitted' versions.)

The results below are culled from a study of six plays: *Hamlet, Julius Caesar, The Winter's Tale, Antony and Cleopatra, Richard 3*, and *1 Henry 4*. Obviously, we are unlikely to find major verbal errors such as multi-line repetitions across several scenes; but given the twentieth-century stress on textual fidelity, and the medium of film which facilitates matters by shooting in small increments, the number and nature of the errors in each film is surprising.

The numbers of errors are as follows. *Hamlet*: 88; *Julius Caesar*: 55; *Winter's Tale*: 94; *Antony and Cleopatra*: 63; *Richard 3*: 135; *1 Henry 4*: 163. With one exception, the errors are distributed relatively evenly across the roles within each play. (The exception is Falstaff in *1 Henry 4*, who has an extraordinary number of errors. If this actor is not just exceptionally careless, it may be that comic actors allow themselves a freer play of memory than more serious characters.) I call all variations from the published BBC text errors although many of the most frequent variants would probably cause little concern to director, audience, or even author. Thus, changes of tense, changes of mood, alterations of singular to plural and vice-versa, and changes in the forms of possessive pronouns (e.g. thy/thine), although frequent, do not feature in the ensuing discussion. Our interest lies in variants that disturb several words or lines, or transform single words into something totally different. (Since the BBC text does not give line numbers, all citations have been taken from Alexander's *The Complete Works*.)

SUBSTITUTION

The largest category is substitution. This general label covers everything from paraphrase:

> Text: Well, that rascal hath good mettle in him.
> Film: Well, there's good mettle in that fellow.
>   (*1H4* 2.4.339–40)

> Text: My Lord of Westmoreland, lead him to his tent.
> Film: My Lord of Westmoreland, go you with him.
>   (*1H4* 5.4.8)

Text: Chop off his head – something we will determine.
Film: Chop off his head, man – somewhat we will do.
    (*R3* 3.1.193)

Text: How now Hastings!
Film: Well met Hastings!
    (*R3* 3.2.98)

to synonym:

Text: his lordly honour
Film: his holy honour
    (*R3* 4.4.369)

Text: What, is my beaver easier than it was?
Film: What, is my armour easier than it was?
    (*R3* 5.3.50)

Text: your good deserts forgot
Film: your just deserts forgot
    (*1H4* 4.3.46)

Text: all the duties of a man
Film: all the virtues of a man
    (*1H4* 5.2.56)

A representative, but by no means exhaustive, list of the range and kind of substitutions in BBC films follows:

Text: What is his strength by land?
Film: What is his force by land?
    (*A&C* 2.2.166)

Text: and then chop him
Film: and then throw him
    (*R3* 1.4.152)

Text: your high-swol'n hearts
Film: your high-swol'n hate
    (*R3* 2.2.117)

Text: to look on death no more
Film: to look on earth no more
 (*R3* 2.4.65)

Text: give order that
Film: give notice that
 (*R3* 3.5.108)

Text: Revenge should have no bounds
Film: Revenge should know no bounds
 (*Ham* 4.7.128)

Text: as I point my sword
Film: as I draw my sword
 (*JC* 2.1.106)

Text: Are you so fond of your young prince
Film: Are you so fond of your young son
 (*WT* 1.2.164)

Text: I think it not uneasy
Film: I think it not hard
 (*WT* 4.2.47)

Text: the down-trod Mortimer
Film: the noble Mortimer
 (*1H4* 1.3.135)

(Here something formulaic has been substituted for something more specific, with consequent redirection of meaning.)

Text: In faith, it is
Film: Upon my life it is
 (*1H4* 1.3.282)

Text: I am a rogue if I were not at half sword
Film: I am a villain if I was not at half sword
 (*1H4* 2.4.157–8)

Text: But as the devil would have it
Film: But as ill luck would have it
 (*1H4* 2.4.214)

Text: If…honour bid me on
Film: If…honour prick me on
  (*1H4* 4.3.10)

(Vernon's line here is presumably indebted to Falstaff's more famous line 'honour pricks me on. Yea, but how if honour prick me off', which appears at 5.1.130–1.)

ADDITIONS

Additions comprise a similarly large category. The additions take several forms, the most frequent of which is extra-metrical induction: the actor provides a run-up to his rehearsed line, usually with a one-word exclamation or oath. Conjunctions constitute another of the most frequent inductions, thus creating the additive style which typifies orality and oral cultures. In the following quotations I bracket the actor's addition.

[O yes], 'tis most true
  (*Ham* 3.1.21)

Ay [truly] sir, but
  (*Ham* 3.2.334)

O [Hamlet] speak to me no more
  (*Ham* 3.4.94)

[Then], will you dine with me?
  (*JC* 1.2.289)

[Why] there's a bargain made
  (*JC* 1.3.120)

[Come], bring me to Octavius
  (*JC* 3.2.272)

[By the gods], I had rather be a dog
  (*JC* 4.3.27)

[Ay,] sure, the gods do this year connive
  (*WT* 4.4.665)

[O] give me thy hand
  (*A&C* 4.2.10)

How [now]? not dead?
    (*A&C* 4.14.103)

[And] if all this will not do
    (*R3* 1.4.267)

[Now,] my lord
    (*R3* 2.2.146)

[See] here breathless lies the King
    (*1H4* 5.3.16)

[Yet] I fear the shot
    (*1H4* 5.3.30)

Other additions provide auxiliary verbs for emphasis, expand contractions, insert connective conjunctions, add vocatives and apostrophes, or round out phrases with epithets which form part of that phrase in another sequence (this last example overlaps with the category of repetition, while several additions provide part of an opening phrase, thus overlapping with induction). I bracket the additional material.

And [yet] truly in my youth
    (*Ham* 2.2.188)

I mean [what is] the matter that you read
    (*Ham* 2.2.194)

[I'll speak to him again]
    (*Ham* 2.2. after 204)

If 'a do [but] blench
    (*Ham* 2.2.593)

Now yours [good] Metellus
    (*JC* 3.1.188)

then you shall [ever] see me pay
    (*JC* 5.3.102)

Come [hither], poor remains of friends
    (*JC* 5.5.1)

Fertile the isle [and] the temple
> (*WT* 3.1.2)

By your most gracious pardon [madam]
> (*A&C* 1.5.72)

'A bears the third part of the world [in arms], man
> (*A&C* 2.7.89)

If [thus] thou vanishest
> (*A&C* 5.2.295)

(NB The same actor's omission of 'thus' from the phrase 'if thus thou' just four lines previously, perhaps triggered the intrusion of the adverb here.)

their ministers [they] attend on him
> (*R3* 1.3.294)

[I pray God he be not, I say]
> (*R3* 3.4.after 59)

Let us be [called] Diana's foresters
> (*1H4* 1.2.24)

(NB The phrase immediately preceding, 'let not us. . .be called thieves', presumably prompted the intrusive repetition here.)

swore the devil his [own] true liegeman
> (*1H4* 2.4.328)

Tut, [man] never fear me
> (*1H4* 4.2.56)

(cf. the same actor just six lines later: '[O] tut, tut [man]')

O would [to God] the quarrel lay upon our heads
> (*1H4* 5.2.48)

And time [itself] that takes survey
> (*1H4* 5.4.82)

OMISSION

Omission comprises another large category. Small units such as conjunctions, inductions, exclamations, and emphatic phrases are frequently omitted (I bracket the omitted material).

And so [once more] return
(*R3* 3.7.91)

Long live [King] Richard
(*R3* 3.7.240)

(The allegedly memorial quarto text of *Richard 3* also omits 'King' at this point.)

Falstaff! [Fast asleep] behind the arras
(*1H4* 2.4.510)

But mine [I am sure] thou art
(*1H4* 5.4.37)

Elsewhere omissions range in length from a complete line or a half-line, to sequences of between two and eight lines. In no case does the BBC text indicate that the material is cut.

[So do not I.] Go coward
(*R3* 1.4.277)

[That ever liv'd]
(*R3* 3.5.34)

[Farewell, and stand fast]
(*1H4* 2.2.69)

[Here's no vanity.]
(*1H4* 5.3.32)

[I could have given less matter / A better ear]
(*A&C* 2.1.31–2)

[Aboard my galley I invite you all]
(*A&C* 2.6.80)

[A sign of dignity, a breath, a bubble]
   (*R3* 4.4.90)

[And I believe it is a fetch of warrant]
   (*Ham* 2.1.38)

[Conceit in weakest bodies strongest works]
   (*Ham* 3.4.114)

[Since no man owes of aught he leaves, what is't to leave betimes?]
   (*Ham* 5.2.209)

[His corporal motion govern'd by my spirit]
   (*JC* 4.1.33)

[and do it with unwash'd hands too]
   (*1H4* 3.3.183)

[ten times more dishonourable ragged than an old-fac'd ancient]
   (*1H4* 4.2.35–6)

Sequences of two lines are omitted at *Antony and Cleopatra* 5.2.111–12, 5.2.254–5, and 5.2.304b–6a. The eight lines which begin *Antony and Cleopatra* 2.6 are omitted (it is hard to believe that this was an accident, but neither the published nor the archives' 'as transmitted' text marks it as a cut).

David Snodin, the script editor, reminds me that 'like most television programmes, BBC Shakespeare plays were made under considerable clock-watching pressure, and at times . . . we simply did not have the time to reshoot accidental omissions and even textual errors'. As an example he cites Act 5 of *Antony and Cleopatra* which was 'shot in its entirety in the last hour of a studio day, almost as if it was "live". Certain textual lapses were therefore inevitable.'[57] It is probably no coincidence that the three two-line omissions I cite above occur in *Antony and Cleopatra* Act 5.

David Burke (Camillo in *The Winter's Tale*) summarises his textual experiences during a thirty-five-year career in which he has performed approximately two-thirds of the Shakespeare canon. Paraphrase in a minor way occurs all the time, he says, with prepositions and conjunctions being the main victims. Although errors are pointed out in rehearsal, and the actor, if conscientious, corrects them, correction tends to stop once a play has opened, and so mistakes get ironed in. Burke explains that, in the weekly repertory system which prevailed in England, an actor could perform in as many as fifty plays per year. 'In these circumstances, paraphrasing became a necessary survival skill, and *nobody* ever spoke the text with absolute faithfulness.'[58] It is noteworthy that several of the single lines which the BBC text marks as cuts are nonetheless retained by the actors (see for example, *1 Henry 4* 2.2.50a and 2.2.100a, spoken by Poins and Hal, respectively).

TRANSPOSITION

Transposition causes the reordering of several speeches in the BBC Shakespeare. At *Richard 3* 4.4.51–4 Queen Margaret speaks her lines in the following order: 53, 52, 54, 51. At *Richard 3* 4.4.374–7 King Richard and Queen Elizabeth reorder their sequence as follows: 375, 376, 374, 377. In both these examples the disturbance is caused by the omission of a line which is duly reinserted a few lines later. In *Richard 3* 1.4.260–5 Clarence causes the disturbance by introducing one line in advance of its proper place, i.e. 260, 264, 261, 262, 263, 265. Iras in *Antony and Cleopatra* omits a half-line 'The gods forbid!' (5.2.212), substituting instead 'O, the good gods!' – which is, of course, her line at 220, where it also appears (thus causing a repetition). The Priest's line 'I'll wait upon your lordship' at *Richard 3* 3.2.113 is transposed to line 123, after Buckingham's 'knowst it not'.

Local transpositions (phrases within the same line) account for a large proportion of the errors in the BBC Shakespeare:

> Text: We could, an if we would
> Film: We would, an if we could
>   (*Ham* 1.5.176)

> Text: Time qualifies the spark and fire of it
> Film: Time qualifies the fire and spark of it
>   (*Ham* 4.7.113)

> Text: do not think of him
> Film: think not of him
>   (*JC* 2.1.185)

Text: Yet in the number I do know but one
Film: Yet I do know but one in the number
   (*JC* 3.1.68)

Text: either push on or pluck back
Film: either pluck back or push on
   (*WT* 4.4.725–6)

Text: In Kent, my liege
Film: My liege, in Kent
   (*R3* 4.4.505)

Text: such beastly shameless transformation
Film: such shameless beastly transformation
   (*1H4* 1.1.44)

Text: had exchang'd / In cradle clothes
Film: in cradle clothes / Had exchang'd
   (*1H4* 1.1.87–8)

Text: look to thy servants, cherish thy guests
Film: cherish thy servants, and look to thy guests
   (*1H4* 3.3.171)

NUMERICAL ERRORS

Errors occur in numerical data.

Text: Caesar's three and thirty wounds
Film: Caesar's three and twenty wounds
   (*JC* 5.1.53)

Text: My lord, old Sir John, with half-a-dozen more, are at the door
Film: Old Sir John, and a few dozen more, are at the door
   (*1H4* 2.4.79–80)

(This is a compound error. 'My lord' is omitted, the preposition 'with' changed to the conjunction 'and', and Falstaff's supporters multiplied from six to about thirty-six.)

Text: ten thousand soldiers
Film: a thousand soldiers
   (*R3* 5.3.218)

> Text: A thousand men
> Film: Ten thousand men
>   (*R3* 1.4.25)

COMPOUND ERRORS

All of the above errors also appear in combination. The following examples combine substitution and transposition:

> Text: Time as long again / Would be fill'd up, my brother
> Film: Time as much again / My brother would be fill'd up.
>   (*WT* 1.2.3–4)

> Text: Of you, and you, Lord Rivers, and Lord Dorset
> Film: Of you, Lord Gray, of you, Lord Rivers
>   (*R3* 2.1.66)

In the next examples we find addition with compensatory omission.

> Text: I thank thee, good Sir John, with all my heart
> Film: I thank thee kindly, good Sir John
>   (*R3* 3.2.111)

> Text: the wrongs I have done thee stir
> Film: the wrongs [that] I have done thee
>   (*WT* 5.1.148)

(Here the addition of 'that' forces the actor to omit 'stir' in metrical compensation.)

Similar examples of singular and compound errors could be continued in abundance, but the pattern is plain to see: twentieth-century actors, products of a print-based culture which values accuracy in textual reproduction, make errors of just the kind Greg *et al.* supposed actors would. As we shall see in the next chapter, other agents may make these errors too. But at least we can state unequivocally that actors do make these errors on a fairly large scale and not just that we imagine they might.

CONCLUSION

It is now necessary to collate our analysis of memorial errors with our earlier discussion of memory, thus raising the question: what standards of memorial/textual accuracy did Shakespeare expect of his actors on the Elizabethan stage?

Here we encounter a problem caused by the difference between six-teenth-century and twentieth-century culture. When the New Bibliographers talked about memorial reconstruction, the ideal they seemed to have in mind was a perfect reproduction: a tape-recording, a fac-simile, memory behaving flawlessly. This is very much a twentieth-century ideal derived from a print-based culture which values textual fidelity. We do not know if Elizabethan actors shared this ideal. But we do know that medieval and Renaissance scribes, whose job was to 'copy' manuscripts, behaved far more cavalierly than we would have assumed. G. L. Brook cites an interesting example of the same scribe (thirteenth century?) copying the same fourteen-line passage, from the same exemplar of Lazamon's *Brut*, twice, probably within a brief period of time, and managing to reproduce very few details the same way both times.[59] In *The Fatal Marriage* the scribe accidentally copied the same twelve-line passage twice but with five sub-stantive variants (lines 1956–65; 2056–67). The Renaissance textual agenda was probably not the one set by the New Bibliographers: the reproduction of copy, noise-free.

We are dealing now with two stages of memorial reconstruction: the original actors' presentation of a new play on the London stage; and puta-tive attempts by auditors or players to reconstruct a text *post hoc*. There can be no doubt that the frequent complaints in authors' prefaces or prologues to 'mangled' or 'maimed' texts indicate authorial disquiet in the face of a version verbally distant from the one originally composed. Hamlet's advice to the players cautions against comic ad libbing; and the claims of the title pages of Q2 *Romeo and Juliet* and *Hamlet* and others to be '*[n]ewly corrected, augmented, and amended*' (the phrasing comes from Q2 *Romeo and Juliet*) suggest that the first quartos were viewed as objects in need of replacement. However, it is frequently pointed out that the corrected or replacement playtexts are far from perfect, and, as we have seen, preachers regularly deplored the textual quality of sermons published from auditors' notes, while nonetheless allowing the reported text to serve as the basis of the cor-rected version. E. A. J. Honigmann comments on the paradox of a Shakespeare sensitive to the quality of the 'bad' quartos but indifferent to the quality of the good.[60]

I am not sure that this is as much of a paradox as it appears. To primary oral cultures, such as that of the Greeks, memory meant remembering, not memorisation; to chirographic cultures, such as that of twentieth-century Britain or North America, memory means memorisation. However, a transitionary culture, with 'secondary' or 'residual' orality, such as that of the Elizabethans, might conceivably aim for memorisation, but be satisfied with remembering. Authors, in other words, might be content to have actors and printers make free with their lines within certain limits.

This is pure speculation, of course. But it is a speculation which Thomas Pettitt's work on formulaic dramaturgy supports, and it is a speculation which Harold Jenkins comes close to articulating when, writing about memorially reconstructed texts, he says, 'such a text would need to be not so much accurate as actable'.[61] Jenkins feels that suspect texts were clearly acceptable to the actors who may have performed them and the audiences who saw them. That they were certainly acceptable to the reading public is seen by the number of editions many of them received. And an author's attitude to his work *in print* would understandably differ from his attitude to that work in performance. (Thus, the verbal problems in Q2 *Romeo and Juliet*, or plot confusions in the dénouement of Folio *The Merry Wives of Windsor* would be tolerable; the staccato dialogue in Q1 *The Merry Wives* might not.)

We are now negotiating uncertain territory. A cautious summary of this territory might content itself with two points: Elizabethan memory was undoubtedly better than ours, but perhaps its aims were different; and in seeking evidence of faulty memory in a suspect text we should perhaps view it not as memorial error but as memorial variation.

What we can say with confidence is that the verbal variations caused by memory seem, on the evidence of Renaissance commonplace books, eighteenth-century ballads, twentieth-century neuropsychology, and twentieth-century BBC actors' slips, not to differ across the centuries. We are now on firmer ground in understanding the textual effects of memory, and so we can, at last, turn our attention to the suspect texts themselves.

Part Two

6 | Introduction

Some circumstantial evidence is very strong, as when you find a trout in the milk.

> Henry David Thoreau, *Journal* 11 November 1854

– Is there any other point to which you would wish to draw my attention?
– To the curious incident of the dog in the night-time.
– The dog did nothing in the night-time.
– That was the curious incident.

> A. Conan Doyle, *The Silver Blaze*

It should be apparent from the previous chapters that much New Bibliographic analysis of suspect texts is confirmatory rather than diagnostic. The features of suspect texts (texts suspected of being reconstructed from memory) are measured against *a priori* expectations of the features a memorially reconstructed text should exhibit. When the features of the material suspect text agree with those of the hypothetical model of memorial reconstruction, this congruence is taken to 'prove' memorial reconstruction. Small wonder that so many texts have been designated memorial reconstructions.

In articles and introductions to editions, New Bibliographers regularly list the features allegedly typical of, and confined to, suspect texts. The following comments on Q *King Lear* are representative:

> Q seems to contain some 'connective' phrases by actors, and many of its misreadings might well be due either to actors' blunders or to mishearing... [M]islineation is a constant feature in Q... Occasionally it is altogether unmetrical. Prose is printed as verse. Still more often is verse printed as prose... I think that the characteristics of Q point to a reported text.[1]

[W]e find in the quarto all the usual stigmas of a reported text: redundancy, whether through the actors' introductions of vocatives, expletives, or connective phrases, or through their lapsing into looser and more commonplace phraseology, merging into paraphrase; anticipation, recollection, and assimilation; vulgarization, and mere breakdown through failure of memory.[2]

Any recto or verso of Q will have opacity elbowing ineptness. Q inadvertently omits. Q has a word or line before or after where it belongs. Anticipation or recollection causes assimilation of similar lines in different passages. Q vulgarizes. Q adds unnecessary words. Q substitutes the well-worn phrase for the Shakespearean phrase. Q misunderstands the meaning of lines. Q misunderstands and misinterprets the action. Q spoils fine touches of characterization. Q does not know who the speaker is and guesses. Q runs together two different speakers' lines. Q, in short, stands solidly in the way of Shakespeare.[3]

Although the New Bibliographers never explain where on the diagnostic scale a neutral *feature* of a suspect text becomes a *symptom* of a memorially reconstructed text, the twin criteria for diagnosis of memorial reconstruction appear to be heterogeneity and accumulation. Thus, the greater the number of features, and the more frequently those diverse features occur, the greater the likelihood of memorial reconstruction.

This is a rather impressionistic strategy, and is clearly unsatisfactory when one considers that critics seeking evidence of revision might claim the same features as evidence of authorial change of intent, while critics seeking evidence of authorial draft or scribal transcription might claim almost all the above features as side-effects of authorial indecision and scribal oversight.

The questions which any survey of suspect texts needs to address are therefore myriad. Are suspect texts the only Renaissance playtexts with extra-metrical connective phrases? (Answer: no). Can mislineation, prose printed as verse, and verse printed as prose be found in non-suspect texts? (Answer: yes). How do we distinguish between omission which is the result of memorial accident and that which stems from purposeful cutting? How do we decide that a word or phrase which comes before or after where we think it belongs is not the result of scribal or compositorial eyeskip? Or a line that we believe misplaced is not the result of authorial experimentation? What do we mean by stylistic redundancy? How do we define vulgarisation? New Bibliographers often acknowledge that several of the alleged features of memorial reconstruction can be found in almost any mode of transmission; it is a question of frequency. But how do we define frequency? When does repetition cease to be rhetorically effective and become a tedious side-effect of memory? These questions form the basis of the following chapters.

In 1952 William Bracy published a monograph on *The Merry Wives of Windsor* in which he attempted a *reductio ad absurdum* of memorial reconstruction. Greg, reviewing the work, objected to Bracy's method of reduction which 'is merely to take instances in which reporting has been assumed and to assert that each is open to another explanation'.[4] Greg's comment unwittingly identifies the central problem in New Bibliographic studies of suspect texts: 'assumed' is the operative word, and Bracy was simply playing the New Bibliographers at their own game by assuming a different scenario. Clearly something is wrong with a textual approach which can cite the same evidence in support of different assumptions.

In the following chapter I eschew teleological assumptions. Without making prejudgments as to origin, and temporarily abandoning the word 'symptom', I list and examine the key features of suspect texts, separately and collectively, to ascertain what they might be symptoms of. In surveying textual features I necessarily cast my net wide, not only examining suspect texts but comparing them with a control group drawn from other plays of the period 1585–1625. Obviously, if the features in suspect texts which critics have designated evidence of memorial reconstruction appear frequently in non-suspect texts (especially in those, such as closet drama, which cannot be affected by actors' memories) those features cannot be ascribed exclusively to memorial reconstruction. The necessity of such a textual control was first realised by McKerrow in 1924 when he reviewed the collection of essays dedicated to proving Shakespeare's hand in *Sir Thomas More*: 'It is not enough to know that wherever A occurs we find B unless we also know that when A does not occur B also is absent.'[5] Similarly, it is not enough to show that putative memorial symptoms appear in suspect texts unless we also show that they do not appear in non-suspect texts.

The features which I list and analyse are, for the most part, familiar, culled from the lists offered by the New Bibliographers in their work on suspect texts. The suspect texts surveyed are forty-one in total, comprising fourteen Shakespearean plays, and twenty-seven non-Shakespearean plays. The principle underlying the choice of texts is straightforward: if a critic has at any time voiced suspicions that a text might be a memorial reconstruction – even if those suspicions never hardened into conclusions or were vociferously rejected – that text is deemed a suspect text. Thus there are 14 Shakespearean suspect texts: *1 Contention* (1594), *Hamlet* (1603), *Henry 5* (1600), *King Lear* (1608), *The Merry Wives of Windsor* (1602), *Pericles* (1609), the Parliament scene in *Richard 2* (1608), *Richard 3* (1597), *Richard Duke of York* (1595), *Romeo and Juliet* (1597), *The Taming of A Shrew* (1594), the fly scene in *Titus Andronicus* (1623), and *1* and *2 Troublesome Reign* (1591; I treat, for the moment, *1* and *2 Troublesome Reign* as two plays, while acknowledging that they may be one long play divided into two quartos for publication).

The twenty-seven non-Shakespearean suspect texts are assembled from the lists offered by Alexander, Kirschbaum, Duthie, Hoppe, *et al.*, supplemented by the explorative suspicions of general editors such as Richard Proudfoot and E. A. J. Honigmann: *Arden of Feversham* (1592), *The Blind Beggar of Alexandria* (1598), *The Death of Robert, Earl of Huntingdon* (1601), *Dr Faustus* (1604), *Edward 1* (1593), *Fair Em* (undated), *The Fair Maid of Bristow* (1605), *The Famous Victories of Henry 5* (1598), *George a Greene* (1599), *1 Hieronimo* (1605), *1 If You Know Not Me You Know Nobody* (1605), *Jack Straw* (1594), *John of Bordeaux* (unpublished MS), *A Knack to Know a Knave* (1594), *A Knack to Know an Honest Man* (1596), *The Maid's Tragedy* (1619), *The Massacre at Paris* (undated), *The Merry Devil of Edmonton* (1608), *Mucedorus* (1598), *Orlando Furioso* (1594), *The Old Wife's Tale* (1595), *Philaster* (1620), the additions to *The Spanish Tragedy* (1602), *Sir Thomas Wyatt* (1607), *Thomas Lord Cromwell* (1602), *The True Tragedy of Richard 3* (1594), and *A Yorkshire Tragedy* (1608).[6] Obviously, there is insufficient room for detailed discussion of all forty-one suspect texts: my primary concern in chapter 7 is investigative method rather than diagnostic conclusion. However, in chapter 8 I present a summary of my analysis of the features of each of the forty-one suspect texts, and offer a textual verdict on each play, in tabular form.

Comparing suspect with non-suspect texts is, as explained above, as important as examining suspect texts associatively. My control comprises all the dramatic texts in the Malone Society Reprint series, and a comprehensively random reading of the printed works of the following dramatists: Anon., Beaumont, Brome, Chapman, Dekker, Fletcher, Greene, Heywood, Jonson, Kyd, Lodge, Lyly, Marlowe, Marston, Middleton, Munday, Nashe, Peele, Shirley, Tourneur, and Webster. This provides sufficient material to help identify those unusual features which are limited to suspect texts (and hence, potentially symptoms of memory) from those which are not.

As we shall see, many of the features in suspect texts which seem unorthodox – so unorthodox as to convince New Bibliographers that the playtexts which contained them were in some way different from others of the period – are more widespread than we have been led to believe. This means either that more plays are memorial than previously suspected or that these features are symptoms of some malfunction in textual transmission which may include, but is not limited to, memorial reconstruction. The ensuing discussion shows that the textual disturbance caused by faulty memory is very difficult to identify because it is identical to the textual disturbance caused by scribes, compositors, forgetful authors, revising authors, adapters, or other playhouse personnel adding to a MS. Thus, while most of the features under discussion may well be textual side-effects of faulty memory, very few are uniquely symptoms of faulty memory.

In my analysis of the features I approach the Shakespearean suspect texts as if no parallel text existed, i.e. I ignore any help or bias offered by a Q2 or F version. This puts the Shakespearean suspect texts on an equal footing with the non-Shakespearean, and facilitates contextual understanding. If the discussion contains fewer illustrations of features from Shakespearean suspect texts than the reader expects, it is because the Shakespearean suspect texts are of a markedly higher textual quality than the non-Shakespearean, and thus provide fewer textual problems for discussion.

I discuss the features of suspect texts under three main headings: the Poem, the Play, and the Text. The Poem is that which the audience would hear and the actors would speak; this category includes verbal features, such as repetition, insertion, and transposition. The Play is that which an audience would see and/or the actors would perform; this category therefore includes features such as plot, reduced casting, and staging. The Text is that material entity which makes a connection between the Poem and the Play possible; this category comprises those material features which are neither seen/acted, nor heard/spoken, such as punctuation, stage directions, and mislining.

I take my distinction between Play and Poem from Webster's prolegomena to the first quarto of *The Duchess of Malfi*. My more immediate prompt, however, is Antony Hammond's astute paper on stage directions. Hammond analyses Webster's prefatory material as follows:

> The title-page announces that the first Quarto is 'The perfect and exact Coppy, with diverse things Printed, that the length of the Play would not beare in the Presentment.' However, in his Dedication to Baron Berkeley, Webster writes 'I offer this Poem to your Patronage.' There is good reason to think that Webster himself may have composed the wording of the title page (in view of the 'authorized' character of the Quarto); if so, he clearly thought that 'the length of the Play' was something related to the performance of the drama in the theatre: that is what a 'play' was. The printed 'perfect and exact Coppy,' then, is a copy of the 'poem.' It was not uncommon at the time for dramatists to refer to their work as a poem, but there are few other examples where the distinction is so directly drawn between 'poem,' meaning the text written by the author, over which the author saw himself as possessing some authority and rights (not in law, but *in esse*, as it were), and the 'play,' which was something that involved a collaborative creation, in which the writer of the script was by no means the first to be considered.[7]

The sense in which I use 'Text', meaning a physical object, runs counter to the meaning established by recent literary theorists. Appealing to the etymology of text as 'woven cloth', Barthes and others have associated the word with plural, indeterminate discourse: 'While the work is held in the hand, the text is held in language: it exists only as discourse. . . In other words, *the Text is experienced only in an activity, a production*. It follows that the Text cannot stop, at the end of a library shelf, for example.'[8] For textual critics, however, 'text' has always meant something material, tangible, something one could grasp physically or trip over, and I refuse to allow literary theory to deprive us of this meaning.[9]

Throughout chapters 7 and 8 I use Play, Poem, and Text with majuscules to refer to the material subsumed by the above definitions. Minuscules are used when I attach the familiar, less specific, meanings to these nouns: play (a four- or five-act drama), poem (a sonnet, an elegy, for example) and text (a material document).

There is a certain unavoidable overlap between these three categories. (I include stage directions in the category of Text but, obviously, stage directions affect what happens in the Play. Aural error could be included in the categories of Poem or of Text.) But separating localised lexical features (the Poem) from structure and staging (the Play) and material presentation (the Text) imposes form on the New Bibliographers' amorphous list, and highlights the area in which the problems in suspect texts are concentrated: the Poem. To this area we must now turn.

7 | Diagnosing memorial reconstruction: the Poem, the Play, the Text

Foul! No repetitions...
Foul! No synonyms!...
Foul! No *non sequiturs*.

Tom Stoppard, Rosencrantz and Guildenstern are Dead

I am not so much concerned with discrediting this method as with trying to discover whether there may not be sound ways of using it.

H. T. Price[1]

A. THE POEM

With suspect texts containing between 757 and 3,416 lines of dialogue (the totals for *A Yorkshire Tragedy* and Q *Richard 3*, respectively), the Poem provides our largest catchment area of material for evaluation. This verbal matter can be affected by a number of agents: revising or indecisive authors, playbook annotators, actors, scribes, and compositors. The amorphous category of repetitions, for instance, which critics cite as strong evidence of memorial reconstruction, is easily attributable to all five of the above. How, then, do we distinguish a memorial repetition from any other?

A.I. REPETITION

A.I.a. External Echoes/Recollection

Harry Hoppe claimed to have identified twenty-four 'true inter-play borrowings' (also known as 'echoes', 'parallels', and 'external recollections') in Q1 *Romeo and Juliet*. All of his 'borrowings' come from Shakespearean texts, twenty of them from plays written in the same period as *Romeo and Juliet* (*Richard 2*, *The Taming of the Shrew*, *3 Henry 6*, *Titus Andronicus*, *The Two Gentlemen of Verona*, and *Richard 3*);[2] thus, the possibility of authorial self-borrowing is strong, and undermines any value Hoppe's parallels may have.

His parallels are of negligible value anyway; they contain proverbial phrases (e.g. *The Merry Wives of Windsor*: 'we burn daylight'), or common sentiments (*Richard 2*: 'And then be gone') or refer to parallel situations (*The Two Gentlemen of Verona*: 'a ladder quaintly made of cords'). A sample will suffice to show how insubstantial a basis these parallels provide for diagnosing faulty memory. (Throughout I cite the alleged source(s) first and the suspect text last.)

> Till we with Trophees *do adorne thy Tombe.*
> > (F *Titus Andronicus* TLN 432)
> With funerall praises *doo adorne thy Tombe.*
> > (QI *Romeo and Juliet*, 14v,23)

> And *how stand you affected to* his wish?
> > (*The Two Gentlemen of Verona* TLN 362)
> *howe stand you affected to* be married?
> > (QI *Romeo and Juliet* B4v,18–19)

> *What* shall *I say more than I* haue inferr'd?
> > (F *Richard 3* TLN 3784)
> *What* should *I say more than I* said before,
> > (QI *Romeo and Juliet* B2v,3)

> When *holy and* deuout *Religious* men
> > (F *Richard 3* TLN 2310)
> He is a *holy and religious* Man
> > (QI *Romeo and Juliet* H4v,25)

> But beg one *fauour at* thy gracious *hand,*
> > (F *Richard 3* TLN 401)
> Accept this latest *fauour at* my *hands,*
> > (QI *Romeo and Juliet* 14v,21)

Although the rhythm of each pair of lines is the same, my italics reveal how unparallel is the verbal content of the lines.

Furthermore, the italicised material is demonstrably conventional, the kind of commonplace which comes easily to any Renaissance author composing in iambic pentameter. As such it is no more significant than the other familiar commonplaces in Renaissance drama: 'the braggingest knave / bluntest wooer / proudest kings / cunningest man in Christendom'; 'Away I say and let me hear no more / talk to me no more / that I may grieve some more'; 'let it be spoke in secret here'; 'I'll beard and brave him proudly to his face'; 'I fear me it will prove too true'; 'I'll send him down to everlasting night'. Characters in Renaissance drama are regularly 'sad and passionate'; painters always 'lay their colours to the life'; anger manifests itself with 'furrows in his frowning brow'. Willard Thorp wrote of 'the common store-house to which all Elizabethan dramatists had a pass-key',[3] and although he was referring to stock situations, his metaphor is equally applicable to language.

One can understand how Hoppe reached his conclusions about memorial reconstruction, for the alleged borrowings frequently appear only in Q1 *Romeo and Juliet*; when they feature in both Q1 and Q2, the Q1 phrasing tends to be closer to that of the putative source than to Q2. However, variance and/or partial agreement may stem from causes other than memorial reconstruction.

It has become a cliché of post-structuralist poetics to assert with Barthes that 'any text is a new tissue of past citations. Bits of codes, formulae, rhythmic models, fragments of social languages, etc. pass into the text and are redistributed within it.'[4] However, this post-structuralist paradigm perfectly conveys the ambiance of Elizabethan drama, and of an age which did not acknowledge textual copyright in the sense that we do. Furthermore, Shakespeare was not alone in being a playwright who was also an actor. Echoes from plays in which an actor–playwright had performed might linger and re-emerge in a new dramatic composition.

Dramatists are, by profession, interested in drama and do not confine their interest to their own compositions. Dorothy Farr points out that in *'Tis Pity She's A Whore* Annabella's 'insistence upon the imminence of death evidently suggested to Ford the episode leading up to the death of the Duchess of Malfi. The verbal parallels are obtrusive.' Andrew Gurr draws attention to the fact that Ben Jonson and Beaumont and Fletcher 'evidently read each other's plays . . . Jonson echoes *The Burning Pestle* and *The Coxcomb* (1610) in *The Alchemist*, and Beaumont and Fletcher echo his *Silent Woman* (1609) and *Alchemist* in *The Scornful Lady* (1610) and *The*

Woman's Prize (1611).'[5] Thus, we must beware lest echoes be authorial rather than reportorial.

We must also take care that echoes are indeed echoes. Appendix I of M. L. Wine's edition of *Arden of Feversham* lists numerous 'Parallels' between *Arden* and other plays, the editor's inverted commas tacitly acknowledging the dubious relevance of the alleged external echoes in the list. '[W]ithout a rigorous definition of what a "parallel" actually is', Wine cautions, '"proof" is always easily forthcoming' (p.141). Despite heroic attempts by H. C. Oliphant and Samuel Schoenbaum to prevent overzealous identification of external echoes, editors and textual critics continue to offer parallels which are highly dubious:

> With greatest pleasures that our Court affords,
>> (*The Spanish Tragedy* (1602) 859)

> With greatest torments that our hel affoords.
>> (A *Dr Faustus* E4v,20)

These lines (cited by Keefer in his edition of *Dr Faustus*, p.81) have too little in common to posit memorial reconstruction.

> And had you cut my body with your swords,
> Or hew'd this flesh and bones as small as sand,
>> (B *Dr Faustus* F2r,14–15)

> This angrie sword should rip thy hatefull chest,
> And hewd thee smaller then the *Libian* sandes,
>> (*The Taming of A Shrew* F2r,25–6)

Greg acknowledges that 'this passage is one of the least convincing of the parallels'.[6] I would go further, and suggest that it is parallel only in sentiment, not expression.

Eric Rasmussen invites us to compare 'shal I haue *Nan Spit*, and to mine owne vse?' (A *Dr Faustus* D3v,3–4) with 'How have ye used my Nan?' (*The Two Angry Women of Abington*). He finds *1 Contention*'s 'this Centricke earth, / And hither come in twinkling of an eye' (c1r,6–7) to be an echo of A *Dr Faustus*' 'of this centricke earth . . . in twinckling of an eie' (c3r,21, E4v,32), and suggests that *1 Contention*'s 'Now *Bullenbrooke* what wouldst thou haue me do?' (c1r,11) echoes A *Dr Faustus*' 'Now *Faustus*, what wouldst thou haue me do?' (BIV,35).[7] Any parallel between the first pair of lines seems negligible; the second and third pairs are too conventional to carry any weight as evidence.

> HUMPHREY: Sirrha, whats a clocke?
> SERVINGMAN: Almost ten my Lord.
>   (*1 Contention* D2r,21–2)

> GLOUCESTER: Sirs, what's a Clock?
> SERVANT: Tenne, my Lord.
>   (*2 Henry 6* TLN 1175–6)

> ARDEN: What a Clock ist sirra?
> MICHAEL: Almost ten.
>   (*Arden of Feversham* 1042–3)

This double parallel (cited by Wine, p.59) is not convincing. The question-and-answer is commonplace; furthermore an author has a one in twelve chance of choosing ten as the hour, and an even better chance of choosing ten as a reasonable hour for bed.

> I have my wish, in that I joy thy sight
>   (*Edward 2* 1.1.151)

> I haue my wishe in that I ioy thy sight.
>   (*Arden of Feversham* 2370)

(See Wine, p.129.) Although the lines are identical, there are a limited number of tag phrases for expressing *politesse* in iambic pentameter; repetition of such an expression is as likely to stem from coincidence as memory.

As Wine recognised, a rigorous definition of external echoes is necessary. It is obvious that our suspect texts are riddled with phrases which resemble those in other plays. But such echoes need not be memorial. Any rigorous definition should, I submit, exclude the following:

(i)   potential echoes or foreshadowings by an author of himself. The parallel phrasing, rhythms, and sentiment of lines which *1 If You Know Not Me* shares with *Sir Thomas Wyatt* could conceivably be authorial self-plagiarism (Heywood, like Greene and Marlowe before him, is a self-repeating writer),[8] and must be dismissed (the sentiment and phrasing are, in any case, commonplace):

QUEEN ELIZABETH: By gods assistance and the power of heauen,
We are instated in our brothers throane,
   (*1 If You Know Not Me* 48–9)

QUEEN MARY: By Gods asistance, and the power of heauen,
after our Troubles we are safely set,
   (*Sir Thomas Wyatt* c3v,26–7)

Pericles echoes *Macbeth* at 4.1.21:

How now, my Lord, why doe you keepe alone?
   (*Macbeth* TLN 1162)

How now *Marina*, why doe yow keep alone?
   (*Pericles* F2v,3)

F. D. Hoeniger judiciously warns that '[a]s *Macbeth* was in Shakespeare's mind all through this scene and IV.iii, the textual echo is not to be blamed on the reporter, as has been suggested'.[9]

(ii) Potential literary echoes by one author of another. Literary landmarks like *The Spanish Tragedy* and *Euphues* had far-reaching textual repercussions, of which Marlowe's 'The hopelesse daughter of a haplesse Jew' (*The Jew of Malta* 1.2.317) in imitation of Kyd's 'The hopeles Father of a haples Sonne' (*The Spanish Tragedy* (1592) 2775) is but one example.

(iii) Stock phrases in the dramatic vocabulary of the time.

(iv) General resemblances of phrase and idea which may be of quite independent origin (no one author had a monopoly on language).

I suggest that, in addition to excluding material from these four categories, any rigorous definition of recollection should be restricted to 1) a run of lines, containing 2) distinctive vocabulary. This restriction provides an important test of memory. A run of lines shows us a mind fumbling for a phrase, and finding, instead, something that comes from elsewhere; distinctive vocabulary helps to distinguish the recollection as unintentional, unlike innocuous recollections (such as Hoppe's examples above), which may stem equally from reporter or author.

Clearly, Hoppe's brief 'innocuous' recollections may be as memorial in origin as lengthy distinctive recollections. But one cannot be sure that they are, and it is imprudent to diagnose a text as memorial on their account. Strictness in diagnostic procedure does not enable us to identify all plays reconstructed from memory; but it ensures that suspect texts whose textual problems stem from non-memorial causes will not be wrongly admitted to the category of memorial reconstruction.

Adhering to such criteria, I cannot view the ensuing oft-cited examples as accidental memorial recollections.

O poore *Horatio*, what hadst thou misdoone?
To leese thy life ere life was new begun.
   (*The Spanish Tragedy* (1592) 964–5)
Ah harmeles Arden how, how hast thou misdone,
That thus thy gentle lyfe is leueld at,
   (*Arden of Feversham* 991–2)

To heare the pittious moane that Rutland made
   (F *Richard 3* TLN 348)
To heare what piteous moane *Philarchus* makes:
   (*A Knack to Know a Knave* 508)

And if the world like not this tragedie,
Hard is the hap of olde *Hieronimo*.
   (*The Spanish Tragedy* (1592) 2605–6)
And if the king like not the tragedy,
Why then belike he likes it not perdy.
   (Q1 *Hamlet* F4v,15–16)

But heere before Prince *Balthazar* and me,
Embrace each other, and be perfect freends.
   (*The Spanish Tragedy* (1592) 2332–3)
      wee'l haue *Leartes*, and our sonne,
Made friends and Louers, as befittes them both,
   (Q1 *Hamlet* I2r,25–6)

(Duthie reinforces this alleged parallel by pointing out that 'in both cases the reconciliation is the prelude to the catastrophe', a statement applicable to a great number of Elizabethan plays.)

We are on firmer ground in identifying an external recollection when it encompasses one or more lines, and contains some distinctive vocabulary:

> Sweete *Mosbie* is the man that hath my hart:
> And he vsurpes it, hauing nought but this,
> That I am tyed to him by marriage.
>   (*Arden of Feversham* 99–101)

> Sweet *Mugeroune*, tis he that hath my heart,
> And *Guise* vsurpes it, cause I am his wife:
>   (*The Massacre at Paris* 795–6)

The first line in each case is conceivably formulaic (we find 'Soranzo is the man that hath her heart' in Ford's *'Tis Pity* 2.3.49, and 'sweet Endimion is he that hath my heart' at *Endymion* 1.4.35). It is the extension into the next line, coupled with the metaphoric verb, 'And he / Guise vsurpes it' which turns the line into identifiable repetition.

The following example is similarly distinctive:

> I haue crost the frosen *Rhine*,
> Leauing faire *Po*, I saild vp *Danuby*,
> As farre as *Saba* whose inhansing streames,
> Cuts twixt the *Tartars* and the *Russians*,
>   (*Old Wife's Tale* 1072–5)

> the frosen Rhene,
> Leauing faire Voya crost vp Danuby,
> As hie as Sabre whose inhaunsing streames,
> Cuts twixt the Tartares and the Russians:
>   (*Orlando Furioso* 73–6)

The tables in chapter 8 show that, using the above criteria, external recollections are surprisingly scarce: it is frequently as plausible to conclude that lines are formulaic (e.g. *TTR3* 2206–7/*KKK* 30–1) as it is to believe that they must be memorial. When external recollections do occur, they generally limit themselves in date, appearing in, and coming from, texts of the early 1590s (see, for example, tables xx and xxii for *A Knack to Know a Knave* and *The Massacre at Paris*). The Shakespeare suspect texts rarely display external recollections.

a.i.b. Internal repetition

In 1948 Harry Hoppe wrote that 'the presence of excessive repetition constitutes one of the best clues to memorial reconstruction of a bad text, and is especially useful when only the bad text is extant'.[10] Although, interestingly, Q1 *Romeo and Juliet*, the text on which Hoppe formulated his theory, is one of the least repetitive of suspect texts, Hoppe's statement has much to recommend it.

In dealing with internal repetitions – as with external echoes – we should heed Hoppe's qualifying adjective 'excessive'. Internal repetition *per se* does not prove memorial reconstruction. Scribal accident resulted in an isolated but lengthy example of repetition in *The Fatal Marriage*; repetitions also occur in *The Faithful Friends*. Kristian Smidt has found repetitions to be relics of authorial revision in several 'good' Shakespeare texts;[11] in a brilliantly incisive article Greg showed how repetitions were evidence of both addition and excision in the mss of *The Second Maiden's Tragedy* and *The Honest Man's Fortune*,[12] and, in his parallel-text edition of *Dr Faustus*, he called attention to recurrent repetition in the B-text (apparently the result of authorial intent combined with carelessness).[13] No reader of Renaissance drama can escape internal repetition:

> *Pisa* renowned for graue Citizens
> (*The Taming of the Shrew* TLN 309)
> Pisa renowned for graue Citizens.
> (*The Taming of the Shrew* TLN 1951)

> What though I kill'd her Husband, and her Father,
> (F *Richard 3* TLN 163)
> What? I that kill'd her Husband, and his Father,
> (F *Richard 3* TLN 427)

Kyd uses repetition bathetically in *The Spanish Tragedy* (1592) to add a poignant dying fall to a line:

> [Nemesis] Enuying at *Andreas* praise and worth,
> Cut short his life to end his praise and woorth.
>> (421–2)

> I know the scarfe, would he had kept it still,
> For had he liued he would haue kept it still,
>> (448–9)

> I lookt that *Balthazar* should haue been slaine:
> But tis my freend *Horatio* that is slaine,
>> (1023–4)

> [Bel-Imperia] On whom I doted more then all the world,
> Because she lou'd me more then all the world.
>> (1026–7)

B *Dr Faustus* repeatedly foreshadows the opening of Faustus' awed speech to Helen:

> Was this that sterne aspect, that awfull frowne,
> Made the grim monarch of infernall spirits,
> Tremble and quake at his commanding charmes?
>> (FIV,23–5)

> Was this that damned head; whose heart conspir'd
> *Benvolio's* shame before the Emperour.
>> (FIV,26–7)

> Was this faire *Hellen*, whose admired worth
> Made *Greece* with ten yeares warres afslict [*sic*] poore *Troy*?
>> (G3r,25–6)

> Was this the face that Launcht a thousand ships,
>> (G4r,26)

Obviously, as with external recollections, we must be careful how we define internal repetitions.

Hoppe defined internal repetition as follows: '[w]ords, phrases or passages that are used more than once'.[14] This broad definition courts trouble. As we saw in chapter 5, repeated 'phrases' – formulae or 'tags' – can be a dramaturgical principle as well as evidence of memorial slip. Repetition of units as small as single 'words' is also precarious as evidence of memorial reconstruction. Greg enthusiastically hailed Sacrapant's phrase 'by poyson, prowesse, or anie meanes of treacherie' (*Orlando Furioso*, 323–4) as an anticipation of Orgalio's lines at 331–2: 'as full of prowesse as policie'. It may be; but the lines have only one word in common, and one word, even one distinctive word, is too insignificant to function as evidence of memorial error.

Nonetheless critics frequently cite repetition of single words as evidence of faulty memory. Duthie sees repetitions in Horatio's account of Rosencrantz and Guildenstern's fate ('He [Hamlet] being set ashore, they went for England'). He believes that the (commonplace) word 'set' comes from Hamlet's letter to Claudius ('I am set naked on your kingdom') and that the (conventional) phrase 'for England' comes from Hamlet's letter to Horatio ('Rosencrantz and Guildenstern hold their course for England'). Duthie tells us that in the Queen's lines ('Then I perceiue there's treason in his lookes / That seem'd to sugar o're his villanie'), 'practically everything can be traced to other passages': he says that 'lookes' is a reminiscence of both 'I'll observe his looks' and 'there is a kind of confession in your looks'; the verb 'perceiue' comes from a phrase used earlier in the play 'Didst perceive?'; 'villanie' comes from 'the King's plots against Hamlet in V ii 29 and 309'; to clinch the argument for faulty memory, we are told that the phrase 'sugar o're' occurs 'in the authorized texts in III i 48'.[15]

No part of this argument do I find convincing: one need only look in concordances for the statistical frequency of 'looks', 'perceive', and 'villainy' in the Shakespeare canon, while Caroline Spurgeon has shown how frequent is the association between sugar and false friends in Shakespeare's imagery. D. L. Patrick's argument for memorial reconstruction in Q *Richard 3* is similarly punctuated with unconvincing examples of one-word repetitions, almost all of which come from the same scene, separated only by a few lines. A scribe or compositor may therefore be the cause of the alleged repetition.

A repetition in the Alleyn MS of *Orlando Furioso* (not reproduced in Q) shows how scribes may introduce one-word repetitions through eyeskip:

Thou seest I now am mightie Hercules:
See [Q Looke] wheres my massie club vpon my necke
   (A *Orlando Furioso* 760–1)

The scribe of *John of Bordeaux* made the same kind of mistake at line 37: 'I know it well that envie hath her splene, and envie lives.' Another hand inserted 'wisdome' above the second 'envie'. At line 774 the *Bordeaux* scribe realised and corrected another such error instantly: 'the prayes that vertue [waite*s*] guide*s* and pittie waighte*s* vpon'. The following two-word repetition in *Dr Faustus* was probably caused by compositorial eye-skip:

> holy *Peters* feast,
> The which **this day** with high solemnity,
> **This day** is held through *Rome* and *Italy*,
>   (B *Dr Faustus* DIV,29–31)

In the second quarto (1619) the passage is emended to read

> holy Peters feast
> The which **in state** and high solemnity
> **This day** is held through Rome and Italy.

Clearly, if we admit one- or two-word repetitions as proof of memorial reconstruction, most printed and manuscript texts will display some memorial symptoms.

In defining a repetition I therefore use the same criteria as I applied to external echoes: length and distinctive vocabulary. Consider the following two accounts of Hal's arrest in *The Famous Victories*, the first narrated by the vintner's boy, the second by the Mayor, both of whom were present at the fray:

> BOY: then whether their Musicke liked them not, or whether they had drunke too much Wine or no, I cannot tell, but our pots flue against the wals, and then they drew their swordes, and went into the streete and fought, and some tooke one part, & some tooke another, but for the space of halfe an houre, there was such a bloodie fray as passeth, and none coulde part them vntill such time as the Maior and Sheriffe were sent for, and then at the last with much adoo, they tooke them,
>   (BIr,16–24)

> MAYOR: and whether it was that their Musicke liked them not, or whether they were ouer=come with wine, I know not, but they drew their swords, and into the streete they went, and some tooke my Lord

the yong Princes part, and some tooke the other, but betwixt them
there was such a bloodie fray for the space of halfe an houre, that
neither watchme[n] nor any other could stay the[m], till my brother
the Sheriffe of London ¢ I were sent for, and at the last with much
adoo we staied them,
> (BIV,33–B2r,6)

For sheer length and distinctive phrasing this repetition cannot be rivalled.
Shorter, but still lengthy, repetitions occur in several suspect texts:

> GEORGE: Vouchsafe a peece of beefe at my poore house,
> You shall haue wafer cakes your fill,
> A peece of beefe hung vp since Martilmas,
> If that like you not, take what you bring for me.
> KENDALL: Gramercies, George.
> (*George a Greene* 607–11)

> GEORGE: Will you to my poore house,
> You shall haue wafer cakes your fill,
> A peece of beefe hung vp since Martlemas,
> Mutton and veale, if this like you not,
> Take that you finde, or that you bring for me.
> ROBIN HOOD: Godamercies, good George,
> (*George a Greene* 1097–1102)

These seem to me to qualify as repetitions. Whether they are memorial
repetitions is less certain: the lengthy repetition in *The Famous Victories*
may easily be the result of authorial indecision. It is important, therefore,
to take into account the frequency of repetition in a suspect text in deciding if and when repetition becomes a symptom of faulty memory. Several
Poems contain only a few internal repetitions: *Edward 1* and *1 Contention*
contain but one set each (as does *David and Bethsabe*, which is not a
suspect text); *Richard Duke of York* is limited to two sets. These frequencies
provide insufficient evidence on which to base a theory of memorial reconstruction, for rewriting (either through authorial indecision, authorial
revision, or an external adapter's patchwork) can result in such oversights.
Frank Hook and Arthur Sampley have provided excellent analyses of the
processes of revision and abridgement in *Edward 1* and *David and*

Bethsabe; since these Poems contain few other features associated with suspect texts, their isolated examples of repetition are unlikely to be memorial.[16]

One should also give characters the benefit of the doubt and permit them to quote themselves once before inferring faulty memory in the transmission of the text. Thus, rather than dismissing two separate sets of repetitions in *The Famous Victories* as memorial, Larry Champion uses them sensitively for thematic interpretation.[17]

Having assessed the frequency of repetition, one should also ask whether a Poem's repetitions are local or pervasive. Although a reporter reconstructing an entire Poem might treat his own role, and his own plot, differently from the rest of the text, he is unlikely to discriminate against one sequential segment. *The Fair Maid of Bristow* contains a possible total of three pairs of repetitions, all of which occur in the middle part of the Poem.[18] However, we should remember that in special circumstances (see chapter 8, table xxx for *Richard 2*, and the discussion of *Sir Thomas Wyatt* and 1 *If You Know Not Me* in A.9 below) memorial reconstruction of one portion of a Poem might be necessary.

Textual critics analysing parallel texts generally divide internal repetitions into anticipations and recollections. Although it is possible to divide internal repetitions in this way in single-text studies, it is precarious to do so. Queen Mary's line in *Sir Thomas Wyatt* – 'Better a poore Queene, then the Subiects poore' (c4r,10) – unexpectedly follows a couplet which has a terminative emphasis to it, and one suspects that the line may be more properly placed seventeen lines later, where a variant occurs:

> Better a poore Prince then the Nation poore,
> The Subiects Treasure, is the Soueraignes store.
> (c4r,27–8)

However, this does not mean that the earlier *phrasing* may not be correct. Nor is the conjectured appropriateness of the lines' situation a reliable determinator of correct placing, for obviously it was the equal suitability of the repeated phrase to two separate occurrences which prompted the agent (author, reporter, or other) to reuse or recall it.

What is beyond dispute is that distinctive, extensive, and pervasive internal repetitions are strong diagnostic evidence of faulty memory.

A.1.c. Paraphrase

Paraphrase is a diluted form of repetition. It may represent legitimate authorial restatement and so merit no critical suspicion, but in some suspect texts paraphrase is characterised by the features which identify repetition: length and distinctive vocabulary. In *The Massacre at Paris* the Queen Mother's lines at 782–90 rephrase and repeat her speech at 625–33. Both sets of lines are delivered to the complicitous Cardinal, and both concern the murder of her sons. Historically, she was involved in the first murder, that of Charles, but there is no evidence for implicating her in the death of Henry, who as the play shows, was poisoned by a Jacobin Friar 'with the connivance of Dumaine'.[19] Thus, the first speech is probably in its correct place (suggesting, incidentally, that we are dealing with recollection and not anticipation), although, as H. J. Oliver cautions, 'this does not mean that the verbal reporting may not be more accurate [in the later scene]'.[20] Certainly, each set of lines is recognisable as a variation on the other:

> I, but my Lord let me alone for that,
> For *Katherine* must haue her will in France:
> As I doe liue, so surely shall he dye.
> And *Henry* then shall weare the diadem.
> And if he grudge or crosse his Mothers will,
> Ile disinherite him and all the rest:
> For Ile rule France, but they shall weare the crowne:
> And if they storme, I then may pull them downe.
> Come my Lord lets vs goe.
>   (625–33)

> Tush man, let me alone with him,
> To work the way to bring this thing to passe:
> And if he doe deny what I doe say,
> Ile dispatch him with his brother presently.
> And then shall *Mounser* weare the diadem:
> Tush, all shall dye vnles I haue my will.
> For while she liues *Katherine* will be Queene.
> Come my Lords, let vs goe seek the *Guise*,

And then determine of this enterprise.
(782–90)

Paraphrase of a sizeable speech, such as this, is potentially strong evidence of faulty memory. However, I am inclined to exercise caution and admit it as evidence only when it is accompanied by more potent forms of repetition (A.1.a and A.1.b).

A.1.d. Connective repetition

Connective repetition or echolalia – immediate echo of the previous line of an interlocutor – is most noticeable in suspect texts in comic scenes. The lines of Perce, the clown, in *John of Bordeaux* furnish an example (I supply punctuation):

> 1 SCHOLAR: how shall we do for monie to pay fort?
> PERCE: how shall we do for moni to pay fort? fayth I thincke thy head was mad of an ould bagpipe . . .
> 2 SCHOLAR: but how yf she will not trust vs?
> PERCE: but how yf she will not trust ous? now comes he in sneking 'how and she will not trust ous'. bring me to a nalle [i.e. an ale] howse . . .
> OLD WOMAN: what meat wod you have Ientellmen?
> PERCE: what meat wod we have? why thow ould mapellfast matrone
> (525–46)

The clown in A *Dr Faustus* indulges in similar tactics:

> WAGNER: the vilaine is bare, and out of seruice, and so hun- /gry, that I know he would giue his soule to the Diuel for a/ shoulder of mutton, though it were blood rawe.
> CLOWN: How, my soule to the Diuel for a shoulder of mut- /ton though twere blood rawe?
> (B3r,12–16)

Connective repetitions need not always be comic. In A *Dr Faustus* we find the following exchange, which serves to emphasise Mephistopheles' statement:

MEPHISTOPHELES: For I am damnd, and am now in hell.
FAUSTUS: How? now in hell? nay and this be hell, Ile wil- /lingly be
damnd here:

    (c2r,12–14)

In Q1 *Romeo and Juliet* we find the following:

BENVOLIO: Call good *Mercutio*.
MERCUTIO: Call, nay Ile coniure too.

    (c4v,9–10)

Similar emphatic repetition occurs in Q *Richard 3*:

2 MURDERER: What shall I stab him as he sleepes?
1 MURDERER: No then he will say twas done cowardly
When he wakes.
2 MURDERER: When he wakes,
Why foole he shall neuer wake till the iudgement day.

    (DIV,4–8)

It is disturbingly easy to locate connective repetitions in comic parts and assume that they represent gratuitous expansion of clowning. Connective repetition, the argument goes, must be a means of extending comic mileage, or a stalling ploy (permitting an actor/reporter to think of what comes next), or part of the tendency towards vulgar emphasis which Greg thought contributed to the dilution of the text. But if the repetition is effective, how do we decide its source: author or actor/reporter? Rhetorically and dramatically, such repetition is an ancient and respected device, and it is impossible to know whether its presence stems from author or reporter: the connective repetition of the clown, Perce, which aroused Harry Hoppe's suspicions of memorial reconstruction in *John of Bordeaux*, is also a feature of Perce's comic predecessor, Miles, in the non-suspect *Friar Bacon and Friar Bungay*.

We can find connective repetitions in many non-suspect texts (where they may still contribute to the dilution of the text); but the fact remains that the phenomenon is not restricted to the forty-one suspect texts under examination.

QUEEN: This bodilesse Creation extasie is very cunning in.
HAMLET: Extasie?
My Pulse as yours doth temperately keepe time,
  (F *Hamlet* TLN 2521–3)[21]

RIVERS: We follow'd then our Lord, our Soueraigne King,
So should we you, if you should be our King.
RICHARD: If I should be? I had rather be a Pedler:
  (F *Richard 3* TLN 616–18)

Clearly, connective repetition cannot be taken as indisputable proof of memorial reconstruction.

A.1.e. Formulae

The Classical scholar, Milman Parry, was the first to provide a working definition of formulae. In his work on Homer, Parry identified and defined the Homeric formula: 'a group of words which is regularly employed under the same metrical conditions to express a given essential idea'.[22] Parry's definition has since been expanded and refined. Paul Kiparsky acknowledges three types of formula: the bound, the flexible, and the free. The bound formula (e.g. 'God from Zion') is unlikely ever to occur in a variant form; the flexible formula is structurally constant but the epithets are variable: 'Moses [God] said to me the other day [night]'; the free formula is formulaic only in that it is 'generated out of deep structure' but 'created anew, roughly at the moment of performance'.[23]

The type of formula most frequently encountered in suspect texts is the flexible formula. *Arden of Feversham* contains a ballad formula familiar to us from chapter 4:

ALICE: And he and Francklin will to London straight.
  (230)

GREENE: I'll vp to London straight,
  (546)

ALICE: Then rydes he straight to London,
  (516)

ALICE: and he is ridden straight / To London,
  (589–90)

In *1 Hieronimo* we find the following:

LORENZO: *Andrea's* gone embassador;
  (A3v,20)

LORENZO: Thou knowest Andreas gone embassador.
  (B2r,12)

LORENZO: You know *andreas* gone embassador,
  (C1r,23)

To this can be added the variants 'So, so, *Andrea* must be sent imbassador' (A3r,30, also spoken by Lorenzo), and 'When first thou camst embassador' (E2r,17, spoken by Balthazar).

Both *The True Tragedy of Richard 3* and *The Famous Victories* describe their respective Princes with the formulaic epithet 'the young prince', and, in the latter play, King Charles of France and King Henry 5 bandy the courteous phrase 'My good brother of France/ England'. *1 Hieronimo* describes characters with the adjective stout ('stout Andrea'). *Arden of Feversham* shares with *The Massacre at Paris*, *1 Contention*, *The True Tragedy of Richard Duke of York* (and the non-suspect *3 Henry 6*) a tendency to preface characters' names with the adjective 'sweet': 'sweet Clarence', 'sweet Ned', 'sweet father', 'sweet Duke of Guise' (thirty-six occurrences in *Arden*, seventeen occurrences in *The Massacre*. A predilection for this adjective is noticeable to a lesser degree in other works by Marlowe.)

Taken individually, verbal formulae have little value as a symptom of faulty memory. As Thomas Pettitt and others have shown, formulae are heavily used by medieval and Renaissance authors. When internal repetitions are also present, then formulae may be considered an important subset of repetition; and when they appear in abundance, as in *The Famous Victories*, they suggest an uninventiveness more likely to stem from a reporter in difficulty than any other agent. In isolation, however, this feature has negligible reliability in a diagnosis of memorial reconstruction.

A.1.f. Banal and stereotyped exit lines

Banal and stereotyped exit lines are a specific category of formulae, and occur frequently in suspect texts. *A Knack to Know a Knave* is full of banal impetus to exit, concluding six of its fourteen scenes (1, 3, 7, 9, 10, 14) with an invitation to Court (including those scenes which are already located at Court). While the line permits varied interpretation (a move from outside the Court to within, for example) the parallel phrasing which characterises it throughout suggests an agent unable to effect an actor's exit with adequate motivation.

The Massacre at Paris terminates scenes with the unimaginative exhortation 'Come, let's go':

> Come my Lord lets vs goe.
> (633)

> Then come my Lords, lets goe.
> (577)

This formulaic exit is shared with *1 Contention* (in abundance) and, to a lesser extent, *Richard Duke of York*. Characters in *Arden* rely regularly on the exit line 'And so farewell'. Alfred Hart suggests that 'pirates were always in trouble when it was necessary to get characters on or off the stage'.[24]

An unimaginative exit line is not automatically a memorially defective line, and there are only a limited number of ways of expressing 'Come, let's go'. But proficient dramatists usually manage to link the exit line with the plot. One of the gentlemen in *Pericles* 4.5 (G3v), exiting from the brothel, asks his companion 'come, I am for no more bawdie houses, shall's goe heare the Vestalls sing?'. This delightful line serves practical, thematic, and tonal functions: it motivates exit, underlines Marina's pure effect, and provides humour. What the Gentleman's line means, of course, when paraphrased is 'Come, let's go', only the agent behind *Pericles* doesn't let him say it so baldly.

The 'Come let's go' formulae of *The Massacre at Paris*, *1 Contention*, and *Richard Duke of York* only occasionally carry dramatic weight, with extensions such as 'Come my Lords, let vs goe seek the Guise' at *The Massacre at Paris* 789 or 'Come cosen lets go tell the Queene' at *Richard Duke of York* A5v,2. That both Marlowe and Shakespeare could provide efficient and varied exits is apparent from the canon of their non-suspect works. In *The Jew of Malta* alone we find such plausible expedients as the following:

BARABAS: Well, goe
And bid the Merchants and my men dispatch
And come ashore, and see the fraught discharg'd.
2 MERCHANT: I goe.
      (1.1.99 102)

LODOWICK: And if she [Abigail] be so faire as you report,
'Twere time well spent to goe and visit her:
How say you, shall we?
MATHIAS: I must and will, Sir, there's no remedy.
      (1.2.388–91)

COURTESAN: Come my deare love, let's in and sleepe together.
      (4.2.129)

CALYMATH: And now, bold Bashawes, let us to our Tents,
And meditate how we may grace us best
To solemnize our Governors great feast.
      (5.3.43–5)

Motivated exit lines involve thinking ahead to the next episode in a given plot sequence, and one suspects that forward planning would not be a top priority in memorial reconstruction. On the other hand, one could also argue that a reporter might resort to commonplace formulae *because* he is concentrating on what is to come. What is certain is that formulaic exit lines are untypical of Renaissance drama as a whole, as the following examples illustrate.[25]

Well, let us depart, the day is far spent.
      (*Gallathea* 1.1.94)

Come, I'll forget him, and go drink some wine.
      (*The White Devil* 3.3.132)

Come, let vs foure to Dinner: I dare say,
This Quarrell will drinke Blood another day.
      (*1 Henry 6* TLN 1066–7)

Hearke you, we'le into another roome and drinke / a while, and then
we'le go seeke out the Doctor.
(B *Dr Faustus* F4v,26–7)

Now let vs in that you may be dispatcht,
I think our councell is already set.
(*The Spanish Tragedy* (1592) 595–6)

TIBERIUS: But in the infancie of our estate,
More priuate consultation better fits,
We and *Seianus*, will into our studie.
JULIA: And we into our walking Gallerie.
(*Tiberius* 503–6)

but and I smell not you and a bawdy house out within these tenne
daies, let my nose be as bigge as an English bag-pudding: Ile followe
your lordship, though it be to the place aforenamed.
(*1 Honest Whore* 1.1.141–3)

I'me full of griefe,
But what she sayd, I'le tell thee as we goe.
('*Tis Pity She's a Whore* F1v,6–7)

Thunder and lightning...
Let's force no *omen* from it, but avoid
The vapors furies now by *Ioue* employd.
(*Caesar and Pompey* 2.4.147–54)

Despite such abundant reassurance that banal exit lines are unusual,
the *caveat* applicable to formulae (1e) is applicable here: unless accompanied by other significant forms of repetition, banal exit lines are too insubstantial a feature to be evidence of memorial reconstruction. For example,
although M. L. Wine observes the five occasions on which characters in
Arden exit with the formulaic 'and so farewell', he ignores the many occasions on which characters lead up to their exit with a sophisticated and
motivated speech.

A.2. INSERTION

Insertion, of words and phrases or of lengthy dramatic episodes, is often associated with memorial reconstruction, partly because of the persistent view that Elizabethan actors irresponsibly tinkered with the text, partly because of the assumption that actors on tour responded to provincial audiences' (assumed) less sophisticated tastes, and partly because of Greg's conclusion that omission and insertion operated in tandem in *Orlando Furioso*. All of these theories can exist independently of the theory of memorial reconstruction.

Greg included insertion (of phrases or episodes) in the amorphous category of 'redundancy', a category in which he also included paraphrase, connective repetitions, formulae, and stereotyped exit lines (1c, 1d, 1e, 1f above). It has seemed to me helpful to separate the kinds of redundancy involved in repetition; and it seems similarly helpful to consider minor insertions such as inductive words and phrases separately from more purposeful additions such as topical references and dramatic episodes.

A.2.a. Extra-metrical connectives

The presence of extra-metrical exclamations, vocatives, and connectives is one of the most frequently cited features of suspect texts: Alfred Hart felt that 'the initial "O" is the sign-manual of the pirate' in Q1 *Hamlet*, and Boas talked of the reporter's 'tell-tale *Tut*' in A *Dr Faustus*.[26] In the list below I enclose the extra-metrical material in square brackets.

Exclamations

[Wel,] if thou be wel aduised, take thy oath,
    (*A Knack to Know a Knave* 874)

[Now] Fortunio let vs see what beautie is,
    (*A Knack to Know an Honest Man* 372)

[No:] as he his eares, so Countie stop thine eye.
    (*Orlando Furioso* 502)

[Tush,] these slender trifles *Wagner* can decide,
    (A *Dr Faustus* c3r,33)

[Oh,] a polyticke speech beguiles the eares of foes,
  (*1 Hieronimo* A2v,32)

[Why] thy speach bewraied an inlye kind of feare.
  (*Arden of Feversham* 1148)

I like that well: [nay] how absolute she's in't,
  (*Pericles* D3v,17)

Vocatives

[Seruio] stand forth, if thy important wronges / be such,
  (*A Knack to Know an Honest Man* 135–6)

Heere [*Faustus*] trie thy braines to gaine a deitie.
  (A *Dr Faustus* A3r,31)

Vocatives can be coupled with expansion:

[I *Dunston,*] now thou speakest as fits a counsellor,
  (*A Knack to Know a Knave* 474)

[Tut Faustus,] marriage is but a ceremoniall toy,
  (A *Dr Faustus* C2r,27)

[Tush *Warwike,*] Thou art deceiued? tis not thy / Southerne powers
  (*Richard Duke of York* A5r,4–5)

Explanatory expansion

And *Edgar* know that I am *Alfrida,* [daughter to *Osrick,*]
  (*A Knack to Know a Knave* 1535)

Well Palmers know that Princes are [in India] arrivd
  (*Orlando Furioso* 1129)

In right of marriage, with [faire Orrelio] [my wedded / wife].
  (*A Knack to Know an Honest Man* 910–11)

(In this instance either of the bracketed phrases may be the explanatory tag; however, the metre is smoother with the first of the bracketed phrases deleted.)

Emphasis

Wee'le make no great a doe, a frend or two [,or so:]
    (Q1 *Romeo and Juliet* G2v,15)

But [heare you] wyfe, while I am master of the Bark,
    (*A Knack to Know a Knave* 1460)

The Earle is thirtie thousand men |strong| in power,
    (*George a Greene* 80)

Sirra, what thinkes the Emperor of my colours,
Because in field I weare both blue and red [at once]?
    (*Orlando Furioso* 282–3)

O Faustus, they are come to fetch [away] thy soule.
    (A *Dr Faustus* c3v,37)

Now by *Appollo* [King] thou swearest thy Gods in vaine.
    (Q1 *King Lear* B3r,17)

Let Princes while they liue haue loue [or feare] 'tis fit,
    (*1 If You Know Not Me* 1501)

[I tell thee] he rose against him being his / Soueraigne,
    (*Richard Duke of York* A4v,21–2)

This is all mistres Arden, is it trew [nor no]?
    (*Arden of Feversham* 481)

My Lord the offer had beene to hye a grace [for him]
For neare did eye behold a fayrer face.
    (*The Blind Beggar of Alexandria* 1553–4)

In this last example, the couplet is spoiled by interpolation of the bracketed material.[27]

Repetition

The connective repetitions described in A.1.d above often reveal themselves by being extra-metrical:

> MARCELLUS: the Prince is now / in armes.
> TURPIN: [In armes?] Whats he that dares annoy so / great a King.
> (*Orlando Furioso* 1099–102)

> SACREPANT: Then know that thou hast slaine Prince / Sacrepant.
> ORLANDO: [Sacrepant.] Then let me at thy dying day / intreate,
> (*Orlando Furioso* 1383–6)

One can at times classify extra-metrical repetitions more specifically. In the following exchange from *Sir Thomas Wyatt* Guilford's farewell, which spoils both metre and rhyme, is possibly an anticipation of his later goodbye on F3v.

> GUILFORD: Intreate not Iane, though shee our bodies/ part,
> Our soules shall meete. [Farwell my loue.]
> JANE: My Dudley, my owne heart.
> (D3v,19–22)

When sentence is passed on the couple five scenes later, we meet the following:

> GUILFORD: Our liues haue plaide their parte,
> Farwell my Iane.
> JANE: My Dudley, mine owne heart.
> (F3v,3–5)

Extra-metrical insertions, as any regular theatre-goer knows, and as chapter 5 demonstrated, often originate with actors in performance, and as such would seem to be reliable evidence of actors' involvement in our suspect texts; and actors' involvement is usually taken to imply memorial reconstruction. The following points must dispel these assumptions.

Greg found several extra-metrical insertions in the 1594 Q of *Orlando Furioso*. What we forget is that he also found – and admitted to being puzzled by – extra-metrical insertions in Alleyn's part of Orlando. For example, at A 408/Q1389–90, A 34/Q632 and A 169/Q1017 we find an extra-metrical 'or no', 'then' and 'ah, ah'. Greg rationalises this problem as follows: 'the insertion of connective phrases, though it might happen *in almost any mode of transmission*, even in plain transcription, would be most easy and natural on the stage'.[28] A feature which can arise 'in almost any mode of transmission' should have no place in a diagnostic study of memory. We are seeking reliable indicators of memory, not possible indicators. Greg frequently acknowledges that extra-metrical additions are not incompatible with the work of 'a rather meddlesome transcriber'.[29] As we saw in chapter 5, transcribers of the period did not behave like photocopiers; we must therefore eliminate extra-metrical connectives as evidence of memorial reconstruction.

One further point endorses this decision: extra-metrical pleonasm is almost as plentiful in non-suspect texts as it is in suspect texts. I bracket the extra-metrical material.

> [Gentlemen,] heauen hath through me, restor'd / the king to health.
> (F *All's Well That Ends Well* TLN 958–9)

> [I,] much is the force of heauen-bred Poesie.
> (F *Two Gentlemen of Verona* TLN 1516)

> [Go Gentlemen,] will you prepare you for this Maske to / night,
> (F *Merchant of Venice* TLN 815–16)

> [Help her,][30] what would she finde? *Lauinia* shal I read?
> (Q1 *Titus Andronicus* F4v,3)

> And [*Lauinia*] thou shalt be imployde in these Armes,
> (Q1 *Titus Andronicus* F3r,33)

> Man delights not me; [no,] nor Woman neither;
> (F *Hamlet* TLN 1355–6)

> [Oh Vengeance!]
> (F *Hamlet* TLN 1622)

> [O] this is the poyson of deepe griefe, it springs all from her Fathers / death, and now behold, [ô Gertrard, Gertrard,]
> (Q2 *Hamlet* K4v,26–7)[31]

> 1 FRIAR: No doubt, [brother,] but this proceedeth of the spirit.
> 2 FRIAR: [I,] and of a moving spirit too [,brother]; but come,
> (*The Jew of Malta* 1.2.327–8)

[Captaine,] we haue receiued Letters from the / king,
(*The Battle of Alcazar* 930–1)

Harold Jenkins has drawn attention to numerous extra-metrical additions in F *Hamlet*, a phenomenon which critics have also found in the first quartos of *Richard 2*, *Richard 3*, and *Othello*. Acknowledging that such additions are characteristic of actors, Jenkins also acknowledges the difficulty of explaining how such additions were incorporated in the Folio text of *Hamlet*. But, he concludes, 'the difficulty of explaining how this happened should not prevent the recognition that it did'.[32]

My survey of the drama of the period shows extra-metrical pleonasm to be a frequent feature of both suspect texts and non-suspect texts. Kristian Smidt suggests that '[o]n the stage they may have been very effective'.[33] What is clear is that extra-metrical connectives hold uncertain symptomatic value for a study of memory.

A.2.b. Local/topical references

One phrase in *A Knack to Know a Knave* reveals itself as an insertion because it is superfluous to requirements of logic and sense. At the conclusion of the play Honesty sentences the hypocritical priest, John the Precise, to 'Stand in Finsburie fields, neere London' (1861). This geographical gloss would be redundant at the Rose (where Henslowe records receipts for the play in 1592–3), and so we may suspect that this is an explanatory insertion for provincial performance.[34]

The external and internal echoes in *A Knack to Know a Knave* support a case for memorial reconstruction; if one concludes that the text is a memorial reconstruction, line 1861 suggests that the report was played in the provinces. Whilst this coincides with the scenario advanced by Greg as explanation for memorial texts, the two circumstances are not automatically linked. The fact that *A Knack to Know a Knave* was played in the provinces does not prove that the text is reported. Thus, the explanatory insertion in the text is unrelated to the topic of memorial reconstruction.

A.2.c. Expanded clowning

There is a tendency among New Bibliographers to suspect as textually corrupt – and by extension, inserted or adapted – episodes of low-life comedy which they judge unseemly in serious drama. This attitude can be seen in approaches to non-suspect texts as well as suspect texts, the most familiar case being that of *The Jew of Malta*. The descent from tragedy into comedy bordering on farce, relished by audiences familiar with Comedy of Cruelty, caused generic problems for E. K. Chambers who concluded that the play 'has only come down to us in a form rehandled to suit an audience of inferior mentality to that aimed at by the original author'.[35] Chambers's conclusion, as J. C. Maxwell points out, is disconcerting 'for those of us who have never detected anything more than a certain unevenness of quality, and now realize that we must have just the inferior mentality the adapter was aiming at'.[36]

Arguments for adaptation in *The Jew of Malta* are based more on a hypothetical vision of Marlowe than on textual evidence. A similar bias informs textual attitudes to A *Dr Faustus*. Simon Trussler jocularly reminds us of the ideology encoded in so much avowedly objective New Bibliographic criticism when he summarises its dissatisfaction with Faustus' Papal prank-playing: 'well, if that's not textual corruption, it's an inexplicable waste of a university education'.[37] Maxwell and Trussler's comments remind us that the New Bibliographers' identification of inserted and adapted episodes in suspect texts may reflect personal taste rather than textual corruption caused by memorial reconstruction.

Greg viewed the mock-Angelica episode in *Orlando Furioso* as an insertion. In this episode Orgalio, instructed to bring Orlando's sweetheart, Angelica, instead presents the mad Orlando with the Clown in female disguise. Since the cues in the Alleyn MS differ from those in the equivalent speeches in Q, Greg concluded that 'the mock-Angelica, at least as a speaking character, proves in all probability to be a pure invention of Q'.[38]

Greg linked this episode with the mock-army scene, in which the clowns function as the mad Orlando's soldiers, and with the earlier scene in which Orlando recruits the clowns. Similarities in tone, and the thematic pointlessness of the 'horseplay' convinced him that these scenes were, like the mock-Angelica episode, 'wholly inserted' to suit 'the taste of a rougher class of spectators'.[39]

Two points unremarked by Greg merit attention here. Mock-sweetheart episodes feature in two, and possibly three, other contemporary plays: *Dr Faustus*, *John of Bordeaux*, and *A Knack to Know a Knave*. In *Dr Faustus*

Faustus requests a wife. Mephistopheles agrees, and the stage directions in A and B read as follows:

> *He fetches in a woman deuill.*
>   (B *Dr Faustus* CIr,36)

> *Enter with a diuell drest like a woman, / with fier workes.*
>   (A *Dr Faustus* C2r,23–4)

The A text thus explains the method of disguise. In the MS *John of Bordeaux* (c.1590) the virtuous Rossalin refuses to succumb to the advances of Prince Ferdinand. The magician Vandermast tries to humour the Prince by summoning a devil, disguised as Rossalin, to appear to Ferdinand at night.

I leave out of the discussion an analogous episode at the dénouement of *A Knack to Know a Knave*, which is rendered ambiguous by an incomplete stage direction (1717). However, it is clear that the episode involves some 'funny business' with a devil, a sweetheart, and a disguise. Thus, the episodes in *Dr Faustus*, *Orlando Furioso*, *John of Bordeaux*, and possibly *A Knack to Know a Knave* suggest that mock-sweethearts enjoyed something of a vogue in plays of the early 1590s (a vogue to which Greene rather than his actors may have contributed: Greene authored *Orlando Furioso*, *John of Bordeaux*, and possibly *A Knack to Know a Knave*).

This does not mean that *Orlando Furioso* could not have been adapted to capitalise on theatrical fashion (in *Dr Faustus*, *John of Bordeaux*, and *A Knack to Know a Knave* the disguised devil is silent, as is Greg's hypothetical original Angelica). But the second point unremarked by Greg, the thematic integration of the clown–Angelica episodes, makes it unlikely that the insertion was done by actors merely to vulgarise a play for an unsophisticated audience.

Orlando Furioso, as Charles Crupi has pointed out, is structured round antitheses: love versus war, madness versus military heroism, chivalry versus self-seeking. Orlando embodies the first of each of these pairs, Sacrepant the second, with Angelica providing the focus of conflict. The contrast is emphasised when 'each briefly takes on the role of the other: Sacrepant tries his hand at love, although he scorns it when rejected, and Orlando rants of war and glory during his madness'.[40]

The comic scenes emphasise this conflict. When Orlando tears off a man's leg to use as a club, knights Angelica for her/his imagined military success, and seizes pots and pans as armour, he 'parodies Sacrepant's devotion to military heroism'.[41] Orlando parodies not only Sacrepant's military excess but his own romantic extravagance, both being extremes of passion/madness which the play will temper. His mistaking of Angelica for a man (thereby showing excessive military zeal) is balanced by excessive romantic zeal when he accepts a clown dressed like Angelica and addresses him/her in hyperbolic Petrarchan terms.[42] The mad scenes, the horseplay, the comedy cannot simply be dismissed as examples of supererogatory provincial placation.

This is not to deny that the comic episodes are insertions or adaptations: their variance from A shows that they represent a different state of the text. But they are an intelligent adaptation, more likely to represent thoughtful rewriting than Greg's gradual degenerative movement towards 'vapid and impromptu' dialogue by actors who 'deliberately set themselves to elaborate after their own fashion the more distinctly comic passages at the expense of what we may conjecture to have been those on which the author set most store'.[43] In 1964 C. L. Barber employed a similar interpretive approach to textual problems in *Dr Faustus*: 'No doubt some of the prose comedy, even in the 1604 Quarto, is not by Marlowe; but when the comic action is a burlesque that uses imaginative associations present in the poetry, its authenticity is hard to doubt.'[44]

Hamlet's injunction (in Q1) against the clown speaking more than is set down for him suggests that insertion occurred on the professional London stage; and although authors may not have approved of the practice, items that were added in the course of performance may in due course have become incorporated in the playbook.[45] Even if one can identify such episodes (as Greg attempted to do in *Orlando Furioso*) this provides no reason to suggest memorial reconstruction. Texts can be expanded and adapted without automatically being memorially reconstructed. Insertion thus remains a feature of many Renaissance playtexts, suspect and non-suspect. It is not a symptom of memorial reconstruction.

Comic insertion and expansion were closely linked in the New Bibliographers' minds with provincial touring. Greg offers as support the observation that '[p]rogressive alteration and impromptu vulgarization of the authorized script are common in touring companies today'.[46] However, there is no evidence one way or the other about Elizabethan provincial tastes. The most we have are scattered references to provincial audiences being fobbed off with old plays. Dekker's *Jests to Make You Merry* (1607) tells how players on tour in the country made 'fooles of the poore country people, in driuing them like flocks of Geese to sit cackling in an old barne: and to swallow downe those plays for new which here euery punck and her squire. . .can rand out by heart they are so stale'.[47]

Cavalier attitudes to verbal content are indicated by Aminadab in Middleton's *Mayor of Queenborough* who tells how the strolling players (in reality a gang of professional thieves) acted from 'a printed play or two, which they bought at Canterbury for sixpence; and what is worse, they speak but what they list of it, and fribble out the rest' (5.1. mislined as 268–70).[48] Certainly, provincial audiences would have less exposure to South Bank plays than London theatre-lovers; Dekker suggests that as a result they were easier to please.[49] But that this paucity of dramatic experience would inevitably mean a preference for jesting and clowning, and a decline in the standards of drama offered by the London companies, is far from clear.

A.3. OMISSION

For obvious reasons few examples of omission can be detected in single-text suspect texts. Sources and analogues can, in principle, shed light on omitted material, although I have come across only one instance where they illuminate localised verbal rather than extensive episodic excision. In *1 If You Know Not Me* Princess Elizabeth asks:

> Hath not proud *Wyat* suffered for his offence,
> And in the purging both of soule and body for heauen,
> Did *Wyat* then accuse *Elizabeth*?
> (391–3)

As Giordano-Orsini observes, line 392 yields 'indifferent sense and bad metre'.[50] Heywood's prose version of the play, *England's Elizabeth* (1631) which might reasonably be expected to represent his view of events, despite its later date, provides help: 'euen at the parting of life and body, hauing prepared his soul for heauen, when no dissimulation can be so much as suspected. . .'.[51] Giordano-Orsini comments: 'the extra-metrical "for heauen" [in 392] turns out to be the end of a sentence which has otherwise disappeared in the dramatic version' (but cf. table xv in chapter 8).[52]

Errors of omission may arise from scribal or compositorial eyeskip, or from the difficulty of reading a manuscript with interlinings, restored deletions, or marginalia. Collation of the ms of Samuel Daniel's *Hymen's Triumph* with the first octavo (1615) illustrates the former circumstance. The ms provides the following arrangement at 797–801:

> She will comaund you nothing, but I wishe
> you would a litle terrifie that boy
> for his presumption, and so charme his tongue
> As hee may neuer dare to vse her name
> But in all reverence as is fitt for her.

In the 1615 edition signature в7r ends with line 104 and the catchword 'For'; however, the verso begins 'As he'.[53] A compositor of Q *Richard 3* made, and then corrected, the same error of eyeskip. Signature c2r ends with the catchword 'Excee', which should begin the next but one line. Signature c2v restores the omitted line:

> If heauen haue any grieuous plague in store,
> Exceeding those that I can wish vpon thee:

Thus, the category of omission, at least in a localised, verbal form, cannot be associated exclusively with memorial reconstruction.

Suspect texts contain a few instances where one can infer episodic omission. In *A Knack to Know an Honest Man* (Q 1596) Annetta and Lucida, accompanied by the clown Gnatto, visit Servio to discover Annetta's brothers' whereabouts. They are told that the brothers are prisoners. The trio then overhear an exchange between Servio and his daughter Phillida in which Phillida reveals the brothers' escape. Annetta responds by laconically dismissing the whole scene:

> How glad am I my brethren are escapt,
> Come sirra, vex the silly wretch no more.
>   (1181–2)

Her last remark implies that an episode of clowning has taken place, which is not provided in the extant text. Unless such an episode was regularly improvised, this text does not support the belief that suspect texts assiduously preserve or expand comic opportunities.

It is important to distinguish between cutting (which is deliberate) and omission (which may be accidental, degenerative, memorial). Cutting is discernible in the part of Stanley in *The True Tragedy of Richard 3* (Q 1594). Several references suggest that this old retainer was originally a character of (comic?) loquacity. Before the confrontation with Richmond, Richard 3 questions Stanley as to Richmond's means. Stanley's reply is succinct:

> And please your grace,
> His power is vnknowne to me,
> Nor willingly would not I be priuy to such causes.
> (1512–14)

and does not seem to merit the King's response:

> Oh good wordes Lord Standley, but giue
> me leaue to gleane out of your golden field of eloquence, how
> braue you pleade ignorance,
> (1515–17)

Stanley asks to defend himself and Richard acquiesces: 'Yea speak Standley, no doubt some fine coloured tale' (1523). Such rebukes may, of course, be sarcastic jokes at the expense of a taciturn character. However, the speech that follows forbids such an interpretation, where Stanley's reply, although short (seven prose lines), switches confusingly from masculine pronouns to feminine without a change of preceding subject, and looks remarkably like an awkward cut:

> for at his departure, was I one of the priuy coun- /cell to your brother
> King Edward the fourth, and that she was / able to relieue him
> without my helpe: I hope her sufficiencie is / knowne to your grace.
> (1527–30)

In a later scene Stanley encounters his stepson Richmond:

> STANLEY: but omitting vain circum- /stances, and to come briefly to
> the purpose, I am now in fewe / words to deliuer much matter . . .

RICHMOND: But omitting this, I pray tell me, shall I looke for your /
helpe in the battell?
　(1827–38)

The injunctions to brevity indicate that, at one stage in the Poem's history,
Stanley was a circumlocutory old man.[54] The excision of his material is conceivably deliberate, and so comes into the category of abridgement, not
memorial omission. While abridgement may operate in tandem with
memorial reconstruction, the former does not presuppose the latter.

A.4. TRANSPOSITION

Suspect texts contain examples of transposition, where a word or line seems
to have the right elements in the wrong order. In *Sir Thomas Wyatt* transposition is probably responsible for the illogic on F3v,10–11 ('Great griefes
speake louder / When the least are dumb'd') where 'great' and 'least' should
be exchanged.

It is an easy step from transposing words to transposing lines in the
immediate area, and there are a few instances when critics have conjectured
that this phenomenon underlies a textual difficulty. In *1 If You Know Not Me*
the wronged Elizabeth tells her household servants:

> 　　weepe not I pray, /
> Rather you should reioyce:
> If I miscarry / in this enterprise, and aske you why, /
> A Virgine and a Martyr both I dy. /
> 　(339–42)

Collier attempted to remedy the defect by relining (slashes indicate his line
endings); Giordano-Orsini suggested that the problem was transposition,
and placed 'If I miscarry in this enterprise' at the beginning of line 340,
giving the following arrangement (I have modernised punctuation for
clarity):

> 　　weepe not I pray.
> If I miscarrie in this enterprise,
> Rather you should reioyce, and aske you why,
> A Virgine and a Martyr both I die.[55]

A passage in *A Knack to Know a Knave* benefits from similar intervention, where the Q reads:

Thy counsell is to me as North stars light,
That guides the Sayler to his wished port:
For by that starre he is so comforted,
That he sailes daungerlesse on daungerous seas,
And in his deepest sadnes comforts him:
> (47–51)

Richard Proudfoot argued that line 51 was misplaced, its logical position being between lines 48 and 49.[56]

As we saw in chapter 5, faulty memory often transposes words and lines. So do scribes and compositors. The example from *A Knack to Know a Knave* could easily be attributed to compositorial eyeskip. In the MS *John of Bordeaux*, for instance, the scribe made an error of transposition which he recognised instantly and corrected: 'wetting his reverent cheke[s] with [grefes trew teres] trew grefes teres' (1115). How can we be sure that other transpositions in this suspect text, and suspected examples in other suspect texts, are not the fault of the scribe? The answer is: we cannot. As a result, transposition is of no value in diagnosing memorial reconstruction.

A.5. SUBMERGED OR WRECKED VERSE

Most Renaissance playtexts contain scattered examples of metrically defective lines. Many Renaissance playtexts also contain lines of iambic pentameter in prose speeches, a phenomenon shared by some stage directions, Spenser's prose, and *The New York Times*. It should come as no surprise that iambic pentameter, the metre closest to English speech, should surface naturally in non-poetic works.

The New Bibliographers were worried by more macaronic mixtures of verse and prose. In 1929 Greg criticised the metrical *congeries* of *The True Tragedy of Richard 3*:

Some parts are written in straightforward if stilted prose, others in tolerable blank verse: the end shows an irregular mixture of quatrains and couplets. In places, however, the prose tends to fall into verse cadence and even contains traces of rime, while at times the verse becomes irregular. There are passages, especially near the beginning, which might equally well be regarded as prose cut up into lengths or verse in the last stages of decay: there are also distinct fragments of fourteener couplets.

He concluded that '[i]t is hard to imagine that the play should have been deliberately composed in this manner'.[57]

Pericles is riddled with speeches apparently intended as verse, but which contain unscannable lines:

> *Antiochus* from incest liued not free:
> For which the most high Gods not minding,
> Longer to with-hold the vengeance that
> They had in store, due to this heynous
> Capitall offence, euen in the height and pride
> Of all his glory, when he was seated in
> A chariot of an inestimable value, and his daughter
> With him; a fire from heauen came and shriueld
> Vp those bodyes euen to lothing, for they so stounke,
>   (*Pericles* D2v,10–18)

Adaptation, revision, and abridgement, independently or in combination, may result in damaged blank verse. Dora Jean Ashe, for instance, suggested that inept cutting lies behind the metrical difficulties in *A Knack to Know an Honest Man*.[58] Greg has shown how revision introduced broken lines into the MS of *The Escapes of Jupiter*.[59] Chapman appears to have left blanks in the text of *Caesar and Pompey* which he presumably intended to fill in later (but on some occasions he didn't, thereby creating broken lines in print). The scribe of *Orlando* left blanks in his transcript whenever his exemplar caused him difficulties (a corrector, who was Alleyn for some if not all of the corrections, filled in all but three). Kristian Smidt has speculated that Shakespeare may have been metrically careless in his first drafts.[60]

Smidt's view was articulated more recently by Robert K. Turner: 'It does not seem unreasonable to suppose that a dramatist writing chiefly for plot and character development, the basic ingredients of his play, might ignore for the time being the metrical structure of his verse and accepted practices of lineation.'[61] The question is whether Turner and Smidt's temporarily metrically careless author could cause total rhythmical wreckage, as in the quotation from *Pericles* above. Consistently wrecked blank verse would seem to indicate someone lacking an ear for verse. Most dramatists seem to have had an internal metronome – even pedestrian verse is identified more by its pedestrian regularity than by any other quality.

Actors, we might suppose, were also metrically sensitive (although Greg suggested the contrary in 1906, and Chambers, in 1930, wrote of actors' 'indifference' to blank verse).[62] But differentiation between prose and verse seems to have been a basic theatrical tenet. Jaques' metatheatrical satire 'Nay god be with you and you talk in blank verse' invites the audience to share this distinction as does Huanebango's wooing of Zantippa in hexameters and prose ('Ile nowe set my countenance and to hir in prose': *The Old Wife's Tale* 821–2). It seems that both audiences and actors were sensitive to metrical variation.

We might also consider the possibility of ancillary theatre personnel as reporters – people whose qualifications need not include a sensitive metrical ear. Greg, it will be remembered, pointed the finger at the book-keeper for Q1 *King Lear*, a person held responsible by Chambers for all the suspect texts in which no single actor–reporter stands out.[63] It is clear that any conclusions on this topic are hampered by lack of evidence.

Persistently wrecked verse cannot be explained away as easily as the other features discussed in Sections A.2–4 above: that is one cannot say confidently, 'this is a phenomenon which may plausibly be attributed to authors, revisers, scribes, etc.'. As such, it seems as important a symptom of faulty memory as external recollections and internal repetitions. However, given the evident uncertainty about authors' attitudes to metre during composition, it might be advisable not to place too much diagnostic weight on this feature if it is the only sustained problem in a Poem (as, for example, in the case of *George a Greene*).

A.6. AURAL ERROR

Aural errors are frequently associated with memorial reconstruction. This is in part because of the great number of aural errors that Greg *et al.* detected in Q *King Lear*, and in part because it is easy to document phonetic spellings in oral tradition. In popular ballads we find 'O'brian' for 'Oberon',[64] 'Anix' for the English place name 'Alnwick' (the 'l' and 'w' are silent), and 'Phenix' for the English family-name 'Fenwick' (the 'w' is silent).[65] The Folio text of *King Lear* frequently indicates aural error in Q1:

> Striuing to better, oft we marre what's well.
>
>> (F TLN 870)
>
> striuing to better ought, we marre whats well.
>
>> (Q D2v,31–2)
>
> No blowne Ambition doth our Armes incite,
>
>> (F TLN 2379)
>
> No blowne ambition doth our armes in sight
>
>> (Q I1v,23)
>
> a Dogg's obey'd in Office.
>
>> (F TLN 2602–3)
>
> a dogge, so bade in office,
>
>> (Q I4r,23)

As diagnostic evidence of memory, aural errors share the objections raised to most of the verbal features we have examined: they can arise in almost any mode of transmission. We cannot exclude the possibility of mis-hearing by a scribe of a dictator, or by a compositor of himself (compositors provide a complicating mnemonic link in that the text is carried from a MS to a composing stick via their memory).

An amusing example of an aural error resulting from dictation can be found in Michael Billington's review of the 1986 RSC production of *A Midsummer Night's Dream*, the copy for which was dictated over the telephone from Stratford to London. In this production the rude mechanicals were portrayed as an amateur dramatics group with Brechtian principles, and, in the printed version, Billington's review read: 'I like the idea of the play-scene being given in blackberries [black berets] and tights'. In a 1993 review of the RSC production of *The Winter's Tale* in London (when dictation was not involved) the same newspaper read 'Cecilia [Sicilia] is racked by the elements as much as John Nettles's Leontes is by jealousy'.[66]

The printed copy of Massinger's *Duke of Milan*, a non-suspect text, prints 'honour' for 'owner' at B1v,3, evidently an aural error, as Greg pointed out, on the part of the compositor.[67] The same homonymic error occurs in Q1 *Hamlet* where H4v,9 reads 'honor' and Q2/F read 'owner'. Memorial error? Certainly; but it is impossible to tell whose. Thus, aural errors cannot function as proof of memorial reconstruction, and the infrequent appearance of such errors in our suspect texts shows that they are not even a strong feature.

A.7. LENGTH OF SPEECHES

Alfred Hart is the only textual critic to view the length of speeches, particularly soliloquies, in suspect texts as significant in diagnosing memory.

One group of suspect texts is characterised by its refusal or inability to develop a speech over fourteen lines: *Fair Em*, *The Famous Victories*, *Mucedorus*, and *George a Greene*, for example. Others, such as *The Massacre at Paris* and Q1 *Romeo and Juliet*, share this characteristic or rise above it only slightly, but are punctuated by an occasional speech in the region of twenty or more lines.[68] A third group (the smallest) contains a number of lengthy speeches and soliloquies. The most notable Poems in this category are *Arden of Feversham*, *The True Tragedy of Richard 3*, *1 Contention* and *Richard Duke of York*, the latter having, for example, nine speeches between twenty and forty lines, over several roles. The consistently lengthy speeches of this last group are a feature shared, of course, with most non-suspect texts.

There is something undeniably suspicious about a play which is unable to develop a speech: *The Famous Victories* is probably the strongest example of a play reduced to perfunctory dialogue, point blank statement, and staccato exchanges. *Richard Duke of York* and *The True Tragedy of Richard 3* are at the other extreme, with erudite and carefully developed speeches across a variety of roles. Although we may not be able to take staccato dialogue like that in *The Famous Victories* as an indicator of memorial reconstruction, any theory about the origin of *Arden of Feversham*, *Richard Duke of York* and *The True Tragedy of Richard 3* should mention their consistently lengthy and coherent speeches.

A.8. FRACTURED ALLUSIONS; FACTUAL ERRORS

The category of fractured allusions and factual errors is small, but potent. Most of our suspect texts contain a few mythological or Classical references, and while disturbances exist, they are minimal. In contrast, some suspect texts contain a high proportion of confused or erroneous mythological and Classical references.

> seest thou not Lycaons son
> The hardie plough-swaine vnto mightie Ioue,
>> (*Orlando Furioso* 396–7)

(It was of course Lycaon's daughter, Callisto, who was changed into the constellation the Bear. See table xxvii for a possible explanation of this error.)

> As eloquent and ful of Oratory, as *Thaly* was, daughter of *Iupiter*
> Whose speaches were so pleasing mong the Greeks
>> (*A Knack to Know a Knave* 208–9)

(Thalia was the muse of Comedy.)

> she is colloured lyke the *Scythia* Maide,
> That challenged *Lucio* at the *Olympian* games,
>> (*A Knack to Know a Knave* 1304–5)

(No plausible relation has yet been established between the Olympic games, Lucio and a Scythian maid.)

We must be careful to distinguish between those allusions which are mangled and those which are merely incomplete. Q *Orlando Furioso* reads

> A furie sure worse than Megera was,
> That reft her sonne from trustie Pilades.
>> (1311–12)

Greg criticises this 'perfectly preposterous mythological statement . . . of which Greene cannot conceivably have been guilty', and concludes that 'in the original text there must have been some mention of Clytemnestra to whom "her" should obviously refer'.[69] One wonders how to distinguish here between careless cutting and memorially induced problems. Elsewhere in his analysis Greg accepts that the adapter in *Orlando Furioso* was careless: 'By a curious piece of carelessness the adapter altered "next know" into "First know" [Q 1567] although no "secondly" follows: the correct phrase would have been "For know". I think the adapter must be responsible; it would be a very unlikely corruption.'[70]

As Greg shows, the adapter's carelessness does not usually apply to *Orlando Furioso*'s mythological content, which is dealt with by cutting. Orlando's 'mythological tirade' (twenty-six lines at A 349–75) is swept away, replaced by 'two lines far more suitable to the dramatic occasion';[71] his 'taunting speech to the dying Sacrapant' (Q 1372–7) is reduced from ten lines to five 'by suitable omission of mythological embroidery';[72] Orlando's twenty-eight lines of mad talk (A 121–48) are reduced to just over five lines in the Q:

> At only one point does Q fail: by substituting 'Tell me' for 'tell thy vlisses' it leaves unexplained the subsequent allusion to Calipso, and this may well be due to a later corruption. Otherwise it is a very skilful piece of adaptation and could not possibly be the outcome of mere failure of memory.[73]

In the midst of such drastic compression it is hard to see why an unexplained allusion to Calipso must be attributed to 'mere memory'. Even the most perfunctory look at the mythologically laden language of A (still heavily laden in Q) is enough to convince one that cutting through Greene's intricate network of allusions could not be an easy task.

Greg absolves Greene of any responsibility for the incomplete Megera reference at 1311–12. New Bibliographers cherish an image of the infallible author. I am sceptical about the infallibility of authorial mythological knowledge, largely because I have spent much time with Greek and Roman literature yet always have to look things up. This is doubtless too personal an observation to carry much critical weight. But even Cicero got things wrong from time to time; and so did Nashe, Marlowe, Shakespeare, Sir Walter Scott, and Robert Browning (to name but a few).

In *The Anatomy of Absurdity* Nashe confuses Io with Europa, and compounds the error by attributing Io's bovine transformation to Jove. In *Dido, Queen of Carthage* Marlowe (or a collaborator) confuses Scylla, the daughter of Nisus, King of Megera, with Scylla the sea-monster.[74] In 2 *Henry 6* Shakespeare refers to Ascanius, instead of Cupid impersonating Ascanius (3.2.116). More glaring errors are made by Shakespeare in the fields of geography and history. Characters in *The Taming of the Shrew* reach Padua, an inland town, by sea from Pisa; the heroes in *The Two Gentlemen of Verona* travel between Verona and Milan, both inland towns, by ship. In *King John*

Shakespeare confused the French King and the Dauphin (2.1.149), while in the second tetralogy he frequently confuses the various Mortimers.

Factual errors and anachronisms permeate the novels of Sir Walter Scott. The sun sets in the east in *The Antiquary*, and characters in *Kenilworth* discuss Shakespeare's plays, although the story concludes in 1560, four years before Shakespeare's birth. Browning's *Fra Lippo Lippi* mentions 'Hulking Tom' (the artist Masaccio) as a disciple of Fra Lippo Lippi, although historically it was Lippi who was the disciple of Masaccio (an error which Browning refused to acknowledge when it was pointed out to him).[75]

Thus, while a reporter may mangle a Classical reference, so may an author. Furthermore, scribes who misunderstand Classical references can introduce nonsense (see, for example, the MS of *The Faithful Friends* 685, 2281). Fractured mythology therefore offers little diagnostic certainty in any study of memorial reconstruction.

A.9. UNEVENNESS

Collier was the first to comment on stylistic unevenness as a symptom of reporting. Having concluded that Q1 *Romeo and Juliet* was a suspect text, he explained '[o]ur principal ground for this notion is, that there is. . . great inequality in different scenes and speeches'.[76] A century later Greg wrote that 'the most striking feature of most of these [suspect texts] is the extraordinary inequality of the text'.[77] E. A. J. Honigmann observed that 'the disparity between clever plotting and very uneven verse (or prose) was a standard feature of "bad" and "derivative" play-texts' while F. D. Hoeniger felt that the 'most pronounced and bewildering feature [of Q *Pericles*] is the extreme unevenness in the literary quality of its language'.[78]

Many factors contribute to unevenness. In *A Knack to Know a Knave*, a Poem notable for the baldness of its imagery, five extended similes stand out because of their quality, their length, and because they are clearly prose in a verse passage:

> But as the tallest Ash is cut down, because it yeelds no fruit, / And an
> vnprofitable cow, yeelding no milke, is slaughtred, / And the idle
> Drone, gathering no honie, is contemned, / So vngrateful children,

that will yeeld no naturall obedience, / Must be cut off, as vnfit to
beare the name Christians.

(*A Knack to Know a Knave* 453–7)[79]

Thomas Lord Cromwell has a clear break in style and content from D2r, and
The Famous Victories improves (relatively speaking) from TLN 846; this coincides with the introduction of the *Henry 5* material. Anomalies in plot and
language affect only the middle third of *The Fair Maid of Bristow*.
Deterioration of quality towards the end is often cited as a feature of
suspect texts (the favoured explanations being the reporter's mental fatigue
or the demise of the character he played), but not all suspect texts disinte-
grate towards the end: *The True Tragedy of Richard 3* actually shows some
improvement, and several texts maintain consistency throughout (e.g.
Richard Duke of York and *John of Bordeaux*).

Beginnings often contribute more than endings to unevenness. The
blunt exposition of *Jack Straw*, scene 1, with its summary of prior action,
differs noticeably from the rest of the Poem, not least in its use of rhyming
couplets: the entire scene is in (clumsy) rhyme, yet rhyme features nowhere
else in the Poem.

The opening scenes of *Sir Thomas Wyatt* and *1 If You Know Not Me* are
nothing but an abrupt interchange of information. *Sir Thomas Wyatt* opens
with the following over-explicit exchange:

SUFFOLK: Is the Kings will confirm'd?
NORFOLK: I, thats the point that we leuel at.
But oh, the confirmation of that will, tis all, tis all.
SUFFOLK: That will confirme my Daughter Queene.
NORFOLK: Right, & my Sonne is marryed to your daughter.
(A2r, 8–12)

Scene 1 of *1 If You Know Not Me* is merely a series of entrances and greetings (although the terseness does effectively convey political unease as the
Lords assemble in Mary's Court, just after the Wyatt rebellion). The final
scenes of this play are marred in the same way: scenes 20–3 contain a
speedy catalogue of deaths and obeisance (although again this is defensi-
ble, serving to stress the role of Providence in protecting Elizabeth). Thus,
the opening scene of both *Sir Thomas Wyatt* and the opening and closing

scenes of *1 If You Know Not Me* do not match the rest of the respective Poems.

Clearly, stylistic unevenness is a large and heterogeneous category, and its overlapping component parts can have many explanations. It is tempting to attribute blunt exposition to memorial reconstruction with a reporter remembering the point but not the detail. However most of the examples cited above can be explained adequately in alternative ways.

Some suspect texts appear to be a condensation of two plays or abridgement of one. Both these processes may necessitate rewriting to cover the joins or to provide summaries of antecedent action; thus, when one comes across blunt exposition creating unevenness in plays which have no other sustained verbal features of faulty memory (such as repetition) – for example, *Thomas, Lord Cromwell*, *David and Bethsabe*, *Jack Straw* – memorial reconstruction can be ruled out.

Two suspect texts, *The Famous Victories* and *Sir Thomas Wyatt*, have some verbal features of faulty memory, notably those from category A.1 (repetition). *The Famous Victories* is probably, and *Sir Thomas Wyatt* probably not, memorially reconstructed. But the texts seem also to be condensations of a two-part original (Henslowe's *1* and *2 Lady Jane* became *Sir Thomas Wyatt*; two plays on the reigns of Henry 4 and Henry 5 became *The Famous Victories*). The bluntness and unevenness may stem from the process of compression rather than (or as much as) the process of memorial reconstruction.

As in all the categories considered above, the identification of verbal problems as either pervasive or local is revealing. We have seen that the opening scene of *Sir Thomas Wyatt* is expositorily blunt, stylistically lame, and unmetrical. A simple (non-memorial) explanation may suffice. The outer leaves of MSS were vulnerable. *The Faithful Friends* lacks both beginning and end leaves, *Woodstock* and *John of Bordeaux* have a leaf missing at the end, and Massinger's *Parliament of Love* has lost two leaves at the beginning. The final sheet of the MS of *Hoffman* was probably lost 'or its verso too soiled to be legible, for the last scene [of the printed quarto] is unfinished'.[80] Someone may have compensated for damage to *Sir Thomas Wyatt* by furnishing a new opening scene; this scene may have been memorially reconstructed, but if so the difference in textual quality reflects the differing abilities of two agents rather than the memorial process *per se*.

For some reason the comic middle third of *The Fair Maid of Bristow* has been cut; the formulaic scene 9 may be a new provision (from memory?) to bridge the hiatus. *Jack Straw* has been drastically cut down and the antecedent action summarised in what is probably a new, but non-memorial, opening scene. The extended similes in *A Knack to Know a Knave* were identified by Richard Proudfoot as coming verbatim from Greene's *The Card of Fancy or Gwydonius*.[81] The agent behind *A Knack to Know a Knave* supplemented his text (be it memorial or authorial) with other material (see tables IX, XVI, and XX for further consideration of these points). Thus while stylistic unevenness can be attributable to memorial reconstruction, there are too many other complicating factors for it to function as a symptom of memory. It is at best a symptom of some hiccup in textual transmission.

A.10. CHARACTER VIGNETTE

The question of character vignette is linked to the category of unevenness, for speeches which serve to develop character in suspect texts are often simply blunt statements of purpose. Here, as earlier (e.g. A.2.c) diagnosis of problems is a matter of taste.

H. J. Oliver comments that 'speeches that have characterisation as their main function are those that a reporter is most likely to spoil'.[82] This seems a reasonable hypothesis; but much depends on our definition of 'spoil'. The RSC production of *The Massacre at Paris* (Stratford, 1985) used the play's many blunt lines and mere *ébauches* of character to good effect. The Queen Mother's opening speech is blunt and tactless:

> Thanks sonne *Nauarre*, you see we loue / you well,
> That linke you in mariage with our daughter heer:
> And as you know our difference in Religion,
> Might be a meanes to crosse you in your loue.
>   (21–5)

In performance this caused visible discomfiture to the Bourbons, and Charles's response, 'Well Madam, let that rest', was both placatory and admonitory. Elsewhere the Poem's bluntness created comic melodrama, grim laughter in the farce of death: the Guise's abrupt four lines which follow Mugeron's murder were given the laconic relish of a Victorian villain.

The mingling of religion and politics which characterises the play found greatest expression in the under-characterisation of Navarre. His bald speeches were used to epitomise religious fervour (he dropped to his knees to deliver speeches as if at prayer) but his religious tunnel vision was tempered by growing political acumen, leading to barbed delivery of even the flattest lines: his solicitous question to the murdered Anjou, 'What, is your highness hurt?' was far from sincere. Throughout the production Navarre was progressively, but silently, aware of all political machinations, emerging in the final scene as an eminently capable leader. The director, Paul Marcus, acknowledged that Navarre's role appears to have suffered most in characterisation, and his directorial approach was as much a duty to the actor of a verbally blunt role as it was a response to the politics of the text.[83]

The motto is *caveat*: what seem lame lines and under-developed characterisation on the page may be very effective theatrically. Any explanation of poor verbal characterisation as being the fault of memory is tenuous.

We should remind ourselves that not all suspect texts skimp on characterisation. Characterisation in *The True Tragedy of Richard 3*, for example, is developed with care. The Jane Shore episodes seem to exist mainly to demonstrate Richard's cruelty, yet even so, they provide touching cameos of the woman's kindness. Scene 3 tells how she has helped the citizens, and this is enough to establish her character, but a telling question sensitively adds to her humanity. On the point of exit she stops to ask Morton 'But how doth thy sonne, is he well?' (321). This kind of attention to character detail is consistent throughout *The True Tragedy of Richard 3*.

A.II. POOR JESTING

Poor jesting is a feature, if not a common denominator, of suspect texts, and it exists in a variety of forms. Verbal comedy is a precise art, more precise than clowning, and if interfered with, the Poem will suffer. The mad men of Gotham scene in *A Knack to Know a Knave* is a feeble catachrestic interlude: 'Now let vs constult among our selues, / How to misbehaue our selues to the Kings worship,' (1365–6). The encounter with the King occupies ten lines, and the scene peters out, although it is this incident which is the title-page attraction of the 1594 Q: '*VVith KEMPS applauded Merrimentes* / of the men of Goteham, in receiuing / the King into Goteham.' The second shoemaker episode (scene 13) in *George a Greene* is affected in a similar way, for the episode provides but the bare structural outline of a comic incident whose importance in the original was sufficient to merit attention in the play's concluding lines (1338–41).

The Fleming shibboleth incident of *Jack Straw* has lost most of its dialogue and all of its humour:

> Let me heare you say bread and cheese.
> Brocke and Keyse.
> (620–1)[84]

Mouse's humour in *Mucedorus* is characterised by predictable verbal misunderstanding. (However, predictability need not lead to tedium: Shakespeare's plays have been praised for the charm of expectation rather than surprise.) Furthermore, given the possibility of extempore comic expansion, it is impossible to decide whether the poor stylistic quality of the examples given is deliberate or memorial in origin. Only the lines of Mouse throughout *Mucedorus* do not demand expansion through improvisation (although they may invite it). Even so, I am reluctant to judge them comically inadequate, since the fifteen editions of this Poem between 1598 and 1668 testify to the public's appreciation of the verbal humour as it is. Poor jesting cannot therefore serve as proof of faulty memory.

B. THE PLAY

B.I. PLOT UNCONFORMITIES

'The plot of a play . . . has a good chance of emerging intact in the process of reporting. This is demonstrated by the Shakespearian bad quartos of which we possess good parallel texts.'[85] Although this seems a reasonable assumption, several suspect texts do contain plot unconformities (Kristian Smidt's helpfully non-judgemental term for 'breaches of continuity or consistency'). By 'plot unconformities' I do not mean mild inconsistency. Audiences accept, and are not confused by, certain kinds of plot inconsistency, as when the three girls in *The Blind Beggar of Alexandria* (who are simply friends) are made sisters so that Cleon can meet them simultaneously under one roof. Inconsistency of this kind is a permitted dramatic licence. Thus, the marriage of Soranzo and Annabella in Ford's *'Tis Pity*

She's A Whore is to take place 'on the Morning-sun' according to F4r,34, but is '[s]ome two dayes hence' at G1r,18. Shakespeare's *King John* asks Hubert to murder Arthur at 3.2.76. Two scenes later we see Hubert preparing to blind Arthur; the change is never explained. Our query is: when does mild inconsistency become unacceptable discrepancy?

One answer is found in *Sir Thomas Wyatt*, which contains extensive plotting contradictions.[86] In scene 3 Wyatt informs Mary that Northumberland and Suffolk have rebelled against Mary's succession to the throne and are in Cambridge, whither Wyatt now travels. However, as Phillip Shaw points out, '[w]hen the Dukes are next seen [scene 4], they are still in London'.[87] Scene 5 concludes with the information that the Duke of Suffolk has just been arrested; scene 9, surprisingly, shows him in hiding; in scene 10 we hear that 'The Duke of Suffolke is not yet apprehended,' (c4r,35); and in scene 12 he is brought in as newly captured.

Historically, Suffolk was arrested twice, but this does not resolve all the above contradictions. That considerable confusions affect this aspect of the plot is further seen in scene 4. Northumberland is taking leave of his fellow peers; Arundell, having lamented that he cannot accompany the Duke, concludes 'Commend vs to the Queene and to your Sonne' (B1v,21) – precisely the people with whom he is staying in London, as he explained in the previous speech:

> I protest,
> Did not the sacred person of my Queene,
> Whose weale I tender as my soules cheefe blisse,
> Vrge my abode, I would not thinke it shame
> To traile a pike where you were generall.
> But wishes are in vaine, I am bound to stay,
>   (B1v,9–14)

Suffolk is on stage throughout this short scene, surprisingly ignored by Northumberland, and saying nothing to his fellow Duke. One may suspect that these lines were originally Suffolk's, for historically Lady Jane 'urged abode', not to Arundell, but to her father, distressed to see him at the head of a band of anti-Mary militants.[88] It was at Jane's request that he remained in London, and such lines would be entirely appropriate to Suffolk.

However, the deferential tone, especially of the concluding lines ('See, on my knees I humbly take my leaue': B1v,16f.) most befits Arundell's position. That they are indeed intended to be spoken by him is evident from Northumberland's recollection of this scene at c1v–c2r:

> when we parted last
> My Lord of Arundel, our farwell was
> Better then our greeting now.
> Then you cride God speede,
> Now you come on me ere you say take heede:
> Then you did owe me your best bloods: nay greeu'd
> You could not spend them in my seruice.
> O then it was a double death to stay behinde,
> (c1v,34–6; c2r,1–5)

The ducal anomalies, and related problems, are a serious barrier to clarity of plot.

The Blind Beggar of Alexandria is an innocuous piece of humours entertainment which lives up to its title-page promise: 'THE BLINDE / begger of Alexan- / dria, most pleasantly discour- / *sing his variable humours* / in disguised shapes full of / *conceite and pleasure*'. However, the play contains confused references to apparently more serious material. The story of Aegiale, whose murder of Cleanthes' wife set the play in motion, is of peripheral importance in the extant text, although scene 7 contains cryptic references to Aegiale's lover, and to her son, which suggest that Aegiale's action originally constituted the serious main plot. The guard's references to 'the branch wherein the kings life remaynes' (1027) and to the 'arborisation' of Aegiale's son, Diones, by Hella (1053) are isolated and purposeless. Cleanthes (in disguise as Count Hermes) urges Aegiale to burn a branch and hence kill the King. Whether by this means, or by warfare, King Ptolemy dies, and Cleanthes becomes King. Ptolemy's conquest of four neighbouring kingdoms is dependent, according to a prophecy to which only brief reference is made (1329–32), on his daughter's marriage to Prince Doricles. This is presumably why Cleanthes murders Doricles (1279), although the prophecy is not mentioned till later. Aspasia, Doricles' sweetheart, subsequently rejects Cleanthes' offer of love, and she and her mother disappear from the play. (Aegiale's disappearance is not due to casting difficulties, for only three of the required four boys appear in the final scene.) T. M. Parrott observes that 'a death like Phaedra's seems the only fitting termination of Aegiale's career'.[89]

In *A Knack to Know a Knave*, scene 7, Ethenwald prepares to return to court with his description of Alfrida, whom he meets for the first time in scene 9. In *Mucedorus*, the King of Arragon returns home triumphant from unspecified wars, bringing with him a prisoner, a young Catalonian prince, of whom nothing further is heard. The scene concludes with an ominous private instruction to Collen (a royal counsellor):

> When thou shalt heare a watch woord from thy king,
> Thinke then some waightie matter is at hand
> That highlie shall concerne our state,
> Then *Collen* looke thou be not farre from me:
>   (B3r,12–15)

No more is heard of this matter either: indeed, Collen appears only once more in the play, in the final scene.

Suspicious though such unconformities may seem, they also appear in many non-suspect texts, where they are caused by a variety of compositional processes from authorial oversight to adaptation. Peter Morrison provides an excellent survey of the many unconformities in *The Changeling*:

> No amount of ingenuity, for example, can make sense out of the play's time scheme, even though a precise understanding of the order of events is essential to render whole sections of the action credible. Piracquo, who apparently has been in Alicante ('five days past') where Beatrice has seen and accepted him, manages to rearrive on two separate occasions ... Piracquo's murder ... at one point apparently occurs immediately following his second arrival, at a second point apparently just prior to the wedding, and at a third point – the actual day of the wedding – 'ten days since,' which leads Vermandero to suspect Franciscus and Antonio even though it is perfectly clear from I.i. that both of them left the castle prior not only to Piracquo's disappearance, but even to his *arrival*. . . Finally, the entire subplot is never resolved, a lapse so glaring that it leads Levin to speculate that the play is missing (by authorial or editorial oversight or omission) an entire scene.[90]

Adaptation caused problems such as the following in the plot of *Hoffman*: 'at l.755 Mathias is reported to be "talking with the lady *Lucibell*" when she has already fled the palace; at l.1091 Lorrique enters "ignorant" of accidents which have happened in his presence'.[91] Webster has accidentally created anomalies in *The White Devil*, the most glaring being Monticelso's statement to Vittoria (3.2.233–4), '[y]ou were born in Venice, honourably descended / From the Vitelli'. The Vitelli were not related to the Accoramboni. However, as Greg realised, it was

> for the murder of one Vincenzo Vitelli that Lodovico Orsini was
> outlawed and obliged to fly from Rome. It is possible therefore that
> Webster intended to work a connection here and make Lodovico the
> murderer of some kinsman of Vittoria's, which would account for
> Brachiano's suit against him, and also give point to his remark about
> Vittoria being in a position to get his pardon from the duke.[92]

Webster's change of purpose in *The White Devil* is minor compared to Chapman's in *Caesar and Pompey*, which resulted in anomalies so severe as to prevent performance of the play.[93] The prize for plot anomalies, however, goes to *The Wit of a Woman* (1604), an anodyne prose comedy about romantic complications in the lives of four women, four men, and their respective fathers. Names and relationships are inconsistent in dialogue, stage directions, and speech prefixes throughout. Merilla appears in scene 1 (line 3) but is called Lodouica elsewhere; Bario has at various times for his daughter Erinta (440–463), Gianetta (1144, 1206), Lodouica (1193 – with whom he has a conversation even though dialogue and stage directions have explicitly instructed her to exit at 1187), and Isabella (1214). His *inamorata* is Isabella at line 1125 and Gianetta at 1206. Veronte's loved one is Erinta at line 722 but Gianetta at 1247; Gerillo loves Gianetta at lines 780–90, even though she is made his sister at 1251. Veronte assumes a schoolmaster's disguise at 200, but appears as a painter at 541; Rinaldo (sometimes called Rimaldo) disguises as an art teacher (190), although appears as a schoolmaster (520), and a doctor (712). Such problems are only the tip of this textual iceberg. Thus authors can create anomalies as bad as, or worse than, those found in suspect texts. Plot anomalies in suspect texts are not necessarily a consequence of the memorial process.

Disordered scenes, such as the Ethenwald–Alfrida sequence in *A*

Knack to Know a Knave, are a pointer to textual disruption rather than to reporting, but since the phenomenon appears in one contemporary manuscript play, *Bonduca,* as a result of memorial uncertainty it must not be excluded from our analysis. The MS of Fletcher's *Bonduca* (BL Add. MS 36758) is a careful, neat, scribal transcript prepared for a private patron. For reasons which the scribe explains, Act 5 suffers a hiatus:

> *The begining of this following Scæne betweene petillius & Iunius / is wanting. – the occasion. why these are wanting here. the / booke where [it] by it was first Acted from is lost: and this hath / beene transcrib'd from the fowle papers of the Authors wch were / found:*

For the two scenes before this, however, the scribe relied on his memory. He began by describing 5.1. in its correct place, then mistrusted his recollection, deleted the scene and placed it after 5.2. Are the disordered scenes in *A Knack to Know a Knave* likewise attributable to memorial error, from a non-scribal source? Perhaps yes, perhaps no. In the non-memorial but textually disordered *A Larum for London,* Stump rallies deserting Walloons in scene 13, although their recovery has been reported in scene 8. Although *A Knack to Know a Knave* has features from categories 1 and 5 of Poem (repetition and submerged/wrecked verse), thus making it likely that the disordered scenes are another indication of faulty memory, it is clear that disordered scenes, taken in isolation, cannot register as a symptom of memorial error.

B.2. REDUCED CASTING

Reduced casts are frequently associated with suspect texts. As we saw in chapter 2 the New Bibliographers developed a scenario of suspect texts as abridged provincial touring texts. The abridgement was deemed to operate in two ways: reduction in playing time to cater to a less sophisticated audience, and reduction of cast to accommodate a reduced touring company. A reduced cast might sometimes necessitate alterations to a play's plot and structure, a scenario parodied in *Rosencrantz and Guildenstern are Dead* where Stoppard's Player offers his audience 'The Rape of the Sabine Women – or rather woman, or rather Alfred. Get your skirt on Alfred.' In *Fair Em* reduced casting is probably the reason behind the senseless dismissal of both Zweno's and William's armies in the final scene: as Standish Henning explains, 'there is no reason for either king to suppose that the outcome of their meeting will not be war'.[94] It would seem that the company had neither the military paraphernalia nor the necessary numbers to stage such a confrontation.

It is the topic of casting which most reveals the New Bibliographers' anti-theatrical thinking. The putative reduced text is frequently referred to as an 'acting version', ignoring the fact that 'good' quartos and folio texts are also acting versions.[95] (As we saw in chapter 2, the New Bibliographers found it convenient to distinguish those texts written for publication from those written for performance.) D. L. Patrick's work on *Richard 3* contains the heaviest concentration of such New Bibliographical bias.

Patrick begins by arguing that Q *Richard 3* is a 'stage abridgement'; he can then turn to other concerns '[w]ith the fact well established that the quarto text is an acting version'.[96] This is an interesting sleight of hand, for 'abridgement' is presented as a synonym for 'acting version', implying that longer plays were not performance texts. A similar rhetorical technique is used elsewhere. Discussing doubling, Patrick argues that '[i]n the quarto, with its known habit of doubling parts, it may well be that one actor took the part of Clarence . . . [and] of Clarence's son' (p.52). Laying aside the improbability of this double, we may note the implication that in the folio text no parts were doubled: doubling occurs when performances are given by small casts.[97] This view of doubling as a problematic and somehow unprofessional activity is related to Patrick's later argument about reporting where, with a logic that I fail to follow, he argues that portions of the play which involve doubling 'will naturally be more faultily transmitted than those which have been left undisturbed' (p.147). To Patrick reduced casting is viewed along with play abridgement, doubling, and performance generally, as a tainted phenomenon that indicates disruption, both theatrical and textual.

While most suspect texts can indeed be performed by a small number of personnel (*A Knack to Know a Knave, Fair Em, Orlando Furioso, The True Tragedy of Richard 3, The Famous Victories*) some require rather large casts. *1 If You Know Not Me* can be acted by twelve men and three boys only if all the dumb shows are omitted; if one incorporates all the dumb shows, the play is unstageable without a vast number of supernumeraries. Scene 23, for instance, requires a cast of twenty-seven, of whom sixteen are mute.[98] It may have been possible to draft in willing stagehands to swell a scene (this tactic is used in Heywood's *The Captives* line 2805, where the MS annotation calls for 'Stagekeepers as a guard') but one would still have to face the burden of costuming.

The fact that a play can be performed by a small cast does not show that it was. The small cast is only a minimum: the play may have been performed by more, although it cannot have been performed by less. (And small casts may, of course, perform non-suspect texts.) Even when one has an example of reduced casting as clear as that in *Fair Em*, where the anticipated military confrontation does not materialise, this does not mean that the play is a memorial reconstruction. The subject of reduced casts therefore has no symptomatic value for our study of memorial reconstruction.[99]

B.3. STAGING REQUIREMENTS

The New Bibliographers glossed over the difficulty of presenting those suspect texts which require complicated or sophisticated staging facilities such as balconies, discovery spaces, and trapdoors (certainly in combination) in other than well-equipped theatres. While a suspect text which requires several of these facilities may be memorially reconstructed, it is less likely to be memorially reconstructed for (or during) a provincial tour;[100] on the other hand, Elizabethan acting companies may have been accustomed to adapting action to the facilities at hand. What is clear is that a survey of staging requirements in our suspect texts sheds no light on the identification of memorial reconstruction.

It does, however, separate those plays which have no special requirements (and therefore can be acted anywhere) from those whose demands are so elaborate as to indicate performance in a fully equipped playhouse. *1 If You Know Not Me*, for instance, requires an upper area which must be capable of holding three people for an entire scene (scene 21). 'Aloft' facilities are also required in *George a Greene*, *The Massacre at Paris*, *The Troublesome Reign of King John*, *Sir Thomas Wyatt*, *The Blind Beggar of Alexandria*, *Edward 1*, and (possibly) *A Knack to Know an Honest Man*, while two stage directions in *The Massacre at Paris* suggest to Thomas Pettitt that the need for an inner stage has been eliminated.[101] Several texts specify the use of doors: two doors in *1 Contention*, *John of Bordeaux*, and *1 Hieronimo*, one door in *A Knack to Know an Honest Man*. A curtained recess is specified or required in *The Famous Victories, The True Tragedy of Richard 3, 1 Contention,* and *Richard Duke of York.*

In one instance we can infer properties which the theatre company lacked. Awkward references in *The Merry Devil of Edmonton* to Smug's fall from a tree, and to his impersonation of St George by mounting the White Horse Inn sign, suggest that the episodes referred to were once staged. The references in the extant text indicate that the company lacked two essential properties: a climbable stage tree, and a mountable property-horse. Episodes that were once presented dramatically have apparently been converted to narrative summary. (For further consideration of this question, see chapter 8, table XXIII.)

Although a suspect text, *The Merry Devil of Edmonton* lacks verbal symptoms of memorial reconstruction. If we accept William Abrams's dating of the play as c.1603,[102] it is evident that the play had little immediate opportunity for London performance, as the theatres were closed from 19 March 1603 to 24 April 1603 and from 17 May 1603 to April 1604.[103] The modest minimum casting requirements (twelve men and three boys) coupled with the lack of necessary props may point to provincial touring, presumably during the extended London closure. What is of interest here is that two out of three New Bibliographical assumptions about the textual circumstances of provincial tours do not apply. *The Merry Devil of Edmonton* is not memorial; its comedy has not been gratuitously expanded; but it has been abridged. This abridgement seems, however, to have been forced upon the company by practical exigencies rather than audience taste.

Restricted conditions of performance can also be discerned in *The Massacre at Paris.* Thomas Pettitt's analysis of the contradictions afflicting the disposal of the Admiral's body suggest a company unable to stage a hanging.[104] This technical property was unavailable, Pettitt argues, and so the Admiral was dragged off to a ditch instead. Unlike *The Merry Devil of Edmonton, The Massacre at Paris* bears verbal symptoms of memorial reconstruction; this staging detail suggests the circumstances in which the reconstructed text was performed, but does not, in the absence of sustained verbal symptoms, prove memorial reconstruction.

C. THE TEXT

C.I. BREVITY

Brevity is one of the most frequently cited features of suspect texts. In fact, the length of suspect texts varies widely, with line totals ranging from the extremely short *A Yorkshire Tragedy* and *Jack Straw* (with 757 and 971 lines of dialogue, respectively) to the 2,180 and 3,416 lines of dialogue in *The True Tragedy of Richard Duke of York* and Q1 *Richard 3*. The longer texts within this range (e.g. *The True Tragedy of Richard Duke of York, 1 Contention, Arden of Feversham*) are more normal than abnormal in length for plays of the period: Alfred Hart calculated the average for plays printed in the years 1592–94 as c.2,250 lines.[105] It seems that concentration on Shakespeare's plays, many of which are approximately 3,000 lines, has created an erroneous impression of the normal length of an Elizabethan play, causing anything which falls below this length to be suspect. However, as Frank Hook observes, 'A play, like Antony's crocodile, is of its own length, and no forceful argument . . . can be based upon comparison with the length of other plays.'[106]

Obviously the brevity of some suspect texts does give grounds for suspicion. John Danter and Edward Allde, printers of Q1 *Jack Straw* and O1 *The Massacre at Paris*, respectively, were sufficiently troubled by these texts' brevity to compensate visually with generous leading, ornamentation, single-line speech prefixes, and unnecessarily turned-over lineation. But brevity is not an automatic pointer to memorial reconstruction. The corpus of Elizabethan drama contains many plays of notable brevity which bear none of the other alleged features of reporting.

At 1,760 lines *The Wit of A Woman* is short and severely defective (relationships are confused beyond hope of emendation); but it contains none of the verbal features analysed in section A.1–11 above. The 1,940 lines of Heywood's *A Woman Killed With Kindness* stem from the play's single-strand domestic plot; and if, at 2,116 lines, Greene's *Alphonsus, King of Aragon* seems short, it is on a par with other Queen's Men's texts, both suspect and non-suspect, of the same period.

Kirschbaum attributes the brevity of some suspect texts to careless memorial omission: 'bad memory and not purposive cutting lies behind the omissions'.[107] This is to ignore the consistent and careful omission of references to the civil war plot in *Fair Em*, or to the Aegiale and Ptolemy stories in *The Blind Beggar of Alexandria*, or to the King/Collen liaison in *Mucedorus*, all of which are more readily attributable to abridgement than degenerative memorial omission.[108]

When a character in a short play refers to that play as lengthy, our textual suspicions may reasonably be aroused. Honesty in *A Knack to Know a Knave* (1,897 lines; 1,853 lines of dialogue) concludes with the apologetic 'And thus though *long at last* we make an end' (1890; my emphasis). At 2,224 lines (2,132 of dialogue), *The True Tragedy of Richard 3* amounts to just over two hours' playing time, yet Truth seems to think it is long: 'Thus gentles, excuse the length by the matter' (70). Brevity coupled with apologies for length suggests abridgement; and while abridgement may operate in tandem with memorial reconstruction, it is not evidence of memorial reconstruction.

C.2. STAGE DIRECTIONS

Various aspects of stage directions aroused the New Bibliographers' critical suspicions about suspect texts. For convenience in discussion I divide this large category into three subsections: descriptive stage directions, ghost characters, and massed entries.

c.2.a. Descriptive stage directions

Descriptive stage directions are traditionally viewed as the hallmark of the reported text, even though, as we saw in chapter 2, New Bibliographic thinking on this subject was often contradictory or inconclusive. Greg urged caution about any hard-and-fast equation of descriptive stage directions with reporting, but as this equation nonetheless hardened into irrefragable truth, he became more inclined to ignore his own caution. Arguing for the textual 'goodness' of *Pericles* Greg offers as support the fact that '[t]he directions . . . are only slightly descriptive'.[109]

Hoppe further muddied the waters. What had begun as an unproven but logical assumption (a reporter is likely to record his impression of events when verbal memory fails; thus he describes the nature of a fight rather than recording its verbal cut-and-thrust) was expanded by Hoppe into a tenuous assumption about Elizabethan acting. Hoppe felt that an actor would not be able to deliver his lines properly in scenes with noise and bustle, and would easily fall into the habit of shouting whatever came into his head until quiet was restored and the normal interplay of dialogue could be resumed. Proper utterance of his lines being virtually impossible, the actor would have neither incentive nor opportunity to fix his speeches in his mind[.][110]

Descriptive stage directions, according to Hoppe, reflect the fact that the reporter was trying to recall something he didn't know accurately in the first place.

Hoppe further speculates that such directions reflect an actor's attempt to remember something he had given up trying to say because of on-stage competition from his fellows. The boy-Ophelia possibly overdid his mad-scene, 'so overwhelming the other players with his singing and bedlam antics as to give them no chance to speak out their parts'.[111] This results in the actor–reporter forgetting his own, and not knowing others', lines and so he provides a descriptive stage direction to cover the action: '*Enter Ofelia playing on a Lute, and her haire downe singing*'.

The New Bibliographers use 'descriptive stage directions' to refer to two phenomena: stage directions which substitute descriptively for dialogue, and those incorporating brief epithets which record mood and impression. The following four examples replace dialogue:

> *Crosse againe, and Faustus hits him a boxe of the eare, / and they all runne away.*
> (A *Dr Faustus* D2v,1–2)
> *He cuts of the Cutpurse eare, for cutting of the / golde buttons off his cloake.*
> (*The Massacre at Paris* 747–8)
> *He stabs the King with a knife as he readeth / the letter, and then the King getteth the / knife and killes him.*
> (*The Massacre at Paris* 1478–80)
> *Enters Dericke roming. After him a Frenchman, / and takes him prisoner.*
> (*The Famous Victories* F2v,5–6)

The brief epithets in the following three examples expand mood:

> *Enter the ghost in his night gowne.*
> (Q1 *Hamlet* G2v,28)

> *Enter Iuliet somewhat fast, and embraceth Romeo.*
> (Q1 *Romeo and Juliet* E4r,31)
> *Enter Sentlo very drousie.*
> (*The Fair Maid of Bristow* D2r,6)

Both types of descriptive direction can also be found in non-suspect texts. *A Woman Killed with Kindness* provides several examples of directions substituting for dialogue.

> *They dance, Nick dancing, speakes stately and scuruily, therest [sic] after the / Country fashion.*
> (B2v,1–2)

> *Sir Charles. Cranwell, Faulkener, and Huntsman, fight against Sir / Francis Wendall, his Faulkener, and Huntsman, and Sir Charles / hath the better, and beats them away, killing one of / Sir Francis his huntsmen.*
> (B3r,20–3)

Ford introduces Act 3, scene 6 of *'Tis Pity She's A Whore* with the descriptive stage direction:

> *Enter the Fryar in his study, sitting in a chayre,* Annabella *kneeling and whispering to him, a Table before them and wax-lights, she weepes, and wrings her hands.*
> (F3v,1–3)

Brian Morris points out that 'Ford frequently sets a scene with considerable exactness, and an eye for significant stage-detail', offering as examples *Love's Sacrifice* 3.4 and 5.3, and *The Broken Heart* 5.3.[112]

The MS of *The Soddered Citizen* yields numerous examples of brief descriptive epithets:

> *Exeunt, arme in arme imbraceinge.*
> (539)
> *Enter... / hastily, in a swett.*
> (1121–2)
> *They looke strangely at each other,*
> (1280)
> *warily exit*
> (1363)

Enter three of the Doctors servants rudely;
   (1892)
Iocondly
   (1901)
exit **in haste,**
   (2788)

The last example provides an important *caveat* for the critic of suspect texts: the descriptive *'in haste'* has been added to the original bare 'exit' by a theatrical reviser.[113] Since several of our suspect texts may be printed from copy used as a playbook, the descriptions may derive from a prompter fulfilling the task of stage choreography. A further *caveat* must be added, for we find that the suspect octavo of *The Massacre at Paris* is actually less descriptive than the contemporary MS (Folger MS J.b.8); whereas the former prints *'Enter a Souldier.'* (972), the MS has *'Enter A Souldier w[t] a Mvskett'*.[114] Descriptive stage directions are therefore not reliably symptomatic of memorial reconstruction.

c.2.b. Vestigial characters

I use the term vestigial instead of the more usual 'ghost', since in this category I discuss characters who are named in a stage direction but do not have a role in the play (ghosts) as well as characters who are named in a stage direction, have no lines in that scene (mutes), but do have a role in the play.

Vestigial characters often occur in suspect texts. In the last scene of *The Fair Maid of Bristow* Richmond and Lester are named as accompanying King Richard; they have no lines (although they are both addressed by Anabell), and do not appear elsewhere in the play. Obviously the monarch must be accompanied by two (or more) attendants, and it matters little whether they are named, so casting exigencies are not affected. But it is odd that two Earls should be brought on by name in one scene only.

In the final scene of *1 Hieronimo* we find the Lord General accompanied by 'Phillippo, and Cassimero, with followers' (F3r,23–4). Phillippo and Cassimero neither speak nor are spoken to, nor do they feature anywhere in the play; yet at some stage they were considered sufficiently distinctive to merit naming. Lines 378–9 of *Orlando Furioso* contain a direction for an otherwise otiose character, Countie Rossillion. In *Jack Straw*, line 682, Tom Miller is given entrance, although the next scene clearly indicates that he was not present in the previous action. Sir Robert Rodston and Sir Harry Isely enter together at *Sir Thomas Wyatt*, E3r, but do not speak. In the same play the stage direction to scene 6 includes Winchester as one of the Lords at the Council in the Tower. He has nothing to say, and in fact, does not belong in the scene, for (historically) he was still in prison.

Vestigial characters are also far from unknown in non-suspect texts. Leonato's wife, Innogen, in *Much Ado about Nothing* 1.2 and 2.1 is probably the most familiar. Webster's *The White Devil* provides several examples. The dumbshow at 2.2 introduces two characters, Christophero and Guid-Antonio, who do not feature elsewhere in the play; the stage direction in 5.1 includes a mysterious Farnese among Franciscus's followers; and in an analogous perplexity, the disguised Lodovico and Gasparo are referred to in the stage directions throughout Act 5 as Pedro and Carlo, although these names do not appear in the dialogue.

The 1600 Q of *2 Henry 4* contains vestigial characters at B4v (*Fauconbridge*), C3v (*sir Iohn Russel*), E4r (*sir Iohn Blunt*; this example comes from Qb, the second issue of the 1600 Q, with a cancel quire E), and F3v (*Bardolfe*). Vestigial characters appear in the MS *Believe As You List*, and in several Queen's Mens' playtexts of the 1590s: Lady Douglas, Sir Egmond, Lord Percy, and Samles in *James 4* (Q 1598), Flaminius, Arcastus and Bajazet in *Alphonsus, King of Aragon* (Q 1599), Trussier (or Thrassier) in *Locrine* (Q 1595).

The category of vestigial characters includes those characters who have but one line and whose roles seem supererogatory. Christophil in *The Spanish Tragedy* (1592) has one cryptic line at 1696 ('Come Madame *Bel-imperia*, this may not be'); he is later referred to by Lorenzo as liberating Bel-Imperia (1705). This apparently superfluous character would pose no textual problem had Kyd simply called him 'Page': the naming of a character sets up (possibly false) expectations about his/her importance (as in the case of *The Fair Maid of Bristow, 1 Hieronimo*, and *Orlando Furioso*, above). Don Pedro in *The Spanish Tragedy* is another character with one line, and Richard Kohler speculates that he is introduced by the author purely for symmetry of staging in 3.14.[115] It seems that authors can cause textual problems as well as reporters.

Vestigial characters can arise from authorial change of intent, revision, and/or abridgement (all of these processes, some overlapping, can be witnessed in *Much Ado About Nothing*, *The White Devil*, *2 Henry 4*, *James 4*, *Alphonsus, King of Aragon*, *Believe As You List*, and *Locrine*). Since all the vestigial characters in suspect texts appear in texts where abridgement can be reasonably inferred, references to them are conceivably remnants of the abridgement process. It is not necessary to attribute them to memorial reconstruction.

c.2.c. Massed entries

Massed entries appear in only two suspect texts, *A Knack to Know a Knave* and *Pericles*. Greg commented on massed entries in *Pericles*, citing them as an example of authorial manuscript:

> Intending a scene between a certain set of characters, the writer may set down their names at the head of it, and then in fact begin say with a soliloquy by one of them before the rest make their appearance.[116]

Given that Greg had earlier accepted (albeit reluctantly) Pollard's designation of *Pericles* as a reported text,[117] his choice of *Pericles* as an illustration of authorial practice is odd. Although F. D. Hoeniger accepts the possibility of a massed entry at *Pericles* 1.4.0 (B4v), he rejects the possibility at 1.2.0 (B1r) on the grounds that 'a mass-entry is difficult to account for in a reported text'.[118]

Neither Hoeniger nor Greg considered straightforward explanations for massed entries in a reported text: the reporter may have had access to a plot, or, more probably, he may have begun by recalling all the characters present in the scene. The massed entries in *A Knack to Know a Knave* and *Pericles* may therefore tell us something about the way a reporter operated. Thus, although not a diagnostic aid (for other scribes may have shared Ralph Crane's predilection for massed entries) massed entries are of interest in suspect texts when the presence of faulty memory has been established by other means.

c.3. MISLINED VERSE

The New Bibliographers frequently equated mislined verse with a memorially reconstructed text. Their intermittent suspicions that shorthand was involved in the reporting possibly accounts for this otherwise tenuous assumption.[119] Several suspect texts do consistently misline blank verse as prose. The manuscript of *John of Bordeaux*, for example, lines verse as prose on most folios until scene 15 (fol.9) where improvement begins; from scene 17 (fol.11) the problem disappears. However, mislining is open to many explanations, and *John of Bordeaux* illustrates one of them: the scribe's concern about the sufficiency of the paper supply forced him to line verse as prose. There is no reason to suppose that a compositor would not have followed this arrangement. Chapman's suspect text, *The Blind Beggar of Alexandria*, mislines verse and prose, a characteristic it shares with Chapman's non-suspect *An Humorous Day's Mirth*, printed the following year by the same printer. Mislining features in so many printed playtexts of the period that it has no diagnostic value for memorial reconstruction.

C.4. PUNCTUATION

The New Bibliographers frequently exclaimed over the paucity of punctuation in Q *King Lear*. They did not consider that this might indicate an author's lightly punctuated manuscript, even though they were well aware of the under-punctuation in hand D of *Sir Thomas More*; and they never explained why they viewed this feature as suspicious (of whatever they suspected) in Q1 *King Lear*. For the record, punctuation has little value in the study of memorial reconstruction, for, as Moxon tells us, it is the responsibility of the compositor:

> For by the Laws of Printing, *a compositor is strictly to follow his* Copy, *viz. to observe and do just so much and no more than his* Copy *will bear him out for; so that his* Copy *is to be his Rule and Authority: But the carelesness of some good Authors, and the ignorance of other Authors, has forc'd* Printers *to introduce a Custom, which among them is look'd upon as a task and duty incumbent on the* Composite, *viz. to discern and amend the bad* Spelling *and* Pointing *of his* Copy, *if it be English*[.][120]

Nonetheless, punctuation may provide illumination concerning the underlying MS copy. Noting the 'chaotic' punctuation in Q *Pericles*, Hoeniger suggested that the compositors were 'so much at a loss that they simply resorted to punctuating the end of each line, whether the sense required it or not'.[121] Fredson Bowers felt that the frequent use of lower case letters at the beginning of verse lines in *Sir Thomas Wyatt* pointed to a compositor following difficult copy rather carefully,[122] and the same explanation may hold for consistently unusual punctuation. On the whole, however, our suspect texts lack any unusual habits in pointing. And since peculiarities of punctuation do not indicate memorial reconstruction, punctuation has no diagnostic relevance.

CONCLUSION

In the above discussion I have concentrated on the twenty-eight features (which I have, for clarity, arranged in three sections under eighteen headings) identified by the New Bibliographers as characteristic of suspect texts and symptomatic of memorial reconstruction. My discussion has considered these features both in practice and in principle, identifying their occurrence in a wide range of Renaissance playtexts, and evaluating possible alternative explanations for their occurrence. My conclusion is that, of all the alleged symptoms of faulty memory, only two, or possibly three, have direct relevance to the subject of memorial reconstruction.

I am drawn to this conclusion by a tri-partite sequence of distinctions which it seems to me prudent to make. The first is a distinction between the verbal fabric of the playtext – the Poem – and its other entities, the Play and the Text. The principal area in which faulty memory can be detected is the Poem. We must cease talking about features from Play and Text, such as vestigial characters and reduced casts, as if they are relevant to diagnosis of faulty memory.

The second distinction relates to the type of faulty memory we should try to identify: short-term or long-term. It is clear that many people involved in the normal transmission of a text, from authors and adapters to scribes and compositors, rely on short-term memory of small sections of text. When short-term memory malfunctions, it will result in a localised textual problem: an aural error, a repetition, an omission. Faulty long-term memory, on the other hand, betrays itself through more pervasive textual problems because it is trying to recall substantial passages, if not the whole, of the Poem, some while after acquaintance with the original text. Thus, evidence of faulty memory is not necessarily evidence of memorial reconstruction. It is only evidence of faulty long-term memory which can lead to a claim for memorial reconstruction.

My third distinction concerns memorial reconstruction (a specific phenomenon, defined below) versus the more amorphous concept of memorial transmission. The diagnostic problems addressed in this chapter might have been foreseen, or avoided, had the term memorial reconstruction been carefully defined and consistently used by the early investigators. Greg's definition of 'reporting' (a synonym for memorial reconstruction) as '*any* process of transmission which involves the memory no matter *at what stage or in what manner*' (my emphasis), was unhelpfully comprehensive.[123] Kirschbaum believed that '[t]he simplest way to describe a bad quarto [the term which became standard for a memorially reconstructed text] is to state that it cannot possibly represent a written transcript of the author's text'.[124]

That there was (and is) a need for a more specific definition of 'memorial reconstruction' is apparent from the fact that critics used (and still use) the term to subsume a variety of processes. Thus, in a recent *TLS* correspondence, Harold Jenkins corrected what he perceived as a misunderstanding on the part of Evert Sprinchorn:

> No one, as far as I know, has ever maintained that the debased Q1 text [of *Hamlet*] represents how Burbage and other leading actors of Shakespeare's Company spoke and remembered their lines ... This [Ophelia's reply to Laertes] is how the speech was reproduced not by an actor who had played Ophelia but by one who had not.[125]

However, the studies cited in chapter 3 show that Greg and Hoppe had in mind, on some occasions at least, memorial reconstruction by an actor who *had* played the role he was attempting to reconstruct. Thus, although Sprinchorn and Jenkins are writing about the same term, they are not writing about the same thing.

This confusion stems from the way in which the blanket-term 'memorial reconstruction' elides identification of the phenomenon of faulty long-term memory with identification of the agent(s) and/or circumstances in which the supposed memorial reconstruction was deemed necessary. Moreover, each critic works from his/her own personal understanding of the term; readers have to infer the critic's definition for it is rarely articulated.

I define memorial reconstruction as: the reproduction of a playtext in whole or in part by someone who had at some stage substantial knowledge of the original playtext as written or performed. It is obvious that this definition does not identify the agent behind reconstruction, the purpose of the reconstruction, or the specific text which is being reconstructed, nor is it intended to do any of these things. My primary aim is to assemble evidence to support or refute a case for memorial reconstruction. This is the subject of chapter 8.

8 | 'Tables...stored full'

> We must . . . be confident that we can clearly distinguish between
> memorial contamination and other forms of corruption, and of this it
> may be easier to convince ourselves than others.
>
> W. W. Greg[1]

Any survey of forty-one suspect texts inevitably assembles a large amount
of textual data. My aim has been to make this material available in as
judicious, unbiased, and neutral a manner as possible. As a discussion of
each play in narrative format is precluded both by limitations of space and
by my desire to focus on textual methodology rather than on conclusion, I
have chosen to present the data from the forty-one suspect texts in tabular
form.

Tabular format minimises the 'cause and effect' scenario inherent in the
narrative method, and also provides an accessible summary of textual quiddities. The layout of the tables and their consecutive presentation permit a
detailed picture of features within an individual play, a comparative overview
of all features of all forty-one playtexts, and of any single feature (e.g. internal
repetitions) across the forty-one texts. The tables record textual features;
they do not generally explain them. In identifying and interpreting the features, I have applied the diagnostic principles of chapter 7.

Table 1 does not itself refer to any playtext: it summarises the criteria
by which the information in tables 11–XLI has been assembled.

Tables 11–XLII contain textual information on each of the forty-one
suspect texts, arranged in twenty categories as follows. The first four
categories comprise factual, historical information: A) Play/Text Used;
B) Stationers' Register/Quarto Dates; C) Printer/Publisher; D) Author/
Company.

The next seven categories comprise evidence from the verbal fabric of each text, the Poem, arranged under headings familiar from, and deduced under, the criteria discussed in chapter 7: E) External Echoes; F) Internal Repetitions; G) Formulae; H) Insertions; I) Expanded Clown's Role; J) Omissions; K) Speech Length. This evidence from the Poem is concluded by the (inevitably impressionistic) category L, Stylistic Summary.

Categories M–Q comprise features from Play and Text: M) Unconformities; N) Staging and Props; O) Length of Text/Length of Dialogue; P) Stage Directions and Speech Prefixes; Q) Vestigial Characters. Category R, Other Observations, includes assorted material not readily assignable to the previous categories (e.g. contemporary references).

Category S lists selected Previous Verdicts on the play's textual origin, and category T provides my own Conclusion. The wide variety of verdicts which previous critics have confidently advanced encourages one to exercise caution in diagnosing each text. I have therefore limited my conclusion to the case for or against memorial reconstruction. This conclusion is based on the evidence provided in categories E–L, the only categories which, as Chapter 7 made clear, have any diagnostic bearing on the question of memorial reconstruction. (Categories M–Q have been included in the tables to provide a full overview of each text's characteristics.) I stress that my Conclusion is the least important part of each table: it is the material leading to that conclusion which is the focus.

I remind the reader that I do not use parallel-text comparisons in formulating the data in the tables. It has been assumed that greater diagnostic certainty can be achieved by admitting parallel texts into the discussion. Of this I remain unconvinced. In considering the competing claims of memorial reconstruction and authorial draft it is evident, as Alan Dessen points out, that the same evidence is 'interpreted in diametrically opposed ways'.[2] Placing a Shakespeare F or Q2 text alongside a Q1 version may narrow the interpretive options instead of increasing them, for it introduces inevitable biases about the direction of dependence: one can rarely have *a priori* confidence in the direction of influence between two texts.[3] It can be argued that Q1 *Hamlet*, for example, must have been revised to become Q2 just as it can be argued that Q2 must be the original of which Q1 is a derivative: evidence, in the form of variants, is readily to hand to support either interpretation. My subsequent examination of the comparative evidence provided by the Shakespeare parallel texts did not change any of my conclusions: that is, it did not compel me to transfer any play from one verdict to another in table XLIII, the summary of conclusions which begins chapter 9, although it may have provided more evidence to support a play's inclusion in the category to which I have assigned it.

TABLE I Criteria for tables I I – XLI I

A **PLAY/TEXT USED**: Self-explanatory.

B **SR/Q DATES**: The abbreviation NE is used to indicate 'no entry' in the Stationers' Register (SR) / Quarto dates are given up to and including 1623. Where the suspect text comprises material added to a text already in print (e.g. *The Spanish Tragedy*) the earlier Q dates are omitted.

C **PRINTER/PUBLISHER**: Names are given in full, even when the stationer is not identified on the title-page, or identified only by initial.

D **AUTHOR/COMPANY**: Speculative attributions are identified as such.

E **EXTERNAL ECHOES**: Identified according to the diagnostic criteria in chapter 7 A.I.a. Repetitions alleged by earlier critics which fall outside these criteria are noted with an indication of why they should be rejected.

F **INTERNAL REPETITIONS**: Comprises verbatim repetition and paraphrase defined according to the criteria in chapter 7 A.I.b and A.I.c.

G **FORMULAE**: Defined according to the criteria in chapter 7 A.I.e.

H **INSERTIONS**: Self-explanatory.

I **EXPANDED CLOWN'S ROLE**: Self-explanatory.

J **OMISSIONS**: Self-explanatory.

K **SPEECH LENGTH**: Long speeches are divided into two groups: those of more than 14 lines, and those between 8 and 14 lines. Of the first group, a parenthetical list of the three highest speech totals is also given.

L **STYLISTIC SUMMARY**: A general overview of theme, metre, and stylistic quality.

M **UNCONFORMITIES**: Major unconformities, as defined in chapter 7 B.I, are listed; minor improbabilities have largely been ignored. Though this category refers mainly to features of plot, some localised verbal unconformities (in the form of *non sequitur*s) are included.

N **STAGING AND PROPS**: 'Staging' refers to the structural features of a playing area, e.g. doors, upper stage. 'Props' refers to portable items, e.g. beds, coffins, banquets. Costumes are excluded.

O **LENGTH**: Two figures are given: (i) total typographic length, from first to final stage direction (i.e. excluding half-title and colophon. If there is no final exit, the count stops at the last line of dialogue), and (ii) total dialogue length (i.e. total typographic length minus single-line stage directions and speech prefixes. Mislining of verse as prose does not affect the count: 1 type line = 1 line).

P STAGE DIRECTIONS/SPEECH PREFIXES: The abbreviations SD and SP are used throughout.

Q VESTIGIAL CHARACTERS: Self-explanatory.

R OTHER OBSERVATIONS: Self-explanatory.

S PREVIOUS VERDICTS: Representative twentieth-century viewpoints. Only the key points of complex and multi-layered arguments are given; those arguments should be consulted in their entirety.

T CONCLUSION: A verdict for or against memorial reconstruction (MR) is given. This verdict, based solely on analysis of the single suspect text, does not preclude associated conclusions such as revision or adaptation.

TABLE II *Arden of Feversham*

A **PLAY/TEXT USED:** *Arden of Feversham* (1592)/MSR (1947 for 1940).

B **SR/Q DATES:** 3 April 1592 to Edward White/Q1 1592, Q2 1599.

C **PRINTER/PUBLISHER:** Edward Allde/Edward White. See *Records of Court of Stationers' Company* vol.1, p.44 for the controversy relating to a confiscated earlier edition of the same year, printed by Abel Jeffes in defiance of White's entry.

D **AUTHOR/COMPANY:** Anon./auspices unknown although usually associated with Pembroke's on basis of alleged external echoes.

E **EXTERNAL ECHOES:** Apart from 99–100 (shared with *MP*; *MP* is probably the debtor: see table XXII) few of any significance and none which cannot plausibly be attributed to the author.

F **INTERNAL REPETITIONS:** 2200/2228. Phrases do recur but they are rarely verbatim; the repetitions are of commonplace vocabulary; and they are seldom more than half a line in length.

G **FORMULAE:** There is a predilection for the adjective 'sweet' (36 times, mainly in first and last Acts), a predilection shared with *MP*. Use of tag phrases ('let it pass', 'I will to London straight') may be authorial or reportorial. Exit lines are generally sophisticated and motivated by plot.

H **INSERTIONS:** Large number of extra-metrical additions. It has been suggested that the Jack Fitten material at 704–40 is a topical insertion. See White (ed., *Arden*, p.29) for cogent refutation of this point.

I **EXPANDED CLOWN'S ROLE:** No.

J **OMISSIONS:** Confused pronoun referents at 32–3 and 99–101 may indicate omission.

K **SPEECH LENGTH:** 20 speeches over 14 lines (highest totals: 30, 31, 47); 52 speeches between 8 and 14 lines.

L **STYLISTIC SUMMARY:** Vigorous language. The Poem is metrically generally good, although the scenes with Black Will and Shakebag vacillate between verse and prose (with some verse embedded in prose). Excellent characterisation of Black Will (among others).

M **UNCONFORMITIES:** Some minor inconsistencies. Mosby knows Greene at 304, yet not at 463. Greene's letter to Alice, written in scene 2, predates the information it contains.

N **STAGING AND PROPS:** 2 entrances ('doors'); interior space with door for 'countinghouse'. Props include: table, bench or stools, chair, broth, stall with shutter ('window': 839), backgammon, torch, prayerbook, glasses of wine.

O **LENGTH:** Total length: 2,574 lines/Length of dialogue: 2,457 lines.

P **STAGE DIRECTIONS/SPEECH PREFIXES:** 'Here enters. . .' collocation throughout. With few exceptions SDs give careful attention to exits and entrances. SDs regularly provide accompanying stage action: e g 'Then Arden drawes forth Mosbies sword' (320); 'Then she throwes down the broth / on the grounde' (380–1); 'Then hee kneeles downe and houldes vp / his hands to heauen' (1475–6); 'Then Will pulles him down with a towell' (2254).

Q **VESTIGIAL CHARACTERS:** No.

R **OTHER OBSERVATIONS:** The play has no sub-plot (see Dolan, 'The Subordinate('s) Plot', pp.329–34 for thematic aptness of this structural feature). The play is concentrated but there is no sense of abbreviation.

S **PREVIOUS VERDICTS:** 'remarkably good' (Brooke ed., *Shakespeare Apocrypha*, p. xiii); 'poor' (Hart, *Stolne and Surreptitious*, p.384); reported text (Jackson, thesis, 'Material for an Edition'; Wine ed., *Arden*, p.xxv).

T **CONCLUSION:** Not MR.

TABLE III *The Blind Beggar of Alexandria*

A **PLAY/TEXT USED:** *The Blind Beggar of Alexandria* (1598)/MSR (1929 for 1928).

B **SR/Q DATES:** c.15 August 1598 to William Jones/Q 1598.

C **PRINTER/PUBLISHER:** James Roberts/William Jones.

D **AUTHOR/COMPANY:** George Chapman/Admiral's Men.

E **EXTERNAL ECHOES:** No; the paraphrases of Marlowe (166 from *1 Tamburlaine*, and 1289ff. from *The Passionate Shepherd*) and of one line (1473) from Kyd's *The Spanish Tragedy* seem to be deliberate burlesque (see Rees, 'Chapman's *Blind Beggar*').

F **INTERNAL REPETITIONS:** 74–5/491–2 (and, more distantly, 98–101); 732–5/780–4/830–3; 1004–5/1101–2.

G **FORMULAE:** With 34 occurrences (and 6 variations such as adverbs and superlatives), the adjective 'sweet' seems overused.

H **INSERTIONS:** 'My Lord' or 'for him' (1553) is extra-metrical (probably the latter if the rhyming couplet is intentional).

I **EXPANDED CLOWN'S ROLE:** The comic plot is full (contrast the political plot which is slight) and is clearly the playtext's *raison d'être*.

J **OMISSIONS:** The serious romantic plot is heavily reduced and actually left unfinished (see Parrott ed., *Plays of George Chapman*, vol.II, pp.674–5). Contradictions in dialogue and SDs concerning Pego's whereabouts in scene I suggest imperfect excision (see also Berry ed., *BBA*, p.8). There are half-lines at lines 9 and 662 where Greg suspected cuts.

K **SPEECH LENGTH:** 9 speeches over 14 lines (highest totals: 18, 21, 22); 41 speeches between 8 and 14 lines.

L **STYLISTIC SUMMARY:** Several unmetrical lines and a few *non sequitur*s, but the overall style is competent, the imagery vigorous, and plot explanations (in the complicated comic disguise plot) lucid. Some verse is printed as prose.

M **UNCONFORMITIES:** Several plot confusions and ambiguities: the murder of Doricles, the 'arborisation' of Dion, and the foreign invasion are unmotivated and unexplained. They are connected with the politics of the sketchy main plot, but the connections are not made plain. Aspasia and Aegiale vanish from the plot before the end of the play without explanation.

N STAGING AND PROPS: Upper stage (354). Props include: a jewel, picture, banquet, goblets for drinking, drum and ensign, 500 crowns, diamonds, pearls, bill, crowns of enemy Kings. Cleanthes' disguises are effected by distinctive costumes and props, noted in the text: patch, nose, velvet gown, pistol.

O LENGTH: Total length: 1,611/Length of dialogue: 1,562 lines.

P STAGE DIRECTIONS/SPEECH PREFIXES: SDS are precise (*'Enter three Lordes'*: 524), often identifying props and sounds (e.g. *'Exit with a sownd of Horns'*: 512; *'Enter* Leon *with his sworde'*: 513) and attentive to blocking (*'Enter* Leon *and* Druso *following him'*: 918; see also 374 and 1428). Some SDS are imperative (*'Offer to goe out'*: 978; 'Count *knocke within'*: 1020). Chapman's *An Humorous Day's Mirth* (1599, apparently printed from an authorial MS) has similarly explicit SDS, identifying props, sounds, and stage movement (e.g. *'Enter her husband behind her'*: 656; *'Enter the King and all the lords with the Trumpets'*: 768) although others are expansively vague (e.g. *'all the rest'*: 801). In *BBA* the SP *Euge.* at 837 seems to be a conflation of Eu./Ge (abbreviations for Euribates (cf. 790) and Gentleman (cf. *Gen.* at 736)), suggesting authorial indecision or conflation. SPS are often omitted when a character speaks immediately following a SD for entry (e.g. 355, 1021, 1336, 1368, 1391, 1531).

Q VESTIGIAL CHARACTERS: References to the deaths of Cleanthes' friends Acates and Acanthes at 1416 and 1419 suggest that they once had roles in play? However, the references, *qua* references, serve an important role, showing that Cleanthes – whose attitude to the action is otherwise very casual – can grieve.

R OTHER OBSERVATIONS: *BBA* was performed at the Rose in February 1595/6 ('ne'), and received 22 recorded performances during its run; the play was revived in 1601 when Henslowe paid for new costumes. There are 6 quotations from 'Irus' (i.e. *BBA*) in Edward Pudsey's commonplace book in the Bodleian. 5 provide variant readings; the sixth is not in the extant text of *BBA*. The punctuation in Q is often chaotic, perhaps suggesting the printer's desperate attempts to make sense of confused or illegible MS copy. *An Humorous Day's Mirth* (like *BBA*, a 'humours' comedy, with slightly drawn figures and prominent comic plot) is 372 lines longer than *BBA*; if *BBA* is cut, *HDM* may shed light on *BBA*'s original complete structure. Much of the verse in *HDM* is printed as prose.

s **PREVIOUS VERDICTS**: Cut and possibly memorially reconstructed text (Greg (1929) ed., *BBA*, p.vi); 'mutilated' text with cuts probably made by actors not Chapman (Parrott ed., *Plays of George Chapman*, vol.II, pp.673–5); an authorial script based on an already 'mutilated' Italian *commedia dell'arte* in which the romantic plot has been cut down and the comic plot expanded (Kaufman, 'The *BBA*'); a deliberate burlesque of Marlowe: the play, 'though probably marred by those who played and published it, is nevertheless a good deal closer to what Chapman wrote than many scholars. . .have hitherto supposed' (Rees, 'Chapman's *Blind Beggar*, p.63); a reported text (Berry ed., *BBA*, p.9).

T **CONCLUSION**: Not MR, but the repetitions are an unexpected stylistic trait in an otherwise competent Poem (cf. *Mucedorus*, table xxv).

TABLE IV *1 Contention*

A PLAY/TEXT USED: *1 Contention* (1594)/Allen and Muir facsimile (1981).

B SR/Q DATES: 12 March 1594 to Thomas Millington/Q1 1594, Q2 1600, Q3 1619 (*2H6*: F 1623).

C PRINTER/PUBLISHER: Thomas Creede/Thomas Millington.

D AUTHOR/COMPANY: William Shakespeare/usually associated with Pembroke's Men.

E EXTERNAL ECHOES: No. The alleged echoes from other plays, cited by Hattaway and Rasmussen (in Hattaway ed., *2H6*, pp.237–41) are not convincing.

F INTERNAL REPETITIONS: A4r,30–1/D4r,3–4.

G FORMULAE: The exit line 'Come let's go' is used 7 times; there is a notable preference for the adjective 'sweet' coupled with a vocative name.

H INSERTIONS: Not detectable.

I EXPANDED CLOWN'S ROLE: No.

J OMISSIONS: Not detectable

K SPEECH LENGTH: 13 speeches over 14 lines (highest totals: 20, 24, 27); 29 speeches between 8 and 14 lines.

L STYLISTIC SUMMARY: Very good. Scene 6 differs stylistically from the rest of the Poem, being abrupt and jerky until Warwick's last speech.

M UNCONFORMITIES: There is a major error in York's pedigree in scene 6 which renders the conflict for the throne otiose, since York's claim is so clearly (albeit inaccurately) *right*.

N STAGING AND PROPS: Trapdoor; two stage doors; upper acting area with direct entrance off, as well as access from the stage; curtained area to conceal a bed. Props include: articles, petitions, glove, hawk, chair, stool, bed, drink and drinking vessels, drums, trumpets, 2 staffs with sandbags attached, white sheet with verses pinned to it, wax candle, bills, halberd, weapons, long staves, Duke of Suffolk's head, London stone (?G1v,9), heads of Lord Say and Sir James Cramer on 2 poles, halters, herbs, head of Jack Cade, sign of the Castle in St Albans, tent (this may be the same as the curtained inner area). Off-stage sound effects include: cannon, chambers, thunder and lightning.

O LENGTH: Total length: 2,219/Length of dialogue: 1,977 lines.

P **STAGE DIRECTIONS**: Very detailed SDs, with careful attention to stage action, character relationships, and attitude: e.g. '*Exet* King, Queene, and Suffolke, and Duke / Humphrey staies all the rest' (A3r,19–20); 'Enter...Dame *Ellanor, / Cobham* his wife' (A4v,18–19); 'Enter the Duke of *Suffolke* with the Queene, and they / take him for Duke *Humphrey*, and giues / him their writings' (B2r,12–14); 'Enter King *Henry*, and the Duke of *Yorke* and the Duke of *So- / merset* on both sides of the King, whispering with him' (B3r,12–13). Several SDs have a narrative flavour, beginning with 'Then' [such-and-such happens]: see, for example, E2r,19, 21, 31. SDs are occasionally indeterminate and permissive ('Enter one or two': B2v,5). One SD anticipates action 2 lines later, where it has a separate SD: 'The Queene lets fall her gloue, and hits the Duches of / *Gloster*, a boxe on the eare' (B4r,12–13; line 15 reads 'She strikes her').

Q **VESTIGIAL CHARACTERS**: No.

R **OTHER OBSERVATIONS**: The text is very sensitive theatrically (see the number of occasions on which Jane Howell's BBC *2 Henry 6* adopts readings and action from *1 Contention*: e.g. B2r,30–2; C2r,13–18; F2v,13). The play requires a cast of at least 20 (12 men, 3 boys, and 5 supernumeraries).

S **PREVIOUS VERDICTS**: MR with access to written material (Alexander, 'II Henry VI', and *Shakespeare's 'Henry VI'*); abridged and reported version of F text (Doran, *Henry VI*); MR made while the London production was still in the reporter's mind (Montgomery, 'The Original Staging'); authorial draft (Urkowitz, '"If I Mistake"'); 'an abridged and corrupt version of Shakespeare's Henry VI, pt.2' (STC 26099); an acting version (Clare, *'Art Made Tongue-tied'*, p.42); MR of a (lost) intermediate abridgement of a Folio-linked script (Irace, *Reforming the 'Bad' Quartos*, pp.124–5); not MR: authorial version by Marlowe (Merriam and Matthews, 'Neural Computation').

T **CONCLUSION**: Not MR.

TABLE V *The Death of Robert, Earl of Huntingdon*

A **PLAY/TEXT USED:** *The Death of Robert, Earl of Huntingdon* (1601)/MSR (1967 for 1965).

B **SR/Q DATES:** 1 December 1600 to William Leak/Q1 1601.

C **PRINTER/PUBLISHER:** Richard Bradock/William Leak.

D **AUTHOR/COMPANY:** Anthony Munday and Henry Chettle/Admiral's Men.

E **EXTERNAL ECHOES:** No.

F **INTERNAL REPETITIONS:** No.

G **FORMULAE:** No.

H **INSERTIONS:** Not detectable.

I **EXPANDED CLOWN'S ROLE:** No.

J **OMISSIONS:** Not detectable.

K **SPEECH LENGTH:** 27 speeches over 14 lines (highest totals: 35, 36, 37); 50 speeches between 8 and 14 lines.

L **STYLISTIC SUMMARY:** Stylistic quality is very good. Speeches are long, well developed, and sustain argument and metaphor. A clear break in plot material is signalled at 861–3; the drama has the material of two plays, although the disjunction is skilfully covered with a 'behind-the-scenes' scene (864–924). The dialogue at 296–309 seems rather clumsy, although it could be villainously comic in effect.

M **UNCONFORMITIES:** Much confusion stems from uncertainty or change of mind about character names, presence, and function. Scene 6 brings on *Salsbury* in a SD (994), but SPS designate him as both 'Sal(s)' and 'Old Anb' (*sic* for 'Old Aub'), while in dialogue he is 'Oxford' (1039); at 1068 he enters as 'Oxford' (SD), but SPS call him 'Sal(s)'. Clearly, there is indecision as to whether he should be Aubrey de Vere, the Earl of Oxford, or Salisbury. Winchester and Chester are confused (both enter at 1527, but they are seemingly intended to be one and the same: see 1578–9). In dialogue, Hubert's son is called 'Hugh' (1175) and 'Moubray' (1181), and appears in SP as both 'Mow'(1182 and subsequently) and 'Hu' (1184, 1187). Confusions also surround the relationships between Fitzwater and his male kinsman, Bruce (variously his son, cousin, and nephew); this confusion is linked to another confusion, the whereabouts of Lord Bruce's two sons (one is/both are at Guildford).

N **STAGING AND PROPS**: Upper stage, curtained recess, 2 doors. Props include: windhorns, bows and arrows, stag's head, purse, flowers, cup, towel, bier, primer and beads, swords, cross, chair, book, mask, bottle of poison, drum, fife, white pennant with *Amoris, Castitatis, & Honoris honos* written in gold, 2 white tapers.

O **LENGTH**: Total length: 3,053/Length of dialogue: 2,893 lines.

P **STAGE DIRECTIONS/SPEECH PREFIXES**: SDs are very detailed, with much specification of action, e.g. '*Marian* kneeles downe': 507; 'She vnwilling, *Iohn* roughly puls her': 1346; 'Matilda taken, led by the haire by / two Souldiers': 1715–16; 'First turns to the Monke, then to the Abbesse': 2508. Props are indicated (e.g. 457, 518, 2403). Many SDs are imperative, and one is permissive: 'Enter, or aboue' (1570; 'above' scenes are used elsewhere so this choice is not a question of uncertain facilities). Two SDs use Latin (excluding the familiar *solus* and *Exit*), 'cum suis' (1449), and 'cum Bruse' (1765). One SD indicates the mimetic: 'Hee seemes to locke a doore' (1921). Bonvile is mute in scene 6 (994ff.; see Vestigial Characters); Hubert, who is not included in the SD at 994, seems to take over Bonvile's role. For further discrepancies in SDs and SPs see Unconformities, above.

Q **VESTIGIAL CHARACTERS**: Lester is mute in scene 4 (331ff.); Bonvile is mute in scene 6 (994ff.) and disappears from the play thereafter. Loreis is a ghost in scene 6 (and appears nowhere else).

R **OTHER OBSERVATIONS**: Philip Henslowe paid Munday and Chettle for a second part of Robin Hood (clearly *The Death of Robert, Earl of Huntingdon*) on 20, 25, 28 February [and probably 8 March] 1598.

S **PREVIOUS VERDICTS**: 'probably a bad quarto' (Honigmann ed., *King John*, p.175, n.3); 'a draft in which the retouchings required for the finished book are not yet present' (Meagher ed., *Death*, p.viii).

T **CONCLUSION**: Not MR.

TABLE VI *Doctor Faustus*

A PLAY/TEXT USED: *Doctor Faustus* (1604)/TFT (1914).

B SR/Q DATES: 7 January 1601 to Thomas Bushell; transferred to John Wright 13 September 1610/Q1 1604, Q2 1609, Q3 1611. (B-text: Q1 1616, Q2 1619, Q3 1620).

C PRINTER/PUBLISHER: Valentine Simmes/Thomas Bushell.

D AUTHOR/COMPANY: Christopher Marlowe and collaborator(s)/ Admiral's Men.

E EXTERNAL ECHOES: No. On the possibly deliberate use (by an author) of the alleged echoes from *A Looking Glass for London and England* see Kuriyama, 'Dr Greg and *Doctor Faustus*'; for variant discussion see Gill, '*Doctor Faustus*: The Textual Problem'.

F INTERNAL REPETITIONS: No.

G FORMULAE: Moderately frequent use of 'tut' and 'tush' (sometimes extra-metrical); the adjective 'sweet' is used 23 times.

H INSERTIONS: The reference to Doctor Lopez (who achieved notoriety in February 1594) on E2r suggests that this is a topical reference post-dating the original composition of the play.

I EXPANDED CLOWN'S ROLE: No.

J OMISSIONS: Not detectable.

K SPEECH LENGTH: 14 speeches over 14 lines (highest totals: 41, 57, 66); 21 speeches between 8 and 14 lines.

L STYLISTIC SUMMARY: Generally very good.

M UNCONFORMITIES: Mephastophilis tells Faustus that he (Mephastophilis) does not appear as a result of Faustus' conjuring (B2r), yet later expresses irritation at his enforced departure from Constantinople because of Robin's conjuring (D4r). One comic scene (scene 9, D3r–D3v) and one chorus (D2v–D3r) are misplaced; Keefer (ed., *DrF*), and Bevington and Rasmussen (eds., *DrF*) insert the former at C2v,19, and the latter at D4r,24). The comic scene 10 has duplicate endings (D3v–D4r).

N STAGING AND PROPS: 'Study' (inner stage?: A2v, B4r). Props include: a chafer of coals, crowns, rich apparel, fireworks and squibs, banquet, books, a pair of horns, chair, false leg, grapes, dagger, silver goblet. Sound effects include: the striking of a clock, thunder and lightning.

o LENGTH: Total length: 1,517/Length of dialogue: 1,450 lines.

p STAGE DIRECTIONS/SPEECH PREFIXES: SDs are careful, competent, and varied. Some are permissive:' *Enter Faustus with two or three Schollers*' (E3v); some are imperative:'*Turne to them*' (C2v), '*Snatch it*' (D2r); some are purposeful:'*Enter Faustus to coniure*' (B1r), '*Enter all the Friers to sing the Dirge*' (D2v). SDs provide for stage action ('*the clowne runnes vp / and downe crying*' (B3v), '*Mepha. giues / him a dagger*' (E4r). Several SDs are in RH margin (a position copied from the playbook?).

q VESTIGIAL CHARACTERS: No.

r OTHER OBSERVATIONS: On 22 November 1602 Philip Henslowe paid William Bird and Samuel Rowley £4 for 'adicyones in docter fostes'.

s PREVIOUS VERDICTS: MR (Kirschbaum, 'The Good and Bad Quartos', and ed., *The Plays of Christopher Marlowe*; Greg (1950), *Marlowe's 'Doctor Faustus'*; Bowers, 'The Text of Marlowe's *Faustus*', and ed., *Marlowe*, vol.II; Ormerod and Wortham eds., *DrF*); a version of the play that was performed in 1594 (Gill ed., *The Complete Works* vol.II, p.xvii); authorial MS 'composed of interleaved scenes by two dramatists' (Bevington and Rasmussen eds., *DrF*, p.64).

t CONCLUSION: Not MR.

TABLE VII *Edward I*

A **PLAY/TEXT USED**: *Edward I* (1593)/MSR (1911).

B **SR/Q DATES**: 8 October 1593 to Abel Jeffes; assigned to William White 13 August 1599/Q1 1593, Q2 1599.

C **PRINTER/PUBLISHER**: Abel Jeffes, to be sold by William Barley.

D **AUTHOR/COMPANY**: George Peele/Admiral's Men? (See Other Observations, below).

E **EXTERNAL ECHOES**: No.

F **INTERNAL REPETITIONS**: 2238–41/2952–4.

G **FORMULAE**: No.

H **INSERTIONS**: Some of the Unconformities listed below (and under SDs) may be misplaced insertions: see, e.g., 763–84, 1122–37, 1724ff., 2964.

I **EXPANDED CLOWN'S ROLE**: No.

J **OMISSIONS**: A line is missing between 562 and 563 (the rhyme is repeated correctly at 572–6).

K **SPEECH LENGTH**: 22 speeches over 14 lines (highest totals: 34, 41, 66); 64 speeches between 8 and 14 lines.

L **STYLISTIC SUMMARY**: Speeches are very good (e.g. 5–45, 74–116), although they sometimes seem to be unmotivated/misplaced (see Unconformities below).

M **UNCONFORMITIES**: Lines 725–7, a paean to Elinor, occur in the middle of an address by Edward to his nobles and seem an odd interruption. '*Queene Elinors speeche*' at 763-84 has no connection with the Queen's preceding 4 lines and little with Edward's following speech. Joan's speech at 1138 has lost its opening (it begins with a subordinate clause). In scene 16 Elinor poisons the Mayoress of London and expresses satisfaction at her act of revenge. This incident is inadequately motivated in the text as it stands; the two meet in scene 3 where the Mayoress is surprisingly dismayed (828–9), and by scene 16 the Mayoress appears as part of the Queen's entourage (2316–19). The characterisation of Elinor is inconsistent: she is both angelic and villainous. The Scottish election is inadequately connected to the main narrative. Rice is included in Edward's entourage at 1819 although he is on Lluellen's side and an enemy to Edward. Reference is made to Elinor's incest at 1869 although the Queen does not reveal her sin publicly until 2747–56. 2567 introduces a messenger to announce '*that Dauid shall be hangd*' yet no such announcement is ever made. Edward's final speech refers to the offstage actions of 2 characters who are dead.

N **STAGING AND PROPS**: Upper stage; inner recess (with canopy; the recess may also function as the 'tent'); trapdoor; doors (for gates). Props and effects include: trumpets, headpieces with garlands, one headpiece with garland and plumes, ensign, swords and bucklers, pikestaff, harp, letters, gold diadem, hot pincers, litter and ladder, Royal bed, baby, cradle, dice, neck halter, lantern, hurdle (on wheels/rollers), Lluellen's head, spear, torches. Possibly also: potter's tools (scene 8). Sound effects include: thunder and lightning.

O **LENGTH**: Total length: 2,977/Length of dialogue: 2,771 lines.

P **STAGE DIRECTIONS/SPEECH PREFIXES**: SDs are inadequate in entrances and exits throughout: Richard has no entrance at 343, the novice must return at 400, the Friar exits at 604 but there is no indication of when he and the novice (who speaks at 610) re-enter. Elinor, Glocester and Joan must enter at 808; Joan must exit at 832; Elinor must enter at 1264. '*Exeunt ambo*' at 1537 seems to refer to the exit of 4 characters. SDs are frequently narrative in their provision of action and blocking: '*the king sitteth in the middest mounted / highest, and at his feete the Ensigne vnderneath him*' (118–19); '*Then Lluellen spieth Elinor and Mortimor, / and saieth thus*' (1013–14). Several SDs appear as headings: '*Queene Elinors speeche*' (763); '*Busling on both sides*' (2016); '*Gloster solus*' (2958). Others are indefinite, permissive: '*Enter.../ ... others as many as may be*' (50–1); '*Here let the Potters wife goe to the Queen*' (2544). Several SDs indicate purpose: '*Enter Iack and the Harper getting a standing / against the Queene comes in*' (1100–1); '*Enter the Nouice and his company to giue the / Queene Musicke at her Tent*' (1897–8). One SD is imperative: '*Make as if yee would fight*' (467), and one is anticipatory: '*Enter Lluellen running out before, and Dauid with a / halter ready to hang himselfe*' (2347–8; David then enters at 2358: '*Enter Dauid*'). SPs fluctuate onomastically: King Edward is both '*Edw[ard].*' (132) and '*Longsh[anks].*' (58) on his first appearance; the 2 forms co-exist subsequently, and a 3rd SP '*King.*' is added at 2707. Similar juxtaposition affects the SDs where Edward is '*Edward*' (131), '*king Edward*' (684), '*Longshank[e]s*' (51–2, 900), '*Edward Longshankes*' (1190), and '*The King*' (2098).

Q   VESTIGIAL CHARACTERS: '*Mary Dutches of Lancaster*' is included as an
attendant in the Queen's nursery at 1597–8. She does not appear
elsewhere and, as Bullen (quoting P. A. Daniel) points out, neither of
Lancaster's 2 wives was named Mary (Bullen ed., *The Works of Peele*
vol.1, p.154, n.1). '*Charles de Moumfort*', mentioned in the SD at 54,
features nowhere else.

R   OTHER OBSERVATIONS: Large cast required: 26 men and 4 boys or 17
men and 13 boys or something in between depending on whether the 9
pages (mute) attending on the 9 lords of Scotland (also mute) at 683 are
played by men and/or boys. Texts for the many songs in the play are not
provided (400, 681–2, 1368–9, 1453, 1907, 2395). One SD specifies the tune:
'*Enter the Harper, and sing to the tune of Who list / to lead a Souldiers life*'
(495–6; a reporter would surely have reproduced the lines he had heard
sung. See Ashe, 'The Text of Peele's *Edward 1*'). L3v contains a colophon
'*Yours. By George Peele Maister of Artes in Oxenford*'. Similar *explicits* can
be found in a holograph letter from Peele to Burghley, 17 January 1595
(BL MS Lansd. 99 art 54), and the title page of Peele's *Anglorum Feriae*
(BL Add. MS 21432). A play called *long shancke* appears in Henslowe's
Diary, 29 August 1595, owned by the Admiral's Men and indicated as
'ne'. Unconformities similar to those in *Ed1* feature in Peele's *David and
Bethsabe*.

S   PREVIOUS VERDICTS: 'a very corrupt text' (Greg (1911) ed., *Ed1*, p.v); a
'bad quarto' (Kirschbaum, 'A Census', p.36); 'the most mutilated'
Elizabethan play extant (Purcell, *George Peele*, p.51); authorial draft,
revised for a provincial audience (Ashe, 'The Text', p.168); authorial
version of the *long shancke* recorded by Henslowe (Hook ed., *Ed1*, p.45).

T   CONCLUSION: Not MR.

TABLE VIII *Fair Em, the Miller's Daughter of Manchester*

A   PLAY/TEXT USED: *Fair Em* (no date)/MSR (1928 for 1927).

B   SR/Q DATES: NE/Q1 undated (STC: 1591? See MSR, p.vi).

C   PRINTER/PUBLISHER: John Danter/Thomas Newman and John Winnington.

D   AUTHOR/COMPANY: Anon./Strange's Men.

E   EXTERNAL ECHOES: No.

F   INTERNAL REPETITIONS: 1151–2/1214–16.

G   FORMULAE: No.

H   INSERTIONS: Two references to Sir Edmund Trafford (101, 1529), a Lancashire nobleman, suggested to Thaler ('*Faire Em*') that the play was prepared for performance (in Lancashire?) in the presence of the Traffords and their friends the Stanleys (Henry, Earl of Derby and his son, Lord Strange. Cf. Author/Company above).

I   EXPANDED CLOWN'S ROLE: No.

J   OMISSIONS: Manville, an important character, is surprisingly silent in scene 1. See also Unconformities below.

K   SPEECH LENGTH: 11 speeches over 14 lines (highest totals: 20, 22, 42); 34 speeches between 8 and 14 lines.

L   STYLISTIC SUMMARY: Very good throughout. Occasional fourteeners and sixteeners among iambic pentameters.

M   UNCONFORMITIES: Scene 13 (1042ff.) introduces the seemingly otiose news of civil war between the two Regents appointed by William in scene 1; this news seems irrelevant/confusing unless it is a remnant of a larger political plot. In scene 17 Dirot guards Blanche, although when last seen he was at war with Demarch: 'Clearly they have made up in order to repel the Danish invasion, but no sign of that action appears' (Henning ed., *Fair Em*, p.27). Sir Thomas Goddard is given scant attention, although Valingford – one of the enemy who has necessitated Goddard's disguise – introduces him in scene 17 (1523–5) as if he had known his true identity all along. Given that so much is made of Em's being 'too fine' to be a miller's daughter, this revelation of identity is oddly casual. The gratuitous dismissal of both armies in the final scene (Henning, p.21: 'there is no reason for either king to suppose that the outcome of their meeting will not be war') suggests a company lacking the numbers and/or military paraphernalia to stage an encounter.

N STAGING AND PROPS: 2 entrance doors. Props include: portrait painted on shield, kerchief, receptacle for urine sample, rapiers, mask for Blanche, drums and trumpets, military apparel, jewel.

O LENGTH: Total length: 1,546/Length of dialogue: 1,479 lines.

P STAGE DIRECTIONS/SPEECH PREFIXES: SDs are very attentive to props and action, indicating gestures, asides, interruptions, off-stage noise, stage choreography, costume, mood, purpose, and relationships (*passim*: see, e.g. *'Here they must call for their gryst within'* (185); *'Blanch speaketh this secretly at one end of the stage'* (235); *'Here he offers to kisse her'* (373); *'Exit in a rage'* (451); *'Here Em cuts him off'* (485); *'He thrusts Em vpon her father'* (926). Several SDs in the RH margin or placed right of centre suggest that the underlying MS was prepared for use as a playbook. Frequent use of 'Here' formula, and of 'to them' formula. The King of Denmark (*'King Den.'* and variants from scene 3) is identified in SPs as *'Zweno K.'* and *'Zweno'* from scene 12 onwards. Henning observes that unmarked entrances and exits increase towards the end of the play.

Q VESTIGIAL CHARACTERS: No.

R OTHER OBSERVATIONS: *Fair Em* was ridiculed by Greene (but not by name) in 'To the Gentlemen Students' in *Farewell to Folly* (SR 11 June 1587, Q 1591).

S PREVIOUS VERDICTS: Abridgement, with some additional factor operative in the second half, but not memorially reconstructed (Greg (1928) ed., *Fair Em*, pp.ix–x); 'as mangled a bad quarto as can be found' (Kirschbaum, 'A Census', p.38); memorial reconstruction and abridgement (Ashe, thesis 'A Survey', p.85; Henning ed., *Fair Em*).

T CONCLUSION: Not MR.

TABLE IX *The Fair Maid of Bristow*

A **PLAY/TEXT USED:** *The Fair Maid of Bristow* (1605)/TFT (1912).

B **SR/Q DATE:** 8 February 1605 to Thomas Pavier/Q 1605.

C **PRINTER/PUBLISHER:** William Jaggard/Thomas Pavier.

D **AUTHOR/COMPANY:** Anon./King's Men.

E **EXTERNAL ECHOES:** No.

F **INTERNAL REPETITIONS:** E4v,13–14/F1r,22–3.

G **FORMULAE:** Possibly paraphrase at C2r,14/C2v,5; formulaic repetitions at A4r,19–20/27–8; E1r,4–5/E1v,8/E1v,27. Florence uses formulaic oaths extensively (7 times) in scene 9 (C1v,23, 26, 30; C2r,2, 11, 19; C2v,23).

H **INSERTIONS:** Not detectable.

I **EXPANDED CLOWN'S ROLE:** No.

J **OMISSIONS:** The SD at C3r,25 ('The drunken mirth') indicates an episode for which dialogue is missing or which is to be performed extempore. (However, it is hard to see how it can fit in with either the preceding or the following scenes. It seems more appropriate to the wedding scene (scene 7), perhaps just before Sir Eustace's odd (drunken?) speech at B2v,32–B3r,5.) Some explanation of Anabell's predicament (for the benefit of King Richard who is to adjudicate it and who seems unaccountably to know that there is a predicament: D3v,24) seems necessary at the beginning of scene 13.

K **SPEECH LENGTH:** 4 speeches over 14 lines (highest totals: 15, 18, 19); 27 speeches between 8 and 14 lines.

L **STYLISTIC SUMMARY:** Some speeches are notably good in the quality of imagery and/or emotion conveyed (e.g. Challener's psychological analysis at F1v,5–22). Mirror imagery is used dexterously throughout the play; thus, Annabell is a true mirror of virtue at A2r,7 whereas Florence is a harlot who makes promises of 'brittle glasse' (E3r,12; see also F1v,27–8, C4v,3, C4v,27). As a 'prodigal son' drama the play makes sustained use of the patient Griselda theme and the mercy/punishment topos. There is some unmetrical verse (e.g. E4v,1–7, E4r,14–15, D1v,1, D4v,3–6).

M **UNCONFORMITIES:** The dénouement occupies one-third of the play: King Richard returns from the Holy Land at TLN 868 (D3v) to be met by advocates for justice, and proceeds to adjudicate action which had reached its height barely 400–500 lines into the play. Unconformities seem highly concentrated in Act 3 (scenes 7–9/B2v–C3r): a double entry for Anabell at B2v,18 and B3r,11; much confusion in SPs on B3v–B4r; a missing scene on C3r; and an anomalously formulaic scene 9. On E2r,30 Harbart, in disguise as Blunt, is referred to as Harbart in dialogue, an odd slip since no-one yet knows Blunt's true identity. Sentlo has 2 lines to speak after he has been instructed to exit on B3v,18; his lines fit logically after B3r,30.

N   STAGING AND PROPS: 2 doors. Props include: weapons, letter, blood, masks, lights, purse with gold, scaffold.

O   LENGTH: Total length: 1,432/Length of dialogue: 1,334 lines.

P   STAGE DIRECTIONS/SPEECH PREFIXES: SDs are a mix of precision and ambiguity: costumes, mood, action and purpose are carefully indicated and described, but entrances and exits are often problematic, e.g. no entrance for Godfrey, Eustace, Anabell, Mother, Challener and Harbart on D3v. (See also Unconformities and Omission.) 'sentloe' is a mistake for 'Blunt' in the SD on C3r,24. SPs and SDs tend to refer to disguised characters by their disguise name (e.g. B3v). Character designations fluctuate in SDs and SPs: Sir Godfrey's wife, Ellen, enters as 'his wife' (A2r,27; A4r,30), 'Mother' (B2v,17) and 'the Mother' (C3v,8), speaking as 'Wom.' (A4v,28; B1r,4; B2v,29) and 'Mo.' (C3v,9, 12, 30; D4r,33). Sir Eustace and Sir Godfrey exit as 'the two old men' on C4v. There are a great number of errors in SPs (13 in all). 'Here' formula (7 times).

Q   VESTIGIAL CHARACTERS: Richmond and Lester, the King's attendants, are mutes in scenes 13 and 15 (although Anabell addresses them by name at E2v,17–18 and a King must be accompanied by nobles, whether named or not).

R   OTHER OBSERVATIONS: The play is printed in a worn-out black-letter font. Strong sense of abbreviation throughout.

S   PREVIOUS VERDICTS: Memorial reconstruction (Kirschbaum, 'The Fair Maid'); group reconstruction for performance in the provinces (Ashe, 'The Non-Shakespearean Bad Quartos'; A Survey).

T   CONCLUSION: Not MR.

TABLE X *The Famous Victories of Henry the Fifth*

A **PLAY/TEXT USED:** *The Famous Victories of Henry the Fifth* (1598)/TFT (1912).

B **SR/Q DATES:** SR 14 May 1594 to Thomas Creede/Q1 1598, Q2 1617.

C **PRINTER/PUBLISHER:** Thomas Creede/unknown.

D **AUTHOR/COMPANY:** Anon./Queen's Men.

E **EXTERNAL ECHOES:** No; however one line – c3r,8–9, a near-hexameter – resembles *The Old Wife's Tale* 813–14, the metre being more distinctive than the vocabulary. The line in *OWT* is a parody of Gabriel Harvey and has point in *OWT*, whose genre is deliberate stylistic arabesque. See Whitworth ed., *OWT*, note to line 640 and Marx, '"Soft, Who Have We Here?"'. Both *FV* and *OWT* are Queen's Men's plays.

F **INTERNAL REPETITIONS:** B1r,16–24 is repeated at B1v,33–5,B2r,1–6. A 6-line sequence on B3r, repeated immediately, is probably dittography by the printer. (Other apparent repetitions, 2 lines in length, contain little distinctive vocabulary and are defendable thematically. See Champion, '"What prerogatiues meanes"', pp.5, 7).

G **FORMULAE:** The Poem is heavily formulaic, especially in comic scenes and in the first half of the play: 'sounds' (18 times), 'Gogs wounds' (15 times), exclamatory 'Why' (43 times) and 'But' (30 times). Prince Henry is 'the young prince' (17 times); Henry 5 and Charles 6 are 'good brother of England/France' (11 times). Prince Henry has a tendency to preface statements with 'Belike' or 'Belike you' (5 times), even when this renders dialogue banal or nonsensical (as, for instance, at B4r,3 and F1r,1–2). 'Faith' ('yfaith', 'in faith') and 'marry' are also used very frequently.

H **INSERTIONS:** Not detectable.

I **EXPANDED CLOWN'S ROLE:** The clowns' roles are prominent and thematically important (see Champion, '"What prerogatiues meanes"') but they do not seem gratuitously expanded.

J **OMISSIONS:** Not detectable.

K **SPEECH LENGTH:** 8 speeches over 14 lines (highest totals: 21, 23, 32); 22 speeches between 8 and 14 lines.

L **STYLISTIC SUMMARY:** Uniformly poor with many staccato speeches, although Katherine of France is fluent and articulate in English, and the political material is also smooth. The comic scenes are verbally abrupt although their thematic relevance as 'ironic counterpointing' is always clear (see Champion, '"What prerogatiues meanes"', pp.5–14). The play is flatly prosaic, colloquial and heavily formulaic; it is prose throughout. There is an especial concentration of formulae in the Henry 4 portion.

M UNCONFORMITIES: *Non sequitur* at D3r,31–3.

N STAGING AND PROPS: Curtained chair or recess. Props include: dagger, crown, cloak of eyelets, 'a Tunne of Tennis balles', potlid, drum and trumpets, shoes and apparel for looters, sword, weapons.

O LENGTH: Total length: 1,710/Length of dialogue: 1,580 lines.

P STAGE DIRECTIONS/SPEECH PREFIXES: SDs refer to Prince Henry as 'the young prince', an epithet reiterated frequently in the dialogue; however, he is 'Henry the fifth' in SPs from the first line of the play (i.e. long before he is King). SDs specify action: a box on the ear (B3v), exit and instant re-entry (B4v), weeping (C2r, C2v, D4v), sleeping (C3v), dying (D1r), beating (D4v), kneeling (F1v), roaming (F2r and v) and roving (F4v), coward's trick (F2v), running away (F2v), asides (F4r), kissing (G2r). Despite such specificity, there are several confusions: on A2v–A3r the King's receivers enter as 'two Receiuers' but exit as one 'Purseuant'; on B3v 'Exeunt the Theefe' should be 'Exeunt Ned and Tom'; on B4r 'Enter Dericke and Iohn Cobler' should be 'Manent. . .'; at D4v,21 a SD is presented as part of the dialogue. On F1r the battle of Agincourt is given the single line 'The Battell'.

Q VESTIGIAL CHARACTERS: No. (The Dolphin is mute throughout even although he is addressed. In scene 19 he is asked to swear allegiance to England; a SD tells us that he kisses the sword (G2r,23) although he remains silent. See Other Observations below.)

R OTHER OBSERVATIONS: Despite its poor verbal quality and abrupt and jerky action, the play has much in common with other Queen's Men's plays of the 1590s (cf. McMillin, 'The Queen's Men'. The Queen's Men split in two for touring in the early 1590s: see Pinciss, 'The Queen's Men'.) *FV* especially merits comparison with *TTR3*: the staging demands and SDs are similar (i.e. the death of the respective Kings in a curtained recess, and the discrepancy between designations in SD and SP for the respective heir to the throne); however, the verbal quality is totally different. Contemporary references: 1) *Tarlton's Jests* (1637) tells how the Queen's Men's clown, Tarlton, doubled the roles of the Lord

Chief Justice with that of Dericke in a version of *FV*. Doubling of these roles is not possible in the extant *FV* text. 2) Thomas Nashe in *Pierce Penilesse* (1592) refers to recent performances of a Henry 5 play in which the Dauphin swears fealty to the English King. This episode is not in *FV* as it stands although there is an indication that it might have been: see G2r,22–3 (and Vestigial Characters above). Sequence of short but dramatically varied and coherent episodes in abrupt dialogue suggests that someone knew the order of events but not the dialogue which should accompany them.

s **PREVIOUS VERDICTS**: 'a bad quarto, if ever there was one' (Price, 'Towards a Scientific Method', p.163); MR (Walter ed., *H5*, p.xxxvii).

T **CONCLUSION**: Probably MR, at least in the first half.

TABLE XI *George a Greene*

A **PLAY/TEXT USED:** *George a Greene* (1599)/MSR (1911).

B **SR/Q DATES:** 1 April 1595 to Cuthbert Burby/1599.

C **PRINTER/PUBLISHER:** Simon Stafford/Cuthbert Burby.

D **AUTHOR/COMPANY:** Anon. (Robert Greene?)/Sussex's.

E **EXTERNAL ECHOES:** No.

F **INTERNAL REPETITIONS:** A mix of repetition and paraphrase: 607–11/1097–1102.

G **FORMULAE:** No.

H **INSERTIONS:** No.

I **EXPANDED CLOWN'S ROLE:** No. In fact, one wonders if the Musgrove plot was meant to be comic. Two references to old Musgrove being over 100 (185, 837) suggest that this is not a numerical error. The old man's obstinacy in the face of Cuddy's attempt to persuade him to lay down arms (scene 3) has comic scope, and King James's defeat at the hands of a centenarian could be similarly amusing.

J **OMISSIONS:** A battle scene may have been cut at line 366. See also Unconformities below.

K **SPEECH LENGTH:** 3 speeches over 14 lines (highest totals: 15, 16, 20); 20 speeches between 8 and 14 lines.

L **STYLISTIC SUMMARY:** Much metrical disruption (e.g. 48–9, 334–6, 633–5, 810–12). Jerky verse and abrupt style throughout, with staccato exchanges. Most prose is printed as verse.

M **UNCONFORMITIES:** The role of the King of Scots as wooer (scene 5) is given more prominence than his political role (see 16–17, 1321–31). The conciliatory ending to the Jane a Barley episode (377–8) implies that a more sustained assault, either on Jane's honour or on her castle, has preceded. The Robin Hood episodes (scenes 10, 12) seem unhappily brief and inexpertly related to the rest of the plot; the shoemaker episode is also tamely episodic. The play seems to deteriorate in structural and verbal quality towards the end.

N **STAGING AND PROPS:** Door, upper stage, trapdoor (?795). Props include: walking staves, shoemaker's tools, swords, dagger, King's garments, commission, wax seals, horn, stand of ale, willow wreath, a gown given to Jenkin, purse, gift from Old Musgrove to King Edward, Ned's bow and arrow.

o **LENGTH:** Total length: 1,341/Length of dialogue: 1,265 lines.

p **STAGE DIRECTIONS/SPEECH PREFIXES:** SDs are attentive to disguises, stage action, relationships (e.g. '*George strikes him*': 528; '*Wily, disguised/ like a woman*': 612–13), sometimes with a narrative flavour: '*Enter a Shoomaker sitting vpon the stage / at worke, Ienkin to him*' (971–2). 'To' formula (613, 659, 972). The SD at 795 is unclear: '*He throwes the ground in, and she comes out*'; this is possibly a reference to a trapdoor, a recess, or a property rock/cave since Jenkin is pretending to conjure up Bettris whom he has concealed. Jenkins enters as '*the Clowne*' at 387 but has the SP '*Ienkin.*' (at 671 the SD calls him '*Ienkin the clowne*').

q **VESTIGIAL CHARACTERS:** Lord Humes is mute in scene 5 (although addressed at line 292), yet seems to be a character of some importance: Cuddy describes how he slew him (373). Three proper names (18, 454, 1178) may refer to actors (now unknown).

r **OTHER OBSERVATIONS:** Strong sense of abbreviation throughout.

s **PREVIOUS VERDICTS:** A 'maimed and deformed' memorial reconstruction (Kirschbaum, 'A Census', p.40); 'an abridgement' (Jenkins, 'Peele's *Old Wive's Tale*', p.180).

t **CONCLUSION:** Not MR.

TABLE XII *Hamlet*

A **PLAY/TEXT USED**: *Hamlet* (1603)/Scolar Press facsimile (1969).

B **SR/Q DATES**: 26 July 1602 to James Roberts/Q 1603 (Q2 version 1604–5, 1611; F 1623).

C **PRINTER/PUBLISHER**: Valentine Simmes/Nicholas Ling and John Trundell.

D **AUTHOR/COMPANY**: William Shakespeare/Chamberlain's–King's Men.

E **EXTERNAL ECHOES**: The oft-alleged echo of *Twelfth Night* (c2v,30; cf. *Twelfth Night* 2.4.118) is clearly a conventional saw (as the quotation marks in Q1 *Hamlet* further attest).

F **INTERNAL REPETITIONS**: No.

G **FORMULAE**: No.

H **INSERTIONS**: Not detectable.

I **EXPANDED CLOWN'S ROLE**: No.

J **OMISSIONS**: Not detectable.

K **SPEECH LENGTH**: 19 speeches over 14 lines (highest totals: 28, 30, 31); 38 speeches between 8 and 14 lines.

L **STYLISTIC SUMMARY**: Pedestrian. Speeches make good (if blunt) general sense, but often suffer from grammatical *non sequitur*s (particularly where antecedents seem missing) and jumbled line order (e.g. D1v,32–3; D4v,8–9, 29–32; F1v,23–5; H3r,15–18). Stylistically uneven text suggests the presence of two hands, and the second hand seems to have a moral agenda (e.g. G2r,1; G3r,24–5; I2r,32–3; I3v,5).

M **UNCONFORMITIES**: Two characters in the dumb show are King and Queen on first appearance but Duke and Duchess thereafter.

N **STAGING AND PROPS**: Trapdoor; possibly an inner stage (for the arras). Props include: drums, trumpets, swords, articles, letter, book, remembrances and tokens from Hamlet to Ophelia, arbour, poison in a vial, rapiers, lute, flowers and herbs, spades, skulls, coffin, daggers, goblets of wine.

O **LENGTH**: Total length: 2,220/Length of dialogue: 2,155 lines.

P **STAGE DIRECTIONS/SPEECH PREFIXES**: SDs are mostly adequate and careful. SDs often refer to characters generically, e.g. '*two Centinels*' (B1r,1); '*two Ambassadors*' (B3r,18; '*Gent.*' in SP and '*Cornelia*' and '*Voltemar*' in dialogue); '*a Bragart Gentleman*' (I2r,34). Entrances and exits are occasionally deficient. Horatio lacks an entrance on F2v, responding 'Heere my Lord' although Hamlet has not called him. SDs indicate action ('*hee kneeles*': G1v,17; '*Leartes leapes into the graue. . .Hamlet leapes / in after Leartes*': IIv,28, 30–1) and characters' appearance ('*Enter the ghost in his night gowne*': G2v,28; '*Enter Ofelia playing on a Lute, and her haire / downe singing*': G4v,27–8), and they also indicate blocking ('*Enter King and Queene, Leartes, and other lordes, / with a Priest after the coffin*': IIv,9–10).

Q **VESTIGIAL CHARACTERS**: Possibly an attempt to delete Barnardo from scene 2? He is not given an entrance and Hamlet does not greet him (although he does greet Horatio and Marcellus with whom Barnardo would obviously have entered). But Horatio twice refers to his watch with 'these Gentlemen' (i.e. Marcellus and another) and Hamlet's questions to the watchers are consistently answered by 'All'.

R **OTHER OBSERVATIONS**: –

S **PREVIOUS VERDICTS**: Abridgement (Burkhart, *Shakespeare's Bad Quartos*); memorial reconstruction (Jenkins ed., *Hamlet*); memorial reconstruction of abridged version (Edwards ed., *Hamlet*; Hibbard ed., *Hamlet*); authorial draft (Urkowitz, '"Well-sayd olde Mole"' and 'Back to Basics'); adaptation of memorially reconstructed version (Irace, 'Origins and Agents').

T **CONCLUSION**: Possibly MR, but if so, a very good one.

TABLE XIII *Henry 5*

A **PLAY/TEXT USED:** *Henry 5* (1600)/Shakespeare Quarto facsimile (1957).

B **SR/Q DATES:** 4 August 1600 to James Roberts (a 'staying' entry); 14 August 1600 to Thomas Pavier: 12 copies 'formerlye printed' including *The historye of Henrye the Vth*/Q1 1600, Q2 1602, Q 3 1619 (F version 1623).

C **PRINTER/PUBLISHER:** Thomas Creede/Thomas Millington and John Busby.

D **AUTHOR/COMPANY:** William Shakespeare/Chamberlain's Men.

E **EXTERNAL ECHOES:** No.

F **INTERNAL REPETITIONS:** No.

G **FORMULAE:** No (Nim's formulaically repetitive 'And there's the humor of it' is appropriate for a humours character).

H **INSERTIONS:** Not detectable.

I **EXPANDED CLOWN'S ROLE:** No.

J **OMISSIONS:** Not detectable.

K **SPEECH LENGTH:** 20 speeches over 14 lines (highest totals: 36, 37, 41); 27 speeches between 8 and 14 lines.

L **STYLISTIC SUMMARY:** Very good verbal texture: speeches are grammatically intact, smooth, and well developed. Stylistically homogeneous (unlike e.g. Q1 *Hamlet*), with the exception of the final scene which is very jerky.

M **UNCONFORMITIES:** On A2v,31 the 'Duke of *Lorain*' has not yet been mentioned and so cannot be 'foresaid'. On F2r the King has Gower summoned twice, first by a soldier and then by Flewellen; it is not clear why, or when, Gower has exited.

N **STAGING AND PROPS:** 2 doors. Props include: tennis balls, swords, rapiers, papers of commission, 2 gloves, hat, leek, crowns, a shilling.

O **LENGTH:** Total length: 1,721/Length of dialogue: 1,640 lines.

P **STAGE DIRECTIONS/SPEECH PREFIXES:** Often inadequate, ambiguous and contradictory, particularly regarding entrances and exits. For example, Pistol is included in the King's entourage at E3v,34. This is unexpected; however, he speaks at the end of the scene and there is no other place for him to enter. On C1r the French King enters with unspecified 'others' who seem to be Orleans, Berry, and possibly the Constable. Speaking characters often have no entry (e.g. Warwick should enter at E1v,11). The entrance for Gloster, Epingam (*sic*) and Attendants on E1r is manifestly wrong; it presumably belongs at the beginning of the scene. This same entry instructs the King to enter, although he is already on stage. The exit for Nim, Bardolfe and Pistol on c2v seems to be 10 lines too low (although if it is higher the Boy must have a separate exit). SDs sometimes designate characters generically but identify them precisely in SPs. Thus Gray, Cambridge, and Masham, identified as such in SPs, enter as '*three Lords*' (B2v–B3r); '*the foure French Lords*' who enter at E3r,13 have the SPs '*Ge.*', '*Const.*', '*Or.*' and '*Bur.*' (for Gebon, Constable, Orleans and Burbon).

Q VESTIGIAL CHARACTERS: Some mute or near-mute characters. Epingam (*sic*) is mute in scene 12; Clarence is silent on all but two occasions; Warwick speaks in scene 13 (although he has no entrance) yet has not previously been part of the King's entourage. See SDs below. Gebon, identified as part of the French party on D2v,7 is not known historically to be a French lord. (This is sometimes explained as being the name of an actor.)

R OTHER OBSERVATIONS: With the exception of the staccato language of the final scene, all the problems in this text stem from SDs and stage choreography. The impression is that the text is being/has been abridged, but SDs from the original version have been erroneously retained or incompletely adapted.

S PREVIOUS VERDICTS: Unauthorised stage adaptation (Okerlund, 'The Quarto Version'); abridgement (Burkhart, *Shakespeare's Bad Quartos*); MR of already abridged text (Hart, *Stolne and Surreptitious*; Taylor ed., *Henry 5*); MR and abridgement as part of a single process (Irace, 'Reconstruction and Adaptation'); a 'theatrical abridgement which has suffered some textual garbling in its passage from promptbook to printed text' (Patterson, 'Back by Popular Demand', p.40); MR of London version 'to provide a reading text of the play' (Craik ed., *Henry 5*, p.28); authorial draft (Berger, 'Seeking *Henry 5*').

T CONCLUSION: Not MR.

TABLE XIV *1 Hieronimo*

A **PLAY/TEXT USED:** *1 Hieronimo* (1605)/STC microfilm.

B **SR/Q DATES:** NE/Q 1605.

C **PRINTER/PUBLISHER:** William Jaggard/Thomas Pavier.

D **AUTHOR/COMPANY:** Kyd?/extant text probably comes from a boys' company; but see Henslowe's *Diary* 23 February–20 June 1592 and the Induction to Q 3 *The Malcontent* for previous owners.

E **EXTERNAL ECHOES:** No.

F **INTERNAL REPETITIONS:** A3r,16–17/33–4; D3v,4/13.

G **FORMULAE:** 'Andrea's gone ambassador' (and variations) appears 5 times: A3r,30/A3v,20/ B2r,12/ C1r,23/ E2r,17.

H **INSERTIONS:** Some extra-metrical phrases, e.g. A2r,27–8; A2v,9.

I **EXPANDED CLOWN'S ROLE:** The whole play is oriented towards comedy.

J **OMISSIONS:** Not detectable.

K **SPEECH LENGTH:** 8 speeches over 14 lines (highest totals: 21, 22, 28); 21 speeches between 8 and 14 lines.

L **STYLISTIC SUMMARY:** Speeches are good, the language competent, and the tone effectively (and presumably deliberately?) farcical (see, e.g., the letter scene at C1v–C2v, and the constant references to Hieronimo's lack of height).

M **UNCONFORMITIES:** The plot is self-consistent. Unconformities only appear if one compares the action with that of *ST* (e.g. Don Pedro is killed in *1 Hier*, yet is alive in *ST*; the final battle in *1 Hier* does not match the account given in *ST*; Hieronimo's farcical paternal pride in *1 Hier* (e.g. E3r,1–9) is at odds with the dignity of his character in *ST*. It is not clear what 'secrets' Revenge is referring to at F2v,34.

N **STAGING AND PROPS:** 2 doors; 'house' (on A2r). Props include: spurs, ceremonial sword, banquet with covered dishes, table, paper, pen, ink, drums and colours, poleaxes, ensigns, hearse, trumpets, ordinance, sennets.

O **LENGTH:** Total length: 1,408/Length of dialogue: 1,278 lines.

P **STAGE DIRECTIONS/SPEECH PREFIXES:** Competent and attentive to staging (e.g: 'ouer heares/ their talke': B2r,14–15; 'Enter Ieronimo trussing of his points': C1v,23; 'They stop his mouth and beare him in': D3r,32; 'The Portugales martch about': E1r,18; 'Exit Horatio carying andrea on his back': F2v,9). The opening SD is a detailed dumbshow, and the SD that follows is contingent upon it ('That done Enter all agen as before': A2r,10). On B2r,20 Horatio is erroneously instructed to exit; Balthasar's exit at E2v,24 is 2 lines too high; Revenge must enter at F2v,22–3 with the Ghost of Andrea.

Q VESTIGIAL CHARACTERS: Phillippo and Cassimero are ghost characters on F3r,23. Castile only appears twice in the play; he speaks 3 words in scene 1 and is mute in scene 8 (D2vff.).

R OTHER OBSERVATIONS: Over 40 per cent of the play is in rhyme. Henslowe records a *Comedy of Don Horatio* (and variant titles) in frequent proximity to *Hieronimo* (i.e. *The Spanish Tragedy*). The Children of the Queen's Revels apparently appropriated *Hieronimo* (tragedy or comedy or both), the property of the King's Men, and the King's Men retaliated by performing the Children's *Malcontent*. This was recent history in 1604, the date of publication of *The Malcontent*, the third impression of which adds an Induction alluding to the quarrel (see chapter 9). Freeman (*Thomas Kyd*) suggests that the reference to 'Ostler' on C2r,14–16 is a play on the name of a Chapel actor, William Ostler. The many references to Hieronimo's diminutive stature throughout *1 Hieronimo* (e.g. B3r,22; B3v,1) possibly indicate Chapel auspices.

S PREVIOUS VERDICTS: Memorial reconstruction (Cairncross ed., *1 Hier*); a revision of the original *Spanish Comedy* made by the Children of the Chapel perhaps in conjunction with their theft of *The Spanish Tragedy* (Freeman, *Thomas Kyd*, pp. 176–7); deliberate burlesque of *The Spanish Tragedy*, and other adult company plays, by Children of the Queen's Revels in 1602–4 (Reibetanz, 'Hieronimo in Decimosexto', pp.120–1).

T CONCLUSION: Not MR.

TABLE XV *1 If You Know Not Me, You Know Nobody*

A **PLAY/TEXT USED:** *1 If You Know Not Me, You Know Nobody* (1605)/MSR (1935 for 1934).

B **SR/Q DATES:** 5 July 1605 to Nathaniel Butter/Q1 1605, Q2 1606, Q 3 1608, Q 4 1610, Q 5 1613, Q6 1623.

C **PRINTER/PUBLISHER:** Thomas Purfoot/Nathaniel Butter.

D **AUTHOR/COMPANY:** Thomas Heywood/Queen Anne's.

E **EXTERNAL ECHOES:** One formulaic line (48) is shared with *STW* (C3v,26) in identical situations. Heywood is probably responsible for both lines.

F **INTERNAL REPETITIONS:** 419–20/1267–8, with paraphrase at 1284–5, 377–9 (and cf. 421). In *England's Elizabeth*, Heywood's prose history of the same events, this trick question – asking Elizabeth to submit so that her acquiescence could be interpreted as guilt – is a last resort. However, it is also good rhetoric and good drama: the same tactic appears in *Death of Robert*, 1996–7 and so may be formulaic. Certainly Elizabeth herself finds it an obvious tactic (380–4). Paraphrase at 619–20/712–13/743.

G **FORMULAE:** Some weak formulae (6–9/1408–10; 361/1250).

H **INSERTIONS:** Not detectable.

I **EXPANDED CLOWN'S ROLE:** No. The Clown's role is soberly complex; he is clearly more a wise fool than comic relief.

J **OMISSIONS:** Line 392, which is unmetrical, possibly contains the end of a sentence which is otherwise absent from the play (see Heywood, *England's Elizabeth*, pp.109–10 and Giordano-Orsini, 'The Copy', p.1037). However, it does make sense as it stands.

K **SPEECH LENGTH:** 3 speeches over 14 lines (highest totals: 15, 16, 21); 21 speeches between 8 and 14 lines. (Like *STW*, *1 If You Know Not Me* has few long speeches and many of moderate length.)

L **STYLISTIC SUMMARY:** Like *STW* the play maintains careful control of its imagery (see the development of sun-justice images at 460–1, 656–7, 1237–8, 1240–1; at 1239–40 Mary misses Philip's metaphorical point but is subliminally aware of it at 1244). The play also sustains the contrast between the mercilessness and religious hatred which typifies Mary and her supporters (e.g. 66–94, 122–31, 714ff., 804) and the innocent and forgiving Elizabeth, supported from some unexpected quarters (e.g.

Sussex at 541ff., Tame at 881ff., and Philip and the Clown throughout. Ironically Philip's justice and mercy towards Elizabeth involves the refusal of mercy to a Spaniard who has killed an Englishman). The change from Elizabeth's distress (in political repression) to Mary's distress (in decline) is emphasised through two uses of the word 'crazey' (150, 1394). The play seems abrupt and compressed in the last scenes, although the hasty, handy deaths do increase the effect of Providence protecting and favouring Elizabeth (I am grateful to Gwendolyn Guth for these points). Several passages are metrically disrupted (e.g. 128–39; 364–7); others are generally good (e.g. scene 4). The play has many short speeches, and it repeats ideas (although not exact phrases); see 299–301/1233–6.

M UNCONFORMITIES: Giordano-Orsini makes a case for Sentlo's lines at 116–19 being originally part of scene 4 ('Thomas Heywood's Play'); however the sequence is coherent as it stands. Mary appoints a Council of 6 (355, 439), only 5 of whom are named in the dialogue (302–3; the Lord Chamberlain completes the quota). In scene 21 Elizabeth moves from talking about herself as Queen Mary's subject (1437–8) to accepting the salutation 'maiesty' without receiving or requesting an explanation for her sudden promotion. (Perhaps Mary's death may be taken for granted, but Elizabeth was wise to verbal tricks at 380–4 and this salutation may be a similar ploy.) Elizabeth addresses her servants, seemingly anomalously, as 'gentlemen' at 324 and 334. This seems less an unconformity than one of a series of references which dignify the working classes: a cook proves to be a Classics scholar (891–5), and Elizabeth is linked with her gentlewoman servant at 1181ff. where Clarentia becomes a milkmaid and Elizabeth a seamstress (1191, and cf. 808–10; Gwendolyn Guth, personal communication).

N STAGING AND PROPS: Two doors; upper stage; arras (to hide behind; is this a curtained inner stage?). Props include: royal purse, mace, sceptre, crown, horn, drum, royal bed, proclamation, jack of beer, dishes of food, 6 torches, 2 petitions, letter, 2 nosegays, gold coins, bells (offstage), chair of state, weapons (including Spanish toledo), cross at Charing Cross, pen, ink, paper, purse, English Bible, goat, writs, seal, faggots, hearse, canopy over the Queen, cap of maintenance, sword royal, 'Coller' (1514), staff, Order of the Garter, Order of the George.

O LENGTH: Total length: 1,598/Length of dialogue: 1,455 lines.

P STAGE DIRECTIONS/SPEECH PREFIXES: SDs are often deficient in entrances and exits, especially towards the end of the play (e.g. 45, 804, 847, 1041, 1045, 1055, 1227). Very often they are specific in their personnel demands ('*three / Houshold seruants*': 309–10; '*three white-cote souldiers*': 465; see also 439, 673, 840, 1225, 1366, 1511, 1514–16). The dumbshows are meticulous in their descriptive choreography (e.g. 673–82). SDs often give useful details of props and actions (e.g. '*They sit, / shee kneeles*': 362–3; see also 651–2 and 1142–3). An aside from behind the arras is indicated at 1282–3. SDs are frequently in RH margin, possibly a sign of annotation for use as a playbook. SDs and SPs display initial onomastic uncertainty about the Constable. He is '*Lo: Chamberlaine*' on his first entrance (1; SP *Cham:/Cha:/Chamb:*), '*Gage*' on his second (47; SP: *Const:*) and *Constable* in SDs throughout the rest of the play (360ff.). (Gage is, confusingly, also the name of Elizabeth's servant who first enters at 146).

Q VESTIGIAL CHARACTERS: Clarentia is mute in scene 21 (1414ff.), but there is nothing surprising about a servant's silence in public.

R OTHER OBSERVATIONS: The play requires a large number of supernumeraries (e.g. scene 23 requires a cast of 27, of whom 16 are mute. I exclude Clarentia from the total of mutes since she has a speaking part in the play). In 1637 Heywood complained that the plot of *1 If You* (and perhaps the play) had been reproduced by stenography and the text printed 'scarce one word trew'. The opening and closing scenes are linked by blunt and sparse exchanges of information. Scene 1 is merely a series of entrances and greetings; scenes 20–3 contain a speedy catalogue of deaths and obeisance (but cf. Stylistic Summary above). The stylistic differences between these scenes and the rest of the text may be accounted for by damage to the outer leaves of the MS; these leaves would then have had to be rewritten/reconstructed. (For similar anomalies see *STW*, also a Queen Anne's play and a partner to *1 If You* in subject matter, and cf. *Philaster*).

S PREVIOUS VERDICTS: Memorial reconstruction (Kirschbaum, 'A Census', p.31; Ashe, thesis, 'A Survey', pp.170–2); memorial reconstruction made by two or more of the actors, perhaps supplemented by actors' parts (Giordano-Orsini, 'Thomas Heywood's Play', p.338).

T CONCLUSION: Insufficient evidence to confirm a case for MR.

TABLE XVI *The Life and Death of Jack Straw*

A **PLAY/TEXT USED:** *The Life and Death of Jack Straw* (1594)/MSR (1957).

B **SR/Q DATES:** 23 October 1593 to John Danter/Q1 1593 (title page; 1594 colophon), Q2 1604.

C **PRINTER/PUBLISHER:** John Danter/sold by William Barley.

D **AUTHOR/COMPANY:** Anon./unknown.

E **EXTERNAL ECHOES:** No.

F **INTERNAL REPETITIONS:** No.

G **FORMULAE:** The adjective 'vnnaturall' is used extensively (11 times); the adverbial form appears twice. This is perhaps no more than one might expect in a play about the Peasants' Revolt.

H **INSERTIONS:** Not detectable.

I **EXPANDED CLOWN'S ROLE:** No. Two comic scenes (2.1 and 2.5) peter out, suggesting the need for comic improvisation to expand the dialogue and action.

J **OMISSIONS:** Couplet lines seem missing after lines 3, 28, 57, 85. Something seems lost after 468. We see/hear nothing of the 'villanies' and 'cruelties' mentioned by Newton at 1042ff. Cf. Other Observations below.

K **SPEECH LENGTH:** 14 speeches over 14 lines (highest totals: 30, 34, 41); 24 speeches between 8 and 14 lines.

L **STYLISTIC SUMMARY:** The style is workmanlike but often bald and blunt; the Poem is mixed metrically (tetrameter, pentameter, couplets, all often faulty). The prevalence of couplets in scene 1, a scene which summarises antecedent action, suggests that this scene has been rewritten: no other scene is entirely in couplets and no other scene summarises so much prior history. Speeches sometimes conclude inconsequentially: e.g. 472–3, 789–90.

M **UNCONFORMITIES:** –

N **STAGING AND PROPS:** Goose, knife, gates of London, bonfire or embers, papers to burn, staff, sword, weapons, letters, King's pardon.

O **LENGTH:** Total length: 1209/Length of dialogue: 970 lines.

P **STAGE DIRECTIONS/SPEECH PREFIXES:** SDs often omit necessary entrances (e.g. King, Bishop, and Treasurer at 336, Morton at 375, Nobs and Hob Carter's Essex men at 682, and rebel prisoners at 1053). Tom

Miller is included in SD at 682, although he is not in this scene (see dialogue in 3.2). The SD for Morton at 488–9 is clearly wrong, and belongs at 499. The set-speech pardon to the rebels (1071–113) is set apart with a heading 'The Kings Pardon deliuered by / *Sir Iohn Morton to the Rebels*' (1071–2). The SD at 845–6 is sensitive to blocking: '*Enter Iacke Strawe, [etc]. . . / Tom Miller being there*'. Two SDs indicating action are positioned in the RH margin at 922–3 ('*The King giues / him the sword*') and 950 1 ('*Here he / stabs him*'). A SD for Tom Miller breaks the law of re-entry at 497–8.

Q VESTIGIAL CHARACTERS: '*County of Salsburie*' enters at 296 with the Queen Mother and Gentleman Usher simply to praise the King for 16 lines. Why should Salsburie be specified, since this dramatic function could be served by any unnamed noble? Perhaps Salsburie once had a larger role which has been cut.

R OTHER OBSERVATIONS: The play is unusual in having only 4 acts. There is no hero (Straw is only nominally the central character); in fact the play's aim seems to be to skim through the rebellion to reach the murder of Straw by Sir William Walworth, Lord Mayor of London. (This may increase the likelihood of the play's association with a Lord Mayor's show). There are several very young or very small characters in the play, e.g. Nobs and Tom Miller; Richard's youth is stressed throughout the play (184, 310), a stress not in the chronicle sources.

S PREVIOUS VERDICTS: 'the mutilated remains of a play' (Greg (1923), *Two Elizabethan Stage Abridgements*, p.286); 'does not display any of the qualities to be found in the acknowledged bad quartos' (Hoppe, *The Bad Quarto*, p.17); 'a strong case for. . .censored promptbook' (Clare, *'Art Made Tongue-tied'*, p.37).

T CONCLUSION: Not MR.

TABLE XVII *John of Bordeaux*

A **PLAY/TEXT USED:** *John of Bordeaux* (MS 507 Alnwick Castle)/MSR (1936 for 1935).

B **SR/Q DATES:** NE/never printed.

C **PRINTER/PUBLISHER:** N/A.

D **AUTHOR/COMPANY:** Anon. (Greene?)/unknown (see Other Observations below).

E **EXTERNAL ECHOES:** No.

F **INTERNAL REPETITIONS:** 507–9/529–31 (the first unit is marked for deletion); 652–3/658–9. Dittography at foot/top of pages on fols. 3r; 3v/4r; 6v, 7r; 8r, 8v.

G **FORMULAE:** 'her/his/my/thy only son/Selimus' appears 5 times within a short space: 190–1/193/205/206–7/227–8.

H **INSERTIONS:** Some extra-metrical phrases (e.g. 115, 218, 225, 497–8, 598–9, 1045).

I **EXPANDED CLOWN'S ROLE:** No. The comic echolalia which characterises Perce's role is also typical of his predecessor, Miles, in *Friar Bacon*. If one includes the secondary comic role of the jester in *Friar Bacon*, the clowning content of *FB* and *JB* is identical (12 per cent in each play).

J **OMISSIONS:** A speech for Bordeaux is missing on fol.11v: 1119 instructs 'her Iohn of Burdaox speckes', followed by a long gap, indicating an expectation that the lacuna would be filled. On the same folio a 12-line gap for a speech of Bordeaux ('her Iohn of Burdiox speake*s* his specth': 1089) was filled in later (by Henry Chettle). The final scene is damaged and incomplete (see McNeir, 'Reconstructing the Conclusion of *JB*' for analysis of what is lost); the last folio contains fragmentary lines, with no indication of where they belong.

K **SPEECH LENGTH:** 11 speeches over 14 lines (highest totals: 15, 16, 18); 35 speeches between 8 and 14 lines.

L **STYLISTIC SUMMARY:** Generally very good with occasional *non sequitur*s, a few unscannable lines, and one mangled mythological reference (924–6). The play has a predilection for balanced and antithetical phrasing (e.g. 7, 115, 267–8, 586–7, 1041–3). The debate about Magic *versus* Nature (despite apparent cuts: 423, 734–6) is reinforced verbally (the word 'art' is used 22 times).

M **UNCONFORMITIES:** The name Rossacler appears frequently instead of Ferdinand in dialogue, SDs and SPs (a major error: Rossacler is John of Bordeaux's son, Ferdinand the son of the Emperor Frederick. See SDs below).

N **STAGING AND PROPS:** 2 doors; trapdoor. Props include: sennets, trumpets, weapons, tablebooks, chains and irons.

O **LENGTH:** Total MS length: 1354 (1348 MS lines plus six fragmentary lines). This would be c.1520 lines of print/Length of MS dialogue: 1474. One scene is missing (1058), and one speech lacking (1119).

P **STAGE DIRECTIONS/SPEECH PREFIXES:** SDs are provided by three hands: S, A, and B. The original SDs (by S) have a tendency to clarify relationships ('Iohn of Burdiox / his wif Rossalin his son Rossacler': 1–2; 'Enter Bacon and perce his man': 126) and to indicate costumes ('Enter Iohn of Burdiox in por appariell': 753; 'Enter yonge Rossaclere in beggour atier': 838). One SD indicates missing dialogue and/or the need for improvisation: 'Enter the seane of the whiper' (1058). SPs, frequently one line too high, seem to have been added after the relevant dialogue was copied out, and often fluctuate: thus, Ameroth is both 'Turk' and 'Emperor', Ferdinand's attendants both 'noble' and 'lord'. In SDs and SPs the scribe regularly writes 'Rossacler' for 'Ferdinand' (this mistake also occurs in dialogue). At 697 the SP 'fredrick' should be 'ferdinand'; and at 1068 'Damod' (*sic* for Damon) should be 'Correbus'. One SD indicates familiarity with the action: 'Exent Bacon / to bring in the showes as you knowe' (446–7). The MS was subsequently tidied with annotations by two annotators, A and B. B seems to be concerned with SDs for sound (408, 436–7, 448). Annotator A deals with props, stage business, sounds, SPs, entrances. He corrects the lining of the SP at 64. He adds many omitted SPs and corrects all of the Rossacler/Ferdinand errors (but misses the 'fredrick'/'ferdinand' error at 697). Those SPs camouflaged by S's continuous lineation have been brought into the margin (e.g. 378, 565) and he has enclosed one of S's SDs in a box to make it more prominent (764). Annotator A supplies entrances (228, 602–3, 801, 948–9) and highlights those already given (254–5, 290, 838, 841). He also adds an actor's name, that of John Holland, at 466–7, 593, 678–9, and 1071.

Q **VESTIGIAL CHARACTERS:** No.

R **OTHER OBSERVATIONS:** McNeir ('Reconstructing the Conclusion of *JB*') believes the company to be the Queen's Men; Renwick (ed., *JB*, p.viii) and McMillin ('The Ownership', p.251) argue for Strange's.

S **PREVIOUS VERDICTS:** 'a shortened version of a longer text' (Renwick ed., *JB*, p.vii); 'a bad quarto that never reached print' (Hoppe, '*JB*').

T **CONCLUSION:** Not MR.

TABLE XVIII *King Lear*

A **PLAY/TEXT USED:** *King Lear* (1608)/Allen and Muir facsimile (1981).

B **SR/Q DATES:** 26 November 1607 to Nathaniel Butter and John Busby /Q1 1608, Q2 1619 (F version 1623).

C **PRINTER/PUBLISHER:** Nicholas Okes/Nathaniel Butter.

D **AUTHOR/COMPANY:** William Shakespeare/King's Men.

E **EXTERNAL ECHOES:** No.

F **INTERNAL REPETITIONS:** No.

G **FORMULAE:** No.

H **INSERTIONS:** Not detectable.

I **EXPANDED CLOWN'S ROLE:** No.

J **OMISSIONS:** Not detectable.

K **SPEECH LENGTH:** 12 speeches over 14 lines (highest totals: 19, 21, 22); 75 speeches between 8 and 14 lines.

L **STYLISTIC SUMMARY:** Excellent.

M **UNCONFORMITIES:** In disguise Kent apparently shaves off his beard ('I raz'd my likenes': C3v,2), yet the steward refers to Kent's 'gray-beard' on E1v,17. (However, this is possibly just a metaphoric way of talking about advanced years.)

N **STAGING AND PROPS:** Upper stage; 2 doors; inner recess. Props include: letters, lights, drums and trumpets, bloody knife, stocks. Sound effects: music to waken Lear.

O **LENGTH:** Total length: 2,986/Length of dialogue: 2,931 lines.

P **STAGE DIRECTIONS/SPEECH PREFIXES:** SDs are attentive to details of staging, e.g. processional order (B1v), action ('*Shee takes a sword and runs at him behind*': H2r; '*Exit King running*': I4v; '*sleepes*': E3r). SDs frequently omit entrances and exits, and sometimes indicate only the first (or the first few) speaking characters in a scene, even when that/those character(s) is/are clearly accompanied by others (e.g. D2v, D4r, E3r). There is one permissive SD ('*two or three*': H1r). 2 scenes give an advance indication of Edgar's entrance in the LH margin (C2v, D3v); the marginal indication '*A Letter*' prefaces the reading aloud of the letter on C1v. There is onomastic fluctuation between SDs and SPs: Edmund is both *Bast[ard]* and *Edmund* (E1r, K3r, K4r), Edgar once appears as '*Tom*' (G3v), Goneril and Regan are simply '*the two Ladies*' on K4v. '*Edmund*' in the SD at I2r is a mistake for Edgar (a mistake which occurs in reverse in the dialogue at H3v,12); '*Leister*' in the SD at F3r is a mistake for Gloster. One SD is imperative: '*draw and fight*' (H1v).

Q VESTIGIAL CHARACTERS: No.

R OTHER OBSERVATIONS: The error of '*Leister*' for '*Gloster*' in the SD on F3r suggests difficulty in reading the handwriting of the copy, a conclusion supported by the large number of press-variants in the 12 extant copies of Q1 (see Wells and Taylor, *Textual Companion*, p.510). Much mislining of verse (Nicholas Okes had never printed a play before).

S PREVIOUS VERDICTS: Q1 copy printed from Shakespeare's autograph MS (Doran, *The Text of 'King Lear'*, retracted 1941 in review of Greg (1933), *Variants*); shorthand report from performance (Greg (1932–3), 'The Function of Bibliography'); MR made by entire company (Duthie ed., *Shakespeare's 'King Lear'*); authorial draft (Warren, 'Quarto and Folio *King Lear*', Urkowitz, *Shakespeare's Revision of 'King Lear'*); shorthand or longhand report by audience member over repeated attendance, compiled for publication (Stone, *The Textual History*); a version of the original text of *King Lear* (Halio ed., *KL*).

T CONCLUSION: Not MR.

TABLE XIX *A Knack to Know an Honest Man*

A **PLAY/TEXT USED:** *A Knack to Know an Honest Man* (1596)/MSR (1910).

B **SR/Q DATE:** 26 November 1595 to Cuthbert Burby/Q 1596.

C **PRINTER/PUBLISHER:** Thomas Scarlet/Cuthbert Burby.

D **AUTHOR/COMPANY:** Anon./Admiral's Men.

E **EXTERNAL ECHOES:** No.

F **INTERNAL REPETITIONS:** 802/834–5.

G **FORMULAE:** The 8 repetitions of the title phrase 'a knack to know a...' (7/8 of which are spoken by Sempronio) are clearly a deliberate rhetorical underlining of the play's moral structure. It is noteworthy that exit lines and conclusions to scenes persistently motivate future action (e.g. 64–8; 231–3; 653–5).

H **INSERTIONS:** Large number of extra-metrical words and phrases (e.g. 253, 366, 368, 372, 442, 446).

I **EXPANDED CLOWN'S ROLE:** No. See Omissions below.

J **OMISSIONS:** Clowning may be cut (or extempore?): scene 12 concludes perfunctorily with an instruction to Gnatto (1182) to cease antics which are not provided in text.

K **SPEECH LENGTH:** 10 speeches over 14 lines (highest totals: 20, 22, 36); 35 speeches between 8 and 14 lines.

L **STYLISTIC SUMMARY:** Many unmetrical passages (e.g. 159–64; 304–6; 997–8). Play is often mislined. Otherwise generally good: there is a predilection for balanced phrasing; contrasts often appear in the form of jingles (e.g. 457–8; 841; 1250–1 and cf. 297–8, 1062–3, 1654–5); careful comic *auxesis* at 404–7. The play is ambitiously large in the scope of its plot yet monitors tone carefully: the scenes of Marchetto's and Fortunio's visits to Annetta and Lucida are alive with threatening bustle, and the atmosphere of dark night and outrage is carefully evoked (see e.g. 1031–41).

M **UNCONFORMITIES:** For confused/abrupt action and dialogue at 739 see SDs below. Lucida half-hints at marriage to Fortunio at 1616–17, but her Father gives her to Sempronio (1746), her Mother's threatened ravisher at the play's outset. Otherwise, very complex plot is free from confusion. *Non sequitur* at 142.

N **STAGING AND PROPS:** 2 doors. Props include: swords, spectacles for

Servio, (needle?)work for Annetta and Lucida, chest of gold/jewels, jewels, *memento mori* skull, book, trumpets, bindings for prisoners, keys, Servio's signet, coals, thumb press, letter, torture instruments (possibly: see 1295), executioner's sword.

O **LENGTH**: Total length: 1,805/Length of dialogue: 1,723 lines.

P **STAGE DIRECTIONS/SPEECH PREFIXES**: SDs provide props, action, specify relationships, and regulate stage movement. A 'here-plus-imperative' formula is frequent (5 times). At one point dialogue is erroneously presented as SD (1357). A cryptic SD ('*Here put them in at doore*': 739) and a succinct SD indicating familiarity of staging ('*Enter the shew on the Stage*': 743) may be illuminated by the St Mark's Day procession in *Women Beware Women* (ed., Gill, 1.3.81–1.3.105). However, line 738 is abrupt and fragmentary and the SD at 739 seems to continue the confused haste. There are some problems in SDs towards the end, e.g. Marchetto must enter bound at 1327 since he seems to be addressed at 1371; Sempronio has duplicate entrances in scene 17 (1469, 1660. In the first part of this scene Sempronio has one speech which must be delivered either chorically or aside, but he seems otherwise redundant before 1660. There may have been an attempt to cut him from 1469–659). Some fluctuation in SDs and dialogue with name of Zepherius (e.g. 993, 1092, 1184, 1357, 1571). Much confusion in SPs: eg. 61, 800-3, 942, 1155, 1231–2, 1379, 1524, 1556.

Q **VESTIGIAL CHARACTERS**: No.

R **OTHER OBSERVATIONS**: 15 extracts from *KKHM* (4 verbatim, 11 in variant form) appear in Bodenham's *Belvedere* (1600). The play was printed surprisingly early in its run: first entered as 'ne' in Henslowe's *Diary* on 22 October 1594, it enjoyed 21 performances between that date and 3 November 1596, yet Burby published it while it was still an attraction of the Admiral's Men's repertory. The play is clearly designed as an answer to *KKK* (table xx): it has the 'comicke end' (1783) which *KKK* lacks, Sempronio is a less cynical version of Honesty in *KKK*, and the play has a greater sense of mercy, most notably in the figure of Sempronio who encourages his attacker, Lelio, to escape (49, 52, 61), and delays Lelio's death (1697ff.) until the Hermit can arrive to clear everything up. (I am grateful to Gwendolyn Guth for these interpretive points).

S **PREVIOUS VERDICTS**: Text is confused, and copy was probably surreptitiously obtained from performance (de Vocht ed., *KKHM*, p.vii); 'a stage version' (Albright, *Dramatic Publication*); 'confused and probably surreptitious' (Sharpe, *The Real War*); memorial reconstruction (Kirschbaum, 'A Census', p.32; Ashe, 'The Non-Shakespearean Bad Quartos'); 'probably a bad quarto even though its corruption is not so deep as texts like *FV*' (Hoppe, *The Bad Quarto*, p.16).

T CONCLUSION: Not MR.

TABLE XX *A Knack to Know a Knave*

A **PLAY/TEXT USED:** *A Knack to Know a Knave* (1594)/MSR (1964 for 1963).

B **SR/Q DATES:** 7 January 1594 to Richard Jones/Q 1594.

C **PRINTER/PUBLISHER:** Widow Charlewood or James Roberts/Richard Jones.

D **AUTHOR/COMPANY:** Anon./Strange's Men.

E **EXTERNAL ECHOES:** Lines 30–1, possibly a formulaic compliment, are shared with *TTR3* 2206–7; line 369 (again possibly formulaic) is shared with B *Dr Faustus*. On 5 occasions chunks of prose, taken near-verbatim from Greene (*The Card of Fancy*) and Lyly (*Euphues*), are chopped into blank-verse lengths and incorporated in the dialogue (see 425–32, 1183–92, 1680–3 from Grosart ed., *Greene*, vol.IV, pp.14, 25, 54; and see lines 453–5, 524–5 from Bond ed., *Lyly*, vol.I, pp.230, 184. See Proudfoot ed., *KKK*, p.vi).

F **INTERNAL REPETITIONS:** 272–3/321–2; 652–3/674–5. Other lengthy repetitions contain conventional vocabulary and so are included under Formulae, below.

G **FORMULAE:** Consistently formulaic. 19–20/28–9; 507–8/569–70; 933–4/1248–9. For formulaic phrases or paraphrases see: 229/568/1327/ 1331/1566; 403/420/440/469. For formulaic invitations to Court see: 240/566/1176/1361/1875 (and cf. 925/1176/1360/1540). There is a fondness for the word 'amiss' throughout: 137/445/448/506/562/641/642/778/1891.

H **INSERTIONS:** Large number of extra-metrical tags (e.g. 53, 188, 190, 195, 197, 219, 231). Explanatory conclusion to 1861 'Finsburie fields, *neere London*' (my emphasis) would be redundant at the Rose and hence must be insertion for provincial performance (see Proudfoot, thesis, pp.xxxviii, 116). The Bailiff of Hexham material may be adaptation of existing material or insertion (see Unconformities, below).

I **EXPANDED CLOWN'S ROLE:** No. In fact, catachrestic interlude of the mad men of Gotham (scene 11), which is a title-page attraction, seems brief and banal. For possible topical expansion of comic material about the Bailiff of Hexham, see Unconformities, below.

J **OMISSIONS:** At 1890 Honesty comments on the length of the play – a seemingly inappropriate remark for the far-from-long 1853-line dialogue.

K SPEECH LENGTH: 21 speeches over 14 lines (highest totals: 28, 31, 34); 56 speeches between 8 and 14 lines.

L STYLISTIC SUMMARY: Metrically macaronic with verse embedded in prose (scenes 1, 8), tumbling verse (152–61), and Alexandrines (e.g. 212). Most of the classical allusions are nonsense (e.g. 123–4, 182–3, 208–10, 1304–5). There are a great number of unmetrical lines, many of them in phrases with classical images. The play is thematically very coherent, dealing with human justice in plot, speech, and image. Several scenes concern refusals for mercy: Philarchus and father (450ff.), the Conicatcher's branding (896), Ethenwald's betrayal of the King (1197–9, 1574–8), and Honesty's final harsh punishments for Cuthbert, Walter, John and Perin (1843ff.). The one act of forgiveness in the play is forced on the King by a spirit (1720–5), suggesting that mercy is not inherent in human nature. Honesty's 'justice' at the end of the play may be seen as a type of the 'fierie doome' that God inflicted on Sodom (cf. 19–20). The Sodom images (19, 26–9) also relate to the stern warnings against adultery issued to the King (1573, 1686, 1703). Honesty begs our pardon at the end of the play (1891), but it is difficult to grant it in the face of the play's sustained darkness; this reluctance to forgive reinforces the play's theme. (I am grateful to Gwendolyn Guth for these points.)

M UNCONFORMITIES: Several problems. In scene 2 the Bailiff encourages his 4 sons in their malpractices and although these sons appear frequently in the rest of the play, no mention is made of the fact that they are brothers (see scenes 6, 8). This is odd, since continual verbal reminders stress the chicanery of the Bailiff and his family (644, 690–4, 695–6, 813–14). Scene 2 presents Walter as an employee, although the play shows he is in business for himself. At 1582 Dunston conjures a spirit to provide him with information he has just heard. Ethenwald arrives to meet Alfrida in scene 5, prepares to return to Court to report his impressions of her in scene 7, yet meets her for the first time in scene 9. Dunston's critical character in scene 14 differs from his earlier sycophantic role (e.g. 21ff., 122ff., 571ff.). There are several *non sequitur*s: e.g. at 742 Osric refers to a 'taske' which Ethenwald has not yet mentioned, and Honesty's speech at 148 does not respond to the King's request at 146–7.

N STAGING AND PROPS: Trapdoor. Props include: money, false writ, robes and sceptre, Bible.

O **LENGTH:** Total length: 1,897/Length of dialogue: 1,853 lines.

P **STAGE DIRECTIONS/SPEECH PREFIXES:** SDs are sometimes in error. Line 1 misses entrance for Honesty, 1278 instructs Perin to exit when he clearly must stay, 1717 should include Ethenwald. A massed entry is given at 575–6. 'To them' SDs occur twice (1106: 'To them'; 1482: 'to Ethenwald'). 2 SDs explain relationships with the phrase 'to wit' (242: 'foure sonnes, to wit, . . .'; 1363: 'mad men of Goteham, to wit, . . .'). 373 is imperative. The SD at 927 'Enter a Knight, Squire, and Farmer' ignores the fact that the latter is not just any farmer, but Walter, the Bailiff's son; 242–4 introduces the Bailiff's offspring ('a / Courtier, a Priest, a Conicatcher, and / a Farmer'), yet the 'a Courtier' is Perin, whom we have just met. The SD at 1717 is confusing. The Devil's presence is necessary to force a pardon from a reluctantly forgiving King (whether by magic or physical threat); this done he disappears (1725). There is no reason for Alfrida to be disguised; her physical appearance (as a result of the disguise?) does seem to cause Edgar problems (1718). Edgar's question, implying incredulity, would be consistent with the devil in disguise as Alfrida (but for what purpose?) but inconsistent with the devil's departure at 1725, for the dialogue implies that Alfrida stays with her husband.

Q **VESTIGIAL CHARACTERS:** No.

R **OTHER OBSERVATIONS:** *KKK* is first mentioned in Philip Henslowe's *Diary* on 10 June 1592. The play has more structural than verbal problems: it is clear that the alliance of Perin, Walter, John, and Cuthbert is a temporary dramatic expedient to create four sons for the Bailiff's death scene.

S **PREVIOUS VERDICTS:** Possibly memorial reconstruction 'although the direct borrowings from Lyly and Greene look more like the work of an author' (Proudfoot ed., *KKK*, p. vii); 'an almost classic specimen of a bad quarto' (Born, *The Rare Wit*, p.viii).

T **CONCLUSION:** Possibly MR.

TABLE XXI *The Maid's Tragedy*

A PLAY/TEXT USED: *The Maid's Tragedy* (1619)/STC MFM.

B SR/Q DATES: 28 April 1619 to Francis Constable and Richard Higginbotham/Q1 1619, Q2 ('Newly perused, augmented, and inlarged') 1622.

C PRINTER/PUBLISHER: Nicholas Okes: sigs.A–G; unknown printer (?): sigs.H–L/Francis Constable and Richard Higginbotham (on separate title-page imprints).

D AUTHOR/COMPANY: Francis Beaumont and John Fletcher/King's Men.

E EXTERNAL ECHOES: No.

F INTERNAL REPETITIONS: DIV,34/36 (this is clearly a deliberate repetition for the benefit of the amazed Amintor).

G FORMULAE: No.

H INSERTIONS: Not detectable.

I EXPANDED CLOWN'S ROLE: No.

J OMISSIONS: Not detectable.

K SPEECH LENGTH: 23 speeches over 14 lines (highest totals: 20, 21, 31); 49 speeches between 8 and 14 lines.

L STYLISTIC SUMMARY: Very good. Verse is frequently mislined as prose.

M UNCONFORMITIES: No.

N STAGING AND PROPS: 2 doors, trapdoor, upper stage. Props include: rock, swords, oboes, recorders, banquet, royal bed, bindings, knife, gold.

O LENGTH: Total length: 2,894/Length of dialogue: 2,861 lines.

P STAGE DIRECTIONS/SPEECH PREFIXES: Generally competent, laconic. SDs indicate asides and noises within. One SD is imperative: '*Kneele*' (H2r,17). Major props and changes of costume are indicated (e.g. '*K. a bed*': 14v,25; '*Enter Aspat. in mans apparell*': K4r,11), as is action: '*Ties his / armes to / the bed*': K1r,15–17; '*Stabs him. . .Kils him*': K2r,24, 32; '*leaues her....Returnes*': L2v,11, 16).

Q VESTIGIAL CHARACTERS: No.

R OTHER OBSERVATIONS: Q2 contains approx. 80 lines not in Q1, and makes many minor verbal changes. Contemporary references: indirect allusion in 1611 when Sir George Buc, Master of the Revels, refers to an untitled MS play as 'This Second Maiden's Tragedy'. On 20 May 1613 payment was made to John Heminge for 14 plays presented at Court inc. *The Maid's Tragedy* (see Turner ed., *MT*, p.3).

s **PREVIOUS VERDICTS**: MR (Kirschbaum, 'A Census', p.43; Duthie, *The Bad Quarto*, p.11, n.1); MS copy made by Beaumont (Gurr ed., *MT*, p.10); 'rough foul papers. . .Beaumont's autograph. . .in a late, but not the final, stage of composition' (Turner ed., *MT*, pp.16, 17); a censored text (Clare, *'Art Made Tongue-tied'*, p.165).

T **CONCLUSION**: Not MR.

TABLE XXII *The Massacre at Paris*

A **PLAY/TEXT USED:** *The Massacre at Paris* (n.d.)/MSR (1929 for 1928).

B **SR/O DATES:** NE/octavo undated, but probably 1593–4 (see Bowers ed., *Marlowe* vol.1, p.357).

C **PRINTER/PUBLISHER:** Edward Allde/Edward White.

D **AUTHOR/COMPANY:** Christopher Marlowe/Admiral's Men (on title-page). Henslowe records performances of a tragedy of the Guise ('ne') in Strange's repertory in January 1592/93 and in the Admiral's repertory in 1594; expenditure on properties indicates revivals in 1598 (? or 1602?) and 1601; in 1602 Henslowe purchased the 'book' from Alleyn.

E **EXTERNAL ECHOES:** Line 953 shared with *TTRDY* c4r, 18; 1376–9 shared with *TTRDY* B4r, 17–18 and F *3H6* TLN 724–5; 795–6 shared with *Arden* 99–100. Further slight resemblances with the *Henry 6* plays may be due to similarity of situation (see Other Observations below). Lines and phrases (1406–8, 1520–1) from *Ed 2* (D4v, B4r) may be authorial.

F **INTERNAL REPETITIONS:** Verbatim repetition, paraphrase, and mosaic (sometimes in combination with external echoes). Queen Mother paraphrases and repeats 625–33 at 782–90; 625 is repeated by the Friar at 1420 (and, in part, by several others: see 'let me alone' under Formulae below); 627 is repeated by Henry 3 at 1090. Both Charles 9 and Henry 3 die (663–5; 1543–4) with symptoms which echo those of the Queen Mother (212–14). Single lines or short phrases are sometimes repeated within the same scene (e.g. 1133–4 and 1142–3 recur at 1158–60).

G **FORMULAE:** Heavily formulaic. The exit line 'Come...let's go', or variants (e.g. 'Come...let's away') is used 17 times; the adjective 'sweet' appears 17 times. (Both tags are also favoured in *1 Cont* and *TTRDY*.) Other tags recur less frequently: 'let me alone' (5 times), 'tush' (5 times), 'gathered a power of men' (2 times).

H **INSERTIONS:** 'I say' is extra-metrical at 501.

I **EXPANDED CLOWN'S ROLE:** No. In fact the scene with the cutpurse is represented merely by a SD (747–8) and 3 lines of dialogue.

J **OMISSIONS:** The extreme concentration – with consequent staging ambiguity – suggests compression and/or omission. For speculation as to two kinds of omission in the text (accidental memorial omission and deliberate cutting) see Other Observations below.

K **SPEECH LENGTH**: 9 speeches over 14 lines (highest totals: 26, 28, 75); 32 speeches between 8 and 14 lines.

L **STYLISTIC SUMMARY**: Very uneven. Long and fluid speeches (e.g. those of the Guise) coexist with short, staccato speeches (e.g. 190–235). Characters are blunt and over-explicit about their motives (e.g. 21–5). Characterisation tends to be two-dimensional, notably in the parts of Navarre and Queen Mother, extremes of good and bad respectively. Verse structure is often lost, although the underlying iambic pentameter is discernible. The verbal quality deteriorates towards the end (compare Guise's soliloquy at 1031–43 with his earlier soliloquy at 108ff.).

M **UNCONFORMITIES**: The remorse expressed by Guise's murderer (1212–19) is surprising and unmotivated (but perhaps this is the nature of remorse). Anjoy's apparent *non sequitur* at 330–2 may simply be a comic example of his cowardice (and was used to comic effect in the RSC production, directed by Paul Marcus, 1985). At 504–8 Guise addresses a question to Anjoy, but Dumaine responds. (Again, the RSC made dramatic mileage out of this moment, underlining Anjoy's incompetence; Guise's next line – 'Tis well aduisde *Dumain*' – stressed '*Dumain*' while the Guise stared pointedly at Anjoy.) Variant suggestions are given for the disposal of the Admiral's dead body (376–82, 579–609; see Pettitt, 'Formulaic Dramaturgy' for the suggestion that the contradictions reflect formulaic adaptation by a company unable to stage a hanging).

N **STAGING AND PROPS**: Upper stage; door (to inner stage? 417, 519); inner stage. Props include: bed, tree or elevated area for hanging Admiral (the 1985 RSC production used the large cross which dominated the action), poisoned gloves, pen, paper, ink, letters, books, gold buttons and an ear, soldier's musket, dagger, poisoned dagger, weapons. See Pettitt, 'Formulaic Dramaturgy' for an analysis of staging.

O **LENGTH**: Total length: 1,586/Length of dialogue: 1,438 lines. The printer has padded a short text typographically (e.g. with unnecessary turn-down of lines) to make the text appear longer; thus, the actual dialogue is only 1,147 lines.

P **STAGE DIRECTIONS/SPEECH PREFIXES**: SDs are often good at specifying necessary stage business (e.g. providing removal of dead bodies: 236, 604, 997, 1583–6) or describing actions (172: '*Pointing to his Sworde*';

747–8, 909, 1343) but are equally often cavalier in exits (characters sometimes exit with escorts but it is not clear who should escort them). Several SDs are imperative ('*Stab him*': 362; '*kill him*': 503). SDs are conscientious in specifying props. Some SDs are very precise ('*Enter two*': 578), others permissive ('*Enter fiue or sixe*': 634).

Q   VESTIGIAL CHARACTERS: No.

R   OTHER OBSERVATIONS: Parallels with Shakespeare's *Henry 6* seem to have been part of the original verbal and structural design of *MP*; e.g. Navarre's speeches begin with a prayer (or thanks to God, or religious reference), like those of Henry in the *H6* plays (see Eriksen, 'Construction in Marlowe's *MP*' for further parallels). Folger MS J.b.8 contains a longer version of scene 15 (972–97). There seems no reason to doubt the MS's authenticity: it clearly exceeds the ability of J. P. Collier, but it is equally clearly not in Marlowe's hand. Comparison of MS with O reveals purposeless variants and disordering in the soldier's speech in O; Guise's 16 lines in MS are reduced to 4 in O (these 4 have only one substantive variant). Comparison of MS with O suggests that the brevity of O has two causes: deliberate cutting and accidental memorial omission.

S   PREVIOUS VERDICTS: 'corrupt version. . .surreptitiously obtained' (Greg (1929) ed., *MP*, p.viii); 'very poor memorial transmission' (Maxwell, 'How Bad is the Text of *JM*?'); 'memorially reported text' (Bowers ed., *Marlowe* vol.1, p.358).

T   CONCLUSION: MR (presumably for performance by Strange's–Admiral's Men, a company which performed both jointly and separately (see Greg (1923), *2ESA*, p.19). If one branch of the company was performing out of town, and Alleyn (who played the Guise and owned the 'book') was in London, reconstruction would be necessary). Not stolen and surreptitious.

TABLE XXIII *The Merry Devil of Edmonton*

A **PLAY/TEXT USED:** *The Merry Devil of Edmonton* (1608)/TFT (1911).

B **SR/Q DATES:** 22 October 1607 to Arthur Johnson/Q1 1608, Q2 1612, Q3 1617.

C **PRINTER/PUBLISHER:** Henry Ballard/Arthur Johnson.

D **AUTHOR/COMPANY:** Anon./King's Men.

E **EXTERNAL ECHOES:** No.

F **INTERNAL REPETITIONS:** No.

G **FORMULAE:** No.

H **INSERTIONS:** Not detectable.

I **EXPANDED CLOWN'S ROLE:** No.

J **OMISSIONS:** Several episodes appear to be cut or abridged. Since the main plot extends over two days and the sub-plot over only one, and the latter contains several references to an episode in which Smug hid in, and fell from, a tree, a sub-plot episode depicting this material may have been cut (see Abrams ed., *MDE*, pp.16–21). Other incidents may be lacking: a scene in which the Lady Prioress gives Raymond 'ghostly counsell' (D4r, 16–17; Abrams suggests that it was the Prioress's approach which parted the lovers at D4r, 3–4), and an incident in which the two fathers find out about Millicent's plan to escape and hide in Brian's lodge. In *A Crew of Kind Gossips* (1609) Samuel Rowlands refers to a catch, sung in *MDE*, which is not in the extant text.

K **SPEECH LENGTH:** 7 speeches over 14 lines (highest totals: 25, 30, 42); 28 speeches between 8 and 14 lines.

L **STYLISTIC SUMMARY:** Stylistically good throughout.

M **UNCONFORMITIES:** The story of Peter Fabell, which opens the play and gives it its title, has little to do with the rest of the plot. Several speeches are misassigned. Errors in character name occur in the dialogue at c2v,30; c3r,29; c4r,25; D1v,16; E4r,28. The ending contains several unconformities. Millicent and Raymond have eloped, and are hiding in the St George Inn, whither Sir Arthur (Millicent's father) and Sir Ralph (the father of the man Sir Arthur intended Millicent to marry) hasten. The Knights enter an inn, summon Blague the host, only to be told by the Chamberlain that Blague is host of the inn across the road. The Chamberlain realises that the two inn-signs have been exchanged, and this device has lured the knights to the wrong inn (apparently The White Horse). The play's concluding lines contradict this: F4r,18–22 make it clear that Smug has straddled the sign of the White Horse to create a second St George. Apparently a property horse was unavailable for Smug, and the episode was replaced by the simpler expedient, conveyed verbally, of switching inn-signs. The extant text contains a conflation of the two incidents. See also Omission above.

N   STAGING AND PROPS: Curtained inner stage. Props include: couch, chimes, chair, and possibly a brake of fern (EIV, 6). A property tree and a property horse seem to have been unavailable (see Omissions and Unconformities). A dog is specified in the SD at EIV,23.

O   LENGTH: Total length: 1,534/Length of dialogue: 1,491 lines.

P   STAGE DIRECTIONS: Entrances and exits are frequently missing or deficient. In the final scene Smug exits, at Blague's invitation, to consume some sack (F3r,1–4). His re-entry is not marked; indeed the extant text has no suitable opportunity in which to bring him back, although he speaks at F4r,16. Several SDs are imperative('*Draw the curtaines*': A3v,8; '*Sit downe*': A4r,28); several SDs specify details of costume and action: '*yong Harry Clare, the men booted, the gentlewomen in / cloakes and safe-guardes*': BIr,3–4; '*Enter . . . trus- / sing their points as new vp*': E4r,28–9; '*Enter Banks. . .wet on his legs*' (E3r,18); '*The Miller comes out very softly*' (E3v,17). The SDs fluctuate between giving characters their names and their generic designations: Banks also appears as '*Miller*' (E3v,17), Sir John also appears as '*Priest*' (E4r,4), a fluctuation shared by SPs. These variants may relate to different sources (see Abrams ed., *MDE*, pp.23–5).

Q   VESTIGIAL CHARACTERS: No.

R   OTHER OBSERVATIONS: Middleton refers to *MDE* in his *Black Book* (SR 22 March 1604), indicating performances in and/or before 1603 (the theatres were closed from 19 March to 24 April 1603 and from 17 May 1603 to April 1604: see Wilson, *The Plague*, pp.110–11). A prose pamphlet, Thomas Brewer's *The Life and Death of the Merry Devil of Edmonton* (SR 5 April 1608) also deals with the events of the play.

S   PREVIOUS VERDICTS: The text is the result of 'the careless author, the indifferent printer, and the injudicious reviser' (Abrams ed., *MDE*, p.36); 'there are a few possible dislocations, and a few facile corruptions and vapid phrases that might point to reporting; but they do not amount to much, and the suggestion is hardly borne out by the general character of the text' (Greg (1944–5), '*MDE*', p.129; 'abridgement on a major scale' of foul papers (Proudfoot, 'Speech Prefixes', p.124).

T CONCLUSION: Not MR.

TABLE XXIV *The Merry Wives of Windsor*

A **PLAY/TEXT USED:** *The Merry Wives of Windsor* (1602)/Allen and Muir facsimile (1981).

B **SR/Q DATES:** 18 January 1602 to John Busby, transferred to Arthur Johnson same day/Q1 1602, Q2 1619 (F version 1623).

C **PRINTER/PUBLISHER:** Thomas Creede/Arthur Johnson.

D **AUTHOR/COMPANY:** William Shakespeare/Chamberlain's Men.

E **EXTERNAL ECHOES:** Although critics cite an echo from *Hamlet* (5.1.89) at F2r,7, and Pistol uses a line from *2H4* (5.3.118) at C1r,9, these do not qualify as accidental memorial echoes: see chapter 7, A.1.b (and see Kinney, 'Textual Signs', pp.207–11 for importance of authorial self-parody in *MWW*). The line from Sidney's *Astrophel and Stella* at D4v,5 is conceivably deliberate/authorial.

F **INTERNAL REPETITIONS:** C4v,31–2/E3v,28–9; E2r,14–15/E2r,18.

G **FORMULAE:** C3v,3–4/E3r,7; Mistress Quickly's 'all goe[s] through my hands' (twice) on B3r and v may be a speech mannerism, like Nym's 'there's the humour of it' or the Host's 'bully rook' or Sir Hugh's 'so kad vdge me'. Falstaff prefaces 4 speeches with exclamatory 'Well' on B1v–B2r; Falstaff refers to 'cuckally knaue[s]' 5 times on C4v–D1r.

H **INSERTIONS:** Not detectable.

I **EXPANDED CLOWN'S ROLE:** No.

J **OMISSIONS:** Not detectable.

K **SPEECH LENGTH:** 3 speeches over 14 lines (totals: 15, 18, 20); 19 speeches between 8 and 14 lines (11 of which are Falstaff's).

L **STYLISTIC SUMMARY:** Jerky and pedestrian style, well below accepted norms of period. A number of passages in rhyming couplets occur in the final scene but nowhere else.

M **UNCONFORMITIES:** Dr Caius' challenge to Sir Hugh (B4r) is pointless, since Simple has not revealed any reason for Caius to suspect Sir Hugh's involvement; Mistress Ford's instruction to her men about her husband's encounter with the buck-basket (F1r) is odd since she has no reason to suspect Ford's arrival. Shallow and Slender do not go to Ford's for dinner at D4r, yet are present on E1v. On C3v Mistress Quickly leaves before arranging a time and place for Mistress Ford to meet Falstaff. There are confusions in the chronology and reasons for Ford's absences, and in the colours of Anne Page's dress in masque (this latter also a problem in F).

N STAGING AND PROPS: Inner area with door, as a counting house (B3v), and probably used for the arras at FIV. Props include: letters, rapier, pen and ink, purse, cup of sack, bag of money, cudgell, weapons, large buck-basket, keys, angels, fowling pieces, satyr costumes, fairy costumes, tapers, a buck's head with horns, £20.

O LENGTH: Total length: 1,622/Length of dialogue: 1,502 lines.

P STAGE DIRECTIONS/SPEECH PREFIXES: SDs are generally careful in choreographing stage action, e.g.: '*There is a noise of hornes, the two women run away. / Enter sir Hugh like a Satyre, and boyes drest like Fayries, / mistresse Quickly, like the Queene of Fayries: they / sing a song about him, and afterward speake*' (G2r). The SD at C1r,25 is 6 lines too high. On E1v and F2r the SDs refer to Sir Hugh as '*Priest*' and the SPs name him '*Sir. Hu.*' and '*Hu.*'.

Q VESTIGIAL CHARACTERS: Slender is mute in scenes 8, 10, 15; Shallow is mute in scenes 10, 13, 15.

R OTHER OBSERVATIONS: Dr Caius seems to usurp some of the Host's lines on D2r,6–10 (which use the Host's colloquialisms; however Dr Caius does use the word 'Bully' on D1v,6).

S PREVIOUS VERDICTS: MR, adaptation, and abridgement (Greg (1954), *The Editorial Problem*, pp.71–2; for Greg's fluctuating opinion between 1910 and 1955 see Roberts, '*The Merry Wives* Q and F', pp.154–9); abridgement (Bracy, *The MWW: The History*; Craig, *A New Look*; Burkhart, *Shakespeare's Bad Quartos*); MR of alternative, adapted London version (Hart, *Stolne and Surreptitious*; Johnson, '*The MWW*, Q1'); 'a grossly inadequate report' edited and partly rewritten to become 'a roughly intelligible and coherent text' (Jowett, *Textual Companion*, p.341); MR for performance or for publication (Craik ed., *MWW*); MR (made by the actors playing the Host, Falstaff, and perhaps Pistol) of a Folio-related script (Irace, *Reforming the 'Bad' Quartos*, p.123).

T CONCLUSION: Probably MR.

TABLE XXV *Mucedorus*

A **PLAY/TEXT USED:** *Mucedorus* (1598)/TFT (1910).

B **SR/Q DATES:** NE/Q1 1598, Q2 1606, Q 3 ('Amplified with new additions') 1610, Q 4 1611, Q 5 1613, Q6 1615, Q 7 1618, Q8 1619, Q 9 1621.

C **PRINTER/PUBLISHER:** Unknown/William Jones.

D **AUTHOR/COMPANY:** Anon./unknown.

E **EXTERNAL ECHOES:** No.

F **INTERNAL REPETITIONS:** A4r,19–23/C2r,31–C2v,1–3 (with paraphrase on D4v,32–E1r,1).

G **FORMULAE:** No.

H **INSERTIONS:** Not detectable.

I **EXPANDED CLOWN'S ROLE:** The Clown's role is the play's *raison d'être*: Mouse is in 10 of the 16 scenes. Mouse's humour is primarily verbal (based on deliberate misunderstanding), not physical (see, for example, D1r–D1v). The additions in Q 3 extend Mouse's part.

J **OMISSIONS:** In scene 3 (B2v) the King of Arragon returns home victorious from war, bringing with him a prisoner, a young Catalonian prince, of whom nothing further is heard; the King announces the betrothal of his daughter to Segasto, who gives no reaction of joy or thanks (he is present: see B2v,21); the scene concludes (B3r) with an ominous private instruction to Collen, but no more is heard of the matter (indeed, Collen appears only once more, in the final scene).

K **SPEECH LENGTH:** 10 speeches over 14 lines (highest totals: 27, 32, 34); 20 speeches between 8 and 14 lines.

L **STYLISTIC SUMMARY:** Occasional loss of verse structure (e.g. B2v,14–17). Iambic pentameter mixed with fourteeners. Perfunctory dialogue is often simply an exchange of information. However, the alternation between scenes of exaggerated tragedy and comedy reflects the generic tug of war between Comedy and Envy in the play's induction (cf. Jupin ed., *Mucedorus*, p.38); the otherwise unexpected lyricism of Bremo, the wild man, at E2r is plausibly part of this design. The Induction and Epilogue scenes between Comedy and Envy seem stylistically superior to the rest of the Poem.

M **UNCONFORMITIES:** Mucedorus' response to Amadine's question about his disguise (F1r,16–17) seems unnecessarily cryptic. See also Omissions, above.

N **STAGING AND PROPS**: Props include: blood, garland of bays and (stringed) musical instrument for Comedy, drums (within), bear, sword, bear head, weapons, cudgel, walking staff, ale pot(s).

O **LENGTH**: Total length: 1,500/Length of dialogue: 1,424 lines.

P **STAGE DIRECTIONS/SPEECH PREFIXES**: SDS have a tendency to clarify the action, indicating movements, props, appearance, offstage action, relationships, and purpose; however, several of these SDS accompany dialogue so self-explanatory as to render the direction superfluous (e.g. DIR: '*Enter Mouse the clowne calling his maister*'). On CIV Mucedorus is identified only as '*the Shepheard*' (an appellation, also in italic, which begins the dialogue).

Q **VESTIGIAL CHARACTERS**: No.

R **OTHER OBSERVATIONS**: Mucedorus' lines at B4V,3–4 are in italic. The patriotic blessing of Elizabeth in the Epilogue (F4V) suggests that the play may have been performed at Court. Q3 (1610) was 'Amplified with new additions': 215 lines were added to QI and 30 lines were cut.

S **PREVIOUS VERDICTS**: MR (Kirschbaum, 'The Texts of *Mucedorus*', p.3); cut version for provincial presentation (Greg (1955), 'The Texts of *Mucedorus*'; Jupin ed., *Mucedorus*, p.11).

T **CONCLUSION**: Not MR.

TABLE XXVI *The Old Wife's Tale*

A **PLAY/TEXT USED:** *The Old Wife's Tale* (1595)/MSR (1909 for 1908).

B **SR/Q DATE:** 16 April 1595 to Ralph Hancock/Q 1595.

C **PRINTER/PUBLISHER:** John Danter/sold by Ralph Hancock and John Hardy.

D **AUTHOR/COMPANY.** George Peele/Queen's Men.

E **EXTERNAL ECHOES:** 1072–5 shared with *OF* 73–6.

F **INTERNAL REPETITIONS:** 634–5/1158–9; 406–7/992–3. The play is, however, extraordinarily repetitive in a deliberate fashion with characters quoting and reminding themselves and others of the words of another, often immediately: see 176–7/179–80; 195–202/205–10/493–7; 535–8/540–3; 593–5/599–601; 786–90/791–3/970–80; 837–8/845.

G **FORMULAE:** The metaphor 'Aprill of my age' appears 3 times (232, 833–4, 861); 'frollicke franion' occurs at 13 and (in the superlative) at 565.

H **INSERTIONS:** Not detectable.

I **EXPANDED CLOWN'S ROLE:** No. There is some evidence that clowning has been reduced by conflating the Clown's role with that of the friend of Jack (see Jenkins, 'Peele's *"Old Wive's Tale"*', p.184).

J **OMISSIONS:** Werstine provides bibliographical information to support the case for omission (by the printer) of material before Erestus' surprising and abrupt question 'Was shee fayre?' (190; Werstine, 'Provenance', p.244). Other suspected omissions cited by critics seem due to economic dramaturgy rather than lacunae (e.g. no scenes in which Huanebango and Booby, released from Sacrapant's spells, discover their wives' true nature/appearance).

K **SPEECH LENGTH:** 5 speeches over 14 lines (highest totals: 18, 20, 27); 15 speeches between 8 and 14 lines.

L **STYLISTIC SUMMARY:** Largely prose, interspersed with mixed metres, in keeping with the shifting genres of this folk tale (see Marx, '"Soft, who have we here?"'). The short abrupt speeches seem suited to the rapid action and concomitant air of wonder. Although one can invoke the folk-tale genre to explain (or rationalise) much in this play, one must nonetheless admit that it is uneven and at times confusing.

M **UNCONFORMITIES:** Madge twice introduces Huanebango (at 315–16 and 653–6). Jack and Eumenides seem not to have enough time to eat between 944 and 957. Sacrapant's magical skill is dependent on a light in a glass (512–17); his life, however, must be dependent on the wreath he wears (1011–13), although this is never articulated. When the 2 brothers discover the light they do not act as the Senex instructed them. Braunmuller provides cogent refutation of more alleged unconformities in *George Peele*, pp.55–6.

N STAGING AND PROPS: Curtained recess, stage trapdoor. Props include: cheese, pudding, lantern, candle, a cross 'that parts three seuerall waies', palmer's staff, alms pennies, pot of honey, two-hand sword, cake, chine of beef, pot of wine, swords, turf, light in a glass, 'little hill', pikestaff, flame of fire, 2 spades, goad, well, 4 pitchers, table with meat on it, fiddles, head with ears of corn, head full of gold, wreath, wool, horn, Sacrapant's head. Sound effects include: thunder and lightning.

O LENGTH: Total length: 1,170/Length of dialogue: 1,081 lines.

P STAGE DIRECTIONS/SPEECH PREFIXES: SDs are very attentive to props and action, and often discursive and detailed, e.g.: '*Enter the Hostes and* Iack, *setting meate on the / table, and Fidlers came to play*, Eumenides / *walketh vp and downe, and will eate no meate*' (916–19); '*Enter Senex at the Crosse stooping to gather*' (173). SDs are very clear about entrances and exits. There is occasional fluctuation between SDs and SPs, e.g. 'Sacrapant' (411)/ '*Coniurer*' (500). The ugly daughter is called '*Celanta*' at 753, 'Zelanto' at 960. The clown is called 'Booby' at 313 (and SPs in same scene), 'Corebus' elsewhere. The Churchwarden (who identifies himself as Steven Loache) is once given the SP '*Simon*' (552), possibly the name of an actor (see Chambers, *Elizabethan Stage*, vol.II, p.III). 2 SDs explain characters: 'Booby *the Clowne*' (313), 'Eumenides *the wandring Knight*' (520). SDs indicate when the verses in songs are to be repeated (307, 646). One SD may have been printed as dialogue: '*Wiggen* sets vpon / the parish with a Pike staffe' (573–4). 2 speeches by 2 Heads are run together at 970–82; presumably the 1st Head speaks until 976 (accompanied by action to which the SD at 972–3 refers), and the 2nd Head speaks at 977–82, although the accompanying action is given in a SD which is placed rather low (983–4).

Q VESTIGIAL CHARACTERS: Venelia is mute throughout. Corebus–Booby and Corebus–friend-of-Jack seem to be two characters conflated into one (see Jenkins, 'Peele's "*Old Wive's Tale*"', p.184; Hook ed., *OWT*, p.346).

R OTHER OBSERVATIONS: —

S PREVIOUS VERDICTS: 'a mutilated text' (Greg (1908) ed., *OWT*, p.vii); 'surely a memorial reconstruction' (Hoppe, *The Bad Quarto*, p.17); an abridged and revised version for a reduced provincial company (Jenkins, 'Peele's "Old Wive's Tale"', p.185); 'an authorial manuscript in a state before final revision' (Hook ed., *OWT*, p.356); scaled-down version made by Peele himself (Whitworth ed., *OWT*, p.xliv); 'a theatrical manuscript, perhaps an abridgement' (Werstine, 'Provenance', p.251).

T CONCLUSION: Not MR.

TABLE XXVII *Orlando Furioso*

A **PLAY/TEXT USED**: *Orlando Furioso* (1594)/MSR (1907).

B **SR/Q DATES**: SR 7 December 1593 to John Danter; assigned to Cuthbert Burby 28 May 1594/Q1 1594, Q2 1599.

C **PRINTER/PUBLISHER**: John Danter/Cuthbert Burby.

D **AUTHOR/COMPANY**: Robert Greene/played by Strange's Men (21 February onwards) 1591/2 (see *Henslowe's Diary*); *A Defence of Cony-Catching* (1592) says Greene sold *OF* to the Queen's Men, and then again to the Admiral's (c3r).

E **EXTERNAL ECHOES**: No.

F **INTERNAL REPETITIONS**: 183–4/201–2.

G **FORMULAE**: No: 'the matchlesse beauty of [fair] Angelica' is part of the rhetorical incantation of the wooers' speeches in scene 1, as are the closing lines of each of their speeches (39–40, 57–8, 79–80, 97–8), heralding Orlando's variant at 134–6. Orlando's journey to hell (and Arthur's to Africa) 'to seeke for Medor and Angelica' (used 3 times) is conceivably the repetitive formula of a madman.

H **INSERTIONS**: Several extra-metrical phrases (e.g. 235, 502).

I **EXPANDED CLOWN'S ROLE**: There is certainly a heavy emphasis on the mad Orlando's encounters with clowns. For the scene in which the Clown is presented to Orlando in disguise as Angelica (1027–8) cf. *A DrF* c2r,23ff., *JB* 679 and *KKK* 1717. These similarities suggest a vogue for fake-sweethearts in drama of the early 1590s.

J **OMISSIONS**: Not detectable.

K **SPEECH LENGTH**: 20 speeches over 14 lines (highest totals: 26, 27, 38); 38 between 8 and 14 lines.

L **STYLISTIC SUMMARY**: At times jerky and resistant to grammatical rules but nonetheless yielding tolerable sense. Occasional relics of verse in prose (e.g. 988–92).

M **UNCONFORMITIES**: 'Hesperides' used as a place name (63); unhistorical linking of Agathocles with the Lacedemonians (349); Lycaon's 'son' for 'daughter' at 396 (although the error may be 'Lycaon' for 'Latona': Latona's son is referred to at 382 and 1264); Brandemart is killed at 981 and never referred to again, although it is Rodamant who is reported dead at 1105; the setting, Africa, is referred to as India at 1081, 1111, 1129, and 1136, but reverts to Africa at 1449 and 1520. The reason for Marsillus' and Mandricard's disguise as Indian palmers (1093ff.) is never given.

N **STAGING AND PROPS**: Upper stage. Props include: trees or something approximating trees on which poems may be pinned, roundelays, false leg, 'spits and dripping-pans', fiddle, glass of wine, fairy wand, drum and trumpets, red banderoll, scarf.

O **LENGTH**: Total length: 1,613/Length of dialogue: 1,518 lines.

P **STAGE DIRECTIONS/SPEECH PREFIXES**: SDS are sometimes vague ('He...sings any odde toy': 1213), permissive ('Then let the musicke play before him': 1285), and imperative ('and so/goe forth': 1285–6). SDS are attentive to details of costume ('Enter Orlando with a scarfe before his face': 1350–1, 1475) and action ('He spyes the Roundelayes': 640; 'Orgalio proffers to goe in': 852; 'He goeth to Angelica and knowes her not': 987). SDS are occasionally inaccurate or incomplete about who enters or remains on stage. The first 5 SPS are given centred, single lines and full names.

Q **VESTIGIAL CHARACTERS**: Rossillion and Aquitaine are mute in scene 2 (378ff.); Rossillion is a ghost character throughout.

R **OTHER OBSERVATIONS**: The MS 'Part' of Orlando in the papers of Edward Alleyn at Dulwich College differs significantly from the role of Orlando in Q.

S **PREVIOUS VERDICTS**: MR, abridgement, and adaptation, designed for provincial performance, in which cuts make room for comic expansions. This MR was supplemented by actors' scrolls (which provided the roundelays); the Latin names were corrected by someone in the printing-house (Greg (1923), *Two Elizabethan Stage Abridgements*).

T **CONCLUSION**: Not MR.

TABLE XXVIII *Pericles*

A **PLAY/TEXT USED**: *Pericles* (1609)/Shakespeare Quarto facsimile (1940).

B **SR/Q DATES**: 20 May 1608 to Edward Blount/Q1 1609, Q2 1609, Q 3 1611, Q 4 1619.

C **PRINTER/PUBLISHER**: (Thomas Creede sigs.B, F–I); William White: sigs.A, C–E/Henry Gosson.

D **AUTHOR/COMPANY**: George Wilkins? and William Shakespeare/King's Men.

E **EXTERNAL ECHOES**: No.

F **INTERNAL REPETITIONS**: No.

G **FORMULAE**: No.

H **INSERTIONS**: Not detectable.

I **EXPANDED CLOWN'S ROLE**: No.

J **OMISSIONS**: Not detectable.

K **SPEECH LENGTH**: 19 speeches over 14 lines (highest totals: 52, 54, 60); excluding the speeches of Gower (see Taylor in Previous Verdicts, below) there are 12 speeches over 14 lines (totals: 15–33). 40 speeches between 8 and 14 lines.

L **STYLISTIC SUMMARY**: Speeches are long and well developed, but occasionally suffer from *non sequitur*s and often from the breakdown of metre. The Poem is stylistically uneven due to the wrecked verse but not as uneven as is frequently alleged.

M **UNCONFORMITIES**: Helicanus' speech about flatterers seems unmotivated (B1v). Cerimon asks whether the sea cast up Thaisa's coffin, having just been told it did (E3v; however, this may merely signal his amazement). Lysimachus says he and others will withdraw (H3v), but clearly they do not.

N **STAGING AND PROPS**: 2 entrance doors. Props include: poison, gold, letters, sword, 5 shields with arms and Latin mottos, heads (bodies?) of dead suitors, napkins, cups, bowl of wine, bags of spices, baby, basket of flowers, casket of jewels, rusty armour, tomb, viol, fishing nets, fire, coffin.

O **LENGTH**: Total length: 2,358/Length of dialogue: 2,271 lines.

P **STAGE DIRECTIONS/SPEECH PREFIXES**: SDs are seriously deficient in entrances and exits. 13 exits are lacking in the play; more important, 5 entrances are missing or incomplete (see D1r,1; E4v,8; G4r,11; H2v,17; H3r,28). Designations in SDs and SPs fluctuate (e.g. *wife/Dion*[yza].: B3v; *three Bawdes / Pander, Boult, Bawd*: F3v; *Pirates/ Sayler*: F4r. One SD is indeterminate (*two or three Lords*: D2v).

Q VESTIGIAL CHARACTERS: No.

R OTHER OBSERVATIONS: Apart from grammatical *non sequitur*s and broken-down/submerged verse, this text is generally very good (as numerous professional productions illustrate). An anonymous commonplace book (c.1650) in the Folger Shakespeare Library (MS v.a.87) contains copious extracts from *Pericles*, 5 of which provide variant readings.

S PREVIOUS VERDICTS: Possibly a reported text, but a good one (Greg (1954), *The Editorial Problem*, p.74); revised authorial copy (Craig, '*Pericles*'); MR (Edwards, 'An Approach to *Pericles*'); 'corrupt' reported copy (Hoeniger ed., *Pericles*); part foul papers, part MR (Musgrove, 'The First Quarto of *Pericles*'); a 'bewilderingly corrupt text', memorially reconstructed by a boy actor, perhaps aided by a hired man with access to Gower's part (Taylor, 'The Transmission of *Pericles*').

T CONCLUSION: Wrecked verse is the only possible indication of MR (see the *caveat* at the end of section A.5 in chapter 7). If a reported text, it is a very good one.

TABLE XXIX *Philaster*

A **PLAY/TEXT USED:** *Philaster* (1620)/STC MFM.

B **SR/Q DATES:** 10 January 1620 to Thomas Walkley/Q1 1620, Q2 ('corrected and amended') 1622.

C **PRINTER/PUBLISHER:** Nicholas Okes/Thomas Walkley.

D **AUTHOR/COMPANY:** Francis Beaumont and John Fletcher/King's Men.

E **EXTERNAL ECHOES:** No.

F **INTERNAL REPETITIONS:** No.

G **FORMULAE:** No.

H **INSERTIONS:** Not detectable.

I **EXPANDED CLOWN'S ROLE:** No.

J **OMISSIONS:** Not detectable.

K **SPEECH LENGTH:** 10 speeches over 14 lines (highest totals: 20, 22, 25); 50 speeches between 8 and 14 lines.

L **STYLISTIC SUMMARY:** Much verse printed as prose; many lines between verse and prose. Exposition in scene 1 seems rather blunt and clumsy. General quality competent.

M **UNCONFORMITIES:** The happy ending in which Gallathea and 'Bellario' accept husbands seems rather hasty. The *non sequitur*s and mishearings cited by Gurr (ed., *Philaster* pp.lxxvi–lxxvii) and Turner (ed., *Philaster*, p.393) seem tenuous.

N **STAGING AND PROPS:** 2 doors; upper stage; inner recess (for arras on D1r and D2v and possibly the prison on H3r). Props include: throne, swords, bush, garland of flowers, purse of money, crown, cornets.

O **LENGTH:** Total length: 2,356/Length of dialogue: 2,283 lines.

P **STAGE DIRECTIONS/SPEECH PREFIXES:** SDs are generally precise in entrances and exits, and very concerned with staging throughout e.g. '*Phy: whisper the King*' (B4r,10); '*They prease / to come in*' (D4v,21–2); '*Giues vm his purse*' (I3v,19); 'PHILASTER *creepes out of a bush*' (H2r,24). Many SDs are in RH margin (cf. Q1 *Othello*, also printed by Okes for Walkley in 1622). SDs sometimes refer to the characters generically (e.g. '*three Gentlemen*' (E2r,7), '*Princesse*' (C1r,25); one SD is explanatory: '*his boy, called* BELLARIO' (C3v,27).

Q **VESTIGIAL CHARACTERS:** No.

R **OTHER OBSERVATIONS:** An address from the publisher to the reader in

Q2 (1622) describes Q1 as 'mained [sic] and deformed', having suffered 'dangerous and gaping wounds' for which neither the printer nor the publisher accepts responsibility.

S PREVIOUS VERDICTS: 'a bad quarto' (Kirschbaum, 'A Census', p.42); 'a botched text throughout. . .printed from a clumsy, dictated transcript of the central part of authorial foul papers, by a scribe familiar with the play in performance' (Gurr ed., *Phil.*, pp.lxxvi, lxxvii); 'I am inclined, but with some reservations, to think it a bad text' (Turner ed., *Phil.*, p.396); censored text (Savage, 'The Gaping Wounds', Clare, *'Art Made Tongue-tied'*, p. 186); 'evidence for reporting is not conclusive' (Ashe ed., *Phil.*, p.xxx).

T CONCLUSION: Not MR.

TABLE XXX The Abdication scene in *Richard 2*

A **PLAY/TEXT USED**: Abdication scene in *Richard 2* (1608), sigs H1v,10–H3v,22/Allen and Muir facsimile (1981).

B **SR/Q DATES**: 29 August 1597 to Andrew Wise; assigned to Matthew Law 25 June 1603/Q4 1608, Q5 1615.

C **PRINTER/PUBLISHER**: William White/Matthew Law.

D **AUTHOR/COMPANY**: William Shakespeare/King's Men.

E **EXTERNAL ECHOES**: No.

F **INTERNAL REPETITIONS**: No.

G **FORMULAE**: No.

H **INSERTIONS**: Not detectable.

I **EXPANDED CLOWN'S ROLE**: No.

J **OMISSIONS**: Not detectable.

K **SPEECH LENGTH**: 3 speeches over 14 lines (totals: 15, 16, 22); 5 speeches between 8 and 14 lines.

L **STYLISTIC SUMMARY**: Excellent. Some mislineation (e.g. H1v,23-7).

M **UNCONFORMITIES**: No.

N **STAGING AND PROPS**: –

O **LENGTH**: Total length: 160/Length of dialogue: 159 lines.

P **STAGE DIRECTIONS/SPEECH PREFIXES**: York's re-entry with Richard at H1v,18 is not indicated.

Q **VESTIGIAL CHARACTERS**: No.

R **OTHER OBSERVATIONS**: –

S **PREVIOUS VERDICTS**: Copy obtained from 'some subordinate person employed about the theatre' or by shorthand (Pollard, *King Richard II*, p.64); MR (Ure ed., *R2*, p.xv); 'a hasty transcript probably made from dictation' (Gurr ed., *R2*, p.176); 'features suggest a reported text' (Jowett in *Textual Companion*, p.307); 'a hasty transcript compiled from dictation or memory' (Clare, *'Art Made Tongue-tied'*, p.48).

T **CONCLUSION**: Not MR.

TABLE XXXI *Richard 3*

A **PLAY/TEXT USED:** *Richard 3* (1597)/Shakespeare Quarto facsimile (1959).

B **SR/Q DATES:** 20 October 1597 to Andrew Wise/Q1 1597, Q2 1598, Q3 1602, Q4 1605, Q5 1612, Q6 1622 (F version 1623).

C **PRINTER/PUBLISHER:** Valentine Simmes: sigs.A–G; Peter Short: sigs.H–M/Andrew Wise.

D **AUTHOR/COMPANY:** William Shakespeare/Chamberlain's Men.

E **EXTERNAL ECHOES:** No.

F **INTERNAL REPETITIONS:** No.

G **FORMULAE:** No. (The ghosts' incantatory 'let me sit heauie on thy soule tomorrow', 'dispaire and die', and 'liue and florish' are clearly rhetorically deliberate.)

H **INSERTIONS:** Not detectable.

I **EXPANDED CLOWN'S ROLE:** No.

J **OMISSIONS:** Not detectable.

K **SPEECH LENGTH:** 34 speeches over 14 lines (highest totals: 34, 37, 44); 56 speeches between 8 and 14 lines.

L **STYLISTIC SUMMARY:** Excellent.

M **UNCONFORMITIES:** '*Ryu.*' (Rivers) is given a speech prefix in scene 12 (G1r,37), despite having been executed in scene 11 (G1r,30).

N **STAGING AND PROPS:** Upper stage; 2 doors. Props include: hearse, ring, sword, letter of commission, indictment, weapons, paper, crown, head of Hastings, throne, armour, drums, trumpets, 2 tents.

O **LENGTH:** Total length: 3,488/Length of dialogue: 3,416 lines.

P **STAGE DIRECTIONS:** SDs frequently omit important speaking characters (e.g. Dorset and Hastings on B3v,16; Catesby on F2v,24 and K3v,29; Ratcliffe on L1v,3). SDs are often vague, concluding lists with '&c' (e.g. D3v,16; E4v,23; M2r,5; M3r,31). SDs indicate stage action, e.g. spitting (B2r,18) and whispering (F4v,31–2, L1v,12); see also: '*Here she lets fall/the sword*' (B2v,8–9); '*Here he ascendeth/the throne*' (H4v,9–10); '*Richard starteth vp out of a dreame*' (L4v,19). The law of re-entry is violated on E4v, where the Cardinal exits at the end of scene 8 (2.4) and enters at the beginning of scene 9 (3.1). There are fluctuations in character designations in SDs and SPs: Richard is '*Ri*' in SD and '*Glo.*' in SP on C3v, Derby is sometimes '*Darby/ie*' in SPs and SDs, sometimes '*Stanley*' (see

D4v,31; F4r,31; K4r,6), and the murderers are sometimes '*murtherers*', sometimes '*Executioners*' (see C4r,11, D1r,28 and 30). The murderer of the princes is called '*Tirrel*' in SD and dialogue on his first appearance (11r; and once Iames Tirrell: 11r), but is given the full name '*Sir Francis Tirrell*' in the SD at 12r,21).

Q VESTIGIAL CHARACTERS: No.

R OTHER OBSERVATIONS: Richmond and Richard's pre-battle speeches to their armies are given the literary headings '*His oration to his souldiers*' (M1v) and '*His Oration to his army*' (M2v).

S PREVIOUS VERDICTS: MR and deliberate abridgement for provincial tour, dictated to scribe writing in shorthand (Patrick, *The Textual History*); MR made collectively by company (Greg (1938), review of Patrick, *The Textual History*; Hammond ed., *R3*); authorial draft (Urkowitz, 'Reconsidering the Relationship'); MR of adapted touring text (Davison, 'Bibliography').

T CONCLUSION: Not MR.

TABLE XXXII *Romeo and Juliet*

A PLAY/TEXT USED: *Romeo and Juliet* (1597)/Allen and Muir facsimile (1981).

B SR/Q DATES: NE/Q1 1597 (Q2 version 1599, 1609, 1622; F 1623).

C PRINTER/PUBLISHER: John Danter: sigs.A–D; Edward Allde (?): sigs.E–K/publisher unknown.

D AUTHOR/COMPANY: William Shakespeare/Hunsdon's Men.

E EXTERNAL ECHOES: No.

F INTERNAL REPETITIONS: H1r,35/H1v,8.

G FORMULAE: No.

H INSERTIONS: Not detectable.

I EXPANDED CLOWN'S ROLE: No.

J OMISSIONS: Not detectable.

K SPEECH LENGTH: 15 speeches over 14 lines (highest totals: 25, 34, 41); 50 speeches between 8 and 14 lines.

L STYLISTIC SUMMARY: Excellent quality: speeches are coherent and well developed.

M UNCONFORMITIES: Romeo mistakenly calls Juliet a 'Mountague' on c4r,3. Friar Lawrence is called Friar Francis on his first appearance (D3v,21); a lost *Friar Francis* play appears in Henslowe's *Diary* and in Heywood's *Apology for Actors*.

N STAGING AND PROPS: Window above; bed within curtains (possibly a curtained property bed, but perhaps a bed within an inner stage with curtains). Props include: weapons, ring, logs and coals, rope ladder, 2 mattocks, crowbar, letters, spade, torch, masks, tomb, lantern, rosemary, 20 ducats, vials, cup, flowers.

O LENGTH: Total length: 2,341/Length of dialogue: 2,225 lines.

P STAGE DIRECTIONS/SPEECH PREFIXES: SDs are often deficient in entrances and exits (entrances are missing for Cousin Capulet and Tybalt at c2v,3, for Romeo at D4r,14, and for Friar Lawrence at 14r,16). There are discrepancies between characters' designations in SDs and in SPs (e.g. '*Capolets wife*' in SD on F2v, '*M.*' or '*Mo.*' in SP; 'Citizens' in dialogue and SD on F2r, '*Watch.*' in SP; '*Page*' in SD on 14v, '*Boy.*' in SP; '*Oldeman*' on 11r in SD, '*Cap.*' in SP. SPs frequently fluctuate: Balthasar is sometimes '*Balth*', sometimes '*Man*'; Lady Capulet is sometimes *Wife*, sometimes *Mo[th]*. SDs are sensitive to staging, e.g. '*Nurse offers to goe in and turnes againe*' (G2r,15); '*Fryer stoops and lookes on the blood and weapons*' (K2r,20); '*They whisper in his eare*' (C4r,7). On H2v,1 the SD '*Enter Paris*' is an error for '*Enter Iuliet*'.

Q **VESTIGIAL CHARACTERS:** No.

R **OTHER OBSERVATIONS:** 'Will will tell thee' (I1r,25) seems to be a reference to Will Kemp. The Nurse's role in scenes 3 and 5 is printed in italic.

S **PREVIOUS VERDICTS:** 'in the main a report' (Greg (1954), *The Editorial Problem*, p.62); abridgement (Burkhart, *Shakespeare's Bad Quartos*); MR of 'a version adapted for acting' (Gibbons ed., *R&J*, p.2, and cf. Mooney, 'Text and Performance'); authorial draft (Urkowitz, '"Do me the kindnes"').

T **CONCLUSION:** Not MR.

TABLE XXXIII *Sir Thomas Wyatt*

A **PLAY/TEXT USED:** *Sir Thomas Wyatt* (1607)/TFT (1914).

B **SR/Q DATES:** NE/Q1 1607, Q2 1612.

C **PRINTER/PUBLISHER:** Edward Allde/Thomas Archer.

D **AUTHOR/COMPANY:** Dekker and Webster on title-page; see also Other Observations, below/Queen Anne's Men.

E **EXTERNAL ECHOES:** No.

F **INTERNAL REPETITIONS:** Paraphrase on C4r,10/C4r,27; F4v,21/27.

G **FORMULAE:** Some formulaic paraphrases and repetitions: A3r,13–15/B4v,18–19/C1r,20, 22; D3v,22/F3v,5; F1r,11–16/F4r,25–9.

H **INSERTIONS:** Extra-metrical phrase 'Farwell my loue' (D3v,21) spoils the couplet and may be an anticipation of the similar phrase on F3v,4, which is integrated into a couplet.

I **EXPANDED CLOWN'S ROLE:** No.

J **OMISSIONS:** See Unconformities below.

K **SPEECH LENGTH:** 7 speeches over 14 lines (highest totals: 21, 22, 36); 41 speeches between 8 and 14 lines.

L **STYLISTIC SUMMARY:** Although there are unmetrical lines (e.g. A2v,5–12) and blunt verse throughout, the play sustains a high standard of imagery. Of numerous examples see especially F2v,26–8 (Dudley); D1v,3–26, D4r,5–11 (Wyatt); A3v,13–15, A4r,19–23 (Jane; the last example is assigned to Dudley but the lines are more probably Jane's). The final scene carefully modulates tone and character: Dudley sarcastically welcomes his enemies (F4v,13–18), has his righteous and poetic anger cautioned by Jane ('Patience': F4v,28), begs, distraught, to precede his wife in death (G1r–v), then engages in a foolish but lovingly protective gesture when he insists that the Hangman beg pardon for Jane's death from her husband (G1v,23–5). By G2v his emotion has become movingly macabre as he uses conventional Petrarchan terms to praise the beauty of Jane's disembodied face/head. (I am grateful to Gwendolyn Guth for these points.) The opening scene differs stylistically from the rest of the text, containing abrupt exchanges of much information quickly and redundantly, and introducing characters very obviously (e.g. A2v,1; A3r,8). Given the vulnerability of MSS' outer leaves, it is possible that the opening scene was damaged and had to be rewritten/reconstructed (cf. *1 If You* for a similar anomaly).

M **UNCONFORMITIES:** There are extensive plotting contradictions concerning Suffolk and Northumberland (see scenes 3, 4, 5, 9, 10, 11, and Shaw, '*Sir Thomas Wyat*'; see also chapter 7, B.1). Martin (thesis, '*If You Know Not Me*', pp.41–3) argues that the speeches of Jane and Guilford on D2v–D3r seem jumbled, and offers a rearrangement; however, the desultory and distracted nature of the conversation seems in keeping with the characters' grief and tension. There is a *non sequitur* at B2v,23–30, presumably because of missing line(s). On F2v,34–F3r,1 Arundell says he will petition the Queen to spare Dudley and Jane but on F3r,16–17 he suddenly sanctions the executions for no apparent reason. At B3r,6 Wyatt is oddly cut off, and Arundell returns to former business. The question at E1v,15 seems odd since Brett has just spoken; perhaps line 14 should belong to Arundell who is otherwise a ghost in this scene.

N **STAGING AND PROPS:** Upper stage. Props include: purse, mace, prayer book, council table, basket for eggs, letters, bottle, bag of food, halter (for suicide by strangling), drum and colours, trumpet, swords, grate (?D2v,26), chairs of state and bar for the trial scene (F1r), severed head of Lady Jane Grey.

O **LENGTH:** Total length: 1,768/Length of dialogue: 1,682 lines.

P **STAGE DIRECTIONS/SPEECH PREFIXES:** Many SDs omit entrances: Arundell speaks in scene 1 without prior entry (A3r,7), as do Sir Harry Isely, Sir George Harper, and Sir Robert Rodston in scene 12 (D3v,23); Ellen has no entry in scene 17 (F4v,1); the '*Clark*' who speaks at F1r,20 has no entrance; presumably a messenger enters at F3r,28 with an amendment to the execution order. 2 SDs appear to be influenced by the dialogue: e.g. '. . .heere lyes young Guilford, / heere the Lady Iane . . . *Enter Young Guilford and the / Lady Iane*' (F4r,30–F4v,1; this is the only SD to refer to Guilford as 'young'. See also A4r,27–9). SDs are generally attentive to action ('*A Trumpet sounds, and no answere*': B4v,24; '*Enter Homes sweating with bottell and* Bag': C2v,1), to stage choreography (A4r,14; E3v,34), to offstage noise (C1r,26; E1r,2), and to details suggesting place and mood ('*Enter Sir Thomas Wyat in the / Tower*': F3v,12–13; see also B2r,28–30). Speeches are sometimes misattributed (e.g. A4r,19; D1v,27).

Q **VESTIGIAL CHARACTERS:** 6 vestigial characters: Arundell speaks without an entrance on A3r,7 (see Stage Directions, above), and is mute on E1v (scene 13); Winchester is a ghost in the SD at B2r,28 (historically he was still in prison); Lord Huntington is addressed in dialogue at C1r,21 (although he has no entrance, he was present historically); Rodston and Isely are mutes in scene 14 (E3r,5), as is Pembroke in scene 16 (F1r,4). The SD at D2v,13 provides an entrance for Guilford and Dudley, who are one and the same.

R **OTHER OBSERVATIONS**: Bowers (ed., *Dekker*, vol.1) discusses compositorial practices regarding punctuation and capitalisation which suggest that the underlying manuscript copy was very difficult. Henslowe paid Chettle, Dekker, Heywood, Smith and Webster for the first part of a Lady Jane play in October 1602 and advanced partial payment on a second part (*Diary*, 15 October–27 October 1602). The impression is that two plays about Lady Jane, in which Sir Thomas Wyatt was the central unifying figure (cf. Hoy, *Introductions* vol.1, p.312), have been compressed into one. *1 Lady Jane* may be represented by TLN 1–679 (A2r–C3v,23), *2 Lady Jane* by TLN 680–1768 (C3v,24–G3r); thus the second part of *STW* is more leisurely paced (cf. *FV*).

S **PREVIOUS VERDICTS**: Reported text (Martin, thesis, '*If You Know Not Me*', p.274; Doran ed., *1 If You*, p.xviii; Kirschbaum 'A Census', p.33); 'an actors' built version of a Wyatt-Lady Jane plot shortened for performance in the provinces' (Halstead, 'Note on the Text', p.589); an unedited version of a reporter's first memorial draft (Bowers ed., *Dekker* vol.1, pp.399–400, n.1); 'a very bad quarto'; nonetheless 'the play as it stands is perfectly intelligible' (Gasper, *The Dragon*, pp.45–6).

T **CONCLUSION**: Probably not MR but the possibility (a slight one) cannot be ruled out. The quality is very similar to *1 If You.*

TABLE XXXIV (Additions to) *The Spanish Tragedy*

A **PLAY/TEXT USED:** Additions to *The Spanish Tragedy* (1602)/MSR (1925).

B **SR/Q DATE:** Transferred to Thomas Pavier 14 August 1600/Q 4 1602, Q 5 1603, Q6 1610–11, Q 7 1615, Q8 1618, Q 9 1623.

C **PRINTER/PUBLISHER:** William White/Thomas Pavier.

D **AUTHOR/COMPANY:** Thomas Kyd is author of *The Spanish Tragedy* as first published in 1592; Ben Jonson was paid by Philip Henslowe in 1601–2 for additions to *Hieronimo*.

E **EXTERNAL ECHOES:** 3138 and 3140, possibly formulaic, are a variant of A *DrF* B2v,29–30.

F **INTERNAL REPETITIONS:** No.

G **FORMULAE:** No.

H **INSERTIONS:** No.

I **EXPANDED CLOWN'S ROLE:** No.

J **OMISSIONS:** No.

K **SPEECH LENGTH:** 2 speeches over 14 lines (totals: 20, 45); 12 speeches between 8 and 14 lines.

L **STYLISTIC SUMMARY:** Metrically fairly erratic. The prose (or verse embedded in prose) in lines 2180–245 is printed partly in prose, partly in verse. The quality of Hieronimo's speeches at 1866–910, 2081–6, 2096–103, 2111–18, 2128–36 is consistently high.

M **UNCONFORMITIES:** No.

N **STAGING AND PROPS:** Door. Props include: sword, dead body of Horatio, torches, taper, tree, seat, book.

O **LENGTH:** Total length: 342/Length of dialogue: 333 lines.

P **STAGE DIRECTIONS:** Competent. Three SDs specify stage action: *'One knockes within at the doore'* (2137); *'The Painter and he sits downe'* (2173); *'He beates the Painter in, then comes out againe / with a Booke in his hand'* (2246–7).

Q **VESTIGIAL CHARACTERS:** No.

R **OTHER OBSERVATIONS:** –

S **PREVIOUS VERDICTS:** New material written by an unknown author for the version of *Hieronimo* owned by the Admiral's Men and noted as 'ne' in Henslowe's *Diary* in 1597 (Greg (1925) ed., *ST 1602*, p.xix); additions 'supplied by a reporter relying on his memory' (Greg and Smith (1949)

eds., *ST 1592*, p.xv); replacement material obtained surreptitiously by
Pavier – 'perhaps by transcript, but conceivably through the actors'
(Edwards ed., *ST*, p.lxiv); indications of memorial reconstruction but
'the problem remains baffling' (Cairncross ed., *1 Hieronimo* and *ST*,
p.xxiv); replacement material by Jonson, showing 'some evidence of
textual corruption' (Barton, *Ben Jonson*, p.14); authorial composition
written by someone more like Shakespeare than Jonson (Craig,
'Authorial Styles').

T CONCLUSION: Not MR.

TABLE XXXV *The Taming of A Shrew*

A **PLAY/TEXT USED**: *The Taming of A Shrew* (1594)/Praetorius facsimile (1886).

B **SR/Q DATES**: 2 May 1594 to Peter Short; sold by Cuthbert Burby to Nicholas Ling 22 January 1607, and transferred from Ling to John Smethwick 19 November 1607/Q1 1594, Q2 1596, Q3 1607 (*The Shrew*: F 1623).

C **PRINTER/PUBLISHER**: Peter Short/sold by Cuthbert Burby.

D **AUTHOR/COMPANY**: Anon./Pembroke's Men (but see Other Observations below).

E **EXTERNAL ECHOES**: Several passages are from Marlowe's works: A2r,17–20 (from Bevington and Rasmussen eds., *Dr. F, A- and B-Texts*, 1.3.1–4); c3r,3–5 (from Bowers ed., *1 Tamburlaine* 3.2.18–20); and c4r,31–4 (a composite from *1 Tamburlaine* 1.2.95–6 and 1.2.194–5). Several passages paraphrase Marlowe's work or are conceived under the influence of it: A4r,29–30 (cf. *2 Tamburlaine* 1.2.9–10); D3v,6–8 (cf. *2 Tamburlaine* 4.3.12–13); B2r,4–8 (cf. *2 Tamburlaine* 2.4.84–8). The Marlowe material is possibly deliberate pastiche, as Polidor's boy seems to acknowledge ('I did but iest') on c4v,13 (see also Marcus, 'The Shakespeare Editor'). Several lines in Kate's submissive speech come from Du Bartas's *The Divine Weeks* (see Taylor, 'The Strange Case').

F **INTERNAL REPETITIONS**: Paraphrase at B1v,6/B1v,10; A2r,17, 21/G2r,20–1.

G **FORMULAE**: Many flat oaths and colloquial fillers: 'souns' (19 times), 'I warrant' (8 times), 'but soft' (6 times), 'tush' (5 times), 'belike' (4 times). The adverb 'presently' appears in phrases 10 times, the adjective 'crystal' or 'crystalline' 7 times. Often the formulae occur in a cluster, as on D1v (6 instances in 24 lines).

H **INSERTIONS**: Not detectable.

I **EXPANDED CLOWN'S ROLE**: Sander's role seems to be one of the highlights of the play, at least to Christopher Slie. The humour is often insipid and at times overstressed (e.g. B4v,6–10), although this need not mean it is expanded.

J **OMISSIONS**: Not detectable.

K **SPEECH LENGTH**: 7 speeches over 14 lines (highest totals: 18, 28, 29); 30 speeches between 8 and 14 lines. The long speeches are predominantly in the sub-plot. Elsewhere speeches tend to be short and staccato, reduced to mere statement of purpose.

L STYLISTIC SUMMARY: Very uneven. The sub-plot contains moments of Marlovian eloquence; the taming plot is verbally abrupt and blunt. Overall, the standard of writing is flatly pedestrian, very prosaic. There are several unmetrical lines.

M UNCONFORMITIES: Scene 3 presents Kate's wedding as being both on Sunday and tomorrow (which is not Sunday); the amounts of the wager in scene 15 vary; in scene 15 Alfonso doubts that Kate will come to Ferando's bidding (F4r,6), although he has not been told that the wager involves a summons, only that it requires an expression of love (F4r,3). In the dénouement Alfonso seems to know Valeria's name and position as servant to the Duke of Cestus' son, although he has not been told this (F2r,31–3). Some speeches make poor sense, lacking main verbs or transitions (e.g. C1v,3–7). Slie's exclamation 'O braue, heers two fine gentlewomen' (C1v,29), which heralds the approach of a man and a woman, is probably a humorous example of Slie's misunderstanding and not a structural unconformity. The disguised characters are never given disguise names but retain their true names in dialogue throughout (e.g. D2r,26. See Miller, thesis, 'A Critical Old-Spelling Edition').

N STAGING AND PROPS: An upper stage is indicated by the dialogue on F3r when the Lord instructs his men to replace Slie 'below'. Stage doors possibly referred to in opening SD. Props include: back packs, table with banquet, chair, wine and drinking vessel, meat, dagger, trumpets, lute, cap, gown, music.

O LENGTH: Total length: 1,627/Length of dialogue: 1,520 lines.

P STAGE DIRECTIONS/SPEECH PREFIXES: SDs frequently refer to characters generically yet the SPs specify names: e.g. 'Enter two yoong Gentlemen' (A4v), *'Pol[i].'* and *'Aurel.'* in SPs; 'Enter the Lord and his men' (A3v), *'Wil.'* and *'Tom.'* in SPs. SDs are attentive to stage presentation e.g. asides, laughter, costume: see B2r,23–4 (*'Saunders/*with a blew coat'), B3v,13 ('Enter S*annder* laughing'), C2v,2 ('She throwes it downe'), E4v,22 (*'Ferando* speakes to the olde man'). The SD at D1v,3 has an additive style, separating the list of 7 characters by 6 uses of the conjunction 'and' ('Enter *Ferando and Kate and Alfonso. . .'*). One SD is indeterminate: *'Enter Sanders with two or three / seruing men'* (D2v,12–13). SDs are sometimes set in italic, sometimes in roman. 2 SDs seem to take their descriptions from the dialogue (or vice-versa); see C3v,13,19 ('Enter *Ferando* baselie attired'. . . 'why art thou thus basely attired?') and D4r,13–14 ('Enter *Sander and his Mistres*'. . . 'Come Mistris').

Q **VESTIGIAL CHARACTERS**: No.

R **OTHER OBSERVATIONS**: Verbal quality is very similar to that of *FV* (SR 1594, Q1 1598; see table x): both texts are heavily formulaic (sharing especially a predilection for 'souns' and 'belike'), prosaic, blunt, and flat. In view of this similarity Honigmann's suggestion ('Shakespeare's Lost Source-Plays') that *A Shrew* is a report made by the Queen's Men merits attention.

S **PREVIOUS VERDICTS**: MR (Alexander, '*The Taming*'); 'stolen and garbled version' (Honigmann, quoted by Morris ed., *The Shrew*); MR which involves 'conscious originality' (Hosley, 'Sources and Analogues', p.293); MR made by actors with or without the assistance of a writer (Morris ed., *The Shrew*); a 'derivative text dependent on *The Shrew*, but. . . rewritten more extensively (especially in the sub-plot) than is usually the case with memorially reconstructed texts' (Thompson ed., *The Shrew*, p.174); MR and thorough adaptation of *The Shrew* (Miller, thesis, 'A Critical Old-Spelling Edition').

T **CONCLUSION**: Part MR (most notably in taming plot).

TABLE XXXVI *Thomas Lord Cromwell*

A **PLAY/TEXT USED:** *Thomas Lord Cromwell* (1602)/TFT (1911).

B **SR/Q DATES:** 11 August 1602 to William Cotton/Q1 1602, Q2 1613.

C **PRINTER/PUBLISHER:** Richard Read/William Jones.

D **AUTHOR/COMPANY:** 'W.S.'/Chamberlain's Men.

E **EXTERNAL ECHOES:** No.

F **INTERNAL REPETITIONS:** No.

G **FORMULAE:** No.

H **INSERTIONS:** Not detectable.

I **EXPANDED CLOWN'S ROLE:** No.

J **OMISSIONS:** Not detectable (but see Unconformities below).

K **SPEECH LENGTH:** 10 speeches over 14 lines (highest totals: 21, 23, 24); 42 speeches between 10 and 14 lines.

L **STYLISTIC SUMMARY:** The verbal quality is generally very good, with some excellent speeches by Cromwell (e.g. A3r,20–A3v,3), and some striking metaphors (e.g. E4r,22). However, there is a clear break in both style and content from scene 11 (D1v–D2r) onwards. Although vestiges of good writing remain, some scenes in the second half contain blunt and clumsy synopses of antecedent developments: e.g. E2r,14–19 and E2v,8–9.

M **UNCONFORMITIES:** The Chorus at D1v–D2 relates events a) whose outcome we know and b) which contradict information already given (France is a hostile enemy (C3r,13–14) yet Bedford cheerfully travels to the enemy country (D1v,29–32)). In scene 13 the Chorus (last seen as recently as scene 11) summarises Cromwell's career with Wolsey and promises events which are dramatised in a mere 13 lines (D4v,11–24) – if indeed they are dramatised at all (Cromwell's highest honours – Order of the Garter, Earldom of Essex, Vice-Regency – are omitted).

N **LENGTH:** Total length: 1,768/Length of dialogue: 1,655 lines.

O **STAGING AND PROPS:** Curtained recess, door. Props include: loose gold coins, purse of coins, bags of money, angels, bills of debt, written bills (advertising distress), gifts to Cromwell (probably in a bag: nutmeg, root of ginger, points, mittens), letters, halberds, trumpet, banquet, music, tipstaff, mace, meat, crucifix, holy water, pen and ink, head of Cromwell.

P **STAGE DIRECTIONS/SPEECH PREFIXES:** SDs regularly specify props, action, and stage choreography (e.g. '*Enter the* Vsher *and the* Shewer, *the meate goes / ouer the Stage*' (E3v,31–2); 'Cromwell *in his study with bagges of money / before him casting of account*' (B1v,19–20). Many SDS have a narrative flavour: '*Here within they / must beate with / their hammers* (A2v,4–6); '*She runnes and imbrases him*' (E2v,34); '*Friskiball riseth, and stands a farre off*' (E1v,17); '*Enter* Cromwell *with his traine*, Bedford *makes as though / he would speake to him: he goes on*' (F2v,9–10); '*The Messenger brings him the / letter, he puts it in his pocket*' (F3r,16–17). Towards the end of the play SDS become remiss about choreographing exits and entrances (e.g. entrances are omitted for Cromwell at D2v,2, for Gardiner's man at F2r,12, a servant at F3r,5,15, and for a hangman at G2v,18; exits are lacking at B1r,8, D2r,35, E4v,17, F2r,13, F3r,4, 9 and G3r,7).

Q VESTIGIAL CHARACTERS: Sir Ralph Sadler is first named and addressed at G2r,2; although line 3 implies his inclusion in the entourage on earlier occasions, he is never included in SDS.

R OTHER OBSERVATIONS: The impression is one of drastic compression: compression of a two-part play, or abridgement of one longer play.

S PREVIOUS VERDICTS: Possibly collaborative, possibly telescoped (Maxwell, *Studies*, p.93); MR (Pettitt, 'Oral Transmission'); 'omission. . . points strongly to. . .censorship' (Champion, '*The Noise*', p.50).

T CONCLUSION: Not MR.

TABLE XXXVII (The fly-scene in) *Titus Andronicus*

A **PLAY/TEXT USED**: *Titus Andronicus* fly-scene (1623)/First Folio facsimile (1968) TLN 1451–539.

B **SR/Q DATES**: 6 February 1594 to John Danter; 1623 F material entered 8 November 1623 to Edward Blount and Isaac Jaggard/F 1623.

C **PRINTER/PUBLISHER**: Isaac Jaggard, Edward Blount/William Jaggard, Edward Blount, John Smethwick, William Aspley.

D **AUTHOR/COMPANY**: William Shakespeare/King's Men.

E **EXTERNAL ECHOES**: No.

F **INTERNAL REPETITIONS**: No.

G **FORMULAE**: 'Come...goe with me' (1535, 1538).

H **INSERTIONS**: Not detectable.

I **EXPANDED CLOWN'S ROLE**: No.

J **OMISSIONS**: Not detectable.

K **SPEECH LENGTH**: 2 speeches over 14 lines (totals: 20, 23); 1 speech between 8 and 14 lines.

L **STYLISTIC SUMMARY**: Competent.

M **UNCONFORMITIES**: No.

N **STAGING AND PROPS**: Banquet.

O **LENGTH**: Total length: 89/Length of dialogue: 86 lines.

P **STAGE DIRECTIONS/SPEECH PREFIXES**: One SD indicates essential action: '*Marcus strikes the dish with a knife*' (TLN 1504).

Q **VESTIGIAL CHARACTERS**: No.

R **OTHER OBSERVATIONS**: Unmetrical lines in Titus' speech at TLN 1513 and 1518. The scene breaks the law of re-entry at 1539–41 which increases the likelihood that it is an addition.

S **PREVIOUS VERDICTS**: MR by King's Men: having lost MS in Globe fire, the company bought a copy of Q3, which represented an unrevised version as acted by Sussex's Men at the Rose in early 1590s, lacking fly-scene (Greg (1919), '*Titus Andronicus*'); Shakespearean addition c.1594 (Wells and Taylor, *Textual Companion*, p.209); Shakespearean addition c. 1597–1602 (Bate ed., *Titus Andronicus*, p.118).

T **CONCLUSION**: Not MR.

TABLE XXXVIII *1 Troublesome Reign of King John*

A **PLAY/TEXT USED:** *1 Troublesome Reign of King John* (1591)/TFT (1911).

B **SR/Q DATES:** NE/Q1 1591, Q2 1611, Q 3 1622.

C **PRINTER/PUBLISHER:** Thomas Orwin/Sampson Clark.

D **AUTHOR/COMPANY:** Anon./Queen's Men.

E **EXTERNAL ECHOES:** No. (The Poem is imitative of Marlowe but not memorially derivative in the sense outlined in chapter 7 A.1.a.).

F **INTERNAL REPETITIONS:** No.

G **FORMULAE:** No.

H **INSERTIONS:** Not detectable.

I **EXPANDED CLOWN'S ROLE:** No; however, the comic scene 8 with the nun and friars, although not otiose, differs stylistically from the rest of the text, notably in its rhyming fourteeners, and may represent a different textual layer.

J **OMISSIONS:** Not detectable.

K **SPEECH LENGTH:** Consistently long. 17 speeches over 14 lines (highest totals: 30, 31, 35). 46 speeches between 8 and 14 lines.

L **STYLISTIC SUMMARY:** Excellent.

M **UNCONFORMITIES:** No.

N **STAGING AND PROPS:** Upper stage ('walls'). Props include: lion's skin, money-chest large enough to conceal a nun, cupboard large enough to conceal a friar, crown, 5 moons, chair, trumpets, weapons.

O **LENGTH:** Total length: 1,819/Length of dialogue: 1,770 lines.

P **STAGE DIRECTIONS/SPEECH PREFIXES:** William Marshal Earl of Pembroke is given his full name and title in the opening SD only. Several SDs explain relationships and position: Limoges is 'the Austrich Duke' (C4r), Arthur is '*Constance*. . .her sonne' (C1r). SDs and SPs fluctuate in character designations: the Bastard is sometimes called '*Philip*' in SPs and SDs, sometimes '*Bastard*' (see D4r). Constance is given two entrances in scene 7 (E3v, E4r), the first clearly erroneous. SDs are attentive to stage action (e.g. 'Enter the Shriue, & whispers the Earle of *Sals* in the eare': A4r,9), but are sometimes deficient in bringing characters on or off stage (an entrance is missing for the Faulconbridge brothers and their mother at A4r,14; Salisbury is not given an exit at A4r,16). One SD summarises the ensuing action and sounds like a narrative heading: 'Enter *Philip* leading a Frier, charging him to show where / the Abbots golde lay' (E4v,1–2).

Q **VESTIGIAL CHARACTERS**: Salisbury is mute in scene 10 (F4v).

R **OTHER OBSERVATIONS**: The Previous Verdicts below are complicated by the uncertainty over the dating of Shakespeare's *King John* (late 1580s/early 1590s *versus* 1595/6).

S **PREVIOUS VERDICTS**: Foul papers of deliberately derivative play [of Shakespeare's *KJ*] written in haste (Honigmann ed., *KJ*); foul papers or authorial fair copy of plot-based derivative of Shakespeare's *KJ* (Sider ed., *TR*); quasi-independent adaptation of Shakespeare's *KJ*, based on plot or scenario of Shakespeare's play (Beaurline ed., *KJ*).

T **CONCLUSION**: Not MR.

TABLE XXXIX *2 Troublesome Reign of King John*

A PLAY/TEXT USED: *2 Troublesome Reign of King John* (1591)/TFT (1911).

B SR/Q DATES: NE/Q1 1591, Q2 1611, Q 3 1622.

C PRINTER/PUBLISHER: Thomas Orwin/Sampson Clark.

D AUTHOR/COMPANY: Anon./Queen's Men.

E EXTERNAL ECHOES: No (see table for *1 Troublesome Reign*).

F INTERNAL REPETITIONS: No.

G FORMULAE: No.

H INSERTIONS: Not detectable.

I EXPANDED CLOWN'S ROLE: No.

J OMISSIONS: Not detectable.

K SPEECH LENGTH: Consistently long. 19 speeches over 14 lines (highest totals: 42, 43, 47); 23 speeches between 8 and 14 lines.

L STYLISTIC SUMMARY: Excellent.

M UNCONFORMITIES: No.

N STAGING AND PROPS: Upper stage. Props include: drums, trumpets, daggers, cloth, drinking vessels for poisoned wine, crown.

O LENGTH: Total length: 1,254/Length of dialogue: 1,215 lines.

P STAGE DIRECTIONS/SPEECH PREFIXES: Both Arthur (A3r) and Henry (E3v) are described in SDs as 'yong' (cf. the princes in *FV* and *TTR3*, also Queen's Men's plays). Entrances and exits are sometimes missing (e.g. Philip lacks an entry on D3r,6; Peter and Hubert lack an exit on B1r,36). SPs fluctuate, once clearly in response to an apostrophe in the dialogue ('*Pandulph*' becomes '*Cardinall*' when so addressed: see B3v,3, 18–B4r,7, 15; he is also '*Legat*' elsewhere: E3v,22); the Bastard is both '*Bastard*' (C1V,19) and '*Philip*' (C4v,10). 2 SDs conclude lists of people expansively with '&c' (B4v,20; E4r,10). One SD is indeterminate: 'Enter King *Iohn* with two or three' (A4v,24). SDs are attentive to staging: 'Enter *King Iohn carried betweene 2. Lords*' (D2v,27); 'Enter two Friers laying a Cloth' (E1V,18). One SD is narrative: 'He leapes, and brusing his bones, after he was (*conj.* wakes) from / his traunce, speakes thus' (A3r,13–14).

Q VESTIGIAL CHARACTERS: No.

R OTHER OBSERVATIONS: Probably a one-part play, albeit a long one, divided in two for publication.

S PREVIOUS VERDICTS: See table XXXVIII.

T CONCLUSION: See table XXXVIII.

TABLE XL *The True Tragedy of Richard the Third*

A **PLAY/TEXT USED**: *The True Tragedy of Richard the Third* (1594)/MSR (1929).

B **SR/Q DATES**: 19 June 1594 to Thomas Creede/Q 1594.

C **PRINTER/PUBLISHER**: Thomas Creede/sold by William Barley.

D **AUTHOR/COMPANY**: Anon./Queen's Men.

E **EXTERNAL ECHOES**: No. (Line 950 echoes *The Spanish Tragedy (1592)* (691) but this is probably deliberate. Kyd's phrase was sufficiently memorable to be ridiculed by Nashe in his preface to Greene's *Menaphon*.).

F **INTERNAL REPETITIONS**: No.

G **FORMULAE**: Possibly formulaic use of 'the young Prince' in dialogue and SDs (13 times) and 'young King' (3 times). (See *FV* (table x) for a similar fondness for this formula.) The adjective 'sweet' appears 20 times.

H **INSERTIONS**: Not detectable.

I **EXPANDED CLOWN'S ROLE**: No.

J **OMISSIONS**: At 1516 and 1523 references to Stanley's garrulity (evident at 1826–38) imply that he was once a loquacious character but this trait has been cut. Line 70 implies that the play or induction is lengthy; neither is.

K **SPEECH LENGTH**: 23 speeches over 14 lines (highest totals: 27, 31, 40); 47 between 8 and 14 lines.

L **STYLISTIC SUMMARY**: Vigorously metaphoric language, with excellent linguistic sense of character development. There is a consistent stress on the play's themes: truth, history, substance, shadow, vengeance, Fortune, authority. There is much prose (some of it with embryonic blank verse, e.g. 430, 476–7). Odd mixture of fourteeners and broken-down verse in scene 7. Otherwise the verbal quality is very good.

M **UNCONFORMITIES**: *Non sequitur* at 1527–30 where confused pronoun referents may indicate a cut. (See Omissions above.)

N **STAGING AND PROPS**: Bed (possibly curtained, or curtained recess). Props include: dagger, letters, pillows to smother the princes, crown, weapons.

O **LENGTH**: Total length: 2,223/Length of dialogue: 2,130 lines.

P **STAGE DIRECTIONS/SPEECH PREFIXES**: Regular use of 'Enters' formula (e.g. 193, 229, 339, 451, etc.). Edward 5 is called 'K[i]ng' in SPS (492ff.) but 'the yoong *Prince*' in SDS (490, 677; cf. *FV*). The Duke of York is named in the SD at 490, although he is not in the scene (nor can he be: he is in sanctuary). The orphaned SD at 586–7 ('Enters the mother Queene. . . / . . .to sanctuarie') may indicate a dumbshow or the heading of a scene for which no dialogue is available. 4 watchmen and a page are instructed to enter at the start of scene 10, although the former seem to belong to scene 9 (as escorts for York) or possibly to 942 (as the 'others' who pull Hastings away). SDS are occasionally problematic in entrances and exits (e.g. 75, 490) but on other occasions are very exact: 'Enters sixe others' (1360). SDS use the 'To' formula at lines 1 and 75. Two SDS indicate purpose: 'Enters men to go to *Richmond*' (1788) and 'Enters *Richmond* to battell againe' (2001).

Q **VESTIGIAL CHARACTERS**: No, although 'To them *Richard*' (75) seems redundant, as neither Richard of York nor Gloucester appears to be in scene (although the dialogue implies Gloucester's presence: 63, 627–8).

R **OTHER OBSERVATIONS**: The playtext has an excellent sense of characterisation, with telling portrayals of Jane Shore's humanity in distress (320–1), and of Richard's change from confident attacker to nervous and unsure defender (see scene 14). Richard's page acts as a Chorus figure (see 475, 896, 932, 1795, 2015), continuing the moral and metatheatrical commentary of the Induction. The text is similar in all but verbal quality to *FV*.

S **PREVIOUS VERDICTS**: 'a strangely amateurish composition' with 'an oral stage in the transmission': '[i]t is hard to imagine that the play should have been deliberately composed in this [metrically mixed] manner' (Greg (1929) ed., *TTR3*, pp.vi–vii); 'a report, or based on a report' (Dover Wilson, 'Shakespeare's *Richard III*', p.300); 'contaminated. . . palimpsest of the original work, with reporter's (and perhaps actors') additions, . . . garbled in transmission' (Hammond ed., *R3*, p.83); authorial composition 'but at a remove distant enough to make room for theatrical production' (McMillin, 'The Queen's Men', p.64).

T **CONCLUSION**: Not MR.

TABLE XLI *The True Tragedy of Richard Duke of York*

A **PLAY/TEXT USED**: *The True Tragedy of Richard Duke of York*
(1595)/Shakespeare Quarto facsimile (1958).

B **SR/Q DATES**: NE; assigned from Thomas Millington to Thomas Pavier 19
April 1602/O1 1595, Q2 1600, Q 3 1619 (*3H6*: F 1623).

C **PRINTER/PUBLISHER**: Peter Short/Thomas Millington.

D **AUTHOR/COMPANY**: William Shakespeare/Pembroke's Men.

E **EXTERNAL ECHOES**: Three lines are shared with *The Massacre at Paris*
(*MP* is probably the debtor: see table XXII). The echoes from other plays
listed by Hattaway ed., *3H6* are not convincing.

F **INTERNAL REPETITIONS**: C8r,11/E7v,10; Warwick's lines on C1r–v are
repeated (with variants) on E2v,27–8; a paraphrase of Clifford's advice to
Henry 6 on B7v,10 appears in the mouth of Henry on C2v,15.

G **FORMULAE**: No.

H **INSERTIONS**: Not detectable.

I **EXPANDED CLOWN'S ROLE**: No.

J **OMISSIONS**: Not detectable.

K **SPEECH LENGTH**: 18 speeches over 14 lines (highest totals: 38, 39, 40); 29
speeches between 8 and 14 lines.

L **STYLISTIC SUMMARY**: Excellent.

M **UNCONFORMITIES**: No.

N **STAGING AND PROPS**: Walls; 2 gates or doors to walls. Props include:
white and red roses for lapels and hats; keys, 3 suns suspended, bows and
arrows, drum and trumpets, ensign, weapons, chambers.

O **LENGTH**: Total length: 2,313/Length of dialogue: 2,181 lines.

P **STAGE DIRECTIONS/SPEECH PREFIXES**: SDs are clear and attentive to
stage action: see 'Enter *Richard* running' (C1v,14), 'Enter *Clifford*
wounded, with an / arrow in his necke' (C3v,15–16), and '*Clifford* grones
and then dies' (C4r,26). Offstage sound effects are indicated: 'Sound for a
post within' (D2r,13), and location is envisaged: 'Enter *Gloster* to king
Henry in the Tower' (E5v,20). 3 SDs have an additive style, separating lists
of characters with 'and' (D3r, E4r, E7r). One SD is indefinite ('*Exeunt*
some with *Edward*': D6r,3); 2 SDs are generalised: 'Enter. . .the
Northerne Earles' (B6r) and 'Enter the house of *Yorke*' (B7v). A narrative
SD occurs at the foot of E4r: 'Then enter the king, *Cla* & *Glo*. & the rest,

/ & make a great shout, and crie, for *Yorke*, for *Yorke*, and / then the *Queene* is taken, & the prince, & *Oxf.* & *Sum.* / and then sound and enter all againe'. The Earl of Rutland's tutor appears in sDs and dialogue as both 'Tutor' and 'Chapl[e]in' (A7v, 14, 18, 19, 25).

Q **VESTIGIAL CHARACTERS**: Montague and Hastings are ghosts (or mutes) in scene 12 (c6r).

R **OTHER OBSERVATIONS**: Remarkably clear and coherent text.

S **PREVIOUS VERDICTS**: MR supplemented by transcription from an actor's part (Alexander, *Shakespeare's 'Henry VI'*); abridgement (Burkhart, *Shakespeare's Bad Quartos*); authorial draft (Urkowitz "'If I Mistake'"); 'an abridged and mangled version of Shakespeare's *Henry VI*, pt.3' (STC 21006); censored text of an acting version (Clare, *'Art Made Tongue-tied'*, p.43); MR, probably made by actors of Warwick and Clifford, of script similar to that of F *3H6* (Irace, *Reforming the 'Bad' Quartos*, p.125).

T **CONCLUSION**: Not MR.

TABLE XLII *A Yorkshire Tragedy*

A **PLAY/TEXT USED:** *A Yorkshire Tragedy* (1608)/MSR (1973 for 1969).

B **SR/Q DATE:** 2 May 1608 to Thomas Pavier/Q1 1608, Q2 1619.

C **PRINTER/PUBLISHER:** Richard Bradock/Thomas Pavier.

D **AUTHOR/COMPANY:** Anon./Queen's Men.

E **EXTERNAL ECHOES:** 493–4 are verbatim from Nashe's *Pierce Penilesse* (ed., McKerrow vol.1, p.157, lines 24–5).

F **INTERNAL REPETITIONS:** No.

G **FORMULAE:** No.

H **INSERTIONS:** First scene may have been added at a later date by another hand (see Cawley and Gaines, ed., *YT*, pp.13–15 and Unconformities below).

I **EXPANDED CLOWN'S ROLE:** No. First scene is comic; rest of play has no opportunity for comedy.

J **OMISSIONS:** Not detectable.

K **SPEECH LENGTH:** 5 speeches over 14 lines (highest totals: 20, 24, 40); 15 speeches between 8 and 14 lines.

L **STYLISTIC SUMMARY:** Verse is mislined and frequently unmetrical. Speeches are abrupt and to the point, but clear, vigorous, and emotionally evocative. There is repeated thematic emphasis on ruined ancient lineage and family name (e.g. 95, 138, 203, 206, 232–3, 237–9 etc.).

M **UNCONFORMITIES:** The opening scene alludes to the servant's mistress, a young woman whose love (the Husband of the play) has married another. Nothing more is heard of this forsaken woman. Scene 1 implies that the Husband's married life is in London (38–40), yet the rest of the play shows it in Yorkshire.

N **PROPS AND STAGING:** Possibly an upper stage and a curtained recess. Props include: souvenirs from London (3 hats with mirrors on 2 of them, 2 rebato wires, a cap-case (travelling bag), 2 poting sticks (metal rods for stiffening the folds of a ruff), brush), weapons, spurs, wine and 2 drinking vessels, spinning top and whip, dagger, chair and/or bed, blood, halberds.

O **LENGTH:** Total length: 794/Length of dialogue: 757 lines.

P **STAGE DIRECTIONS/SPEECH PREFIXES:** Exits are occasionally missing (see 220, 397, 794). Sam's entrance at 27 is incomplete (because it fails to bring Sam on stage although it describes him). Otherwise SDs are detailed, descriptive, and informative: '*Furnisht with things from London*' (27); '*spurns / her*' (178–9); '*Seruant in a feare*' (373); '*Drink both*' (450); '*Husb, takes vp the childe by the skirts of his long / coate in one hand and drawes his dag- / ger with th'other*' (506–8); '*Enter a lusty seruant*' (563); '*Enter Husband as being thrown off his horse, And falls*' (632). The frequency with which SDs are placed in the RH margin (40 times) may suggest that the underlying MS has been prepared for use as a playbook.

Q   **VESTIGIAL CHARACTERS:** No.

R   **OTHER OBSERVATIONS:** With the exception of the first scene, characters are designated generically (the Husband, Wife, Son) as befits the allegorical nature of the play (and/or its desire to deny its relation to the Calverley murders which it depicts). The half-title describes the play as 'One of the foure Plaies in one', suggesting it was performed with 3 other short plays.

S   **PREVIOUS VERDICTS:** Foul papers (Cawley and Gaines ed., *YT*, p.29).

T   **CONCLUSION:** Not MR.

9 | Conclusion

> It is always a source of regret when hypotheses and evidence together
> fail to yield immediate and satisfyingly universal results.
>
> Thomas Clayton[1]

Table XLIII on pp.324–5 summarises my conclusions *vis à vis* memorial
reconstruction (in descending order of probability) for each of the suspect
texts surveyed in chapter 8. It is easier to argue that a playtext is not memorially reconstructed than it is to prove that it is; hence, the first row in table
XLIII, that which confidently proclaims its contents to be plays which are
'Unquestionably Memorially Reconstructed', is blank.

In the discussion which follows this table I consider some of the
general points revealed by the tabulated material in chapter 8, highlight
pertinent textual details (and lack thereof), and offer some conclusions on
the material surveyed.

MEMORIAL RECONSTRUCTION

In editing Beaumont and Fletcher's *The Maid's Tragedy* and *Philaster*,
Robert K. Turner considered the possibility of memorial reconstruction in
the respective QI versions of the plays, scrutinising the texts for the 'classical stigmata' (defined by Turner as brevity, external echoes, internal repetitions, actors' gags, and expanded comedy) of reported texts.[2] Tables XLII in
chapter 8 reveal the enormous variety of features and problems in texts
grouped together as suspect, and show that 'classical stigmata' do not exist
(either in suspect texts collectively, or in the seven for which a case for
memorial reconstruction can be made). Everything we have been taught to
identify as paradigmatic is for the most part conspicuously absent. Let us
consider the more celebrated stereotypes.

TABLE XLIII A summary of the diagnoses

UNQUESTIONABLY MEMORIAL RECONSTRUCTION:
None

A STRONG CASE CAN BE MADE FOR MEMORIAL RECONSTRUCTION:
The Famous Victories (1598)
The Massacre at Paris (undated)
The Merry Wives of Windsor (1602)
The Taming of A Shrew (1594)

A CASE CAN BE MADE FOR MEMORIAL RECONSTRUCTION:
Hamlet (1603)
A Knack to Know a Knave (1594)
Pericles (1609)

PROBABLY NOT MEMORIAL RECONSTRUCTION:
1 If You Know Not Me (1605)
Sir Thomas Wyatt (1607)

NOT MEMORIAL RECONSTRUCTION:
Arden of Feversham (1592)
The Blind Beggar of Alexandria (1598)
1 Contention (1594)
The Death of Robert, Earl of Huntingdon (1601)
Doctor Faustus (1604)
Edward 1 (1593)
Fair Em (undated)
The Fair Maid of Bristow (1605)
George a Greene (1599)
Henry 5 (1600)
1 Hieronimo (1605)
Jack Straw (1594)
John of Bordeaux (undated)
King Lear (1608)
A Knack to Know an Honest Man (1596)
The Maid's Tragedy (1619)
The Merry Devil of Edmonton (1608)
Mucedorus (1598)
The Old Wife's Tale (1595)

TABLE XLIII (*cont.*)

Orlando Furioso (1594)

Philaster (1620)

The abdication scene in Richard 2 (1608)

Richard 3 (1597)

Romeo and Juliet (1597)

Additions to The Spanish Tragedy (1602)

Thomas Lord Cromwell (1602)

The fly-scene in Titus Andronicus (1623)

1 and 2 Troublesome Reign (1591)

The True Tragedy of Richard the Third (1594)

The True Tragedy of Richard Duke of York (1595)

A Yorkshire Tragedy (1608)

DIVERSITY

It is verbal features such as external echoes and internal repetitions, which, as chapter 7 argued, most reliably indicate faulty long-term memory. However, of the forty-one suspect texts, less than one quarter have serious or sustained verbal problems. Of this quarter only four texts can support a strong case for memorial reconstruction (*The Massacre at Paris, The Famous Victories, The Taming of A Shrew,* and *The Merry Wives of Windsor*) while for only three more can a possible case for memorial reconstruction be made (*A Knack to Know a Knave, Hamlet,* and *Pericles*).

Even within these two groups there is a remarkable divergence of features. Of the first group only *The Massacre at Paris* contains significant external echoes; *The Famous Victories* is internally repetitive and formulaic; *The Taming of A Shrew* shares some of its formulae with *The Famous Victories* but also contains stylistically different (new?) material in a second hand alongside the material which seems to be memorially reconstructed. *The Merry Wives of Windsor* suffers from jerky and pedestrian style. Within the second group, *Pericles* is characterised mainly by submerged verse; *A Knack to Know a Knave* also suffers from submerged verse, but is, in addition, externally and internally repetitive; *Hamlet* is competent (albeit pedestrian) overall, but has some garbled passages.

Thus despite our desire to find patterns – for example to associate external echoes with plague-year suspect texts (when company amalgamation and disbandment, and touring may have created textual flux) – there is insufficient evidence from which to extract a paradigm. Better this acknowledgement of untidiness than a false and distorting order.

'BAD' VERSUS 'GOOD'

Even when one has reason to believe oneself to be on firm ground in diagnosing a Poem as memorially reconstructed, complications occur. The tables include two Queen's Men's texts entered in the Stationers' Register in 1594: *The Famous Victories* (Q 1598) and *The True Tragedy of Richard 3* (Q 1594). *The Famous Victories* shows sustained verbal characteristics of memorial reconstruction: it is internally repetitive and heavily formulaic; *The True Tragedy* is at the other end of the diagnostic scale, free of external and internal repetitions. Whereas *The Famous Victories* is stylistically poor, prosaic, and banal in its colloquialism, with short staccato speeches, *The True Tragedy* exhibits long and well-developed speeches with careful and sensitive verbal characterisation. In matters relating to the Poem these two plays are worlds apart.

However, two notable features suggest that the texts have more in common than their respective Poems would lead one to believe. Stage directions (consistently) and dialogue (frequently) refer to the royal hero in each play as 'the young prince',[3] while speech prefixes unusually designate the plays' respective heirs to the throne as 'King' from their first entrance as prince. This seems to indicate that the underlying manuscripts were written or overseen by the same hand. The company may have made no distinction between the two texts, seeing them as satisfactorily playable, their different textual quality irrelevant. Here clearly, at least in stage directions and speech prefixes, the distinction between memorial and non-memorial playtexts breaks down.

Scott McMillin has argued this point in his study of those Queen's Men's playtexts which reached print in 1594. Finding one system (the alteration of texts to suit a cast of fourteen) operative across three texts, suspect and non-suspect,[4] McMillin suggested that the company did not discriminate between so-called 'good' and 'bad' texts. Such contextual consideration is important, precisely because it complicates the textual picture.

STATIONERS

It used to be common to link suspect texts with a suspect stationer and declare both to be 'bad' (the career of John Danter being the most frequent target). More recently the stationers have been absolved on the grounds that they cannot be responsible for the textual quality of a play which they have legitimately bought.[5] Nonetheless, textual quality is still wrongly linked with stationers' activities through the inaccurate and emotive use of the word 'pirate'. As chapter 1 explained, 'piracy' refers technically to the publication by one stationer of a work belonging to another stationer. The first quartos (no longer extant) of *The Spanish Tragedy* (published by Edward White) and of *Arden of Feversham* (published by Abell Jeffes) were both 'pirated' in that Jeffes had the right to *The Spanish Tragedy* and White had the right to *Arden of Feversham*. Such piracy was a transgression in the eyes of the Stationers' Company and, if the matter came to grievance, resulted in the destruction or confiscation of the offending print run. In the case of White and Jeffes, 'yt is agreed that all the booke[s] of eche ympression shalbe as confiscated and forfayted accordinge to thordonnance[s], disposed to thuse of the poore of the companye'.[6]

Richard Head explains how, when he became a printer of plays in the seventeenth century, his fellow stationers did not share his professional scruples about printing copies to which they had no title: 'they. . . made choice of the best Playes then extant; though the Copies were other mens, *I* thought this criminal, but they made a tush at it'.[7] Printing other stationers' copies is piracy. Reconstructing a text from memory for sale to a stationer is not; publishing a text which has been reconstructed from memory is not.

If an unorthodox source were to offer a stationer the text of a play, the stationer would not necessarily have reason to feel suspicious. Stationers were accustomed to receive textual copy from diverse sources. In the case of dramatic copy, acting companies and authors would appear to be the most legitimate sources. But other parties had copies of texts or access to them. Brian Vickers has recently drawn attention to a text published in 1629, Sir Edwin Sandys's *Europae Speculum*, designed to replace a 'spurious stolne Copie' of 1605.[8] The 1629 replacement, 'authentic' copy is not, however, the author's manuscript; the printer explains how he obtained '*by a direct meanes, of a deere friend, a perfect Copie*, verbatim, *transcribed from the Authours Originell, and legitimate one, of his own hand=writing'* (2v). Thus, a friend of the author had a copy. Moseley's preface to the Beaumont and Fletcher First Folio similarly shows that friends of the actors had a copy of some plays, and the epistle 'to the Reader' in Q2 *Gorboduc* implies that acquaintances or servants of the authors had access to a copy. With such diversity of potential vendors, few stationers would be likely to check on the derivation of a text before agreeing to purchase it.[9]

Furthermore, we must remind ourselves that the professional public theatre as we know it began only with the building of The Theatre in 1576. Of the forty suspect texts that reached print, twenty-two were published in the 1590s. While it is customary to explain this correlation of date and suspect text by the theory of provincial plague-year memorial reconstruction, it is more probably a reflection of the diverse and unforeseen practices which inevitably occur when a new social phenomenon is being established before codes of practice have been formulated (cf. attitudes to computer software, videotapes). Thus various theatrical personnel from stage-trotters to hired men could have taken it upon themselves to sell a draft of a text, seeing the occasion as a fortunate opportunity rather than a sin.

Nonetheless, it is clear that some stationers were opportunistic, as was Jaggard in 1599 (with the publication of *The Passionate Pilgrim*, a collection of poetry designed to simulate Shakespeare's sonnet sequence, then circulating in manuscript), and as were Jaggard and Pavier in 1619 (with the publication of the falsely dated 'Pavier Quartos', in which the false dates circumvented the ban on new printings of King's Men's texts). However, there is no evidence that stationers, even opportunistic stationers, aggressively sought popular playtexts, regardless of textual quality, or hired agents to report or steal them. It is notable that in his lengthy and detailed accounts of stationers' chicanery (written forty years after the period of suspect texts) Richard Head does not mention the reporting of plays, although he does tell how his master learned shorthand for the purpose of reporting sermons.

COMIC EXPANSIONS

Tables II–XLII in chapter 8 show that, contrary to Greg's widely cited belief, not one of the forty-one suspect texts surveyed has otiose comic expansion. Two texts – *The Blind Beggar of Alexandria* and *Mucedorus* – do display prominent comedy and clowning, but there is no evidence that this has been gratuitously expanded; the textual evidence (see tables III and XXV) suggests that serious, political frameworks, to which vestigial references remain, have been eliminated in both plays, making the comic antics each play's *raison d'être*. Even so, neither playtext has any convincing verbal characteristic of memorial reconstruction, abridgement being, in both cases, a more plausible explanation for the extant text. Thus, on the available evidence, any connection between expanded comic action and memorial reconstruction is not substantiated.

PROVINCIAL AUDIENCES

William Jones, who published *Mucedorus* and *The Blind Beggar of Alexandria* in the same year, clearly thought that these short comic romps were commercially viable and, if the publishing history of *Mucedorus* is any indication, the London book-buying public showed his instincts to be correct. *Mucedorus* was reprinted sixteen times between 1606 and 1668, prompting one critic to call it the 'most popular Elizabethan play'.[10] Although one cannot discount the play's amateur appeal (the doubling chart prefixed to the quarto is of use to performers, not readers), this publishing record should urge us to beware of dismissing enthusiasm for comedy as an unsophisticated provincial predilection: if the provinces had a taste for comic relief, it was a taste shared by London readers. One can argue, as Greg did, that Jones was publishing mainly for a provincial market,[11] but this seems special pleading.

We know of only one provincial playgoer whose theatrical sensibilities privileged clowning over other dramatic moments and he is fictional: Christopher Sly, old Sly's son of Burton-heath, who expresses interest in 'a Christmas gambold or a tumbling tricke'.[12] Christopher Sly excepted, the tables in chapter 8 reveal that there is no evidence for the theory that provincial playgoers preferred comic escapades. This theory should therefore be abandoned.

PROVINCIAL PERFORMANCES

There is, however, some evidence to associate one, and possibly two, suspect texts with provincial playing. *A Knack to Know a Knave* concludes with the sentencing of the hypocritical priest, John the Precise, to death by shooting 'in Finsburie fields, neere London' (1861). The explanatory tag 'neere London' might have been ironically, comically (and deliberately) redundant at the Rose, but seems more likely to be genuinely explanatory, benefiting an audience unfamiliar with the geography of London and its environs: in other words, a provincial audience.

The supposition that the extant text of *A Knack to Know a Knave* was played outside London receives tentative support from a complex textual tangle surrounding one of the play's villains, the Bailiff of Hexham. Some description of this tangle, which seems to have been caused by adaptation to satirise an infamous local official, is necessary.

The corrupt bailiff is first introduced in scene 2 where he catechises his offspring about their malpractices. All four sons measure up admirably to their father's hypocritical standards, and, satisfied and unrepentant, the bailiff expires and is carried off to Hell by a devil. It is the last we see of the bailiff, although not the last we hear of him, for several *post mortem* references (644, 690–2, 694–7, 805–8) ensure that he is never far from our thoughts.

Although the four sons (Perin, Walter, Cuthbert, and John) feature frequently in the rest of the play, no mention is made of the fact that they are siblings. In scene 6, Perin, in disguise as a judge, tricks Cuthbert, a coneycatcher, in most unfraternal fashion; in scene 8 Perin and Walter deal with each other purely as fellow business men; and in the concluding arraignment, when all brothers are punished, no reference is made to their family association at the point where we most expect it. This anomaly might be unremarkable were it not for the continual verbal reminders of the bailiff and his family.

There are further discrepancies in the plot: Walter tells us he received no paternal bequest, a fact contradicted by scene 4 (which presents him as an employee when the play shows that he is in business for himself). Stage directions compound the problem. '*Enter a Knight, Squire, and Farmer*'

(927) obscures the fact that the latter is not just any farmer, but Walter, the bailiff's son; scene 2 is introduced with the explanatory 'Enter Baylief of Hexham, and his foure sonnes, to wit, a Courtier, a Priest, a Conicatcher, and a Farmer' (242–4), yet the 'a Courtier' is Perin, whom we have just met. The indications are that the alliance of Perin, Walter, John, and Cuthbert, is a temporary dramatic expedient to get four crooked sons together for the bailiff's death-bed scene.

This, at least, seems a reasonable interpretation of the evidence. From here I advance to speculation. The most likely reason for this rearrangement – and for the repeated bailiff references – is topical: bailiff material in the play may have been played up and adapted to satirise a local bailiff (probably in the Hexham region of Northumberland), where many proto-types of the fictional corrupt bailiff can be found.[13]

If *A Knack to Know a Knave* is a memorial reconstruction (and there is some evidence to suggest that it might be: see table xx) it is a memorial reconstruction which has a good claim to be associated with provincial per-formance. Notwithstanding, we must beware of making an automatic con-nection between memorial reconstruction and provincial performance, for the conditions are not symbiotic. Plays may be performed in the provinces without necessarily being memorially reconstructed – as *The Merry Devil of Edmonton* (table xxiii) shows.

The extant text of *The Merry Devil of Edmonton* (1608) was arranged for and/or by a company which seems to have lacked two large but essential props: a climbable tree and a White Horse inn-sign (large and strong enough for an actor to straddle). The incident involving the putative tree episode receives full attention in William Abrams's edition (pp.17–21); accordingly my discussion focuses on the contradictory references to the inn-signs in the play's dénouement.

The lovers, Millicent and Raymond, have succeeded in marrying against the will of Sir Arthur, Millicent's father, and are safely lodged in the George Inn, whither Sir Arthur and Sir Ralph (the father of the man intended for Millicent) hasten in anger. The fathers enter an inn (FIr), which they believe to be the George, and summon Blague, the host of the George Inn, only to be told by the Chamberlain that Blague is host of the inn across the road. After a few lines of comic misunderstanding the

Chamberlain declares 'Sfoote our signes remooud, this is strange' (F2r,12). It appears that the two inn-signs – that of the George, the other unidentified but (from subsequent conversation) apparently that of the White Horse – have been exchanged deliberately to lure the knights to the wrong inn.

The play's concluding lines present another version of events:

SMUG: I will be by and by, I will be Sir *George* againe,
SIR ARTHUR: Take heed the fellow do not hurt himselfe.
SIR RALPH: Did we not last night find two S. *Georges* here.
FABELL: Yes Knights, this martialist was one of them.
SIR ARTHUR: Then thus conclude your night of meriment.
    (F4r,18–22)

From this it appears that Smug, the clown, evading arrest for deer-poaching, has straddled the sign of the White Horse to create the impression of Saint George.[14]

The simplest explanation for the conflicting references in the text seems to be practical, related to touring. A property-horse inn-sign would be cumbersome on tour; it might be easier to replace the entire episode with the simpler expedient of switching inn-signs. If this is the case, the extant text contains a conflation of the two incidents, with imperfectly deleted references to Smug's impersonation remaining.

Thus a case can be made for *The Merry Devil of Edmonton* as an abridged and adapted text. The playing company seems to have been away from its regular playing space and facilities; a provincial venue may provide the reason. If so it is important to remember that *The Merry Devil of Edmonton*, which is not a memorially reconstructed text, was adapted for a provincial venue because of practical circumstances. The perceived aesthetic sensibilities or attention span of the provincial audience are not a factor (although they may be in relation to the Peter Fabell framework, which is begun but not completed. But that is speculation).

PLAGUE YEARS

It is true that many suspect texts reached print in periods of plague. The reason generally given is that, on return to London, an acting company had no further use for the reconstructed text it had performed in the provinces and so sold it to a stationer. But if there is no evidence to connect provincial performance with memorial reconstruction we should re-examine the traditional assumptions about plague-year publication.

A connection between a 'bad' text and plague-period publication was made long before there was such a phenomenon as professional companies playing regularly in purpose-built London theatres from which they were temporarily evicted during plague. In 1570 the printer of Q2 *Gorboduc* explained how the text of the 'exceedingly corrupted' Q1 (1565) was acquired by a young man who 'lacked a little money and much discretion, in the last great plague, *an[no]* 1565. . .while the said Lord [Sackville] was out of England, and T. Norton far out of London'. The inference is that the authors' absence left them vulnerable (to domestic betrayal) and their manuscript draft(s) accessible.[15]

By analogy one might argue that in the plague-years of the 1590s, with leading players and company managers absent, manuscripts kept in the playhouse, where they were normally safe, became similarly vulnerable. Although the playhouses were closed for business (that is, closed to crowds), there is no suggestion that the actors could not enter to retrieve costumes and playbooks in preparation for touring; and once the touring company had departed, the playhouse must still have been accessible to those left behind. Selling an author's draft to a stationer may not have seemed a heinous crime to a starving actor deprived of regular income, and, if the payment was the glass of wine, meal, half a crown, and six to twelve copies of the book which Head tells us was the reward for authors in the seventeenth century, this would have been substantial. [16]

Q2 *Gorboduc* at least provides external contemporary testimony to a connection between plague-year publication and illicit acquisition of a 'corrupted' text, but in a scenario which differs from the traditional correlation between plague-year publication and memorial reconstruction.

ABRIDGEMENT, REVISION, ADAPTATION

The data in the tables in chapter 8, and from other plays (see below), indicate adaptation of the kind I have suggested for *A Knack to Know a Knave* and *The Merry Devil of Edmonton* to be the norm rather than the exception on the Renaissance stage. Of the thirty-four suspect texts which I have deemed 'Not Memorial', eleven show clear signs of abridgement.[17] Several more seem to be revised, and two are themselves additions: the fly-scene in *Titus Andronicus*, and the Additions to *The Spanish Tragedy*.

The alterations in the eleven plays which contain signs of abridgement or 'mending' (Henslowe's useful synonym for adaptation) are of different kinds. *Thomas Lord Cromwell* seems to compress material from two plays into one.[18] *Fair Em* appears to be abridged by or for a company which was forced to tailor the text to the limited resources of a small cast seemingly unable to stage the expected final confrontation between two armies. The opening scene of *Jack Straw* contains blunt summary of antecedent action and differs stylistically from the rest of the text; the extant text seems designed to move to the Peasants' Revolt as rapidly as possible, with a focus on the heroic achievements of Sir William Walworth, the Lord Mayor of London, rather than on the civic discontent which motivated the uprising. The unusually concentrated nature of the drama, and the extreme brevity of the text (at 971 lines of dialogue it amounts to less than an hour's playing time) suggest abridgement. Perhaps, critics have speculated, the play was abridged so that it could be performed as a prelude to another on the reign of Richard 2, or presented as part of a Lord Mayor's show. (The Lord Mayor of London in 1590 was, like Sir William Walworth, a fishmonger. *Jack Straw* may have been performed as a tribute to him, although the guild association which one might expect to be stressed is not mentioned.)[19]

External testimony shows the adaptation of *1 Hieronimo* to be part of a complex sequence of theatrical theft, counter-theft, and rivalry between a boys' and an adult company. The play was published as *The First Part of Hieronimo* in 1605. According to Henslowe's *Diary*, Kyd's *The Spanish Tragedy* (1592) was often performed in close proximity to a related piece: 'the comodey of doneoracio' or the 'spanes comodye donne oracioe' or 'the comodey of Jeronymo'. If these titles refer to one and the same play, now known as *1 Hieronimo*, it is clear that the partner-piece to *The Spanish Tragedy* was a comedy.

In the topical and metatheatrical Induction to the third impression of *The Malcontent* (1604) Sly questions Condell about the daring decision to perform a play belonging to another company, to which Condell replies: 'Why not Maleuole in folio with vs, as Ieronimo in Decimo sexto with them. They taught vs a name for our play, wee call it *One for another*' (A4r). From this it would seem that, at a time when *1 Hieronimo* was owned by the King's Men, it was acquired and performed by a children's company, the Queen's Revels, in retaliation for which the King's Men performed Marston's *The Malcontent*, written originally for the Queen's Revels but subsequently 'lost', found, and expanded by the King's Men. In appropriating *1 Hieronimo* the Queen's Revels appear to have burlesqued the play. Hieronimo is a risible figure throughout, references to his 'pygmy' stature are stressed, and discrepancies between (literally) lofty, martial dignity and decorum, and its representation by child actors, are played up.[20]

Such regular rewriting and adaptation is, as we shall see, not confined to suspect texts; its frequency, and the contractual obligation for a dramatist to 'mend' others' plays,[21] suggests that Renaissance drama is closer to what we know as journalism than it is to literature. I refer not to the quality but to the process: the (re)adjustment of one's writing at short notice to take account of new developments, topical, circumstantial, or aesthetic.

Several of the texts which I have deemed 'Not Memorial' appear to be authorial drafts,[22] and many contain major revisions. *Edward 1* (table VII) shows substantial rewriting of the character of Queen Elinor. Two characterisations of the Queen exist in the text – a villainous personality, and a loving monarch. It is apparent that the latter, historically correct, characterisation has been incompletely replaced by the former, probably in a burst of anti-Spanish sentiment.

Like *Edward 1*, *The Death of Robert, Earl of Huntingdon* (1601) shows signs of authorial draft, most notably in uncertainty or change of mind about character names (see table v). These are coupled with major *currente calamo* revisions which affect character relations and plot: it seems that the author first planned to give Fitzwater a son, then decided to make this son the elder child of Bruce and nephew of Fitzwater. Thus, Fitzwater's kinsman, young Bruce, is on various occasions Fitzwater's son, cousin, and nephew, while Old Bruce's two sons are variously represented as both at Guildford (without family relationship to Fitzwater), and one at Guildford and the second *chez* Fitzwater. These two sets of filial problems map onto each other. The text contains the author's earliest choices, his final choices, and a transitional stage between the two, for, as the Malone Society editor explains in discussing the confusions in scenes 6, 7, and 8: 'Apparently, the three scenes were composed *seriatim*; the alteration made in the second of them has determined the handling of the third, though the first has not yet been corrected to conform to the change in plot.'[23]

Contradictions and confusions in plot and character are not confined to the texts represented in the tables. The anonymous *Selimus* (Q 1594), *Locrine* (Q 1595), *A Larum for London* (Q 1602), *The Wit of a Woman* (Q 1604), *Captain Thomas Stukeley* (Q 1605), Brome's *The Antipodes* (Q 1640), Chapman's *Caesar and Pompey* (Q 1631), Ford's *'Tis Pity She's A Whore* (Q 1633), Greene's *James 4* (Q 1598), Greene and Lodge's *A Looking Glass for London and England* (Q 1594), Massinger's *Believe As You List* (undated MS), Middleton's *The Witch* (undated MS), Middleton and Rowley's *The Changeling* (Q 1653), Peele's *The Battle of Alcazar* (Q 1594), and *David and Bethsabe* (Q 1599), Shakespeare's *Much Ado About Nothing* (Q 1598), *The Two Gentlemen of Verona* (F 1623), *The Taming of the Shrew* (F 1623), *Timon of Athens* (F 1623), to name but a few, have similar problems to a greater or lesser degree, showing that flux and confusion resulting from adaptation, abridgement, revision (or failure to revise) are the normal conditions of Renaissance playtexts. *Stasis* is not a condition endemic in drama. If contradictions, anomalies, and loose ends in Renaissance playtexts are a problem, they are primarily a twentieth-century critical problem.

If the texts of Renaissance drama are often closer to twentieth-century 'bad' than 'good' on the scale of textual quality, we must ask why we do not always notice this. There are many possible reasons. Some badness we tolerate (e.g. minor plot inconsistencies, geographic errors, or localised anomalies such as the problems of logic and sequence in *The Taming of the Shrew*, TLN 2245–93).[24] Some badness we disguise rhetorically, as when editors refer to the 'imperfections' of a Folio text as opposed to the 'corruptions' of a suspect text.[25] Some badness we edit away (e.g. ghost characters are relegated to footnotes). And since we read and teach Renaissance plays in modernised versions in which many problems are edited out, the unedited suspect texts are left exposed as the sole repositories of 'badness'. Thus, we see badness substantially where we choose to see it: as Hamlet says in the line which forms the epigraph to this book, 'there is nothing either good or bad, but thinking makes it so'.

CONCLUSION

With the textual features of suspect texts readily available in tabular form in chapter 8 it should be impossible for critics to make the kind of generalisations which have been familiar up to now: very few of the individual cases and features permit expansion into generally applicable hypotheses. Thus Fredson Bowers's '[e]ach "bad quarto" ... seems to be something of a law to itself' proves remarkably accurate.[26]

The assembled data should also caution against trickle-down dependence such as contemporary critics' reliance on earlier critics' reliance on Greg. As earlier chapters have made clear, Greg's study of the area of suspect texts is partial (in both senses of the word, one of which Greg acknowledged) and larger context is crucial when one wishes to postulate a practice, a system, a widespread phenomenon. In extending the study of suspect texts from a narrow Shakespearean focus and from parallel-text 'good' versus 'bad' comparison, the tables provide some of this wider context.

But there is a still wider context to be considered. Reading the non-suspect works of the authors listed in chapter 6, I have been made continually aware of the textual mobility, fluidity and adaptability of Renaissance drama. Furthermore, although the tables signal a clear division of texts into those with verbal problems (and hence possibly memorially reconstructed) and those with structural problems (and hence less likely to be memorially reconstructed) the evidence that companies or audiences observed such a division is exiguous. Title-pages and prefatory epistles castigate earlier editions even as they are influenced by the earlier texts,[27] and of the forty suspect texts which reached print, the reader could buy and enjoy 'improved' versions of only twelve.[28] Even more pointed is the fact that several suspect texts enjoyed multiple reprintings (e.g. *Mucedorus* and *1 If You Know Not Me*). Thus, whether they liked it or not, Renaissance readers were bombarded with 'badness'.

In analysing the forty-one texts which critics have deemed memorial I have been continually reminded of Alan Dessen's perspicacious pessimism in judging the case for memorial reconstruction 'possible but by no means proven (or perhaps even provable)'.[29] My study concludes that memorial reconstruction remains what it has always been: a possibility. It is an ingenious possibility and an attractive possibility, but let us not mistake it for fact.

If memorial reconstruction is too readily assumed by critics when studying problematic texts, the result is misdiagnosis. Misdiagnosis can have two serious consequences. First, it may conceal a much more interesting textual history, as table XVII (on the MS play *John of Bordeaux*) shows.[30] Secondly, misdiagnosis adversely affects the data on which our critical judgements and understanding of Elizabethan/Jacobean theatrical practice are based. Gower (ironically one of the alleged reporters of *Henry 5*) voices such implications more succinctly:

> you must learne
> To know such slaunders of this age,
> Or else you may maruellously be mistooke.
> (Q1 *Henry 5*, DIV,2–5)

Notes

1 McGann, *A Critique of Modern Textual Criticism*, p.4.
2 *The Merry Wives of Windsor* claimed to present the text 'As it hath bene
  diuers times Acted . . . Both before her Maiestie, and else-where'; the title-
  page of *Hamlet* advertised performance 'in the Cittie of London: as also in
  the two Vniuersities of Cambridge and Oxford, and else-where'; that of
  Pericles claimed performance at the Globe. *Romeo and Juliet* and *Henry 5*
  claimed simply to have been performed, and named the appropriate
  company.
3 *Pericles*, however, was never superseded by a longer version.
4 All quotations from the First Folio come from the facsimile edition
  prepared by Charlton Hinman. The address '*To the great Variety of Readers*'
  is on A3r (p.7). For discussion about the exclusion of *Pericles* from the Folio
  see Wells and Taylor, *William Shakespeare. A Textual Companion*, pp.70–2,
  130–31; for Pollard's analysis see *Shakespeare Folios and Quartos*, pp.64–80.
5 *Hamlet* represents something of a special case in that there are three texts
  of this play: the 'bad' text of 1603 was followed by a 'good' text in 1604–5,
  which was itself replaced by a different 'good' text in 1623. Nevertheless,
  the essential fact is that Heminge and Condell shunned the copy of the
  'bad' text when preparing the First Folio; in this respect *Hamlet* resembles
  the other plays under discussion.
6 Greg (1910) ed., *The Merry Wives of Windsor, 1602*, pp.xxxix–xli.
7 Following William B. Long, I use the term 'playbook' to refer to what is
  more usually known as the 'promptbook'. As Long explains, promptbook
  is a modern term with modern associations. See Long, "'A bed / for
  woodstock'", p.93, and *Co-operative Ventures*.
8 Jenkins ed., *Hamlet*, p.19.
9 Critics often disagreed about what kind of memorial reconstruction these

ten plays represented, but the central premise of memorial reconstruction was, with few exceptions, unchallenged.

10 Werstine, 'Texts on Tour'; see also 'Touring and the Construction of Shakespeare Textual Criticism'. Dillon, 'Is There a Performance in this Text?' Memorial reconstruction by actors for performance is the quintessential New Bibliographic contribution to a debate which had begun by postulating memorial reconstruction (and allied note-taking) by a reporter in the London playhouse for publication (see chapter 3).

11 See Werstine, *ibid.*

12 Greg (1923), *Two Elizabethan Stage Abridgements*, pp.5, 134, 351.

13 So prevalent are these assumptions that Stoppard was able to rely on them in *Rosencrantz and Guildenstern are Dead* when Rosencrantz and Guildenstern view a sample of the touring players' repertory:

> GUILDENSTERN: No enigma, no dignity, nothing classical, portentous, only this – a comic pornographer and a rabble of prostitutes . . .
> PLAYER: (*acknowledging the description with a sweep of his hat. Bowing; sadly*) You should have caught us in better times. We were purists then.

For perpetuation of the connection between comic adaptation and provincial touring see Irace, who cites the 'comic additions in QI *Hamlet* as clues to its origin as a popular adaptation, perhaps for a company on tour' (*Reforming the 'Bad' Quartos*, p.158).

14 Greg (1923), *Two Elizabethan Stage Abridgements*, p.334.

15 Duthie, *The 'Bad' Quarto of 'Hamlet'*, p.50. The phrase 'quite miserable ineptitude' is a subjective one: there seems to me nothing miserable or inept about *1 Contention* or *Richard Duke of York*, for example.

16 Warren, 'Quarto and Folio *King Lear*', p.99.

17 The studies of Hibbard and of Taylor complicated the textual picture by showing how revision could complement rather than replace the memorial scenario; in each case the memorial first Quarto was viewed as a report of a revised version. (Greg had suggested a similar scenario for QI *The Merry Wives of Windsor*, but his argument about revision was not pursued. See Werstine, 'Narratives', p.76, and chapter 3).

18 McLeod, 'The Marriage of Good and Bad Quartos'; McMillin, 'The Queen's Men in 1594' and 'Casting the *Hamlet* Quartos'.

19 Brian Vickers is the staunchest defender of New Bibliographic orthodoxy: see '*Hamlet* by Dogberry'; Y. S. Bains's 'The Incidence of Corrupt Passages' argues that Q1 *Hamlet* is an authorial first draft. For a good overview of the case for revision see Ioppolo, *Revising Shakespeare*.

20 The case for memorial reconstruction in Q *King Lear* had first been stated by Chambers in 1930 (*William Shakespeare*, vol.1, pp.465–6).

21 Cairncross ed., *2 Henry 6*, p.xxi.

22 Gibbons ed., *Romeo and Juliet*, p.2.

23 Oliver ed., *The Taming of the Shrew*, pp.20–1.

24 Wilders, introduction to Alexander *et al.* eds., *Richard III*, p.7.

25 Hoppe, '*John of Bordeaux*: A Bad Quarto that Never Reached Print'.

26 Greg (1954), *The Editorial Problem*, pp.105–6.

27 Kirschbaum, 'A Census', pp.25, 32, 40.

28 See Irace, 'Reconstruction and Adaptation'; 'Origins and Agents'; *Reforming the 'Bad' Quartos*. Irace's work quantifies Greg's semi-quantitative observations.

29 For Greg's identification of *Orlando Furioso* as memorial, see (1919), '"Bad" Quartos Outside Shakespeare'; for the fly-scene in *Titus Andronicus*, see Greg (1919), '*Titus Andronicus*'. For Alexander's work see '*II Henry VI* and the Copy for *The Contention*', '*3 Henry VI* and *Richard Duke of York*', '*The Taming of a Shrew*', and *Shakespeare's Henry VI*. For Chambers on Q1 *King Lear* see *William Shakespeare*, vol.1, pp.465–6. For Q1 *Richard 3* see Patrick, *The Textual History of 'Richard III'*.

30 Kirschbaum, 'A Census', p.21.

31 Kirschbaum, '*The Faire Maide of Bristow*', and 'The Good and Bad Quartos of *Dr Faustus*'.

32 Price, 'Towards a Scientific Method', p.163. Greg had earlier condemned this quarto for its 'shortness and fatuity', but had not labelled it a 'bad' quarto. See Greg (1929), *The Massacre at Paris*, p.x.

33 Duthie, *The 'Bad' Quarto of 'Hamlet'*, p.11, n.1.

34 Abrams ed., *The Merry Devil of Edmonton*, pp.39–40 and cf. Proudfoot, 'Speech-Prefixes', p.124.

35 Greg (1949) and Nichol Smith eds., *The Spanish Tragedy*, p.xv; Honigmann ed., *King John*, pp.174–6.

36 Kirschbaum, 'The Texts of *Mucedorus*'.

37 For the identification of *A Knack to Know a Knave* see Proudfoot ed., *A Knack to Know a Knave* (BLitt thesis, 1961; MSR 1963); for *Arden of*

Feversham see Jackson (BLitt thesis), 'Material for an Edition'; for
1 Hieronimo see Cairncross ed., *Hieronimo and The Spanish Tragedy*; for
A Yorkshire Tragedy see Cawley and Gaines eds., *A Yorkshire Tragedy*,
pp.28–9; for *Thomas, Lord Cromwell* see Pettitt, 'Oral Transmission,
Incremental Repetition, and the "Bad" Quarto'. For suspicions about *Jack
Straw* I am indebted to Richard Proudfoot (personal communication). I
exclude from the total Alice Walker's identification of Q1 *Othello* (1622) as
an abridged playbook transcribed by a copyist who introduced corruptions
based on his memory of performance (Walker and Wilson eds., *Othello*,
p.125, and Walker, 'The 1622 Quarto'). This is not 'memorial
reconstruction' in the same sense as is postulated for the other suspect
texts in the list.

38 Edward Alleyn's MS 'part' of Orlando in *Orlando Furioso* (now in Dulwich
College) and the MS fragment of one scene of *The Massacre at Paris* (now
in the Folger Library) do not create parallel texts for *Orlando Furioso* and
The Massacre at Paris in the sense that Q2 *Hamlet* does for Q1; I therefore
classify *Orlando Furioso* and *The Massacre at Paris* as single texts.

39 Taylor, *Three Studies*, p.148.

40 McLeod (Random Cloud), 'The Marriage of Good and Bad Quartos',
p.421.

41 Thomas, 'The Myth of the Authorized Shakespeare Quartos';
Honigmann, *The Stability of Shakespeare's Text*; McMillin, 'The Queen's
Men in 1594'; and 'Casting the *Hamlet* Quartos'; Werstine, 'Narratives';
Holderness and Loughrey eds., *The Tragicall Historie of Hamlet*. In his
review of Holderness and Loughrey's edition, Brian Vickers mocks the
laudable effort to avoid the term 'bad' quarto: the editors introduce 'a new
type of euphemism: instead of calling Q1 a "Bad Quarto", let it be known
as "a text which has by-passed the crucial relationship to an authorial
manuscript"'. Vickers, '*Hamlet* by Dogberry', p.5.

42 Wilson, *Shakespeare and the New Bibliography*, p.82. This essay, first
published in 1945, was written approximately three years earlier.

43 Hoppe, '*John of Bordeaux*', p.121.

44 Cf. Kirschbaum, 'An Hypothesis', p.709.

45 Holderness and Loughrey eds., *The Tragicall Historie of Hamlet*, p.13. For
consideration of 'bad' quarto dramaturgy, see Leggatt, *Shakespeare's
Political Drama*, p.246, n.17 and 20, p.247, n.24 and 36, and Irace, *Reforming
the 'Bad' Quartos*, *passim*. Irace 'takes the "bad" quartos seriously,

evaluating them as theatrical scripts in their own right and comparing their features with those of known adaptations' (p.12).

46 Green ed., *The Merry Wives of Windsor*, p.148; Cairncross, introduction to the Arden editions of *2 Henry 6* and *3 Henry 6*.

47 Gibbons ed., *Romeo and Juliet*, p.1; Bowers, *On Editing Shakespeare*, p.41.

48 Wilson, *Shakespeare and the New Bibliography*, p.27.

49 Taylor, *Three Studies*, p.110, n.1.

50 Gibbons ed., *Romeo and Juliet*, pp.4, n.2, and 6, n.1.

51 For an excellent analysis of the rhetoric and hypotheses in studies of suspect texts, see Patterson, 'Back by Popular Demand', pp.29–41.

52 Wine ed., *Arden of Feversham*, p.xxvi.

53 See, for example, Greg (1955), 'Richard Robinson', p.411. More recent, and more sustained, objections to Pollard's proposal have been made by Blayney in 'Shakespeare's Fight with *What* Pirates?', 'A Groatsworth of Evidence', and *The Bookshops in Paul's Cross Churchyard*.

54 Gasper, *The Dragon and the Dove*, p.47.

55 Moseley, *Richard III*, p.114.

56 Greg (1923), *Two Elizabethan Stage Abridgements*, p.256.

57 Duthie, *Elizabethan Shorthand*. Although Greg did cling to the shorthand scenario for *King Lear*, he did so reluctantly (see my chapter 2).

58 For criticism of the New Bibliographic desire for narrative, see Werstine, 'Narratives' – a criticism unconsciously voiced by Alexander in 1924: 'In the days before the *romance* of Shakespeare's fight with the pirates was a familiar *story* . . .' ('*II Henry VI* and the Copy for *The Contention*', p.629; my italics). For judicious praise of New Bibliographic compilation, see Kuriyama, 'Dr Greg and *Doctor Faustus*', p.177: 'though the case for A [*Dr Faustus*]'s being a reported téxt rather than a heavily cut and otherwise debased text is hardly conclusive, . . .one remains indebted to him [Greg], as one often does, for a rather full list of A's actual and possible weaknesses'.

CHAPTER 2

1 Greg (1956), Review of Bowers, *On Editing Shakespeare*, p.102.

2 McKerrow, *A Note on the Teaching of 'English Language and Literature'*, p.31.

3 Greg (1930–1), 'The Present Position of Bibliography', p.251.

4 Anon., Review of Greg, *Principles of Emendation*, p.526.

5 Sisson, Review of McKerrow, *Introduction to Bibliography*, p.479;
Lawrence, Review of Greg, *Dramatic Documents*, p.219; Adams, Review
of Greg, *Two Elizabethan Stage Abridgements*, p.606.

6 Albright, 'A Reply', p.201, referring to Greg's review of Chambers.

7 Greg (1925), Review of Chambers, *The Elizabethan Stage*, p.98.

8 These are very rough totals, for the categories sometimes overlap. For a
complete list of Greg's writings see *Library*, 4th series, 26 (1945–6): 72–97;
ibid., 5th series, 15 (1960): 42–6. Corrections and addenda to the first list
are as follows: 'The Swiss Hotels.' *Economist* 26 December 1914; 'Ben
Jonson's "Conversations."' *TLS* 27 August 1925; 'Nathaniel and Nathan
Field.' *TLS* 15 April and 3 June 1926; *'The Taming of the Shrew.' TLS* 24
May 1928; 'Woode's "Conflict of Conscience."' *TLS* 26 October 1933; 'Alice
and the Stationers.' *Library*, 4th series, 15 (1935): 499–500; 'The Use of
Capitals.' *TLS* 12 February 1938; 'Basic English.' *TLS* 25 March 1944. For
an unpublished article by Greg, see Ioppolo, 'The Final Revision of
Bonduca'; for three further additions to the Greg canon, see Sherbo, 'Three
Additions'.

9 Kuriyama, 'Dr Greg and *Doctor Faustus*', p.176; and see pp.171–81.

10 Warren, *'Doctor Faustus*: The Old Man and the Text', pp.118, 121.

11 For the problems in Greg's definition of foul papers see Werstine,
'Narratives', pp.69–75. For Long's replacement of the familiar term
'promptbook' by 'playbook' see p.339, n.7.

12 McLeod, 'The Psychopathology of Everyday Art'.

13 Long, 'Bookkeepers in Action'; Thomson, 'One Quarto > Two
Bookkeepers > Three Texts?'.

14 McMillin, *The Elizabethan Theatre*, p.19.

15 Greg (1916), 'The Handwritings of the Manuscript', p.46.

16 Stoppard, *The Real Thing*, p.41.

17 McMillin, *The Elizabethan Theatre*, pp.32–3; p.8.

18 For iconographic analyses of Moors see Jones, *Othello's Countrymen*,
and Hunter, 'Othello and Colour Prejudice', pp.31–59.

19 Bradley, *From Text to Performance*, pp.37, 155.

20 Taylor, *Three Studies*, pp.120–3; quotations are from pp.122 and 123.

21 For editions of the A-text of *Dr Faustus* see Ormerod and Wortham
(1985), Gill (1989), Keefer (1991), and Bevington and Rasmussen, *Doctor
Faustus A- and B-Texts* (1993); in a spirit of textual positive discrimination
this last edition gives the A-text the commentary for pasages which are in

both A and B. For revisions of Alexander's conclusions see Urkowitz, '"If I
Mistake"', and McMillin, 'Casting for Pembroke's Men'. For Blayney's
seminal work see *The Texts of 'King Lear' and their Origins*, 'Shakespeare's
Fight with *What* Pirates?', 'A Groatsworth of Evidence', and *The
Bookshops in Paul's Cross Churchyard*. The collection of essays edited by
Williams is *Shakespeare's Speech-Headings*. For Taylor's work on *Henry 5* see
Three Studies, and his Oxford edition of the play (1982). Patterson's
challenge, 'Back by Popular Demand', is reprinted in *Shakespeare and the
Popular Voice*. A representative selection of Sams's work includes
'Viewpoint: Shakespeare's Text', 'The Timing of the *Shrews*', 'The
Troublesome Wrangle', 'Shakespeare, or Bottom?' and 'Taboo or Not
Taboo?'.

22 For casting see Berger, 'Casting *Henry V*' and 'The Disappearance of
MacMorris'; Johnson, '*The Merry Wives of Windsor*, Q1'; McMillin,
'Casting the *Hamlet* Quartos'; Dessen, 'Conceptual Casting'; King,
Casting Shakespeare's Plays; and Foster, 'Reconstructing Shakespeare 1'. For
touring see Wasson, 'Elizabethan and Jacobean Touring Companies';
MacLean, 'Tour Routes'; Ingram, 'The Costs of Touring'; and Werstine,
'Texts on Tour' and 'Touring and the Construction of Shakespeare Textual
Criticism'. For Knutson's work see '*Henslowe's Diary*', 'Influence of the
Repertory System' and *The Repertory of Shakespeare's Company*. The case
for revision can be found in Urkowitz, *Shakespeare's Revision of 'King Lear'*,
'Reconsidering the Relationship', '"Well-sayd olde Mole"', '"If I
Mistake"', 'Five Women Eleven Ways', and 'Good News About "Bad"
Quartos'; Honigmann, 'Shakespeare as Reviser', 'The Date and Revision
of *Troilus and Cressida*', and 'Shakespeare's Revised Plays'; Ioppolo,
Revising Shakespeare; and Berger 'Looking for *Henry V*'. For studies of
suspect texts see Irace, 'Origins and Agents', 'Reconstruction and
Adaptation', and *Reforming the 'Bad' Quartos*, and cf. my chapters 7 and 8.

23 For Trousdale see 'Diachronic and Synchronic', and 'A Second Look'. For
de Grazia see 'The Essential Shakespeare', and her collaborative article
with Stallybrass, 'The Materiality of the Shakespearean Text'; for
Werstine see 'McKerrow's "Suggestion"', 'The Textual Mystery of
Hamlet', and 'Narratives'. For Marcus, see *Puzzling Shakespeare*, 'Textual
Indeterminacy', 'Levelling Shakespeare', 'The Shakespearean Editor', and
Unediting the Renaissance, chapter 3. For the analyses by Grady and Taylor
see Grady, *The Modernist Shakespeare*, pp.57–63, Taylor, *Reinventing*

Shakespeare, pp.231–60, and cf. Howard Felperin, 'Historicizing Bardolatry'. Werstine's phrase comes from 'Narratives', p.86.

24 'New Bibliography' embraces the wider textual climate (analysis of variants in printed and manuscript texts, understanding of commercial Elizabethan theatre and dramatic repertory practices, application of rigorous editorial method, etc.) of which 'bibliography' (the study of the printed or manuscript book as material object) forms but a part.

25 Trinity College, Cambridge, Greg MSS 1^{97}.

26 Wilson, *Shakespeare and the New Bibliography*, p.1; originally published in Francis ed., *The Bibliographical Society 1892–1942*.

27 Greg (1940), 'Ronald Brunlees McKerrow', p.494. See also Greg (1960), *Biographical Notes*, pp.10–11.

28 Pollard, *Shakespeare Folios and Quartos*, p.86.

29 Wilson, *Shakespeare and the New Bibliography*, p.9; Greg (1908), 'On Certain False Dates'.

30 Greg (1903), 'The Bibliographical History of the First Folio'.

31 Rather than simply using his surname, I refer throughout this chapter to John Dover Wilson as Dover Wilson to avoid any confusion with F. P. Wilson, whom I also mention.

32 Wilson, 'Alfred William Pollard', p.268.

33 *Ibid.*, p.286.

34 For the connection between grief and textual work see Taylor, 'The Rhetoric of Textual Criticism', pp.50–1.

35 See Alexander, '*II Henry VI* and the Copy for *The Contention*', '*3 Henry VI* and *Richard Duke of York*', and *Shakespeare's 'Henry VI' and 'Richard III'*.

36 For good analyses of the scientific pretensions of Greg and McKerrow, see Trousdale, 'Diachronic and Synchronic' and 'A Second Look', and de Grazia, 'The Essential Shakespeare'.

37 Greg (1940), 'Ronald Brunlees McKerrow', p.496.

38 McKerrow, Review of K. Deighton, *The Old Dramatists*, pp.13–14.

39 Oates *et al.* 'Walter Wilson Greg', p.151.

40 He invokes it in (1927), *The Calculus of Variants*; (1930–1), 'The Present Position of Bibliography'; (1932–3), 'Bibliography – an Apologia'; (1950) *Marlowe's 'Doctor Faustus'*; and prefixes a quotation from it to (1923), *Two Elizabethan Stage Abridgements*.

41 Oates *et al.*, 'Walter Wilson Greg', p.151.

42 See Greg (1927), *The Calculus of Variants*, p.v, and cf. Shepard, 'Recent Theories of Textual Criticism', p.131.

43 Greg (1904), 'Tottel's Miscellany', p.123, n.1.

44 Greg (1923), *Two Elizabethan Stage Abridgements*, p.200.

45 Chambers, Review of Greg, *Two Elizabethan Stage Abridgements*, p.247.

46 Greg (1960), *Biographical Notes*, p.15.

47 Bryce, 'Peter Alexander', pp.383, 382.

48 *Ibid.*, p.381.

49 Pollard, Note on 'The Aims of Bibliography', pp.257, 258.

50 Dover Wilson, 'Alfred William Pollard', p.259.

51 See Jenkins, 'John Dover Wilson', pp.394, 405, 413, 415.

52 Dover Wilson, *Milestones on the Dover Road*, p.26

53 Jenkins, 'John Dover Wilson', p.397.

54 Greg (1930-1), 'The Present Position of Bibliography', p.253.

55 See Greg (1956), Review of Bowers, *On Editing Shakespeare*, p.101.

56 Dover Wilson's revision theories are readily accessible in his editions
    of the New Cambridge Shakespeare. For his comments about
    punctuation see *The Manuscript of Shakespeare's 'Hamlet'*, vol. II, p.197.
    Greg notes Dover Wilson's reaction to punctuation with amusement:
    (1935), Review of Dover Wilson, *The Manuscript of Shakespeare's
    'Hamlet'*, p.82.

57 Gary Taylor provides a good summary of the developing desire for fact in
    the early twentieth century in *Reinventing Shakespeare*, pp.240-58. Cf. de
    Grazia, 'The Essential Shakespeare' and Trousdale, 'Diachronic and
    Synchronic' and 'A Second Look'.

58 Greg (1911-13), 'What is Bibliography?', p.48.

59 Greg (1945), 'Bibliography: A Retrospect', p.27.

60 Greg (1911-13), 'What is Bibliography?', p.46.

61 Greg (1935), 'The Genuine Text', p.364. This surprisingly postmodern
    remark introduces a topic which I touch on only briefly in this chapter
    – that bibliography is the original material criticism. Cf. de Grazia,
    'The Essential Shakespeare', and Holderness, Loughrey, and Murphy,
    '"What's the matter?"'.

62 Greg (1920), 'Transcription in the Pirated Plays', p.320.

63 Quoted by Willey, *Cambridge and Other Memories*, p.12.

64 *Ibid.*

65 See Baldick, *The Social Mission*; Court, 'The Social and Historical
    Significance'; Eagleton, *Literary Theory*, pp.17-53; Firth, *The School of
    English Language and Literature*; Gross, *The Rise and Fall of the Man of
    Letters*; Palmer, *The Rise of English Studies*; Potter, *The Muse in Chains*;

Tillyard, *The Muse Unchained*; Willey, *Cambridge and Other Memories*, pp.12–36; and cf. Graff, *Professing Literature*.

66 Firth, *The School of English Language and Literature*, p.10.

67 Witness to Royal Commission, quoted by Palmer, *The Rise of English Studies*, p.111.

68 See Collins, *Life and Memoirs*.

69 This insult is quoted as a fact by Charteris ed., *The Life and Letters of Sir Edmund Gosse*, p.197; Sutcliffe, *The Oxford University Press*, p.137; Palmer, *The Rise of English Studies*, p.89. In fact, as Ann Thwaite points out, it is apocryphal. Although Edmund Gosse circulated the story, the phrase derives from Smollett's *Humphrey Clinker*; what Tennyson apparently said was 'he [Churton Collins]'s a jackass. That's what he is.' It was, Thwaite reminds us, 'typical of Gosse to improve on stories with time'. Thwaite, *Edmund Gosse*, pp.295–7 (quotation from p.297). I am grateful to Janet Ing Freeman for drawing my attention to this reference.

70 Freeman, 'Literature and Language', pp.562–3, 566.

71 Margaret Atwood, 'Witches', p.4.

72 Eagleton, *Literary Theory*, p.29.

73 Greg (1930–1), 'The Present Position of Bibliography', p.254.

74 For Tillyard's and others' memories of Q's gossipy criticism, see Tillyard, *The Muse Unchained*, pp.65–9 and 83–4.

75 Baldick, *The Social Mission*, p.77.

76 *Ibid.*, p.78; my emphasis.

77 Bradley, *Shakespearean Tragedy*, p.167.

78 Collins's approach to research seems not to have been as cavalier as Greg's review would indicate. He had an appetite for factual detail: Laurence Collins offers the example of his father's search through forty-two parish registers in Norwich to ascertain Robert Greene's exact date of birth (Collins, *Life and Memoirs*, p.232). Unfortunately for Churton Collins his care for biographical accuracy was not matched by care for textual accuracy; and textual accuracy was the kind that Greg felt to be most important.

Greg continued his critical campaign against Collins's *Greene* with barbed comments in (1923), *Two Elizabethan Stage Abridgements*, (1931), *Dramatic Documents*, and a passing reference to an unidentified book from Oxford University Press which 'was a real disgrace' (see (1930–1), 'The Present Position of Bibliography', p.244). Collins had unwittingly set a

trap for himself with his hostile review of Greg's 'unintelligible' and
'confused' book on *Pastoral Poetry and Pastoral Drama* (1906), concluding
in defence 'the duty of a reviewer is quite as much to comment on
deficiencies as to expose errors'. Greg seized his opportunity: 'That I
cordially agree with Professor Collins's view that a critic has a duty to
perform to his public in exposing both the errors and deficiencies of a
book under review will sufficiently appear from an article by me on a work
of Professor Collins, which appeared almost simultaneously with his
article on mine'. (See Collins, 'The Hybrid-Academic.' *The Tribune* 20
April 1906; Greg's reply, *ibid.*, 26 April 1906; Collins's reply, *ibid.*, 30 April
1906; Greg's counter-reply, *ibid.*, 4 May 1906.) On 6 May 1906
H. Friedrichs sent Greg some cautionary advice: 'It is a gift, to write just
such letters as yours, but a dangerous one, and – if I may say so on the
strength of my superior age and experience with practical journalism – one
w.[hic]h your friends would rather see you use very sparingly' (Greg MSS
4^2 in Trinity College Library). For a good overview of the undying
hostility between Collins and Greg, see Sutcliffe, *The Oxford University
Press*, pp. 128–39.

79 Greg (1905–6), Review of Collins ed., *The Plays and Poems of Robert
Greene*, pp.248, 249.
80 Greg (1903), Review of Bond ed., *The Complete Works of John Lyly*, p.24.
81 Greg (1925–6), 'Type-Facsimiles and Others', p.321.
82 Greg (1903), Review of Nutt ed., *The Mabinogion*, p.96; (1903), Review of
McKerrow ed., *The Works of Thomas Nashe*, p.153; (1904), Review of
Carpenter ed., *The Life and Repentaunce of Marie Magdalene*, p.170.
83 Greg (1929), Review of Ward, *The Seventeenth Earl of Oxford*, p.221.
84 Greg (1904), Review of Carpenter ed., *The Life and Repentaunce of Marie
Magdalene*, p.170.
85 Greg (1947), 'Accuracy and Scholarship', p.535.
86 Greg (1903), Review of Fischer ed., *Das 'Interlude of the Four Elements'*,
p.96.
87 Greg (1937), Review of Carver ed., *The Comedy of Acolastus*, p.602. For
examples of Greg's continued efforts at bibliographical education, see
(1903), Review of Bond ed., *The Complete Works of John Lyly*, note 1; (1904),
Review of Hart ed., *The Alchemist*, p.28; (1914), Review of Judson ed.,
Cynthia's Revels, pp.261–2; (1921), '*Everyman* and John Scott', p.144; (1926),
'The "Issues" of *The Pilgrim's Progress*', p.549; (1928), Review of Lucas ed.,

The Complete Works of John Webster, p.452; (1943), Review of *The English Institute Annual*, p.322.

88 Greg (1902), 'Bacon's Bilateral Cipher', p.41.

89 Greg (1911), Review of Smith ed., *Laelia*, p.529; the remark applies to an anonymous critic's comment on the relationship between *Laelia* and *Twelfth Night*.

90 Greg (1924), Review of de Groot, '*Hamlet': its Textual History*, p.228.

91 Greg (1903), Review of Wallace ed., *The Birth of Hercules*, p.150.

92 Greg (1935), Review of Wood ed., *The Plays of John Marston*, pp.90, 94.

93 See (1928), 'Bibliography', p.80: 'I rather regret the defunct "bibliology".' By 1932 Greg had rejected this term in favour of 'Bücherkunde'; see (1932–3), 'Bibliography – An Apologia', p.114.

94 Greg (1911–13), 'What is Bibliography?', pp.40–1.

95 *Ibid.*, p.42.

96 *Ibid.*, p.42; and (1911–13), abstract of 'What is Bibliography?', pp.10–11.

97 Greg (1911–13), 'What is Bibliography?', p.41.

98 Greg (1932–3), 'Remarks on "The Aims of Bibliography" by Sir Stephen Gaselee', p.252.

99 Greg (1930–1), 'The Present Position of Bibliography', p.256.

100 *Ibid.*, p.257.

101 Greg (1903), Review of Quinn ed., *The Faire Maide of Bristow*, p.95.

102 Greg (1901), Review of Boas ed., *The Works of Thomas Kyd*, p.190.

103 Greg (1925), Review of Kellner, *Restoring Shakespeare*, p.465.

104 *Dictionary of National Biography*.

105 Greg (1908), 'On Certain False Dates', p.389.

106 Collins ed., *The Plays and Poems of Robert Greene* vol.1, p.vii. Both Palmer (*The Rise of English Studies*, p.133) and Kernan (*The Death of Literature*, p.39) state unequivocally that Collins committed suicide. He may well have done so: he had suffered from bouts of severe depression all his life, and his movements on the afternoon and evening of his death contradict his announced intentions. However, the coroner's verdict was accidental death, and the events of Collins's last day remain a mystery. See Collins, *Life and Memoirs*, pp.282–93.

107 Taylor, 'The Rhetoric of Textual Criticism', p.49.

108 Greg (1902), 'On the Date of the *Sad Shepherd*', p.71.

109 Greg (1925–6), '*The Spanish Tragedy* – A Leading Case?', p.47.

110 Greg (1931), *Dramatic Documents* vol.1, p.196.

111   Greg (1939–40), 'The Date of *King Lear*', p.385. Cf. (1942), *The Editorial Problem*, p.96; (1946), Review of Kirschbaum, *The True Text*, p.231.

112   Greg (1942), *The Editorial Problem*, p.iii.

113   Greg (1950), *Marlowe's 'Doctor Faustus'*, p.viii.

114   Greg (1920), 'Was *Sir Thomas More* Ever Acted?'. Greg adds that the *TLS* correspondent to whom he is replying has not given him reason to change his mind.

115   Greg (1931), *Dramatic Documents*, p.93.

116   Greg (1910), '*The Trial of Treasure*', p.35.

117   Greg (1925), Review of Sykes, *Sidelights on Elizabethan Drama*, p.200.

118   Greg (1932–3), 'The Function of Bibliography', p.262.

119   Greg (1943), Review of *The English Institute Annual*, p.322.

120   Greg (1930–1), 'The Present Position of Bibliography', p.249. For disagreement as to whether Bradshaw wrote 'rigorously' or 'vigorously' see Greg, *ibid.*, and Needham, *The Bradshaw Method*, p.8.

121   Greg (1947–8), 'The Date of the Earliest Play-Catalogues', p.191. Cf. Greg (1934–5), 'Was There a 1612 Quarto of *Epicene*?', p.314: 'I am afraid that after reviewing all the evidence which, so far as I am aware, has any relevance to the problem, we must remain in some doubt as to what actually happened.'

122   Greg (1931), *Dramatic Documents*, p.xi.

123   *Ibid.*, p.201.

124   Greg (1942), *The Editorial Problem*, p.ix.

125   *Ibid.*, pp.56–7.

126   Greg (1931), *Dramatic Documents*, p.216.

127   *Ibid.*, p.209.

128   Greg (1923), *Two Elizabethan Stage Abridgements*, p.1.

129   Greg (1931), *Dramatic Documents*, p.221.

130   McKerrow, 'A Suggestion Regarding Shakespeare's Manuscripts', p.460, n.1. For an analysis of the unquestioning way in which McKerrow's suggestion has been accepted, see Werstine, 'McKerrow's "Suggestion"'. The contributors to Williams, ed., *Shakespeare's Speech-Headings* re-examine McKerrow's suggestion and provide much evidence to refute it. On several occasions even Greg seems to distance himself from wholehearted support of McKerrow's suggestion; see, for example, (1942), *The Editorial Problem*, p.140 and (1944–5), '*The Merry Devil*', p.130, n.2.

131 McKerrow, Review of Pollard ed., *Shakespeare's Hand in the Play of 'Sir Thomas More'*, p.239.

132 I am grateful to Harold Jenkins for informing me of the commissions which prompted these articles.

133 Quoted in Oates *et. al.*, 'Walter Wilson Greg', p.162.

134 McKerrow, *Prolegomena*, p.vii.

135 The situation is complicated by the fact that, although Greg frequently expressed caution in his writings, he did not always practise the caution he advocated. Furthermore, he was impatient with expressions of caution by others. See his reviews (1925) of Chambers, *The Elizabethan Stage* and (1928) of Albright, *Dramatic Publication*. Both these reviews also reprimand Chambers and Albright for the naive expectation that the world of theatre history or textual study could ever approach the certainty of science – an expectation for which Greg is partly responsible.

136 See Blayney, *The Texts of 'King Lear'*, pp.2–8.

137 Maxwell ed., *W. W. Greg. Collected Papers*; Greg (1913), 'Chaucer Attributions in MS. R. 3. 19'; (1925), 'A Collier Mystification'; (1931–2), 'Three Manuscript Notes'; (1938–9), 'A Fragment from Henslowe's Diary'; (1926–7), 'Derby his Hand – and Soul'; (1946–7), '*The Triumph of Peace*'; and cf. (1947), Review of Fletcher ed., John Milton's *Complete Poetical Works*, p.134.

138 Greg (1931–2), 'Three Manuscript Notes', pp.315–16.

139 Greg (1928), 'Act-Divisions in Shakespeare', p.158.

140 McKerrow, *Prolegomena*, p.9, n.2.

141 Greg (1932–3), 'Bibliography – An Apologia', p.128.

142 Greg (1917), 'Hamlet's Hallucination' (many people, including Greg himself, were unsure just how serious Greg was in his argument about the Ghost); (1946), 'The Damnation of Faustus'; (1940), 'Time, Place, and Politics in *King Lear*'. Further references to this last article appear parenthetically in the text.

143 This conclusion is lamely practical. For a more stimulating account see Flahiff, 'Lear's Map'. Flahiff argues that the geography of the play is embodied in the characters' names: for example, Perillus in *King Leir* becomes Kent in Shakespeare's version. The characters' peregrinations therefore dramatise the division of the kingdom.

144 Empson, '*The Spanish Tragedy*'.

145 F. P. Wilson remarks that, as a bibliographer, Greg was 'never content

merely to print records; he had always to interpret them' (Wilson, 'Sir Walter Wilson Greg', p.322). Tom Davis points out the folly of assuming textual criticism to be less personal or ephemeral than critical interpretation: 'Literary critics make an entire profession out of not agreeing with each other: interpretations must be individual, or they are worthless. But textual critical judgments aren't like that: their job is not to be interesting, but (in some sense) to be "true".' Davis proceeds to illustrate the similarity of attitude and procedure in textual and literary criticism. See 'The Monsters and the Textual Critics'.

146 Greg (1942), *The Editorial Problem*, p. 91.
147 The epithet comes from (1932–3), 'The Function of Bibliography', p.248.
148 *Ibid.*, p.256.
149 Greg (1928), Review of Albright, *Dramatic Publication*, p.98.
150 In 'Who is it that can tell me who I am?' Robert Clare argues that the New Revisionists of the 1980s and 1990s also rely on rhetorical gestures as proof.
151 Greg (1942), *The Editorial Problem*, p.85.
152 This statement is a paraphrase of remarks made by Greg (1942) in *The Editorial Problem*, pp.xix, 89. Cf. Hart, *Stolne and Surreptitious Copies*, p.447.
153 Greg (1942), *The Editorial Problem*, p.93.
154 In his personal copy of *The Editorial Problem* (now in the library of Trinity College, Cambridge) Greg has underlined Q's 'Use' and added a footnote reservation: 'perhaps this is to put more weight on the word than it will bear'.
155 Price, 'Towards a Scientific Method', p.167.
156 Wells and Taylor, with Jowett and Montgomery, *William Shakespeare. A Textual Companion*, p.18. This inability to cope with plurality extends even to the New Bibliographers' personal lives: McKerrow's gloom when his wife gave birth to twin boys was well known.
157 See Maas, *Textual Criticism*, pp.37, 49.
158 I am indebted to Richard Proudfoot for the points in this paragraph.
159 Greg (1942), *The Editorial Problem*, pp.111–12.
160 Housman, 'The Application of Thought', p.1064.
161 Greg (1945), 'Bibliography – A Retrospect', p.29.
162 Greg (1925), Review of Kellner, *Restoring Shakespeare*, pp.476–7.
163 Knutson, *The Repertory of Shakespeare's Company*, p.214, n.12.

164 Greg (1900), 'Webster's *White Devil*', p.122.

165 Long, 'Perspective on Provenance', pp.42–3, n.10.

166 Greg (1950), Review of Hoppe, *The Bad Quarto of 'Romeo and Juliet'*, p.66.

167 Pollard and Wilson, 'The "Stolne and Surreptitious" Shakespearian Texts', p.18. Werstine examines Pollard and Wilson's hypothesis in 'Texts on Tour' and 'Touring and the Construction of Shakespeare Textual Criticism'.

168 See Montgomery, *The Contention of York and Lancaster* (DPhil thesis) vol.II, p.li.

169 Greg (1923), *Two Elizabethan Stage Abridgements*, p. 335.

170 *Ibid.*, p.134.

171 Greg (1910), *The Merry Wives of Windsor*, p.xlii.

172 Greg (1905–6), Review of Robertson, *Did Shakespeare Write 'Titus Andronicus'?*, p.341; Greg (1946), Review of Kirschbaum, *The True Text*, p.233. By 1923 Greg had changed his 1906 view about actors and metre: 'the actors . . . [were] naturally most sensitive to rhythm'. (1923), *Two Elizabethan Stage Abridgements*, p.354.

173 Greg (1932–3), 'The Function of Bibliography', p.256.

174 Greg (1942), *The Editorial Problem*, p.xix. This dismissal did not prevent Greg from invoking revision when convenient, as in his account of the ending of *The Merry Wives of Windsor*.

175 Pollard, *Shakespeare's Fight with the Pirates*, p.xxvi.

176 Greg (1946), Review of Kirschbaum, *The True Text*, p.233.

177 *Ibid.* Greg repeats this point more forcefully in (1949), Review of Duthie ed., *King Lear*, p.397.

178 Greg (1932–3), 'The Function of Bibliography', p.254.

179 Greg (1932–3), 'Bibliography – An Apologia', p.114. For the relationship between the development of New Bibliography and the rare-book trade, see Loewenstein, 'Authentic Reproductions'.

180 For an excellent analysis of the bias against theatre in the nineteenth century, see Barish, *The Antitheatrical Prejudice*, pp.295–399 and cf. Taylor, *Reinventing Shakespeare*, p.230.

181 Greg (1902), 'Old Plays and New Editions', p.422.

182 Greg may simply be being anachronistic here, thinking of artificial lighting on the contemporary stage, rather than being anti-theatrical. Cf. the stage directions in his 'new vamp't' edition (1911) of Peele's *The*

Old Wife's Tale: '*After a time footsteps are heard and three page-boys, whom, were it light enough, you would at once know by the fashions of their dress to be Antic, Frolic, and Fantastic, straggle out of the wood on the right, groping their way* (p.5). However, in 'A Suggestion Regarding Shakespeare's Manuscripts', McKerrow twice associates Shakespeare's plays with novels (the second in a passage that clearly envisages Shakespeare as writing plays for publication, not performance): in F *Comedy of Errors* character designations change 'much as they do in a novel'; 'Is it not natural that . . . he [Shakespeare] should at times follow the practice of the novelist rather than of the person writing a play for the Press' (pp.460, 464–5).

183 Greg (1942), *The Editorial Problem*, p.100. The adjectives regularly attached to the collocation 'bad quarto' are 'just' and 'mere'. See Pollard's introduction to Alexander, *Shakespeare's 'Henry VI' and 'Richard III'*, p.3, and McKerrow, 'A Note on *Henry VI, Part II*', p.157.

184 Cf. Berger, 'Looking for *Henry V*'. Even John Russell Brown, renowned for his theatrical approach, shows the influence of the New Bibliography when he writes that the text of Chapman's *Caesar and Pompey* (apparently never performed) is 'uncontaminated by the theatre'. Brown, 'Chapman's *Caesar and Pompey*', p.469. Cf. Chambers: Marlowe's 'popularity . . . kept his plays alive, or rather, *slowly decaying* upon the stage' (Review of Bennett ed., 'Marlowe, *The Jew of Malta*', p.77; my emphasis). As recently as 1985 Philip Edwards could write that when Shakespeare handed his text of *Hamlet* to the theatre 'degeneration began . . . the nearer we get to the stage, the further we are getting from Shakespeare'. Edwards ed., *Hamlet*, p.32.

185 Greg (1954), *The Editorial Problem*, p.108.

186 Greg (1917), 'Hamlet's Hallucination', p.421; (1936), 'Stage or Study?'. Here, as elsewhere, Greg's influence is wide-reaching. In 1958 G. R. Elliott could write, 'So while he [Shakespeare] wrote immediately for the stage he wrote ultimately for reflective readers – for those who (*like himself*) would be interested in and aided by, *but never satisfied by*, stage-performances of his plays.' Elliott, *Dramatic Providence in 'Macbeth'*, p.10 (my emphasis).

187 Greg (1940), 'Ronald Brunlees McKerrow', p.514.

188 Greg (1950–1), 'The Rationale of Copy-Text', p.26.

189 Greg (1941), 'McKerrow's "Prolegomena" Reconsidered', p.143.

190 Greg (1932–3), 'Bibliography – An Apologia', p.127. Cf. Randall
     McLeod: 'We can found [an edition] only on what we ... *surmise*
     [Shakespeare] wrote.' 'The Marriage of Good and Bad Quartos', p.430.
191 I am grateful to Paul Werstine for drawing my attention to this sequence.
192 Greg (1919), 'The *Hamlet* Texts', p.384.
193 Greg (1932–3), 'The Function of Bibliography', p.241.
194 Greg (1930–1), 'The Present Position', p.260; (1911–13), 'What is
     Bibliography?', p.41; Adams, Review of Greg, *Two Elizabethan Stage
     Abridgements*, p.606.
195 Greg (1956), Review of Bowers, *On Editing Shakespeare*, p.103.
196 Greg (1959), Review of Bowers ed., *The Dramatic Works of Thomas
     Dekker. Vol. III*, p.415.
197 Greg (1915), 'Detachment in War Time', p.69.
198 Bateson, 'The Application of Thought', p.323.
199 *Ibid.*, p.324.
200 Greg (1950–1), 'The Rationale of Copy-Text', p.33.
201 Quoted by Kernan, *The Death of Literature*, p.103.
202 Cf. Davis, 'The Monsters and the Textual Critics'.
203 Greg (1925), Review of Kellner, *Restoring Shakespeare*, pp.476–7.
204 Greg (1902), Review of Schücking, *Studien über die stöfflichen
     Beziehungen*, p.81.
205 Greg (1903), Review of Wallace ed., *The Birth of Hercules*, p.150.
206 Greg (1940), Review of Bartlett and Pollard, *A Census of Shakespeare's
     Plays*, p.211.
207 Greg (1954), Review of Bowers ed., *The Dramatic Works of Thomas
     Dekker. Vol. I*, p.418.
208 See Taylor, *Reinventing Shakespeare*, pp.162–96.
209 Quoted by Grady, *The Modernist Shakespeare*, p.43.
210 Quoted by Taylor, *Reinventing Shakespeare*, p.166.
211 For a fuller discussion, to which I am indebted, see Grady, *The Modernist
     Shakespeare* and 'Disintegration and its Reverberations'.
212 Grady, 'Disintegration and its Reverberations', p.115.
213 Greg (1927), Review of Baldwin, *The Organization and Personnel*, p.954.
214 Marsh, 'The Shakespeare First Folio', p.621.
215 Greg (1955), 'The Shakespeare First Folio', p.639; Bald, 'The Shakespeare
     First Folio', p.639.
216 Greg (1942), *The Editorial Problem*, p.12, n.1.

217 Keefer ed., *Christopher Marlowe's Doctor Faustus*, p.xvi.

218 *Ibid.*, p.lxiv.

219 McMillin, 'Building Stories', p.60.

220 *Ibid.*, p.57.

221 *Ibid.*, p.58.

222 Greg (1899), 'Pre-Malorean Romances', p.10.

223 Greg (1906), *Pastoral Poetry and Pastoral Drama*, p.9.

224 Werstine draws a connection between Pollard's *Shakespeare Folios and Quartos* and Conan Doyle's *Hound of the Baskervilles* in 'Narratives', p.65.

225 See, for example, Greg (1910), '*The Trial of Treasure*', p.32.

226 See Greg (1932–3), 'The Function of Bibliography', p.249.

227 Greg (1925), 'The Escapes of Jupiter', p.176.

228 See Bryce, 'Peter Alexander', p.400. Harold Jenkins finds in Dover Wilson's *What Happens in 'Hamlet'* 'some of the excitement of a detective story' adding that 'it is perhaps no coincidence that it belongs to the period of the detective story's vogue'. Jenkins, 'John Dover Wilson', p.407. John Churton Collins, who tried to be a bibliographical detective and failed, was notwithstanding a zealous amateur criminologist, receiving murder-mystery clues by mail from a society of cryptographers. See Collins, *Life and Memoirs*, p.183.

229 See Oates *et al.*, 'Walter Wilson Greg', pp.167–8; F. P. Wilson recounts how Greg submitted detective novels 'to the same kind of scrutiny he gave to the variants in the first quarto of *King Lear*'. Wilson, 'Sir Walter Wilson Greg', p.331.

230 Quoted on the dust-jacket of the 1978 edition.

231 Sayers ed., *Great Short Stories of Detection*, vol.1, pp.11–13.

232 See Ong, *Orality and Literacy*, p.150 for examples of two detective novels which self-consciously promote the connection between textual and detective mysteries.

233 Anon., Review of Greg, *Principles of Emendation*, pp.526–7.

234 The quotations come from Doyle, *A Study in Scarlet*, p.47, *The Valley of Fear*, p.33, and Len Deighton's introduction to *The Valley of Fear*, p.9.

235 Werstine's 'The Textual Mystery of *Hamlet*' provides a sophisticated interrogation of the very attitude its title seems to perpetuate.

236 Jenkins ed., *Hamlet*, p.20. Jenkins's terms curiously echo those of Warwick in *1 Contention* when he is asked to defend his suspicions that the Duke of Gloucester was murdered:

> Who sees a hefer dead and bleeding fresh,
> And sees hard-by a butcher with an axe,
> But will suspect twas he that made the slaughter? . . .
> Euen so suspitious is this Tragidie.
>
> (E3r)

237 Dover Wilson, quoted by Jenkins, 'John Dover Wilson', p.394.
238 Lawrence, 'The "Stolne and Surreptitious" Shakespearian Texts', p.449.
239 Werstine, 'Texts on Tour', and 'Touring and the Construction of Shakespeare Textual Criticism'.
240 Greg (1919), 'The "Stolne and Surreptitious" Shakespearian Texts', p.461.
241 Chambers, Review of Greg, *Two Elizabethan Stage Abridgements*, p.245.
242 This had been earlier noted independently by W. H. Widgery, Grant White, and H. D. Gray. See Jenkins ed., *Hamlet*, pp.20–1.
243 Albright assumes here that an actor retained his written part (so he could refresh his memory) for the duration of a run. However, it may be that parts were sufficiently valuable as capital property of the company to be recalled as soon as possible. We have no information on this point.
244 Albright, *Dramatic Publication*, p.302.
245 *Ibid.*, p. 296.
246 Greg (1928), Review of Albright, *Dramatic Publication*, pp. 92, 98, 100. Greg's Notebook, and his personal copy of his edition of Q1 *The Merry Wives of Windsor* (1910) record many of Albright's suggestions, showing that he took her criticisms seriously. (Both items are in the library of Trinity College, Cambridge.)
247 Greg (1928), Reply to Albright, p.202.
248 Price, 'Towards a Scientific Method', p.151.
249 McKerrow, Review of Pollard ed., *Shakespeare's Hand*, p.239.
250 'I fully admit the necessity of examining all related examples before formulating any general theory. But *Orlando* offers such exceptionally secure foundations for criticism that, so far as textual analysis is concerned, I prefer to treat it by itself'. Greg (1923), *Two Elizabethan Stage Abridgements*, p.290, n.1.

CHAPTER 3
1 Greg (1928), Review of Albright, *Dramatic Publication*, p.100.
2 Alexander Schmidt, *Zur Textcritik des King Lear* (1789), quoted by Kirschbaum, *The True Text of 'King Lear'* (1945), p.80.

3 Hart, *Stolne and Surreptitious Copies*, p.vii.

4 Duthie, *The 'Bad' Quarto of 'Hamlet'*, p.5.

5 Sisson, Review of McKerrow, *Introduction to Bibliography*, p.479.

6 Duthie, *The 'Bad' Quarto of 'Hamlet'*, p.45; Thomas, '*Hamlet* Q1: First Version or Bad Quarto?', p.249.

7 Collier ed., *The Works*, vol.VI, p.369 and vol.VII, p.191.

8 Mommsen, '*Hamlet*, 1603 and *Romeo and Juliet*, 1597', p.182.

9 Daniel, *The Merry Wives*, p.ix.

10 In questioning Greg's study of *The Merry Wives*, I am following the lead established by Werstine ('Narratives'), to whose work I am deeply indebted.

11 Greg (1910), *The Merry Wives*, p.xiv. Subsequent references to this edition are cited parenthetically in my text.

12 Cf. Werstine, 'Narratives', p.76.

13 Greg (1928), Reply to Albright, *Dramatic Publication*, p.202. Cf. Werstine, 'Narratives', p.77.

14 Chambers, *William Shakespeare*, vol.I, p.430.

15 Duthie, *The 'Bad' Quarto of 'Hamlet'*, p.28.

16 Greg (1942), *The Editorial Problem*, p.71.

17 Hoppe, *The Bad Quarto of 'Romeo and Juliet'*, p.71.

18 Oliver notes that Greg changed his mind but concludes that he was wrong to do so. Oliver ed., *The Merry Wives*, p.xxvi.

19 Greg (1953), Review of Bracy, *The Merry Wives*, p.77. In *The Shakespeare First Folio* (1955) Greg describes Q1 *The Merry Wives* as a memorial reconstruction made by an independent reporter helped by the actors of Falstaff and the Host (p.334).

20 Green ed., *The Merry Wives*, p.148.

21 This last suggestion is one of the most extraordinary in the entire narrative. *Henslowe's Papers* frequently record payments for altering ('mending') plays. Revision was an expected activity for 'attached' dramatists (those under contract), and could hardly have come as a surprise to the players. In a letter to Henslowe, Daborne explains that he has made some alterations to scenes in his play *Machiavel* which the players already have in Parts (*Henslowe Papers* ed., Foakes vol.II, p.81). Henslowe's *Diary* and *Papers* suggest that if the players were 'resentful', they must have been so on a regular basis.

22 Werstine, 'Narratives', p.76.

23 Cf. Werstine, 'Narratives', p.77.

24 Leah Marcus exposes a similar attitude in T. W. Craik's introduction to the Oxford edition of *The Merry Wives*. See Marcus, *Unediting the Renaissance*, chapter 3.

25 Kirschbaum, 'An Hypothesis', p.703; Bracy, *The Merry Wives*, p.41.

26 Bracy, *The Merry Wives*, p.40.

27 Duthie, *The 'Bad' Quarto of 'Hamlet'*, p.28.

28 The imprint on both volumes reads '1907'. They actually appeared in December 1906.

29 Greg (1905–6), Review of Collins ed., *The Plays and Poems of Robert Greene*, p.249.

30 Greg (1919), '"Bad" Quartos Outside Shakespeare'; (1923), *Two Elizabethan Stage Abridgements*. Subsequent references to *Two Elizabethan Stage Abridgements* are cited parenthetically in the text as *2ESA*.

31 Greg (1919), '"Bad" Quartos Outside Shakespeare', p.200.

32 Bradley, *From Text to Performance*, p.146.

33 Cf. de Grazia, *Shakespeare Verbatim*, pp.17–18; Trousdale, 'A Second Look', pp.90–1; and de Grazia and Stallybrass, 'The Materiality of the Shakespearean Text', pp.259–60, n.12. In his account book Philip Henslowe changes the year in March, January, or April.

34 Many of Greg's problems stem from the way in which he is only able to consider the quarto in relation to the Plot, and is driven to assume that the former must be an adaptation of the latter. See Bradley, *From Text to Performance*, *passim*.

35 For a careful analysis of the thematic necessity and symmetry of the clowning episodes which troubled Greg as otiose expansion, see Crupi, *Robert Greene*, pp.110–12. In an excellent essay Michael Warren defends the dramaturgy of *Orlando Furioso*; see 'Greene's *Orlando*'.

36 Bradley, *From Text to Performance*, p.188; see also his comments at pp.144–5.

37 See lines 82–90; 270–1; 315–22; 412–18; 498–505; 535–9; 575–83; 1450–4. We are perhaps too severe in analysing the grammar rather than the ambiance of speeches in Elizabethan drama. Q 4 *A Looking Glass for London*, prepared for use as a playbook by Prince Charles's Men in the first decade of the seventeenth century, contains meaningless, mistaken, and misprinted lines. We do not know that these were transferred to the

actors' Parts; but the evidence of the printed text indicates that textual problems did not trouble Renaissance stage performers the way they trouble textual critics. See Baskervill, 'A Prompt Copy'.

38 See Chettle, *Kind Heart's Dream*, A4r.

39 Scott McMillin, 'The Queen's Men in 1594', shows that all Queen's Men's playtexts printed in 1594 have been abridged. McMillin's argument can, with minor modification, be extended to all but one of the Queen's Men's quartos of the 1590s. The exception is *The Old Wife's Tale*, which may have been written originally for a boys' company.

The title-page of *Orlando Furioso* does not name an acting company. Henslowe's *Diary* (21 February 1591/2) records a play called 'orlando' at the Rose Theatre, acted by Strange's Men. The anonymous *Defence of Cony-Catching* (entered in the Stationers' Register 21 April 1592) associates the play with both the Admiral's Men and the Queen's Men. Addressing Robert Greene, the persona in *Defence* says: 'Aske the Queens Players, if you sold them not *Orlando Furioso* for twenty Nobles, and when they were in the country, sold the same Play to the Lord Admirals men for as much more. Was not this plaine Conny-catching Maister R.G.?' (1592, sig.c3r). See Greg (1923), *Two Elizabethan Stage Abridgements*, pp.125–34.

40 Subsequent studies by Patrick (*The Textual History of 'Richard III'*), Duthie (*The 'Bad' Quarto of 'Hamlet'*) and Hart (*Stolne and Surreptitious Copies*) are guilty of the same prejudicial approach to verbal details. See chapter 7 for further discussion of this point.

41 Peter Alexander's seminal study of the *Henry 6* plays, published six years after Greg's work on *Orlando Furioso*, also found it necessary to supplement the theory of memorial reconstruction. Stage directions in *1 Contention* which are identical with those in F *2 Henry 6* were explained by transcription, an explanation also held to account for material in 1.1 and 1.4. Similarly, certain speeches in *Richard Duke of York* were so complete and so accurate 'as to suggest that they were transcribed from a part in possession of the reporter'. Alexander, *Shakespeare's 'Henry VI'*, pp.84–90.

42 Chambers, Review of *Two Elizabethan Stage Abridgements*, p.248.

43 This *desideratum* was repeated by W. J. Lawrence in 1931 when he called for an 'associative inquiry' into "bad quartos". Lawrence, 'The Secret of "The Bad Quartos"', p.447.

44 Kirschbaum, 'An Hypothesis', p.697, n.2; '*The Faire Maide of Bristow*

(1605)'. Kirschbaum's total pointedly excludes *The Taming of A Shrew* (1594), first identified as a suspect text by Peter Alexander.

45 Greg (1942), *The Editorial Problem*, p.96.

46 Kirschbaum, *The True Text*, p.6, n.17.

47 *Ibid.*, p.21.

48 Alan Dessen notes how the evidence that can be used 'to buttress or challenge' memorial reconstruction is 'often the same evidence interpreted in diametrically opposed ways'. (Dessen, 'Weighing the Options', p.66.) Greg came close to realising this in 1953 when he objected to Bracy's interrogation of memorial reconstruction in *The Merry Wives*: 'his method . . . is merely to take instances in which reporting has been assumed and to assert that each is open to another explanation'. What Greg objects to in Bracy's method is, of course, the staple of the New Bibliographic approach to memorial reconstruction. Greg (1953), Review of Bracy, *The Merry Wives*, pp.77–8.

49 Kirschbaum, 'An Hypothesis', p.704, n.16; Greg (1910), 'The *Hamlet* Quartos', pp. 196–7; Wilson, *Shakespeare and the New Bibliography*, p.82; Duthie, *The 'Bad' Quarto of 'Hamlet'*, pp.47–8.

50 This sleight of hand was first acknowledged by Duthie (*The 'Bad' Quarto of 'Hamlet'*, p.90) when he analysed the work of the disintegrators, but his insight did not extend to studies of memorial reconstruction.

51 Kirschbaum, 'The Good and Bad Quartos', p.277; 'An Hypothesis', p.706, n.21.

52 Greg (1950), *Marlowe's 'Doctor Faustus'*, p.21. D. L. Patrick issues a similar challenge at *Richard 3* 3.5.75–6, 103, 108: 'Can any other theory account for the quarto text in this passage?' (Patrick, *The Textual History of 'Richard III'*, p.57.) Greg, in his review of Patrick's work, agrees with Patrick in rhetoric and style as well as in opinion: 'To suppose that Shakespeare, or for the matter . . . any competent writer, could have written the quarto text as it stands, seems to me out of the question: given the quarto text, to suppose that the folio was produced by a process of revision, mere fatuity'. Greg (1938–9), Review of Patrick, *The Textual History*, p.118.

53 Thomas, '*Hamlet* Q1', p.251.

54 Cf. Miller, '*A Shrew* and the Theories'. A recent exception which may herald a new trend is Janis Lull, who writes about 'the authors of Q1 [*Hamlet*]'. 'Forgetting *Hamlet*', p.141.

55 Kirschbaum, 'The Good and Bad Quartos', p.292. Evidence of such an

author may perhaps be found on the final page of the quarto: '*Terminat hora diem, Terminat Author opus*'. This epigraph is unlikely to have been appended by the printer as Greg suggested. Greg (1950), *Marlowe's Doctor Faustus*, pp.71–2. Bevington and Rasmussen believe the motto to be conventional (it also appears at the end of the MS *Charlemagne*) and agree with Greg that the printer may have added it (Bevington and Rasmussen eds., *Doctor Faustus*, p.198); however, given that the *Charlemagne* MS appears to be an authorial copy, the tag may be conventionally used by authors rather than printers.

56 See Rasmussen, *A Textual Companion*, pp.8–10 for a discussion of Greg's illogical attitude concerning the alleged reporter and the *English Faust Book* in A *Dr Faustus*.

57 Greg (1910), *The Merry Wives*, p.xix, n.1; (1950), *Marlowe's 'Doctor Faustus'*, p.97; Kirschbaum, *The True Text*, p.30; Alexander, 'The Original Ending', p.114. In his edition of *Hamlet*, G. R. Hibbard perpetuates the stereotype of the dull reporter: 'The reporter could not reconstruct the speech because he had never properly understood it. A failure to comprehend compounds the errors due to a failure to remember.' Hibbard ed., *Hamlet*, p.85.

58 Irace's work provides a significant exception to this critical attitude: she finds a dramatic intelligence operating behind the structural alterations in the six Shakespearean suspect texts she examines. See Irace, *Reforming the 'Bad' Quartos*. For a careful analysis of the sub-plot of *A Shrew*, showing that the reporter consciously adapted the material, see Miller, '*A Shrew* and the Theories'.

59 Kirschbaum, 'The Good and Bad Quartos', p.284 (my emphasis).

60 Werstine, 'Narratives', pp.82–3.

61 Greg (1942), *The Editorial Problem*, p.74; Pollard, *Shakespeare Folios and Quartos*, pp.78–9; Hart, *Stolne and Surreptitious Copies*, p.79; Greg (1940), *The Variants in the First Quarto of 'King Lear'*, p.138, n.; Hart, *Stolne and Surreptitious Copies*, p.80.

62 Hoppe, *The Bad Quarto of 'Romeo and Juliet'*, p.76, n.1. See also my note 44.

63 Greg (1950), Review of Hoppe, *The Bad Quarto of 'Romeo and Juliet'*, p.65.

64 Hoppe, *The Bad Quarto of 'Romeo and Juliet'*, p.76.

65 Alexander, *Shakespeare's 'Henry VI' and 'Richard III'*, p.72; Steven Urkowitz has recently argued that the verbal quality of the two Sheridan reconstructions is far inferior to that of the Shakespearean suspect texts. See Urkowitz, '"If I Mistake"', p.234.

66 Hoppe, *The Bad Quarto of 'Romeo and Juliet'*, p.78.

67 *Ibid.*, p.161.

68 Alexander makes a similar point in *Shakespeare's 'Henry VI' and 'Richard III'*, p.95.

69 For analysis of the problems caused by Greg's failure to accept the additions as those of Bird and Rowley, see Bowers, 'Marlowe's *Doctor Faustus*: The 1602 Additions' and 'Textual Introduction' to *Dr Faustus*, in Bowers ed., *The Complete Works of Christopher Marlowe*, vol.II, pp.123–59; Keefer, 'Verbal Magic', pp.324–30.

70 Barber, '"The form of Faustus' fortunes good or bad"', p.93, n.2.

71 Ornstein, 'Marlowe and God', p.1378.

72 Brockbank, *Marlowe: Doctor Faustus*, p.61.

73 The one early-twentieth-century exception seems to be Chambers (*William Shakespeare* vol.I, p.344); I am grateful to Paul Werstine for bringing this to my attention. For discussion of the complex nature of Q2 see Goldberg, '"What? in a names"'.

74 Dessen, 'Weighing the Options', p.66.

75 Fenton, 'In the Study and On the Stage', pp.989–90.

76 Fuller, *TLS* 3 January 1986, p.11, reprinted in Fuller, *Consolations*. Fuller was evidently much interested in the details of Q1 *Hamlet*. See 'On the 160th Anniversary of the Discovery of the First Quarto of *Hamlet*' in Fuller, *New and Collected Poems 1934–84*.

CHAPTER 4

1 Quoted by Simpson, *A Study of the Prose Works of John Donne*, p.261.

2 This process was doubtless facilitated by the structure of the sermon, which was designed to be easily followed. Donne's sermons are models of clarity; Henry Smith's style was simple and straightforward; 'one Clappam' heard by John Manningham in December 1602 was blunt, eloquent, and witty, linking the scarlet images of Song of Solomon 4.3 ('Thy lips are like a thred of skarlett') with Joshua 2.21 ('Shee bound the skarlet threed in the windowe') in a manner which aroused both Manningham's imagination and admiration (Sorlien ed., *The Diary of John Manningham*, pp.157–9). Sermons were structured to be as memorable rhetorically as they were theologically. See Mitchell, *English Pulpit Oratory*; Simpson, *A Study*; Owst, *Preaching in Medieval England*; Hayward, 'A Note on Donne'; Sorlien ed. *The Diary of John Manningham*; Mulryan, 'Literacy in an Illiterate Medium'.

3 Egerton, *A Lecture preached by Maister Egerton, at the Blacke-friers*, A6v–A7r.

4 Egerton, *An Ordinary Lecture Preached at the Blacke-Friers*. The second (corrected) edition of the sermon (see note 3, above) reduces these claims slightly. Charactery is no longer described as having satisfied the desire for a system of reporting speech accurately, but as having *endeavoured* to satisfy that desire. Similarly, A. S. qualifies the confident 'I haue not missed one word' with the adverb 'wittingly'.

5 There is reason to believe that some sermons were preached from notes, in which case the preacher would not have had a full copy of a text to give to the printer. Both John Donne and Thomas Playfere had to create a text from notes and/or memory when petitioned by friends for copies. See Hayward, *A Note on Donne*, p.80; and Playfere, Preface to 'The Pathway to Perfection', in *The Whole Sermons*, 17r–v.

6 Sorlien ed., *The Diary of John Manningham*, p.152.

7 For analysis of the different verbal quality of the reported versions and their corrected counterparts, see Price, *A Fruitful Sermon*, and 'Another Shorthand Sermon'.

8 Price points out that the publisher of Bright's *Characterie* was also the publisher of Egerton's *An Ordinary Lecture Preached at the Blacke-Friers* (1589) and so the insistence on accuracy in the preface to the sermon may be no more than an advertising ploy. Price, 'Another Shorthand Sermon', p.176.

9 Buc, *The Third University of England*, 401r, p.984.

10 For an analysis of the (in)ability of shorthand to report plays see Duthie, *Elizabethan Shorthand*.

11 Kirkman and Head, *The English Rogue*, part II (1668), p.202.

12 Hall, *Henry VIII* in *Hall's Chronicle*, vol.I, p.145.

13 *Ibid.*, vol.II, p.354.

14 Pollard, 'The First MP Journalist', p.12.

15 These lines do not appear in Q2 or F. In Q1 they form part of Hamlet's warning that the clown should speak no more than is set down for him; if Q1 is memorially reconstructed by actors, these interpolated lines provide a clever metatheatrical joke.

16 Dekker may have table-books in mind when he advises gallants to 'hoord vp the finest play-scraps you can get, vp-pon which your leane wit may most sauourly feede for want of other stuffe'. *The Gull's Hornbook* 1609, E4v.

17 McKenzie ed. *The Hog Hath Lost His Pearl*, pp.vi–viii. Cf. Clare, '*Art Made Tongue-tied*', pp.171–2.

18 The sonnet is found in one copy only, now in the library of the University of Texas at Austin. I quote from Holaday gen. ed., *The Plays of George Chapman: The Comedies*, p.235.

19 Cf. Cotgrave's *Dictionarie* (1611), which defines the adjective *trotier* (m.), *ère* (f.) as follows: 'wandering much vp and downe; as in the Prouerbe, Fille fenestrière, & trotière, rarement bonne mesnagière' (seldom proves gazer or gadder a good housewife).

20 See the printer's epistle to the reader in Q2 *Gorboduc* (1570), A2r.

21 Epistle 'To the Reader', prefaced to *The Rape of Lucrece*.

22 Heywood, *Pleasant Dialogues and Dramas*, R5r, quoted from Doran ed., *1 If You Know Not Me*, p.xxxviii.

23 Giordano-Orsini, 'Thomas Heywood's Play', p.338.

24 The possibility of Heywood's ignorance may be supported by the vagueness of several other testimonies, from his own statement of 1608, to the Earl of Pembroke's letter to the Company of Stationers on 10 June 1637: 'I am informed that some copies of playes belonging to the king and queenes servants, the players . . . having been lately stollen *or gotten from them by indirect means*, are now attempted to be printed[.]' (See Chambers, *William Shakespeare*, vol.I, p.136; my emphasis.)

25 Shapiro, 'Stenography', p.305.

26 Webster's *The Devil's Law Case* refers to textual theft through Brachygraphy. In a scene in a Neapolitan law court, but clearly indebted to Elizabethan England, Sanitonella tells the officers 'You must take special care, that you let in / No brachygraphy men, to take notes'; this caution is advised lest 'scurvy pamphlets, and lewd ballads [be] / Engendered of it presently' (Brennan ed., 4.2.26–7; 29–30).

27 Greg (1925–6), '*The Spanish Tragedy* – A Leading Case?', pp.51–2.

28 Jenkins ed., *Hamlet*, p. 20.

29 Blayney, 'Shakespeare's Fight with *What* Pirates?'.

30 Mahood, *Bit Parts in Shakespeare's Plays*, p.13.

31 Quoted in Rennert, *The Spanish Stage*, p.175.

32 *Ibid.*, p.176.

33 Ruano de la Haza, 'An Early Rehash of Lope's *Peribañez*'. Further references to this article are included parenthetically in the text.

34 Quoted by Wright, 'A Note on Dramatic Piracy', p.256.

35 Quoted by Alexander, *Shakespeare's 'Henry VI'*, pp.70–1.
36 Alexander, *Shakespeare's 'Henry VI'*, p.72.
37 Urkowitz, "'If I Mistake'", p.234.
38 Greg (1907), *Henslowe Papers*, p.38.
39 Cited by Wilson, *Shakespeare and the New Bibliography*, p.86.
40 In Grosart ed., *The Non-Dramatic Works*, vol.II, p.353. The Spanish actor
    who foiled Ramirez's reconstruction was clearly performing to an
    audience who knew the play, hence their protests at the actor's inaccuracy.
41 Chapman, *Jane Austen's Letters*, letter 21, p.67.
42 *Ibid.*, letter 17, p.52.
43 Chapman, *The Novels of Jane Austen*, vol.II, p.xi, n.1.

CHAPTER 5

1 Ong, *Orality and Literacy*, p.41, citing Jack Goody.
2 Silk, *Homer. The Iliad*, p.17.
3 The Bible provides a good illustration of this structural technique. The
   New Testament Gospels, for example, eschew a chapter-by-chapter Life
   of Jesus, presenting instead, individual scenes, selected highlights. (See
   Ong, 'Text as Interpretation', p.155.)
4 For an excellent analysis of formulae in *The Faerie Queene*, to which I am
   indebted, see Webster, 'Oral Form and Written Craft'.
5 See Ong, 'Milton's Logical Epic'; Trousdale, 'Shakespeare's Oral Text',
   p.101. For examples of recent works with deep roots in the oral tradition,
   see Bayer, 'Narrative Techniques and the Oral Tradition in *The Scarlet
   Letter*', and Sybil Marshall's novel *A Nest of Magpies* (1993).
6 Ong, 'Oral Residue in Tudor Prose Style', p.150.
7 Ronald Wright explains how European explorers/invaders had to acquire
   'a rich metaphorical language' to deal with the Six Nations of North
   America, for colourful phrases like 'planting the tree of peace', 'stoking the
   council fire' were ubiquitously used 'to fix each clause in memory, like
   headings and illustrations in a text'. Wright, *Stolen Continents*, p.126.
8 See Potter, "'Nobody's Perfect'", p.94. Interviewed about her novel *A Nest
   of Magpies*, the eighty-year-old writer Sybil Marshall explained the
   colourful style of the dialogue as a residue of oral tradition: 'We all spoke
   in metaphor. Country people always do.' *The Guardian*, 9 February 1993.
   There is a direct line between Marshall's metaphoric country style and
   Renaissance writing. Finding his fiddle bewitched in *The Witch of*

Edmonton, Father Sawgut declares that he can 'make no more music than a beetle of a cow-turd' (3.4.45–6), and in the same play Old Carter boasts of his good health: he is 'as sound as an honest man's conscience when he's dying' (Corbin and Sedge eds., 4.2.126–7).

9 Pettitt, 'Formulaic Dramaturgy'.

10 *Ibid.*, p.184.

11 Long, 'Perspective on Provenance', pp.25–6.

12 For details of these and other repetitions, see Trousdale, 'Shakespeare's Oral Text'.

13 Socrates, *Phaedrus* 274 C–5 B, quoted by Yates, *The Art of Memory*, p.38.

14 Thomas, 'The Meaning of Literacy', p.108. Cited from Hinde, *A Faithful Remonstrance*, pp.56–8.

15 Letters, vol. 1, 63–4; quoted in Lowes, *The Road to Xanadu*, p. 40. The fact that Le Grice's memoirs were written some time after the event may diminish the reliability of this anecdote.

16 The examples of Julius Caesar and William of Ockham are noted by Carruthers, *The Book of Memory*, pp.7, 99.

17 Luria, *The Mind of a Mnemonist*. The main character in Jorge Luis Borges's short story 'Funes, the Memorious' has mnemonic abilities similar to those of Shereshevskii. See Borges, *Fictions*, pp.97–105.

18 'Declarative' memory, sometimes called 'that' memory, refers to identification (that 'that' is a traffic-light, a toothbrush, a Shakespeare play) and is distinct from 'how' memory (how to ride a bike) which does not suffer attrition in the same accelerated way. Declarative memory can be divided into two parts: semantic memory (verbal recall) and episodic memory (recall of actions). See Rose, *The Making of Memory*, p.120.

19 McKerrow ed., *Works of Thomas Nashe*, vol.II, p.299.

20 Carruthers, *The Book of Memory*, p.29.

21 These powers often prevented him coping with quotidien necessities. For example he was unable to recognise people because an individual's different facial expressions were filed separately (with separate associations) in his memory, rather than integrated to form a whole.

22 On occasion Shereshevskii would omit an object when recalling the sequence. The omission inevitably had a physical, visual explanation: the object's colour blended with that of its background, or it was in a dark niche 'so I couldn't see it'. Luria, *The Mind of a Mnemonist*, p.37.

23 Carruthers, *The Book of Memory*, p.109.

24 Cowley, *Poems*, pp.82–4.

25 Hoppe, *The Bad Quarto of 'Romeo and Juliet'*, pp.75–6.

26 Patrick, *The Textual History*, p.34.

27 Bartlett, *Remembering*. I quote his results from the convenient summary in Hunter, *Memory*.

28 Although it is sometimes felt that Bartlett overemphasised the case for contextualisation and interpretation (see Conway, *Autobiographical Memory*, pp.24–5), his premise has not been seriously challenged. For more recent discussion of contextualised, interpretive memory, see Gillespie, *The Mind's We*, pp.107–51.

29 Hunter, *Memory*, p.150.

30 *Ibid.*, p.152.

31 *Ibid.*, p.129.

32 *Ibid.*, pp.17–18.

33 Pettitt, 'Introduction' in Andersen, Holzapfel, and Pettitt, *The Ballad as Narrative*, p.9.

34 *Ibid.*, p.12.

35 Andersen and Pettitt, 'Mrs Brown of Falkland', p.4.

36 Quoted by Fowler, *A Literary History of the Popular Ballad*, p.312.

37 Child, *The English and Scottish Popular Ballads*, vol.IV, p.231, from which all ballad quotations are taken.

38 Andersen and Pettitt, 'Mrs Brown of Falkland', p.17.

39 In the discussion of 'The Lass of Roch Royal', 'Bonny Baby Livingston', and 'Child Waters', I am indebted to the thorough and stimulating research of Thomas Pettitt, and his collaborator Flemming Andersen. My choice of three ballads from the thirty-five supplied to collectors by Mrs Brown is based on Pettitt and Andersen's conclusion that only these three and their parallel variant versions were 'provided . . . under circumstances which render comparative analysis a legitimate exercise for the purpose of determining the processes of oral transmission'. For the background to this reasoning, see Andersen and Pettitt, 'Mrs Brown of Falkland', p.12.

40 *Ibid.* Elsewhere Pettitt examines and rejects the possibility of Mrs Brown having known alternative versions, or of having extemporised the texts from a known story; Pettitt, 'Mrs Brown's "Lass of Roch Royal"', pp.13–31.

41 Pettitt, 'Mrs Brown's "Lass of Roch Royal"', p.25.

42 *Ibid.*, p.27.

43 Oliver ed., *'Dido Queen of Carthage' and 'The Massacre at Paris'*, p. 126.

44 For a full and careful description of the MS see Kelliher, 'Contemporary Manuscript Extracts'.

45 The following survey is based on commonplace books in the collections of the Folger Shakespeare Library, the British Library Manuscript Room, and the Stratford-on-Avon Record Office. See also Beal, '"Notions in Garrison"'.

46 Fane's commonplace books are in the Stratford-on-Avon Record Office (ER 93/1 and 93/2) and the Folger Library (v.a.180).

47 The example of this practice most familiar to students of Elizabethan drama is found in Philip Henslowe's *Diary*. This theatrical account book originally belonged to Philip's brother, John, who used the volume for 'accounts relating to mining and smelting operations. . .1576–81' (Foakes and Rickert eds., *Henslowe's Diary*, p.xi). Philip reversed and inverted the volume to provide a fresh start for his theatrical dealings.

48 For dramatists' use of commonplace books, see Schoell, 'G. Chapman's "Commonplace Book"'; Dent, *John Webster's Borrowing*'; and Beal, '"Notions in Garrison"', p.146. Beal describes Jonson's *Timber* as 'based on some kind of commonplace book if not virtually amounting to one in itself'.

49 For detailed support of this probability see Kelliher, 'Contemporary Manuscript Extracts', pp.165–71.

50 The author began with Act 1 on folio 47v (volume reversed), continued on folio 48r (volume reversed), before running out of space and continuing on folio 47r (volume reversed).

51 These marginalia are lined up against extract 2 also.

52 These marginalia relate to extract 14, against which they are placed.

53 The use of one of the current shorthand systems – Bright's *Characterie* (1588), Bales's *Brachygraphy* (1590), or, if the play was performed after 1602, Willis's *Stenography* (1602) – to take brief notes or key lines in the playhouse may be discounted. The palimpsestic nature of the MS indicates that this is the first copy; it is clearly not based on a prior version, whether longhand or shorthand. The reference to the Queen in extract 4 shows that the playgoer made his copy before 1603.

54 My terminology betrays my roots in a print-based culture: oral societies viewed remembering as a creative act of composition, and would not have distinguished conceptually between the activities as I have done.

55 Gaskell, *From Writer to Reader*, pp.261, 260, 249. I am grateful to Michael Warren for drawing my attention to this reference.

56 Snodin, 'The Text' in Alexander *et al.* eds., *All's Well That Ends Well*, p.32.
  Similar disclaimers appear in the introductions to all the BBC
  Shakespeare texts.

57 David Snodin, personal communication.

58 David Burke, personal communication.

59 Brook, 'A Piece of Evidence', pp. 25–8.

60 Honigmann, *The Stability of Shakespeare's Text*, p. 190.

61 Jenkins ed., *Hamlet*, p.20.

CHAPTER 6

1 Chambers, *William Shakespeare*, vol.1, p.465.

2 Greg (1954), *The Editorial Problem*, p.90.

3 Kirschbaum, *The True Text*, p.10.

4 Greg (1953), Review of Bracy, *The Merry Wives of Windsor*, pp.77–8.

5 McKerrow, Review of Pollard ed., *Shakespeare's Hand in the Play of 'Sir Thomas More'*, p.239.

6 For explanations about the compilation of this list see chapter 1.

7 Hammond, 'Encounters of the Third Kind', p.72, n.2.

8 Barthes, 'From Work to Text', p.75.

9 Jerome McGann deals with this point in 'The Text, the Poem, and the Problem of Historical Method'.

CHAPTER 7

1 Price, 'Towards a Scientific Method', p.152.

2 Hoppe, *The Bad Quarto of 'Romeo and Juliet'*, pp.161–5. The later plays
  which contain the remaining alleged 'borrowings' are *1 Henry 4*, *The Merry
  Wives of Windsor*, *Hamlet*. But since Hoppe dates the reconstruction as
  1597, how can Q1 *Romeo and Juliet* echo two plays not yet written?

3 Thorp, *The Triumph of Realism*, p.91.

4 Barthes, 'Theory of the Text', p.39.

5 Farr, *John Ford and the Caroline Theatre*, p.50; Gurr ed., *Philaster*,
  pp.xxii–xxiii.

6 Greg (1950), *Marlowe's 'Doctor Faustus'*, p.28.

7 Rasmussen, *A Textual Companion*, p.75, n.30; Rasmussen, cited in
  Hattaway ed., *2 Henry 6*, p.240.

8 For good illustrations of Greene's tendency towards self-plagiarism, see
  Goree, 'Concerning Repetitions in Robert Greene's Romances'; Hart,

'Robert Greene's Prose Works'; and Vincent, 'Further Repetitions in the Works of Robert Greene'. Trousdale, 'Shakespeare's Oral Text' illustrates Shakespeare's habit of borrowing from himself. Lowes, in *The Road to Xanadu*, demonstrates Coleridge's habit of re-using his own phrases and lines.

9 Hoeniger, ed., *Pericles* 4.1.21, n.

10 Hoppe, *The Bad Quarto of 'Romeo and Juliet'*, p.168.

11 Smidt, 'Repetition, Revision, and Editorial Greed.'

12 Greg (1930), 'A Question of Plus or Minus'.

13 Greg (1950), *Marlowe's 'Doctor Faustus'*, p.55. Repetitions characteristic of 'very bad reporting' were noted in B *Dr Faustus* by Roma Gill with some perplexity: 'I confess I cannot see how this fits in with any theory about the nature of the B-text'; Gill ed., *Dr Faustus* (1965), p.78, n.

14 Hoppe, *The Bad Quarto of 'Romeo and Juliet'*, p.128.

15 Duthie, *The 'Bad' Quarto of 'Hamlet'*, pp.155, 153–4.

16 Hook ed., *Edward 1*; Sampley, 'The Text of Peele's *David and Bethsabe*'.

17 Champion, '"What prerogatiues meanes"', pp.5, 7.

18 Analysis of the Play of *The Fair Maid of Bristow* shows that plotting anomalies are likewise concentrated in this section. While this part of the playtext may have been affected by memorial transmission, the bulk of the playtext itself is not a memorial reconstruction.

19 H. J. Oliver ed., *'Dido Queen of Carthage' and 'The Massacre at Paris'*, p. liv.

20 *Ibid.*, p.lv.

21 This connective repetition does not feature in Q2; Q1 has a different connective repetition at the equivalent point.

22 Parry, *The Making of Homeric Verse*, p.272.

23 Kiparsky, quoted by Rosenberg, 'Oral Literature in the Middle Ages', p.447.

24 Hart, *Stolne and Surreptitious Copies*, p.318.

25 I quote from Lancashire ed., *Gallathea*; Brennan ed., *The White Devil*; Bowers ed., *1 Honest Whore*, in *The Dramatic Works of Thomas Dekker*, vol.II; and Berger and Donovan eds., *Caesar and Pompey*. *Tiberius* is quoted from Greg (1915) MSR.

26 Hart, *Stolne and Surreptitious Copies*, p.216; see Boas, quoted by Greg (1950), *Marlowe's 'Doctor Faustus'*, p.332.

27 It is, however, possible that the supposed couplet is coincidental, and that the interpolated phrase is 'My Lord'.

28 Greg (1923), *Two Elizabethan Stage Abridgements*, pp.317-18, my emphasis.

29 *Ibid.*, p.304, n.1.

30 H. T. Price notes that the editors of the old Cambridge series emended 'Help her' to 'Helping her', viewing it as a stage direction rather than extra-metrical pleonasm. Price, 'Towards a Scientific Method', p.158.

31 F omits the phrase 'and now behold'.

32 Jenkins, 'Playhouse Interpolations', p.47.

33 Smidt, *Iniurious Impostors*, p.132.

34 This was first noted by Proudfoot, BLitt thesis.

35 Chambers, Review of Bennett ed., *The Jew of Malta*, p.78.

36 Maxwell, 'How Bad is the Text of *The Jew of Malta?*', p.435.

37 Trussler, *Dr Faustus*, p.xiv.

38 Greg (1923), *Two Elizabethan Stage Abridgements*, p.306.

39 *Ibid.*, pp.307, 310.

40 Crupi, *Robert Greene*, p.107.

41 *Ibid.*, p.110.

42 *Ibid.*, p.112.

43 Greg (1923), *Two Elizabethan Stage Abridgements*, p.310.

44 Barber, 'The form of Faustus' fortunes', p.109.

45 See Eric Rasmussen's suggestion about the Clown's role in *Sir Thomas More* ('"Setting Down What the Clown Spoke"'), and Harold Jenkins's study of repetitions and additions in F *Hamlet* ('Playhouse Interpolations').

46 Greg (1942), *The Editorial Problem*, p.56, n.3.

47 Dekker, *Jests to Make You Merry* in Grosart ed., *The Non-Dramatic Works*, vol.II, pp.352-3.

48 I quote from Bullen ed., *The Mayor of Queenborough*. The *OED* defines 'fribble' as 'to falter, stammer (*out*)'.

49 Dekker, *Jests to Make You Merry* in Grosart, ed., *The Non-Dramatic Works*, vol.II, p.353.

50 G. N. Giordano-Orsini, 'The Copy for *If You Know Not Me*', p.1037.

51 Heywood, *England's Elizabeth*, F7r-v, pp.109-10.

52 Giordano-Orsini, 'The Copy for *If You Know Not Me*', p.1037. On the use of sources and analogues for successful textual reconstruction and diagnosis, see Eugene Vinaver's work on Malory's French sources, detailed in the introduction to his edition of *The Works of Thomas Malory*, pp.cxiv-cxviii.

53 See Greg (1903), '*Hymen's Triumph* and the Drummond MS', p.61. I quote the MS from Pitcher's MSR transcription.

54 The incident in which Richard rebukes Stanley for his speech habits when discussing Richmond's means is paralleled in Shakespeare's *Richard 3*, in both Q and F. I quote from F with Q variants in square brackets:

> RICHARD: *Stanley* [Q: How now], what newes with you?
> STANLEY: None, good my Liege [Q: Lord], to please you with ye
> > hearing,
> Nor none so bad, but well may be reported [Q: it may well be told].
> RICHARD: Hoyday, a Riddle, neither good nor bad:
> What need'st thou runne so many miles about [Q: Why doest thou
> runne so many mile about],
> When thou mayest tell thy Tale the neerest [Q: a neerer] way?
> > TLN 3253–8

This is the only indication of Stanley's circumlocutory verbal trait in Shakespeare's play, and may suggest that the anonymous *True Tragedy of Richard 3*, in its extant version, served as source.

55 Giordano-Orsini, 'Thomas Heywood's Play on *The Troubles of Queen Elizabeth*', pp.319–20.

56 See Proudfoot, BLitt thesis, p.83.

57 Greg (1929) ed., *The True Tragedy of Richard the Third*, p. vii.

58 Ashe, 'A Survey', PhD thesis, p.91.

59 Greg (1925), *The Escapes of Jupiter*, pp. 165–75.

60 Smidt, '*Iniurious Impostors*', *passim*.

61 Turner ed., *Philaster*, pp.389–90.

62 Greg (1905–6), Review of J. M. Robertson, *Did Shakespeare Write 'Titus Andronicus'?*, p.341; Chambers, *William Shakespeare*, vol.1, p.157. However, in 1923 Greg wrote that actors were 'naturally most sensitive to rhythm' (*Two Elizabethan Stage Abridgements*, p.354).

63 Chambers, *William Shakespeare*, vol.1, p.158.

64 Greg (1925), Review of Mead ed., *The Famous Historie of Chinon of England*, p.108.

65 Child, *The English and Scottish Popular Ballads*, vol.IV, pp.311–27.

66 See *The Guardian*, 10 July 1986 and 25 June 1993.

67 Greg (1923–4), 'Massinger's Autograph Corrections', pp.213–14.

68 Guise's opening soliloquy is seventy lines.

69 Greg (1923), *Two Elizabethan Stage Abridgements*, p.298.

70 *Ibid.*, p.296.

71 *Ibid.*, p.292.

72 *Ibid.*, p.296.

73 *Ibid.*, p.295.

74 See McKerrow ed., *The Works of Thomas Nashe*, vol.IV, pp.18, 301.

75 For these and other examples see Smart, *Shakespeare: Truth and Tradition*, pp.187–90.

76 Collier ed., *The Works of William Shakespeare*, vol.VI, p.369.

77 Greg (1942), *The Editorial Problem*, p.59.

78 Honigmann ed., *King John*, p.176; Hoeniger ed., *Pericles*, p.xxviii.

79 The other examples can be found at lines 425–9, 520–6, 1183–92, 1680–3. See Proudfoot, *A Knack to Know a Knave* (MSR), p.vi, and table xx in chapter 8.

80 See Jenkins ed., *Hoffman*, p.vi.

81 This was first pointed out by Proudfoot ed., *A Knack to Know a Knave* (MSR), p. vi.

82 Oliver, ed., *'Dido Queen of Carthage' and 'The Massacre at Paris'*, p.109.

83 Paul Marcus, personal communication.

84 The point of this question, as explained in lines 616–19, receives confirmation in a parallel but later episode recounted in Sorlien ed., *The Diary of John Manningham*, p.235.

85 Born, *The Rare Wit*, p.14.

86 For an excellent discussion of plot unconformities in *Sir Thomas Wyatt*, see Phillip Shaw's discussion '*Sir Thomas Wyat* and the Scenario of *Lady Jane*', to which I am indebted.

87 *Ibid.*, p.230, n.11.

88 'the ladie Iane his daughter . . . taking the matter heauilie, with weeping teares, made request to the whole councell, that hir father might tarrie at home in hir companie'. Holinshed, *The Chronicles of England, Scotland and Ireland* (1587), vol.III, 5M1v (p.1085).

89 Parrott ed., *The Plays and Poems of George Chapman*, p.675.

90 Morrison, 'A Cangoun in Zombieland', p.222–3. The wide-ranging detail of Morrison's lengthy analysis is inadequately represented by my extract; the essay merits consultation in full.

91 Jenkins ed., *Hoffman*, p.vii.

92 Greg (1900), 'Webster's *White Devil*', p. 113.

93 Brown, 'Chapman's *Caesar and Pompey*', p.468.

94 Henning ed., *Fair Em*, p.21.

95 For a sensitive discussion of this point, illustrated in the Q1 text of *Romeo and Juliet*, see Mooney, 'Text and Performance'.

96 Patrick, *The Textual History of Richard III*, p. 18.

97 Although this may stem from a (justifiable?) confidence in the large resources of the London companies, it fails to consider the thematic and economic advantages of doubling. Recent work on this topic includes: Mahood, *Bit Parts in Shakespeare's Plays*; Berger, 'Casting *Henry V*'; Meagher, 'Economy and Recognition'; Melchiori, 'Peter, Balthasar, and Shakespeare's Art of Doubling'; Booth, 'Speculations on Doubling in Shakespeare's Plays'.

98 I have excluded characters who do not speak but who feature regularly in the play (e.g. Clarentia, Elizabeth's waiting-woman) from the total number of mutes.

99 Scott McMillin has recently analysed two suspect texts in relation to the question of reduced casts. See 'The Queen's Men in 1594', and 'Casting the *Hamlet* Quartos'. Cf. also King, *Casting Shakespeare's Plays*.

100 William Montgomery negotiates this difficulty in *1 Contention* by arguing that the reconstruction was made while the London performance (and concomitant facilities) were still fresh in the mind of the reporter. See 'The Original Staging'.

101 See Pettitt, 'Formulaic Dramaturgy'.

102 Abrams ed., *The Merry Devil of Edmonton*, p.34.

103 Wilson, *The Plague in Shakespeare's London*, pp.110–11.

104 Pettitt, 'Formulaic Dramaturgy'.

105 Hart, 'The Length of Elizabethan and Jacobean Plays'; 'The Time Allotted for Representation of Elizabethan and Jacobean Plays'; 'Acting Versions of Elizabethan Plays'.

106 Hook ed., *The Old Wife's Tale*, p.344.

107 Kirschbaum, 'An Hypothesis', p.705, n.17.

108 For discussions about cutting in *Fair Em* and *The Blind Beggar of Alexandria*, see Hennning ed., *Fair Em*, and Parrot ed., *The Plays and Poems of George Chapman*.

109 Greg (1942), *The Editorial Problem*, p.74.

110 Hoppe, *The Bad Quarto of 'Romeo and Juliet'*, p.92.

111 *Ibid.*, p.93.

112 Morris ed., *'Tis Pity She's A Whore*, p.57, n.

113 See Pafford ed., *The Soddered Citizen*, p.ix.

114 Despite the fact that this MS leaf (Folger MS J.B.8) was discovered by the notorious forger, John Payne Collier, there is little reason to doubt the leaf's authenticity. Collier was simply not capable of this standard of palaeographical forgery in the 1820s and 1830s (when he announced the discovery of the leaf). The Hall commonplace-book ballads (Folger MS v.a.339), which he forged in the 1850s, are characterised by jerky and angular letters in contrast to the competent, if disjunct, letter formation in the leaf. For an earlier general discussion of the validity of the leaf, see Petti, *English Literary Hands*, pp.84–5; for the ballad forgeries, see Dawson, 'John Payne Collier's Great Forgery'.

115 Kohler, 'Kyd's Ordered Spectacle', pp.41–2.

116 Greg (1942), *The Editorial Problem*, p.136.

117 *Ibid.*, p.74.

118 Hoeniger ed., *Pericles*, p.20.

119 Chambers, *William Shakespeare*, vol.1, p.521; Pollard, *Shakespeare Folios and Quartos*, p.62.

120 Moxon, *Mechanick Exercises on the Whole Art of Printing*, p.192.

121 Hoeniger ed., *Pericles*, p.xxxi.

122 Bowers ed., *The Dramatic Works of Thomas Dekker*, vol.1, p.400.

123 Greg (1923), *Two Elizabethan Stage Abridgements*, p.256. By such a definition, almost any Renaissance playtext can be deemed reported.

124 Kirschbaum, 'A Census', p.20. This is the definition offered recently by Holderness and Loughrey, but without Kirschbaum's pejorative tone: a suspect text is 'a text which has bypassed the crucial relationship to an authorial manuscript'. See *The Tragicall Historie of Hamlet*, p.20.

125 Jenkins, 'Shakespeare's Bad Quarto', *TLS* 15 April 1994.

CHAPTER 8

1 Greg (1955), *The Shakespeare First Folio*, p.382.

2 Dessen, 'Weighing the Options', p.66.

3 For a cautionary *exemplum* see Bradley's analysis of Greg's study of *The Battle of Alcazar* in *From Text to Performance*.

CHAPTER 9

1 Clayton, 'Today We Have Parting of Names', p.84.

2 Turner ed., *Philaster*, p.393 and *The Maid's Tragedy*, p.15.

3 This characteristic also occurs in another Queen's Men's playtext, *2 Troublesome Reign*.

4 The texts are *The True Tragedy of Richard 3*, *Friar Bacon and Friar Bungay*, and *Selimus*.

5 See Judge, *Elizabethan Book Pirates*, and Kirschbaum, *Shakespeare and the Stationers* for good discussions of Elizabethan publishing. For recent studies of stationers see Ferguson, *Valentine Simmes*, Bracken, 'William Stansby's Early Career', and Gerald D. Johnson's series of articles: 'John Busby', 'The Stationers', 'William Barley', 'Thomas Pavier', 'Nicholas Ling', 'John Trundle'.

6 Quoted by Greg and Nichol Smith (1949) in their introduction to *The Spanish Tragedy (1592)*, p. vii.

7 Kirkman and Head, *The English Rogue*, part II, 'The Preface to the Reader', A7r.

8 Vickers, 'Shakespeare's Bad Quarto', *TLS* 29 July 1994, p.15. I am grateful to Professor Vickers for corresponding with me about this text.

9 Or, if a stationer's suspicions were aroused, he might not act on them (as the trade in 'Gucci' handbags and 'Dior' scarves exemplifies today).

10 Reynolds, '*Mucedorus*, Most Popular Elizabethan Play?'

11 Greg (1955), 'On the Text of *Mucedorus*', p.322.

12 The Sly of *A Shrew*, who is not explicitly identified with a provincial village, asks specifically 'when will the foole come againe?' (*A Shrew*, CIV,22).

13 If one is justified in seeking a Northumbrian prototype, Sir John Forster, the Warden of the Middle Marches (the geographic area extending south of Flodden and west of Alnwick, with its administrative headquarters in Hexham) is as good a candidate as any. He emerges as more corrupt than others by virtue of longevity as much as lifestyle. Born in 1501 he died in 1602, and was Warden of the Middle March from 1560 to his death (with a brief hiatus in 1586–7). By virtue of his position Forster occupied a large house in Hexham, but also set up house in Hexham Abbey, an action which outraged the local population. When his wife died, Forster lived with a common-law wife, by whom he had many bastard children, as peculative and as licentious as their father.

Several points of contact arise between the family in *A Knack to Know a Knave* and the historical Forster dynasty. For example, two references in the play suggest that Perin was a bastard son of the bailiff (106–9; 168). At line 348 the bailiff says 'Here haue I bene a Bayliefe three score yeares.' Even Sir John Forster did not rule for sixty years, and when the

Gravedigger in *Hamlet* wishes to underline his long service he chooses only half this figure. The bailiff's 'three score yeares' may be an exaggerated joke at the expense of an equally aged official, and in 1593, Sir John, although warden for only thirty-three years, was aged ninety-two.

    For material on this subject see: Bates, *The History of Northumberland*; Blair, 'Wardens and Deputy Wardens'; Bain ed., *The Border Papers*; Pease, *The Lord Wardens of the Marches*; Tomlinson, *Life in Northumberland*; Watts and Watts, *From Border to Middle Shire Northumberland*.

14 This is what happens in the equivalent anecdote in T. B.'s prose pamphlet, *The Life and Death of the Merry Devil of Edmonton* (SR 1608, Q 1631) with slight variation: Smug tries to escape from the gamekeepers after an evening poaching; when the keepers see two St George signs, they believe they are in Hodsdon, which has two St George Inns; thinking themselves seriously out of their way, they retreat, leaving Smug safe. This episode was obviously the high-spot of the pamphlet, and is summarised on the 1631 title-page, where it is also depicted in a woodcut.

15 Despite castigating Q1, the printer of Q2 relied on it for his own edition. See Cauthen, '*Gorboduc, Ferrex and Porrex*'.

16 Kirkman and Head, *The English Rogue*, part II, p.203.

17 These eleven texts are: *The Blind Beggar of Alexandria, Fair Em, The Fair Maid of Bristow, Henry 5, 1 Hieronimo, Jack Straw, John of Bordeaux, The Merry Devil of Edmonton, Mucedorus, Thomas Lord Cromwell, The True Tragedy of Richard 3*.

18 For similar structural leaps and changes in pace see *The Famous Victories* and *Sir Thomas Wyatt*; both these texts show signs of compression from two plays into one, with the probable complication of memorial reconstruction in the case of *The Famous Victories*.

19 For discussion of some of the possibilities, see Shapiro, '*Richard II* or *Richard III* or ...?', and de Bruyn, *Mob-Rule and Riot*.

20 See Reibetanz, 'Hieronimo in Decimosexto'.

21 See Haaker, 'The Plague, the Theater, and the Poet' and Bentley, *The Profession of Dramatist*.

22 *1 Contention, The Death of Robert, Earl of Huntingdon, Dr Faustus, Edward 1, King Lear, Philaster, Richard 3*, the Additions to *The Spanish Tragedy*, the fly-scene in *Titus Andronicus, 1* and *2 Troublesome Reign*. (My list of authorial drafts is, in fact, longer than this because it includes plays from

the list of altered texts offered above, as some authorial drafts are also adapted.)

23 Meagher ed., *The Death of Robert, Earl of Huntingdon*, p.viii.

24 The Oxford Shakespeare deals with this problem by creating a new scene at TLN 2258.

25 For a good discussion of this point, see Leah Marcus, *Unediting the Renaissance*, chapter 3, in which Marcus analyses the rhetoric in editions of *The Merry Wives of Windsor*.

26 Bowers ed., *The Complete Works of Christopher Marlowe*, vol.II, p.125.

27 Q2 *Hamlet*, '[n]ewly imprinted . . . according to the true and perfect Coppie', reprinted most of Act I from Q1; the printers of the '[n]ewly corrected' edition of *Romeo and Juliet* relied heavily on Q1; Heminge and Condell's preface to the First Folio seems to denigrate all previous quartos, while reprinting the texts of several of them. For Q2 *Gorboduc* see note 15.

28 Marlowe (*et al.*)'s *Dr Faustus*; Shakespeare's *Hamlet*, *Henry 5*, *2* and *3 Henry 6*, *King John*, *The Merry Wives of Windsor*, *Richard 3*, *Romeo and Juliet*, *The Taming of the Shrew*; and Beaumont and Fletcher's *The Maid's Tragedy* and *Philaster*.

29 Dessen, 'Weighing the Options', p.66.

30 Cf. my '(Mis)Diagnosing Memorial Reconstruction in *John of Bordeaux*', in preparation.

Bibliography

PRIMARY SOURCES

MANUSCRIPTS

Anon. Academic Plays. Folger Library: MS J.a.2.
  The Comedy of July and Julian. Folger Library: MS v.a.159.
  Commonplace Book. Folger Library: MS v.a.87.
  Dick of Devonshire. British Library: MS Egerton 1994.
  Extracts from *1 Henry 4*. British Library: MS Add. 64078.
  The Wasp. Alnwick Castle: MS 507.
Beaumont, Francis and John Fletcher. *Bonduca*. British Library: MS Add.
  36758.
Fane, Sir Francis. Commonplace Books. Stratford-on-Avon Record
  Office: MS ER 93/1 and 93/2, Folger Library: MS v.a.180.
Greene, Robert. *John of Bordeaux*. Alnwick Castle, Northumberland: MS
  507.
Greg, W. W. MSS. Trinity College, Cambridge.
  Letters. National Library of Scotland.
Heywood, Thomas. *The Captives*. British Library: MS Egerton 1994.
Hoby, Margaret. *The Diary of Lady Margaret Hoby 1599–1605*. British
  Library: MS Egerton 2614.
Marlowe, Christopher. *The Massacre at Paris* Leaf. Folger Library: MS J.b.8.
Massinger, Philip. *Believe As You List*. British Library: MS Egerton 2828.
Peele, George. *Anglorum Feriae*. British Library: MS Add. 21432.
Letter to Burghley, enclosing *The Tale of Troy*. British Library: MS Lansd.
  99.

SIXTEENTH- AND SEVENTEENTH-CENTURY PRINTED PLAYS
(PLACE OF PUBLICATION IS LONDON THROUGHOUT)

Anon. *A Larum for London*. 1602.
  A Yorkshire Tragedy. 1608.

    Alphonsus, King of Aragon. 1599.

    Arden of Feversham. 1592.

    Captain Thomas Stukeley. 1605.

    1 Contention. 1594.

    Fair Em. Undated.

    The Fair Maid of Bristow. 1605.

    The Famous Victories of Henry the Fifth. 1598.

    George a Greene. 1599.

    Jack Straw. 1594.

    A Knack to Know an Honest Man. 1596.

    A Knack to Know a Knave. 1594.

    Locrine. 1595.

    The Merry Devil of Edmonton. 1608.

    Mucedorus. 1598.

    Selimus. 1594.

    The Taming of A Shrew. 1594.

    1 and *2 Troublesome Reign*. 1591.

    The True Tragedy of Richard Duke of York. 1595.

    The True Tragedy of Richard 3. 1594.

    The Wit of A Woman. 1604.

Beaumont, Francis, and John Fletcher. *The Maid's Tragedy*. 1619.

    Philaster. 1620.

    Comedies and Tragedies. 1647.

Brome, Richard. *The Antipodes*. 1640.

Chapman, George. *The Blind Beggar of Alexandria*. 1598.

    An Humorous Day's Mirth. 1599.

    Caesar and Pompey. 1631.

Dekker, Thomas, John Webster, *et al. Sir Thomas Wyatt*. 1607.

Ford, John. *'Tis Pity She's A Whore*. 1633.

Greene, Robert. *Friar Bacon and Friar Bungay*. 1594.

    James 4. 1598.

    Orlando Furioso. 1594.

Greene, Robert and Thomas Lodge. *A Looking Glass for London
    and England*. 1594 and Q4 undated.

Heywood, Thomas. *1 If You Know Not Me You Know Nobody*. 1605.

    A Woman Killed with Kindness. 1607.

    The Rape of Lucrece. 1608.

Kyd, Thomas. *1 Hieronimo*. 1605.
 The Spanish Tragedy. 1592 and 1602.
Marlowe, Christopher. *The Massacre at Paris*. Undated.
Marlowe, Christopher *et al*. *Dr Faustus*. 1604 and 1616.
Marston, John. *The Malcontent*. 1604.
Middleton, Thomas. *A Chaste Maid in Cheapside*. 1630.
Middleton, Thomas and William Rowley. *The Changeling*. 1653.
Munday, Anthony, Drayton, M., Wilson, R., and Hathaway, T.
  1 Sir John Oldcastle. 1600.
Munday, Anthony, and Henry Chettle. *The Death of Robert, Earl
  of Huntingdon*. 1601.
Peele, George. *Edward 1*. 1593.
 The Battle of Alcazar. 1594.
 The Old Wife's Tale. 1595.
 David and Bethsabe. 1599.
Sackville, Thomas, and Thomas Norton. *Gorboduc*. 1565 and 1570.
Shakespeare, William. *Hamlet*. 1603 and 1604–5.
 Henry 5. 1600.
 King Lear. 1608.
 The Merry Wives of Windsor. 1602.
 Pericles. 1609.
 Richard 2. Q4 1608.
 Richard 3. 1597.
 Romeo and Juliet. 1597 and 1599.
Taylor, R. *The Hog Hath Lost His Pearl*. 1614.
'W. S.' *Thomas Lord Cromwell*. 1600.

SERMONS

Dove, J. *A Sermon Preached at Pauls Crosse*. 1594.
Egerton, Stephen. *An Ordinary Lecture Preached at the Blacke-Friers*. 1589.
 A Lecture preached by Maister Egerton, at the Blacke-friers, 1589. 1603.
Playfere, Thomas. 'The Pathway to Perfection'. In *The Whole Sermons of
  that Eloquent Divine, of Famous Memory, Thomas Playfere,
  Doctor in Divinitie. Gathered into One Vollume*. 1623.
Saunderson, R. *Twelve Sermons*. 1637.
Smith, Henry. *The Benefit of Contentation*. 2nd edition, 1590.
 The Wedding Garment. 1590.

The Benefit of Contentation. 1591.

The Affinity of the Faithful. 1591.

The Affinity of the Faithful. 2nd edition, corrected and augmented, 1591.

The Sermons of Master Henry Smith, Gathered into One Volume. 1592.

OTHER CONTEMPORARY PRINTED MATERIAL

Anon. *The Defence of Coney-Catching.* 1592.

Bales, Peter. *The Writing Schoolmaster.* 1590.

Bright, Timothy. *Characterie, An Art of Short, Swift, and Secret Writing.* 1588.

Buc, George. *The Third University of England.* 1615. Addendum to John
     Stow, *Annals.* 1614.

Chettle, Henry. *Kind Heart's Dream.* 1592.

Cotgrave, Randall. *A Dictionarie of the French and English Tongues.* 1611.

Dekker, Thomas. *The Gull's Hornbook.* 1609.

Hall, Edward. *Hall's Chronicle...(1548 and 1550).* 1809.

Heywood, Thomas. *England's Elizabeth.* 1631.

     Pleasant Dialogues and Dramas. 1637.

Hinde, William. *A Faithful Remonstrance of the Holy Life and Happy Death
     of John Bruen.* 1641.

Holinshed, Raphael. *The Chronicles of England, Scotland and Ireland.* 3 vols.
     1577, 1587.

Kirkman, Francis and Richard Head. *The English Rogue.* Part II, 1671.

Marston, John. *The Scourge of Villainy.* 1599.

Nashe, Thomas. *The Unfortunate Traveller.* 1633.

Willis, John. *Stenography.* 1602.

SECONDARY SOURCES

THESES

Ashe, D. J., 'A Survey of Non-Shakespearean Bad Quartos'. PhD thesis,
     University of Virginia, 1953.

Jackson, MacDonald P. 'Material for an Edition of *Arden of Feversham*'.
     BLitt thesis, University of Oxford, 1963.

Martin, E. M. F. 'A Critical Edition of *1 If You Know Not Me*'. MA thesis,
     University of London, 1930.

Miller, Stephen R. 'A Critical Old-spelling Edition of *The Taming of A
     Shrew*, 1594'. PhD thesis, University of London, 1993.

Montgomery, William. '*The Contention of York and Lancaster*: A Critical
Edition'. DPhil thesis, 2 vols., University of Oxford, 1985.

Proudfoot, G. R. 'A Critical Edition of *A Knack to Know a Knave*'. BLitt
thesis, University of Oxford, 1961.

BOOKS, ARTICLES, AND EDITIONS (EDITIONS OF PLAYTEXTS ARE
LISTED UNDER THE NAME OF THE EDITOR)

Abrams, William Amos ed. *The Merry Devil of Edmonton*. Durham, NC:
Durham University Publications, 1942.

Adams, J. Q. Review of W. W. Greg, *Two Elizabethan Stage Abridgements*.
JEGP 23 (1924): 605–9.

Albright, E. M. *Dramatic Publication in England, 1580–1640*. New York:
Modern Language Society of America, 1927.

'*Dramatic Publication in England, 1580–1640*: A Reply'. *RES* 4 (1928):
193–202.

Alexander, Peter. '*II Henry VI* and the Copy for *The Contention* (1594)'.
TLS 9 October 1924: 629–30.

'*3 Henry VI* and *Richard, Duke of York*'. *TLS* 13 November 1924: 730.

'*The Taming of a Shrew*'. *TLS* 16 September 1926: 614.

Shakespeare's 'Henry VI' and 'Richard III'. Cambridge University Press,
1929.

'The Original Ending of *The Taming of the Shrew*'. *SQ* 20 (1969): 111–16.

Alexander, Peter ed. *William Shakespeare. The Complete Works*. London and
Glasgow: Collins, 1951.

Alexander, Peter *et al*. eds. *Henry IV Part 1*. BBC TV Text. London: BBC
Books, 1979.

Julius Caesar. BBC TV Text. London: BBC Books, 1979.

Hamlet. BBC TV Text. London: BBC Books, 1980.

Antony and Cleopatra. BBC TV Text. London: BBC Books, 1981.

All's Well That Ends Well. BBC TV Text. London: BBC Books, 1981.

The Winter's Tale. BBC TV Text. London: BBC Books, 1981.

Richard III. BBC TV Text. London: BBC Books, 1983.

Allen, Michael J. B. and Kenneth Muir eds. *Shakespeare's Plays in Quarto*.
Berkeley: University of California Press, 1981.

Andersen, Flemming G. and Thomas Pettitt. 'Mrs Brown of Falkland:
A Singer of Tales?' *Journal of American Folklore* 92 (1979): 1–24.

Andersen, Flemming G., Otto Holzapfel and Thomas Pettitt. *The Ballad as Narrative*. Odense University Press, 1982.

Anon. Review of W. W. Greg. *Principles of Emendation. Life and Letters* 1 (1928): 526–7.

Ashe, Dora Jean. 'The Non-Shakespearean Bad Quartos as Provincial Acting Versions'. *RP* (1954): 57–62.

'The Text of Peele's *Edward I*'. *SB* 7 (1955): 153–70.

Ashe, Dora Jean ed. *Philaster*. London: Edward Arnold, 1974.

Atwood, Margaret. 'Witches: The Strong Neck of a Favorite Ancestor'. *Radcliffe Quarterly* 66, no. 3 (1980): 4–6.

Bain, Joseph ed. *The Border Papers*. State Papers No. 36, vols. 1 and 11. Edinburgh: H. M. General Register House, 1894–6.

Bains, Y. S. 'The Incidence of Corrupt Passages in the First Quarto of Shakespeare's *Hamlet*'. *N & Q* 40 (1993): 186–92.

Bald, R. C. 'The Shakespeare First Folio'. *TLS* 28 October 1955: 639.

Baldick, Chris. *The Social Mission of English Criticism 1848–1932*. Oxford: Clarendon Press, 1983.

Bang, W. ed. *1 Selimus*. MSR. Oxford, 1909.

Barber, C. L. 'The form of Faustus' fortunes good or bad'. *Tulane Drama Review* 8 (1964): 92–119.

Barish, Jonas. *The Antitheatrical Prejudice*. Berkeley, Los Angeles and London: University of California Press, 1981.

Barthes, Roland. 'From Work to Text'. In Josué V. Harari ed. *Textual Strategies: Perspectives in Post-Structuralist Criticism*. Ithaca: Cornell University Press, 1979, pp.73–81.

'Theory of the Text'. In Robert Young ed. *Untying the Text*. London: Routledge, 1981, pp.31–47.

Barton, Anne. *Ben Jonson, Dramatist*. Cambridge University Press, 1994.

Bartlett, Frederic. *Remembering. A Study in Experimental and Social Psychology*. Cambridge University Press, 1932.

Baskervill, C. R. 'A Prompt Copy of *A Looking Glass for London and England*'. *MP* 30 (1932–3): 29–51.

Bate, Jonathan ed. *Titus Andronicus*. Arden 3. London: Routledge, 1995.

Bates, Cadwallader, J. *The History of Northumberland*. London: E. Stock, 1895.

Bateson, F. W. 'The Application of Thought to an Eighteenth-Century

Text: *The School for Scandal'*. In René Wellek and Alvaro Ribeiro.
*Evidence in Literary Scholarship: Essays in Memory of James
Marshall Osborn*. Oxford: Clarendon Press, 1979, pp.321–35.

Bayer, John G. 'Narrative Techniques and the Oral Tradition in *The Scarlet
Letter'*. *American Literature* 52 (1980–1): 250–63.

Beal, Peter. '"Notions in Garrison": The Seventeenth-Century
Commonplace Book'. In W. Speed Hill ed. *New Ways of Looking
at Old Texts. Papers of the Renaissance English Text Society,
1985–1991*. Binghamton, NY: Center for Medieval and Early
Renaissance Studies, 1993, pp.131–47.

Beaurline, L. A. ed. *King John*. Cambridge University Press, 1990.

Bentley, G. E. *The Profession of Dramatist in Shakespeare's Time 1590–1642*.
Princeton University Press, 1971.

Berger, Thomas L. 'The Disappearance of MacMorris in Shakespeare's
Henry V'. *RP* (1985–6): 13–26.

'Casting *Henry V'*. *Shakespeare Studies* 20 (1988): 89–104.

'Looking for *Henry V*: A Fiction'. In Berger and Maguire eds. *Textual
Formations and Reformations (q.v.)*.

Berger, Thomas L. and Dennis G. Donovan eds. *Caesar and Pompey*. In Allan
Holaday gen. ed. *The Plays of George Chapman: The Tragedies (q.v.)*.

Berger, Thomas L. and Laurie Maguire eds. *Textual Formations and
Reformations*, in preparation.

Berry, Lloyd ed. *The Blind Beggar of Alexandria*. In Allan Holaday gen. ed.
The Plays of George Chapman: The Comedies (q.v.).

Bevington, David and Eric Rasmussen eds. *Doctor Faustus A- and B-texts
(1604, 1616)*. Revels. Manchester University Press, 1993.

Blair, C. H. Hunter. 'Wardens and Deputy Wardens of the Marches'.
Archeologia Aeliana, 4th series, 28 (1950): 18–95.

Blayney, Peter. *The Texts of 'King Lear' and their Origins. Vol. I: Nicholas Okes
and the First Quarto*. Cambridge University Press, 1982.

'Shakespeare's Fight with *What* Pirates?' Paper presented at the Folger
Shakespeare Library, May 1987.

'A Groatsworth of Evidence'. Paper delivered at the SAA annual
meeting, Austin, TX, April 1989.

The Bookshops in Paul's Cross Churchyard. London: The Bibliographical
Society, 1990.

Bond, R. Warwick ed. *The Complete Works of John Lyly*. Vol.1. Oxford: Clarendon Press, 1902, reprinted 1967.

Booth, Stephen. 'Speculations on Doubling in Shakespeare's Plays'. In *Shakespeare: The Theatrical Dimension*. Edited by Philip McGuire and D. A. Samuelson. New York: AMS Press, 1979, pp.103–31.

Borges, Jorge Luis. 'Funes, the Memorious'. In *Fictions*. London: Calder, 1965, reprinted 1974, pp.97–105.

Born, Hanspeter. *The Rare Wit and the Rude Groom*. Berne: Francke Verlag, n.d. (c.1970).

Bowers, Fredson. 'The Text of Marlowe's *Faustus*'. *Modern Philology* 49 (1951–2): 195–204.

    On Editing Shakespeare. Charlottesville, VA: University Press of Virginia, 1966.

    'Marlowe's *Doctor Faustus*: The 1602 Additions'. *SB* 26 (1973): 1–18.

Bowers, Fredson ed. *The Dramatic Works of Thomas Dekker*. 4 vols. Cambridge University Press, 1953–61.

    The Complete Works of Christopher Marlowe. 2 vols. Cambridge University Press, 1973.

Bracken, James K. 'William Stansby's Early Career'. *SB* 38 (1985): 214–16.

Bracy, William. *The Merry Wives of Windsor. The History and Transmission of Shakespeare's Text*. *University of Missouri Studies* 25. Columbia, MO: University of Missouri Press, 1952.

Bradley, A. C. *Shakespearean Tragedy*. London: Macmillan, 1904.

Bradley, David. *From Text to Performance in the Elizabethan Theatre*. Cambridge University Press, 1992.

Braunmuller, A. R. *George Peele*. Boston, MA: Twayne, 1983.

Brennan, Elizabeth M. ed. *The Duchess of Malfi*. New Mermaids. London: Ernest Benn, 1964.

    The White Devil. New Mermaids. London: Ernest Benn, 1966.

    The Devil's Law Case. New Mermaids. London: Ernest Benn, 1975.

Brockbank, J. P. *Marlowe: Dr. Faustus*. London: Edward Arnold, 1962.

Brook, G. L. 'A Piece of Evidence for the Study of Middle English Spelling'. *Neophilologische Mitteilungen* 73 (1972): 25–8.

Brooke, C. F. Tucker ed. *The Shakespeare Apocrypha*. Oxford: Clarendon Press, 1908.

Brown, Arthur ed. *The Captives*. MSR. Oxford, 1953.

Brown, John Russell. 'Chapman's *Caesar and Pompey*: An Unperformed
Play?' *MLR* 49 (1954): 466–9.

Bryce, J. C. 'Peter Alexander 1893–1969'. *PBA* 66 (1980): 379–405.

Bullen, A. H. ed. *The Mayor of Queenborough*. In *The Works of Middleton*.
Vol. ii. London: John C. Nimmo, 1885.

    The Works of Peele. 2 vols. 1888. Reissued Port Washington, NY:
Kennikat Press, 1966.

Burkhart, Robert E. *Shakespeare's Bad Quartos: Deliberate Abridgements
Designed for Performance by a Reduced Cast*. The Hague and Paris:
Mouton, 1975.

Cairncross, A. S. ed. *King Henry VI Part 1*. Arden. London: Methuen, 1962.

    King Henry VI Part 2. Arden. London: Methuen, 1957, reprinted 1962.

    King Henry VI Part 3. Arden. London: Methuen, 1964.

    Hieronimo and The Spanish Tragedy. Regents Renaissance Drama
Series. London: Edward Arnold, 1967.

Carruthers, Mary. *The Book of Memory: A Study of Memory in Medieval
Culture*. Cambridge University Press, 1990.

Cauthen, I. B. '*Gorboduc, Ferrex and Porrex*: The First Two Quartos'. *SB* 15
(1962): 231–3.

Cawley, A. C. and Barry Gaines eds. *A Yorkshire Tragedy*. Manchester
University Press, 1986.

Chambers, E. K. *The Elizabethan Stage*. 4 vols. London: Oxford University
Press, 1923.

    Review of Greg, *Two Elizabethan Stage Abridgements*. *Library*, 4th
series, 4 (1923–4): 242–8.

    William Shakespeare. A Study of Facts and Problems. 2 vols. Oxford:
Clarendon Press, 1930.

    Review of H. S. Bennett ed. Marlowe, '*The Jew of Malta*' and '*The
Massacre at Paris*'. *MLR* 27 (1932): 77–9.

Champion, Larry S. '"What prerogatiues meanes": Perspective and
Political Ideology in *The Famous Victories of Henry V*'. *South
Atlantic Review* 53, no. 4 (1988): 1–19.

    '*The Noise of Threatening Drum*'. Newark, NJ: University of Delaware
Press, 1990.

Chapman, R. W. ed. *Jane Austen's Letters*. 2nd edition. London: Oxford
University Press, 1952.

   The Novels of Jane Austen. Vol.II. London: Clarendon Press, 1923.

Charteris, Evan ed. *The Life and Letters of Sir Edmund Gosse.* London: Heinemann, 1931.

Child, F. J. *The English and Scottish Popular Ballads.* 5 vols. 1882–1905. Reprinted New York: Dover Publications, 1965.

Clare, Janet. *'Art Made Tongue-tied by Authority': Elizabethan and Jacobean Dramatic Censorship.* Manchester University Press, 1990.

Clare, Robert. '"Who is it that can tell me who I am?": The Theory of Authorial Revision between the Quarto and Folio Texts of *King Lear'. Library,* 6th series 17 (1995): 34–59.

Clayton, Thomas. *The 'Hamlet' First Published (Q1, 1603).* Newark, NJ: University of Delaware Press, 1992.

   'Today we have Parting of Names: Editorial Speech-(Be)Headings in *Coriolanus'.* In George Walton Williams ed. *Shakespeare's Speech-Headings (q.v.),* pp.61–99.

Cloud, Random. See McLeod, Randall.

Collier, John Payne ed. *The Works of William Shakespeare.* 8 vols. London: Whittaker, 1842–4.

Collins, J. Churton. *The Study of English Literature.* London: Macmillan, 1891.

   'The Hybrid-Academic'. *The Tribune* 20 and 30 April 1906.

Collins, J. Churton. ed. *The Plays and Poems of Robert Greene.* 2 vols. Oxford: Clarendon Press, 1905.

Collins, L. C. *Life and Memoirs of John Churton Collins.* London: John Lane, The Bodley Head, 1912.

Conway, Martin A. *Autobiographical Memory. An Introduction.* Milton Keynes: Open University Press, 1990.

Corbin, Peter and Douglas Sedge eds. *Three Jacobean Witchcraft Plays.* Manchester University Press, 1986.

Court, Franklin E. 'The Social and Historical Significance of the First English Literature Professorship in England'. *PMLA* 103 (1988): 796–807.

Cowley, Abraham. *Poems.* Edited by A. R. Waller. Cambridge University Press, 1905.

Craig, D. H. 'Authorial Style and the Frequencies of Very Common Words: Jonson, Shakespeare, and the Additions to *The Spanish Tragedy'. Style* 26 (1992): 199–210.

Craig, Hardin. '*Pericles* and *The Painfull Aduentures*'. *SP* 45 (1949): 100–5.
    A New Look at Shakespeare's Quartos. Stanford University Press, 1961.
Craik, T. W. ed. *The Merry Wives of Windsor*. Oxford: Clarendon Press,
    1989.
    King Henry 5. Arden 3. London: Routledge, 1995.
Crupi, Charles W. *Robert Greene*. Boston, MA: Twayne, 1986.
Daniel, P. A. *The Merry Wives of Windsor*. London: W. Griggs, 1888.
Davis, Tom. 'The Monsters and the Textual Critics'. In Thomas L. Berger
    and Laurie Maguire eds. *Textual Formations and Reformations*
    (*q.v.*).
Davison, Peter. 'Bibliography: Teaching, Research and Publication.
    Reflections on Editing the First Quarto of *Richard III*'. *Library*,
    6th series 17 (1995): 1–33.
Dawson, Giles E. 'John Payne Collier's Great Forgery'. *SB* 24 (1971): 1–26.
de Bruyn, Lucy. *Mob-Rule and Riot: The Present Mirrored in the Past*.
    London: Regency, 1981.
de Grazia, Margreta. 'The Essential Shakespeare and the Material Book'.
    Textual Practice 2 (1988): 69–86.
    Shakespeare Verbatim. Oxford: Clarendon Press, 1991.
de Grazia, Margreta and Peter Stallybrass, 'The Materiality of the
    Shakespearean Text'. *SQ* 44 (1993): 255–83.
de Vocht, H. ed. *A Knack to Know an Honest Man*. MSR. Oxford, 1910.
Dent, R. W. *John Webster's Borrowing*. Berkeley: University of California
    Press, 1960.
Dessen, Alan. 'Weighing the Options in *Hamlet* Q1'. In Thomas Clayton
    ed. *The 'Hamlet' First Published (Q1, 1603)* (*q.v.*), pp.65–78.
    'Conceptual Casting in the Age of Shakespeare: Evidence from
    Mucedorus'. *SQ* 43 (1992): 67–70.
Dillon, Janette. 'Is There a Performance in This Text?' *SQ* 45 (1994):
    74–86.
Dolan, Frances E. 'The Subordinate('s) Plot: Petty Treason and the Forms
    of Domestic Rebellion'. *SQ* 43 (1992): 317–40.
Doran, Madeleine. '*Henry VI, Parts II and III*': Their Relation to the
    '*Contention*' and the '*True Tragedie*'. University of Iowa Press, 1928.
    The Text of 'King Lear'. Stanford CA: Stanford University Press, 1931.
    Review of Greg, *The Variants in the First Quarto of 'King Lear'*. *RES* 17
    (1941): 468–74.

Doran, Madeleine, ed. *1 If You Know Not Me, You Know Nobody*. MSR. Oxford, 1934.

Doyle, Sir Arthur Conan. *A Study in Scarlet*. London: John Murray and Jonathan Cape, 1974.

    The Valley of Fear. London: Pan Books, 1980.

Duthie, G. I. *The 'Bad' Quarto of 'Hamlet'*. Cambridge University Press, 1941.

    Elizabethan Shorthand and the First Quarto of 'King Lear'. Oxford: Blackwell, 1949.

Duthie, G. I. ed. *Shakespeare's 'King Lear': A Critical Edition*. Oxford: Blackwell, 1949.

Eagleton, Terry. *Literary Theory. An Introduction*. Oxford: Basil Blackwell, 1983.

Edwards, Philip. 'An Approach to the Problem of *Pericles*'. *Shakespeare Survey* 5 (1952): 25–49.

Edwards, Philip ed. *Hamlet*. New Cambridge. Cambridge University Press, 1985.

Elliott, G. R. *Dramatic Providence in 'Macbeth'*. Princeton University Press, 1958.

Empson, William. '*The Spanish Tragedy*'. *Nimbus* 3, no.3 (1956):16–29. Reprinted in R. J. Kaufmann ed. *Elizabethan Drama: Modern Essays in Criticism*. New York: Oxford University Press, 1961, pp.60–80.

Eriksen, Roy T. 'Construction in Marlowe's *The Massacre at Paris*'. In Stig Johanson ed. *Proceedings of the First Nordic Conference for English Studies*. Oslo, 1981, pp.41–54.

Evans, G. B. gen. ed. *The Riverside Shakespeare*. Boston, MA: Houghton Mifflin, 1974.

Fabian, Bernhard and Kurt Tetzeli von Rosador eds. *Shakespeare: Text, Language, Criticism*. Hildesheim, Zurich and New York: Olms–Weidmann, 1987.

Farr, Dorothy. *John Ford and the Caroline Theatre*. London: Macmillan, 1979.

Felperin, Howard. 'Bardolatry Then and Now'. In Jean I. Marsden ed. *The Appropriation of Shakespeare* (q.v.), pp.129–44.

    The Uses of the Canon. Oxford: Clarendon Press, 1990.

    'Historicizing Bardolatry: Or, Where Could Coleridge Have Been Coming From?' In *The Uses of the Canon* (q.v.), pp.1–15.

Fenton, James. 'In the Study and on the Stage'. Review of Harold Jenkins
ed. *Hamlet*. *TLS* 17 September 1982: 989–90.

Ferguson, W. Craig. *Valentine Simmes*. Charlottesville, VA: University of
Virginia Press, 1968.

Firth, C. H. *The School of English Language and Literature*. Oxford: Basil
Blackwell, 1909.

Flahiff, Frederick T. 'Lear's Map'. *Cahiers Élisabéthains* 30 (1986): 17–33.

Foakes, R. A. ed. *The Henslowe Papers*. 2 vols. London: Scolar Press,
1977.

Foakes, R. A. and C. T. Rickert eds. *Henslowe's Diary*. Cambridge
University Press, 1961.

Foley, John Miles ed. *Oral Traditional Literature*. Columbus, OH: Slavica
Publishers, 1980.

    Oral Tradition in Literature: Interpretation in Context. Columbia, MO:
University of Missouri Press, 1986.

Foster, Donald W. 'Reconstructing Shakespeare 1: The Roles that
Shakespeare Performed'. *SN* 41 (1991): 16–17.

Fowler, David C. *A Literary History of the Popular Ballad*. Durham, NC:
Duke University Press, 1968.

Francis, F. C. ed. *The Bibliographical Society 1892–1942: Studies in Retrospect*.
London: The Bibliographical Society, 1945.

Freeman, Arthur. *Thomas Kyd: Facts and Problems*. Oxford: Clarendon
Press, 1967.

Freeman, Edward A. 'Literature and Language'. *The Contemporary Review*
52 (1887): 549–67.

Fuller, Roy. 'The Marcellus Version'. *TLS* 3 January 1986: 11.

    New and Collected Poems 1934–84. London: Secker and Warburg, 1985.

    Consolations. London: Secker and Warburg, 1987.

Gaskell, Philip. *From Writer to Reader. Studies in Editorial Method*. Oxford:
Clarendon Press, 1978.

Gasper, Julia. *The Dragon and the Dove: The Plays of Thomas Dekker*.
Oxford: Clarendon Press, 1990.

Gibbons, Brian ed. *Romeo and Juliet*. New Arden. London: Methuen, 1980.

Gill, Roma. '*Doctor Faustus*: The Textual Problem'. *University of Hartford
Studies in Literature* 20 (1988): 52–60.

Gill, Roma ed. *Dr Faustus*. London: Ernest Benn, 1965.

    Women Beware Women. London: Black, 1988.

Dr Faustus. London: A & C Black, 1989.

The Complete Works of Christopher Marlowe. Vol.II. Oxford: Clarendon Press, 1990.

Gillespie, Diane. *The Mind's We. Contextualism in Cognitive Psychology*. Carbondale and Edwardsville: Southern Illinois University Press, 1992.

Giordano-Orsini, G. N. 'The Copy for *If You Know Not Me, You Know Nobodie* Part 1'. *TLS* 4 December 1930: 1037.

'Thomas Heywood's Play on *The Troubles of Queen Elizabeth*'. *Library*, 4th series, 14 (1933–4): 313–38.

Goldberg, Jonathan. '"What? in a names that which we call a Rose": The Desired Texts of *Romeo and Juliet*'. In Randall McLeod ed. *Crisis in Editing: Texts of the English Renaissance*. New York: AMS Press, 1994.

Goree, Roselle Gould. 'Concerning Repetitions in Greene's Romances'. *PQ* 3 (1924): 69–75.

Grady, Hugh. *The Modernist Shakespeare. Critical Texts in a Material World*. Oxford: Clarendon Press, 1991.

'Disintegration and its Reverberations'. In Jean I. Marsden ed. *The Appropriation of Shakespeare* (*q.v.*), pp.111–27.

Graff, Gerald. *Professing Literature*. University of Chicago Press, 1987.

Green, William ed. *The Merry Wives of Windsor*. Signet Classic. New York and Toronto: New American Library, 1965.

Greg, W. W. (1899) 'Pre-Malorean Romances'. *MLQ* 2 (1899): 10–13.

(1900) 'Webster's *White Devil*. An Essay in Formal Criticism'. *MLQ* 3 (1900): 112–26.

(1901) Review of F. S. Boas ed. *The Works of Thomas Kyd. MLQ* 4 (1901): 185–90.

(1902) 'On the Date of the *Sad Shepherd*'. *MLQ* 5 (1902): 65–71.

(1902) 'Old Plays and New Editions'. *Library*, 2nd series, 3 (1902): 408–26.

(1902) 'Bacon's Bilateral Cipher and its Applications'. *Library*, 2nd series, 3 (1902): 41–53.

(1902) Review of L. L. Schücking. *Studien über die stöfflichen Beziehungen der englischen Komödie zur italienischen bis Lilly. MLQ* 5 (1902): 80–1.

(1903) Review of R. B. McKerrow ed. *The Works of Thomas Nashe.* *MLQ* 6 (1903): 152–3.

(1903) Review of M. W. Wallace ed. *The Birthe of Hercules.* *MLQ* 6 (1903): 148–50.

(1903) 'The Bibliographical History of the First Folio'. *Library*, 2nd series, 4 (1903): 258–85.

(1903) Review of R. W. Bond ed. *The Complete Works of John Lyly.* *MLQ* 6 (1903): 17–25.

(1903) '*Hymen's Triumph* and the Drummond MS'. *MLQ* 6 (1903): 59–64.

(1903) Review of A. H. Quinn ed. *The Faire Maide of Bristow.* *MLQ* 6 (1903): 94–5.

(1903) Review of Alfred Nutt ed. *The Mabinogion.* *MLQ* 6 (1903): 96.

(1903) Review of J. Fischer ed. *Das 'Interlude of the Four Elements'.* *MLQ* 6 (1903): 95–6.

(1904) Review of F. I. Carpenter ed. *The Life and Repentaunce of Marie Magdalene.* *MLQ* 7 (1904): 170.

(1904) Review of H. C. Hart ed. *The Alchemist* and C. M. Hathaway Jr. ed. *The Alchemist.* *MLQ* 7 (1904): 26–9.

(1904) 'Tottel's Miscellany'. *Library*, 2nd series, 5 (1904): 113–33.

(1904) 'On the Editions of *Mucedorus*'. *Shakespeare Jahrbuch* 40 (1904): 95–107.

(1905–6) Review of J. Churton Collins ed. *The Plays and Poems of Robert Greene.* *MLR* 1 (1905–6): 238–51.

(1905–6) Review of J. M. Robertson. *Did Shakespeare Write 'Titus Andronicus'?* *MLR* 1 (1905–6): 337–41.

(1906) 'The Hybrid-Academic'. *The Tribune* 26 April and 4 May 1906.

(1906) ed. *The Battle of Alcazar.* MSR. Oxford, 1906.

(1906) *Pastoral Poetry and Pastoral Drama.* London: A. H. Bullen, 1906, reprinted New York: Russell & Russell, 1959.

(1907) *Henslowe Papers.* London: A. H. Bullen, 1907.

(1908) 'On Certain False Dates in Shakespearian Quartos'. *Library*, 2nd series, 9 (1908): 113–31 and 381–409.

(1909) ed. *The Old Wives Tale.* MSR. Oxford, 1909 (for 1908).

(1910) 'The *Hamlet* Quartos, 1603, 1604'. *MLR* 5 (1910): 196–7.

(1910) ed. *The Merry Wives of Windsor, 1602*. Oxford: Clarendon Press, 1910.

(1910) '*The Trial of Treasure*, 1567. A Study in Ghosts'. *Library*, 3rd series, 1 (1910): 28–35.

(1911) ed. *Sir Thomas More*. MSR. Oxford, 1911.

(1911) Review of G. C. Moore Smith ed. *Laelia*. *MLR* 6 (1911): 528–9.

(1911) ed. *The Old Wife's Tale, New Vamp't and Adorned with Figures*. London: Sidgwick and Jackson, 1911.

(1911–13) 'What is Bibliography?' *Transactions of the Bibliographical Society* 12 (1911–13): 39–53. Abstract, pp.10–12.

(1913) 'Chaucer Attributions in MS. R. 3. 19 in the Library of Trinity College, Cambridge'. *MLR* 8 (1913): 539–40.

(1913) ed. *A Larum for London*. MSR. Oxford, 1913.

(1913) ed. *Edward 1*. MSR. Oxford, 1913.

(1914) Review of A. C. Judson ed. *Cynthia's Revels*. *MLR* 9 (1914): 259–62.

(1915) 'Detachment in War Time: Atrocities'. *The Economist* 9 January 1915: 69–70 (this article is signed 'X').

(1915) ed. *The Tragedy of Tiberius*. MSR. Oxford, 1915.

(1916) 'The Handwritings of the Manuscript'. In A. W. Pollard ed. *Shakespeare's Hand in the Play of Sir Thomas More* (*q.v.*), pp.41–56.

(1916) 'Supplies of Capital after the War'. *The Economist* 26 August 1916: 371.

(1916) 'A Critical Mousetrap'. In Israel Gollancz ed. *A Book of Homage to Shakespeare*, pp.179–80. Oxford University Press, 1916.

(1917) 'Hamlet's Hallucination'. *MLR* 12 (1917): 393–421.

(1919) 'The "Stolne and Surreptitious" Shakespearian Texts'. *TLS* 28 August 1919: 461.

(1919) '"Bad" Quartos Outside Shakespeare – "Alcazar" and "Orlando"'. *Library*, 3rd series, 10 (1919): 193–222.

(1919) 'The *Hamlet* Texts and Recent Work in Shakespearian Bibliography'. *MLR* 14 (1919): 380–5.

(1919). '*Titus Andronicus*'. *MLR* 14 (1919): 322–3.

(1920) 'Transcription in the Pirated Plays of Shakespeare'. *TLS* 20 May 1920: 320.

(1920) 'Was *Sir Thomas More* Ever Acted?' *TLS* 8 July 1920: 440.

(1921) '*Everyman* and John Scott'. *TLS* 3 March 1921: 144.

(1923) *Two Elizabethan Stage Abridgements: The Battle of Alcazar and Orlando Furioso.* The Malone Society. Oxford: Frederick Hall, 1923.

(1923–4) 'Massinger's Autograph Corrections in *The Duke of Milan, 1623*'. *Library*, 4th series, 4 (1923–4): 207–18.

(1924) Review of H. de Groot. *'Hamlet': its Textual History. MLR* 19 (1924): 228–30.

(1925) Review of H. Dugdale Sykes. *Sidelights on Elizabethan Drama. MLR* 20 (1925):195–200.

(1925) Review of E. K. Chambers. *The Elizabethan Stage. RES* 1 (1925): 97–111.

(1925) 'A Collier Mystification'. *RES* 1 (1925): 452–4.

(1925) Review of W. E. Mead ed. *The Famous Historie of Chinon of England* by C. Middleton. *Library*, 4th series, 6 (1925–6):104–8.

(1925) Review of L. Kellner. *Restoring Shakespeare. RES* 1 (1925): 463–78.

(1925) *The Escapes of Jupiter.* In J. C. Maxwell ed. *W. W. Greg. Collected Papers (q.v.)* pp. 156–83.

(1925–6) '*The Spanish Tragedy* – A Leading Case?' *Library*, 4th series, 6 (1925–6): 47–56.

(1925–6) 'Type-Facsimiles and Others'. *Library*, 4th series, 6 (1925–6): 321–6.

(1926) ed. *Friar Bacon and Friar Bungay.* MSR. Oxford, 1926.

(1926) ed. *Alphonsus, King of Aragon.* MSR. Oxford, 1926.

(1926) 'The "Issues" of *The Pilgrim's Progress*'. *TLS* 19 August 1926: 549.

(1926–7) 'Derby his Hand – and Soul'. *Library*, 4th series, 7 (1926–7): 39–45.

(1927) Review of Baldwin. *The Organization and Personnel of the Shakespearean Company. TLS* 15 December 1927: 954.

(1927) *The Calculus of Variants.* Oxford: Clarendon Press, 1927.

(1928) Review of E. M. Albright. *Dramatic Publication in England, 1580–1640. RES* 4 (1928): 91–100.

(1928) 'Bibliography'. *TLS* 2 February 1928: 80.

(1928) Reply to Albright. *RES* 4 (1928): 202–4.

(1928) 'Act-Divisions in Shakespeare'. *RES* 4 (1928): 152–8.

(1928) ed. *The Massacre at Paris.* MSR. Oxford, 1928 (1929).

(1928) Review of F. L. Lucas ed. *The Complete Works of John Webster*. *RES* 4 (1928): 449–56.

(1929) ed. *The True Tragedy of Richard the Third*. MSR. Oxford, 1929.

(1929) Review of B. M. Ward. *The Seventeenth Earl of Oxford*. *MLR* 24 (1929): 216–21.

(1929) ed. *The Blind Beggar of Alexandria*. MSR. Oxford, 1929.

(1930) 'A Question of Plus or Minus'. *RES* 6 (1930): 300–4.

(1930–1) 'The Present Position of Bibliography'. *Library*, 4th series, 11 (1930–1): 241–62.

(1931) *Dramatic Documents from the Elizabethan Playhouse*. Vol.1. Oxford: Clarendon Press, 1931.

(1931–2) 'Three Manuscript Notes by Sir George Buc'. *Library*, 4th series, 12 (1931–2): 307–21.

(1932) ed. *A Looking Glass for London and England*. MSR. Oxford, 1932.

(1932–3) 'Remarks on "The Aims of Bibliography" by Sir Stephen Gaselee'. *Library*, 4th series, 13 (1932–3): 250–5.

(1932–3) 'Bibliography – An Apologia'. *Library*, 4th series, 13 (1932–3): 113–43.

(1932–3) 'The Function of Bibliography in Literary Criticism Illustrated in a Study of the Text of *King Lear*'. *Neophilologus* 18 (1932–3): 241–62.

(1934–5) 'Was There a 1612 Quarto of *Epicene*?' *Library*, 4th series, 15 (1934–5): 306–15.

(1935) Review of H. Harvey Wood ed. *The Plays of John Marston. Vol. 1*. *MLR* 30 (1935): 90–4.

(1935) 'The Genuine Text', *TLS* 6 June 1935: 364.

(1935) Review of J. Dover Wilson. *The Manuscript of Shakespeare's 'Hamlet'*. *MLR* 30 (1935): 80–6.

(1936) 'Stage or Study?' *TLS* 2 May 1936: 379.

(1937) Review of P. L. Carver ed. *The Comedy of Acolastus*. Translated by John Palsgrave. *MLR* 32 (1937): 601–5.

(1938) ed. *An Humorous Day's Mirth*. MSR. Oxford, 1938.

(1938–9) Review of D. L. Patrick. *The Textual History of 'Richard III'*. *Library*, 4th series, 19 (1938–9): 118–20.

(1938–9) 'A Fragment from Henslowe's Diary'. *Library*, 4th series, 19 (1938–9): 180–4.

(1939) ed. *King Lear. 1608*. Shakespeare Quarto Facsimiles. London: The Shakespeare Association and Sidgwick and Jackson, 1939.

(1939–40) 'The Date of *King Lear* and Shakespeare's Use of Earlier Versions of the Story'. *Library*, 4th series, 20 (1939–40): 377–400.

(1940) 'Time, Place, and Politics in *King Lear*'. *MLR* 35 (1940): 431–46.

(1940) Review of H. C. Bartlett and A. W. Pollard. *A Census of Shakespeare's Plays in Quarto, 1594–1709*. *RES* 16 (1940): 208–11.

(1940) *The Variants in the First Quarto of 'King Lear'. A Bibliographical and Critical Inquiry*. London: Bibliographical Society, 1940.

(1940) 'Ronald Brunlees McKerrow 1872–1940'. *PBA* 26 (1940): 489–515.

(1941) 'McKerrow's "Prolegomena" Reconsidered'. *RES* 17 (1941): 139–49.

(1942) *The Editorial Problem in Shakespeare. A Survey of the Foundations of the Text*. Oxford: Clarendon Press, 1942. See also Greg (1954).

(1943) Review of *The English Institute Annual: 1941*. *RES* 19 (1943): 320–3.

(1944–5) '*The Merry Devil of Edmonton*'. *Library*, 4th series, 25 (1944–5): 122–39.

(1945) 'Bibliography – A Retrospect'. In F. C. Francis ed. *The Bibliographical Society 1892–1942: Studies in Retrospect* (*q.v.*), pp.23–31.

(1945–6) 'A List of Dr Greg's Writings'. Compiled by F. C. Francis. *Library*, 4th series, 26 (1945–6): 72–97.

(1946) Review of L. Kirschbaum. *The True Text of 'King Lear'*. *RES* 22 (1946): 230–4.

(1946) 'The Damnation of Faustus'. *MLR* 41 (1946): 97–107.

(1946–7) '*The Triumph of Peace*: A Bibliographer's Nightmare'. *Library*, 5th series, 1 (1946–7): 113–26.

(1947) Review of H. F. Fletcher ed. John Milton's *Complete Poetical Works. Vol. II*. *MLR* 12 (1947): 133–7.

(1947–8) 'The Date of the Earliest Play-Catalogues'. *Library*, 5th series, 2 (1947–8): 190–1.

(1949) and Nichol Smith eds. *The Spanish Tragedy (1592)*. MSR. Oxford, 1949 (for 1948).

(1949) Review of G. I. Duthie ed. *King Lear*. *MLR* 44 (1949): 397–400.

(1950) *Marlowe's 'Doctor Faustus' 1604–1616*. Oxford: Clarendon Press, 1950.

(1950) *The Tragical History of the Life and Death of Doctor Faustus by Christopher Marlowe. A Conjectural Reconstruction*. Oxford: Clarendon Press, 1950.

(1950) Review of H. Hoppe. *The Bad Quarto of 'Romeo and Juliet'*. *RES* n.s. 1 (1950): 64–6.

(1950–1) 'The Rationale of Copy-Text'. *SB* 3 (1950–1): 19–36.

(1951) ed. *Bonduca*. MSR. Oxford: 1951.

(1953) Review of W. Bracy. *The Merry Wives of Windsor. The History and Transmission of Shakespeare's Text*. *SQ* 4 (1953): 77–9.

(1953) Review of C. H. Herford and P. and E. Simpson eds. *Ben Jonson. Vol. XI. RES* n.s. 4 (1953): 285.

(1954) Review of F. Bowers ed. *The Dramatic Works of Thomas Dekker. Vol. I. RES* n.s. 5 (1954): 414–19.

(1954) *The Editorial Problem in Shakespeare. A Survey of the Foundations of the Text*. 3rd edition. Oxford: Clarendon Press, 1954.

(1955) *The Shakespeare First Folio*. Oxford: Clarendon Press, 1955.

(1955) 'The Shakespeare First Folio'. *TLS* 28 October 1955: 621, 639.

(1955) 'On the Text of *Mucedorus* and the Meaning of Copyright'. *MLR* 50 (1955): 322.

(1955) 'Richard Robinson and the Stationers' Register'. *MLR* 50 (1955): 407–13.

(1956) Review of Fredson Bowers. *On Editing Shakespeare. SQ* 7 (1956): 101–4.

(1959) Review of F. Bowers ed. *The Dramatic Works of Thomas Dekker. Vol. III. RES* n.s. 10 (1959): 413–15.

(1960) *Biographical Notes 1877–1947*. Oxford: New Bodleian Library, 1960.

(1960) 'The Writings of Sir Walter Greg, 1945–59'. Compiled by D. F. McKenzie, edited by J. C. T. Oates. *Library*, 5th series, 15 (1960): 42–6.

Grosart, Alexander B. ed. *The Non-Dramatic Works of Thomas Dekker*. 5 vols. 1885. Reissued New York: Russell and Russell, 1963.

The Life and Complete Works in Prose and Verse of Robert Greene. Vol.IV. Reissued New York: Russell and Russell, 1964.

Gross, John. *The Rise and Fall of the Man of Letters*. London: Weidenfeld and Nicolson, 1969.

Gurr, Andrew ed. *The Maid's Tragedy*. Edinburgh: Oliver and Boyd, 1969.
Philaster. Revels. London: Methuen, 1969.
Richard 2. Cambridge University Press, 1984.

Haaker, Ann. 'The Plague, the Theater, and the Poet'. *RD* n.s. 1 (1968): 283–306.

Habicht, Werner, D. J. Palmer, and Roger Pringle eds. *Images of Shakespeare*. Newark, NJ: University of Delaware Press, 1988.

Halstead, W. 'Note on the Text of *The Famous History of Sir Thomas Wyatt*'. *MLN* 54 (1939): 585–9.

Hammond, Antony. 'Encounters of the Third Kind in Stage-Directions in Elizabethan and Jacobean Drama'. *SP* 89 (1992): 71–99.

Hammond, Antony ed. *King Richard III*. Arden. London: Methuen, 1981.

Harbage, Alfred. *Annals of English Drama, 975–1700*. Revised by S. Schoenbaum. London: Methuen, 1964.

Harris, Bernard ed. *The Malcontent*. New Mermaids. London: Ernest Benn, 1967.

Hart, Alfred. 'The Length of Elizabethan and Jacobean Plays'. *RES* 8 (1932): 139–54.
'The Time Allotted for Representation of Elizabethan and Jacobean Plays'. *RES* 8 (1932): 395–413.
'Acting Versions of Elizabethan Plays'. *RES* 10 (1934): 1–28.
Stolne and Surreptitious Copies. Melbourne University Press, 1942.

Hart, H. C. 'Robert Greene's Prose Works'. *N & Q*, 10th series, 4 (1905): 81–4; 162–4; 224–6.

Hattaway, Michael ed. *2 Henry 6*. Cambridge University Press, 1991.

Hayward, John. 'A Note on Donne'. In Theodore Spencer ed. *A Garland for John Donne 1631–1931*. Cambridge, MA: Harvard University Press, pp.73–97.

Henning, Standish ed. *Fair Em*. New York: Garland, 1980.

Henslowe, Philip. See Foakes, R. A.

Hibbard, G. R. ed. *Hamlet*. Oxford University Press, 1987.

Hinman, Charlton ed. *The Norton Facsimile. The First Folio of Shakespeare*. New York: Norton, 1968.

Hoeniger, F. D. ed. *Pericles*. London: Methuen, 1963.

Holaday, Allan gen. ed. *The Plays of George Chapman: The Comedies*.
    Urbana, IL: University of Illinois Press, 1970.
    The Plays of George Chapman: The Tragedies. Cambridge: D. S. Brewer,
        1987.
Holderness, Graham. 'Shakespeare's Bad Quarto'. *TLS* 8 April 1994: 19.
Holderness, Graham and Bryan Loughrey. 'Shakespeare's Bad Quarto'.
    TLS 4 February 1994: 15.
Holderness, Graham, Bryan Loughrey, and Andrew Murphy. '"What's the
    matter?" Shakespeare and Textual Theory'. *Textual Practice* 9
    (1995): 93–119.
Holderness, Graham and Bryan Loughrey eds. *The Tragicall Historie of
    Hamlet Prince of Denmarke*. Hemel Hempstead: Harvester
    Wheatsheaf, 1992.
Honigmann, E. A. J. 'Shakespeare's "Lost Source-Plays"'. *MLR* 49 (1954):
    293–307.
    The Stability of Shakespeare's Text. London: Edward Arnold, 1965.
    'Shakespeare as Reviser'. In Jerome J. McGann ed. *Textual Criticism
        and Literary Interpretation (q.v.)*, pp.1–22.
    'The Date and Revision of *Troilus and Cressida*'. In Jerome J. McGann
        ed. *Textual Criticism and Literary Interpretation (q.v.)*, pp.38–54.
    'Shakespeare's Revised Plays: *King Lear* and *Othello*'. *Library*, 6th
        series, 4 (1982): 142–73.
Honigmann, E. A. J. ed. *King John*. Arden. London: Methuen, 1954.
Hook, Frank S. ed. *Edward I*. In C. T. Prouty, gen. ed. *The Life and Works of
    George Peele*. Vol. II. New Haven and London: Yale University Press,
    1961.
    The Old Wife's Tale. In C. T. Prouty, gen. ed. *The Life and Works of
        George Peele*. Vol. III. New Haven and London: Yale University
        Press, 1970.
Hoppe, Harry. '*John of Bordeaux*: A Bad Quarto that Never Reached Print'.
    In *Studies in Honor of A. H. R. Fairchild, University of Missouri
    Studies* 21 (1946): 119–32.
    The Bad Quarto of 'Romeo and Juliet'. Ithaca, NY: Cornell University
        Press, 1948.
Hosley, Richard. 'Sources and Analogues of *The Taming of the Shrew*'.
    Huntington Library Quarterly 27 (1963–4): 289–308.

Housman, A. E. 'The Application of Thought to Textual Criticism'. In J. Diggle and F. R. D. Goodyear eds. *The Classical Papers of A. E. Housman*. Vol.III. Cambridge University Press, 1972, pp.1058–69.

Hunter, G. K. 'Othello and Colour Prejudice'. In *Dramatic Identities and Cultural Traditions*. Liverpool University Press, 1978, pp.31–59.

Hunter, Ian M. L. *Memory*. Harmondsworth: Penguin Books, 1957, revised 1964, reprinted 1968.

Hunter, Robert G. *Shakespeare and the Comedy of Forgiveness*. New York: Columbia University Press, 1965.

Ingram, William. 'The Costs of Touring'. *MaRDiE* 6 (1993): 57–62.

Ioppolo, Grace. '"The Final Revision of *Bonduca*": An Unpublished Essay by W. W. Greg'. *SB* 43 (1990): 62–80.

    Revising Shakespeare. Cambridge, MA: Harvard University Press, 1991.

Irace, Kathleen O. 'Reconstruction and Adaptation in Q *Henry V*'. *SB* 44 (1991): 228–53.

    'Origins and Agents of Q1 *Hamlet*'. In Thomas Clayton ed. *The 'Hamlet' First Published* (*q.v.*), pp.90–122.

    Reforming the 'Bad' Quartos: Performance and Provenance of Six Shakespearean First Editions. Newark, NJ: University of Delaware Press, 1994.

Jackson, Russell ed. *The Importance of Being Earnest*. London: Ernest Benn, 1980.

Jenkins, Harold. 'Peele's *Old Wive's Tale*'. *MLR* 34 (1939): 177–85.

    'Playhouse Interpolations in the Folio Text of *Hamlet*'. *SB* 13 (1960): 31–47.

    'John Dover Wilson 1881–1969'. *PBA* 59 (1973): 383–416.

    'Shakespeare's Bad Quarto'. *TLS* 15 April 1994: 17.

Jenkins, Harold ed. *Hoffman*. MSR. Oxford, 1950 (1951).

    Hamlet. New Arden. London: Methuen, 1982.

Johnson, Gerald D. 'John Busby and the Stationers' Trade, 1590–1612'. *Library*, 6th series, 7 (1985): 1–5.

    'Nicholas Ling, Publisher 1580–1607'. *SB* 38 (1985): 203–14.

    'William Barley, Publisher & Seller of Bookes 1591–1614'. *Library*, 6th series, 11 (1985):10–46.

    'John Trundle and the Book-Trade 1603–1626'. *SB* 39 (1986): 177–99.

'*The Merry Wives of Windsor*, Q1: Provincial Touring and Adapted Texts'. *SQ* 38 (1987): 154–65.

'The Stationers Versus the Drapers'. *Library*, 6th series, 10 (1988): 1–17.

'Thomas Pavier, Publisher, 1600–25'. *Library*, 6th series, 14 (1992): 12–50.

Jones, Eldred D. *Othello's Countrymen: The African in English Renaissance Drama*. London: Oxford University Press, 1965.

Jowett, John. See Wells and Taylor.

Judge, C. B. *Elizabethan Book Pirates*. Cambridge, MA: Harvard University Press, 1934.

Jupin, Arvin H. *A Contextual Study and Modern-Spelling Edition of 'Mucedorus'*. New York: Garland, 1987.

Kaufman, H. A. '*The Blind Beggar of Alexandria*: A Reappraisal'. *PQ* 38 (1959): 101–6.

Keefer, Michael H. 'Verbal Magic and the Problem of the A and B Texts of *Doctor Faustus*'. *JEGP* 82 (1983): 324–46.

'History and the Canon: The Case of *Doctor Faustus*'. *UTQ* 56 (1987): 498–522.

Keefer, Michael H. ed. *Christopher Marlowe's Doctor Faustus – A 1604-Version*. Peterborough, ONT: Broadview Press, 1991.

Kelliher, Hilton. 'Contemporary Manuscript Extracts from Shakespeare's *Henry IV, Part 1*'. *English Manuscript Studies 1100–1700* 1 (1989): 144–81.

Kernan, Alvin. *The Death of Literature*. New Haven: Yale University Press, 1990.

King, T. J. *Casting Shakespeare's Plays. London Actors and their Roles, 1590–1642*. Cambridge University Press, 1992.

Kinney, Arthur. 'Textual Signs in *The Merry Wives of Windsor*'. *Yearbook of English Studies* 23 (1993): 206–34.

Kirschbaum, Leo. 'A Census of Bad Quartos'. *RES* 14 (1938): 20–43.

The True Text of 'King Lear'. Baltimore, MD: The Johns Hopkins Press, 1945.

'An Hypothesis Concerning the Origin of the Bad Quartos'. *PMLA* 60 (1945): 697–715.

'*The Faire Maide of Bristow* (1605), Another Bad Quarto', *MLN* 60 (1945): 302–8.

'The Good and Bad Quartos of *Dr Faustus*'. *Library*, 4th series, 26 (1945–6): 272–94.

'The Texts of *Mucedorus*'. *MLR* 50 (1955): 1–5.

Shakespeare and the Stationers. Columbus, OH: Ohio State University Press, 1955.

Kirschbaum, Leo ed. *The Plays of Christopher Marlowe*. Cleveland OH: World Publishing, 1962.

Knutson, Roslyn L. '*Henslowe's Diary* and the Economics of Play Revision for Revival 1592–1603'. *Theatre Research International* 10 (1985): 1–18.

'Influence of the Repertory System on the Revival and Revision of *The Spanish Tragedy* and *Dr Faustus*'. *ELR* 18 (1988): 257–74.

The Repertory of Shakespeare's Company 1594–1613. Fayetteville: University of Arkansas Press, 1991.

Kohler, Richard C. 'Kyd's Ordered Spectacle: "Behold . . . / What 'tis to be subject to destiny"'. *MaRDiE* 3 (1986): 27–49.

Kuriyama, Constance Brown. 'Dr Greg and *Doctor Faustus*: The Supposed Originality of the 1616 Text'. *ELR* 5 (1975): 171–97.

Lancashire, Anne ed. *Gallathea* and *Midas*. Regents Renaissance Drama Series. 1969. London: Edward Arnold, 1970.

Lavin, J. A. ed. *Friar Bacon and Friar Bungay*. New Mermaids. London: Ernest Benn, 1969.

Lawrence, W. J. 'The "Stolne and Surreptitious" Shakespearian Texts'. *TLS* 21 August 1919: 449.

'The Mystery of the *Hamlet* First Quarto'. *Criterion* 5 (1927): 191–201.

'The Pirates of *Hamlet*'. *Criterion* 8 (1929): 642–6.

'The Secret of "The Bad Quartos"'. *Criterion* 10 (1931): 447–61.

Review of W. W. Greg. *Dramatic Documents*. *RES* 8 (1932): 219–28.

Lea, K. M. ed. *Parliament of Love*. MSR. Oxford, 1928.

Leggatt, Alexander. *Shakespeare's Political Drama*. London: Routledge, 1988.

Loewenstein, Joseph F. 'Authentic Reproductions: On the Origins of the New Bibliography'. In Thomas L. Berger and Laurie Maguire eds. *Textual Formations and Reformations* (*q.v.*).

Long, William B. '"A bed / for woodstock": A Warning for the Unwary'. *MaRDiE* 2 (1985): 91–118.

'Bookkeepers in Action: *The Two Merry Milkmaids* and the

Manuscript Playbooks'. Paper delivered to SAA annual meeting, Albuquerque, NM, 14 April 1994.

'Perspective on Provenance: The Context of Varying Speech-heads'. In George Walton Williams ed. *Shakespeare's Speech-Headings* (*q.v.*), pp.21–44.

Co-operative Ventures: English Manuscript Playbooks 1590–1635. (Forthcoming).

Loughrey, Bryan and Graham Holderness. 'Shakespearean Features'. In Jean I. Marsden ed. *The Appropriation of Shakespeare* (*q.v.*), pp.183–201.

Lowes, John Livingston. *The Road to Xanadu.* 1927. Revised 1930, and reprinted London: Picador, Pan Books, 1978.

Lull, Janis. 'Forgetting *Hamlet*: The First Quarto and the Folio'. In Thomas Clayton ed. *The 'Hamlet' First Published (Q1, 1603)* (*q.v.*), pp.137–50.

Luria, A. R. *The Mind of a Mnemonist.* Translated by Lynn Solotaroff. 1968. Reprinted Cambridge, MA: Harvard University Press, 1987.

Maas, P. *Textual Criticism.* Translated by Barbara Flower. 3rd edition. Oxford: Clarendon Press, 1958.

Macdonald, Hugh and D. Nichol Smith eds. *Arden of Feversham.* MSR. Oxford, 1940 (1947).

MacLean, Sally-Beth. 'Tour Routes: "Provincial Wanderings" or Traditional Circuits?' *MaRDiE* 6 (1993): 1–14.

McGann, Jerome, 'The Text, the Poem, and the Problem of Historical Method'. *NLH* 12 (1980–1): 269–88.

A Critique of Modern Textual Criticism. University of Chicago Press, 1983.

McGann, Jerome ed. *Textual Criticism and Literary Interpretation.* University of Chicago Press, 1985.

McKenzie, D. F. ed. *The Hog Hath Lost His Pearl.* MSR. Oxford, 1972.

McKerrow, R. B. Review of K. Deighton. *The Old Dramatists. MLQ* 4 (1901): 13–14.

A Note on the Teaching of 'English Language and Literature', with Some Suggestions. English Association Pamphlet 49. London: English Association, 1921.

Review of Pollard, A. W. ed. *Shakespeare's Hand in the Play of 'Sir Thomas More'. Library*, 4th series 4 (1923–4): 238–42.

'The Elizabethan Printer and Dramatic Manuscripts'. *Library*, 4th series, 12 (1931–2): 253–75.

'A Note on *Henry VI, Part II*, and *The Contention of York and Lancaster*'. *RES* 9 (1933): 157–69.

'A Suggestion Regarding Shakespeare's Manuscripts'. *RES* 11 (1935): 459–65.

Prolegomena for the Oxford Shakespeare. Oxford: Clarendon Press, 1939.

McKerrow, R. B. ed. *The Works of Thomas Nashe*. 5 vols. London: A. H. Bullen, 1904–10.

Locrine. MSR. Oxford, 1908.

McLeod, Randall. 'The Psychopathology of Everyday Art'. *The Elizabethan Theatre* 9 (1981): 100–168.

'The Marriage of Good and Bad Quartos'. *SQ* 33 (1982): 421–31.

'What's the Bastard's Name?' In George Walton Williams ed. *Shakespeare's Speech-Headings* (q.v.), pp.133–209.

McManaway, James G. and Mary R. eds. *Dick of Devonshire*. MSR. Oxford, 1955.

McMillin, Scott. '*The Book of Sir Thomas More*: A Theatrical View'. *Modern Philology* 68 (1970–1): 10–24.

'Casting for Pembroke's Men: The *Henry VI* Quartos and *The Taming of A Shrew*'. *SQ* 23 (1972): 141–59.

'The Ownership of *The Jew of Malta, Friar Bacon*, and *The Ranger's Comedy*'. *ELN* 9 (1972): 249–52.

'The Queen's Men in 1594: A Study of "Good" and "Bad" Quartos'. *ELR* 14 (1984): 55–69.

The Elizabethan Theatre and 'The Book of Sir Thomas More'. Ithaca, NY: Cornell University Press, 1987.

'Building Stories: Greg, Fleay, and the Plot of *2 Seven Deadly Sins*'. *MaRDiE* 4 (1989): 53–62.

'Casting the *Hamlet* Quartos: The Limit of Eleven'. In Thomas Clayton ed. *The 'Hamlet' First Published (Q1, 1603)* (q.v.), pp.179–94.

McNeir, Waldo F. 'Robert Greene and *John of Bordeaux*'. *PMLA* 44 (1949): 781–801.

'Reconstructing the Conclusion of *John of Bordeaux*'. *PMLA* 66 (1951): 540–43.

Mahood, M. M. *Bit Parts in Shakespeare's Plays*. Cambridge University Press, 1992.

Marcus, Leah S. *Puzzling Shakespeare: Local Reading and Its Discontents*. Berkeley: University of California Press, 1988

'Textual Indeterminacy and Ideological Difference: The Case of *Doctor Faustus*'. *RD* n.s. 20 (1989): 1–29.

'Levelling Shakespeare: Local Customs and Local Texts'. *SQ* 42 (1991): 168–78.

'The Shakespearean Editor as Shrew-Tamer'. *ELR* 22 (1992): 177–200.

Unediting the Renaissance: Shakespeare, Marlowe, Milton. London: Routledge, forthcoming.

Marsden, Jean I. ed. *The Appropriation of Shakespeare: Post-Renaissance Reconstructions of the Works and the Myth*. New York: St Martin's Press, 1991.

Marsh, R. C. 'The Shakespeare First Folio'. *TLS* 21 October 1955: 621.

Marshall, Sybil. Interview in *The Guardian*. 9 February 1993.

A Nest of Magpies. London: Michael Joseph, 1993.

Marx, Joan C. '"Soft, Who Have We Here?": The Dramatic Technique of *The Old Wives Tale*'. *RD* n.s. 12 (1981): 117–43.

Maxwell, Baldwin. *Studies in the Shakespeare Apocrypha*. New York: Columbia University Press, 1956.

Maxwell, J. C. 'How Bad Is the Text of *The Jew of Malta*?' *MLR* 48 (1953): 435–8.

Maxwell, J. C. ed. *W. W. Greg. Collected Papers*. Oxford: Clarendon Press, 1966.

Meads, Dorothy M. *Diary of Lady Margaret Hoby 1599–1605*. London: George Routledge & Sons, 1930.

Meagher, John C. 'Economy and Recognition: Thirteen Shakespearean Puzzles'. *SQ* 35 (1984): 7–21.

Meagher, John C. ed. *The Death of Robert, Earl of Huntingdon*. MSR. Oxford, 1967 (for 1965).

Melchiori, Giorgio. 'Peter, Balthasar, and Shakespeare's Art of Doubling'. *MLR* 78 (1983): 777–92.

Merriam, Thomas V. N. and Robert Matthews. 'Neural Computation in Stylometry II: An Application to the Works of Shakespeare and Marlowe'. *Literary and Linguistic Computing* 9 (1994): 1–6.

Meyer, Ann R. 'Shakespeare's Art and the Texts of *King Lear*'. *SB* 47 (1994): 128–46.

Miller, Stephen. '*A Shrew* and the Theories'. In Thomas L. Berger and Laurie Maguire eds. *Textual Formations and Reformations* (*q.v.*).

Mitchell, W. F. *English Pulpit Oratory from Andrewes to Tillotson*. London: SPCK, 1932.

Mommsen, Tycho. '*Hamlet*, 1603 and *Romeo and Juliet*, 1597'. *The Athenaeum* 29 (1857): 182.

Montgomery, William. 'The Original Staging of *The First Part of the Contention*'. *Shakespeare Survey* 41 (1988): 13–22.

Mooney, Michael E. 'Text and Performance: *Romeo and Juliet*, Quartos 1 and 2'. *Colby Quarterly* 26 (1990): 122–32.

Morris, Brian ed. '*Tis Pity She's a Whore*. New Mermaids. London: Ernest Benn, 1968.

Morrison, Peter. 'A Cangoun in Zombieland: Middleton's Teratological *Changeling*'. In Kenneth Friedenreich ed. '*Accompaninge the Players*'. *Essays Celebrating Thomas Middleton, 1580–1980*. New York: AMS Press, 1983, pp.219–41.

Moseley, C. W. R. D. *William Shakespeare: Richard III*. Harmondsworth: Penguin, 1989.

Moxon, Joseph. *Mechanick Exercises on the Whole Art of Printing*. Edited by Herbert Davis and Harry Carter. 2nd edition. London: Oxford University Press, 1962.

Muir, Kenneth and F. P. Wilson eds. *Jack Straw*. MSR. Oxford, 1957.

Mulryan, John. 'Literacy in an Illiterate Medium: The Paradox of Learned Clarity in the Sermons of Lancelot Andrewes'. In Gordon Coggins and C. Stuart Hunter eds. *Literacy and Illiteracy in the Renaissance*. St Catherines and Guelph, ONT: Victoria College, 1987, pp.131–43.

Musgrove, S. 'The First Quarto of *Pericles* Reconsidered'. *SQ* 29 (1978): 389–406.

Needham, Paul. *The Bradshaw Method*. Hanes Foundation Lecture. Chapel Hill: University of North Carolina Press, 1988.

Oates, J. C. T. *et al.* 'Walter Wilson Greg 9 July 1875–4 March 1959'. *Library*, 5th series, 14 (1959): 151–74.

Okerlund, Gerda. 'The Quarto Version of *Henry V* as a Stage Adaptation'. *PMLA* 49 (1934): 810–34.

Oliphant, E. H. C. 'How Not to Play the Game of Parallels'. *JEGP* 28 (1929): 1–15.

Oliver, H. J. ed. '*Dido Queen of Carthage*' and '*The Massacre at Paris*'. London: Methuen, 1968.

 The Merry Wives of Windsor. New Arden. London: Methuen, 1971.

 The Taming of the Shrew. Oxford: Clarendon Press, 1982.

Ong, Walter J. 'Historical Backgrounds of Elizabethan and Jacobean
Punctuation Theory'. *PMLA* 59 (1944): 349–60.

'Oral Residue in Tudor Prose Style'. *PMLA* 80 (June, 1965): 145–54.

'Milton's Logical Epic and Evolving Consciousness'. *Proceedings of the
American Philosophical Society* 120 (1976): 295–305.

'African Talking Drums and Oral Noetics'. *NLH* 8 (1977): 411–29.

'Text as Interpretation: Mark and After'. In John Miles Foley ed. *Oral
Tradition in Literature* (*q.v.*), pp.147–69.

Orality and Literacy. The Technologizing of the Word. London:
Methuen, 1982, reprinted Routledge, 1991.

Ormerod, David and Christopher Wortham eds. *Dr Faustus: The A-Text*.
Nedlands: University of Western Australia Press, 1985.

Ornstein, Robert. 'Marlowe and God: The Tragic Theology of *Dr Faustus*'.
PMLA 83 (1968): 1378–85.

Owst, G. R. *Literature and Pulpit in Medieval England*. Oxford: Basil
Blackwell, 1961.

Preaching in Medieval England. Cambridge University Press, 1926.

Pafford, J. H. P. ed. *The Soddered Citizen*. MSR. Oxford, 1936.

Palmer, D. J. *The Rise of English Studies*. Oxford University Press, 1965.

Parrott, T. M. ed. *The Plays and Poems of George Chapman. Vol. II: The
Comedies*. London: Routledge, 1914.

Parry, Adam ed. *The Making of Homeric Verse: The Collected Papers of
Milman Parry*. Oxford: Clarendon Press, 1971.

Patrick, David Lyall. *The Textual History of 'Richard III'*. Stanford
University Press, 1936.

Patterson, Annabel. 'Back by Popular Demand: The Two Versions of *Henry
V*'. *RD* n.s. 19 (1988): 29–62.

Shakespeare and the Popular Voice. Oxford: Blackwell, 1989.

Pease, Howard. *The Lord Wardens of the Marches of England and Scotland*.
London: Constable, 1913.

Petti, Anthony G. *English Literary Hands from Chaucer to Dryden*. London:
Edward Arnold, 1977.

Pettitt, Thomas. 'Mrs Brown's "Lass of Roch Royal" and the Golden Age
of Scottish Balladry'. *Jahrbuch für Volkslieder Forschung* 29 (1984):
13–31.

'Formulaic Dramaturgy in *Doctor Faustus*'. In Kenneth Friedenreich,
Roma Gill, and Constance B. Kuriyama eds. *'A Poet and a filthy*

Playmaker': New Essays on Christopher Marlowe. New York: AMS
    Press, 1988, pp.167–91.

'Oral Transmission, Incremental Repetition, and the "Bad" Quarto:
    Folkloristic Perspectives on the Text of *Doctor Faustus*'. Paper
    circulated to the workshop on '*Doctor Faustus*, A and B Texts',
    Marlowe Society of America Second International Conference,
    Oxford, August 1988.

Pinciss, G. M. 'The Queen's Men, 1583–1592'. *Theatre Survey* 11 (1970): 50–65.

Pinciss, G. M. and G. R. Proudfoot eds. *The Faithful Friends*. MSR.
    Oxford, 1975.

Pitcher, John ed. *Hymen's Triumph*. MSR. Oxford, 1994.

Pollard, A. F. 'The First MP Journalist. A Reporter of Things Seen'. *The
    Times* 1 October 1932: 11–12

Pollard, A. W. *Shakespeare Folios and Quartos*. London: Methuen, 1909.

    King Richard II. A New Quarto. London: Bernard Quaritch, 1916.

    Shakespeare's Fight with the Pirates. Cambridge University Press, 1920,
    reprinted 1967.

    'Elizabethan Spelling as a Literary and Bibliographical Clue'. *Library*,
    4th series, 4 (1923–4): 1–8.

    Note on 'The Aims of Bibliography'. *Library*, 4th series, 13 (1932–3):
    255–8.

Pollard, A. W. ed. *Shakespeare's Hand in the Play of 'Sir Thomas More'*.
    Cambridge University Press, 1923.

Pollard, A. W. and J. Dover Wilson. 'The "Stolne and Surreptitious"
    Shakespearian Texts I: Why Some of Shakespeare's Plays were
    Pirated'. *TLS* 9 January 1919: 18.

Potter, Lois. '"Nobody's Perfect": Actors' Memories and Shakespeare's
    Plays of the 1590s'. *Shakespeare Survey* 42 (1990): 85–97.

Potter, Stephen. *The Muse in Chains: A Study in Education*. London:
    Jonathan Cape, 1937.

Price, Hereward, T. *A Fruitfull Sermon by Henrie Smith*. Halle: Max
    Niemeyer, 1922.

    'Another Shorthand Sermon'. *Essays and Studies in English and
    Comparative Literature. University of Michigan Publications in
    Language and Literature* 10 (1933): 161–87.

    'Towards a Scientific Method of Textual Criticism for the Elizabethan
    Drama'. *JEGP* 36 (1937): 151–67.

Proudfoot, G. R. ed. *A Knack to Know a Knave*. MSR. Oxford, 1963.
　　'Speech Prefixes, Compositors and Copy in Plays from the
　　　　Shakespeare *Apocrypha*'. In George Walton Williams ed.
　　　　Shakespeare's Speech-Headings (*q.v.*), pp.121–32.
Purcell, Sally. *George Peele*. South Hinksey: Carcanet, 1972.
Rasmussen, Eric. 'Setting Down What the Clown Spoke: Improvisation,
　　　　Hand B, and *The Book of Sir Thomas More*'. *Library*, 6th series, 13
　　　　(1991): 126–36.
　　'Rehabilitating the A-Text of Marlowe's *Doctor Faustus*'. *SB* 46 (1993):
　　　　221–38.
　　A Textual Companion to 'Doctor Faustus'. Manchester University Press,
　　　　1993.
Rees, Ennis. 'Chapman's *Blind Beggar* and the Marlovian Hero'. *JEGP* 57
　　　　(1958): 60–3.
Reibetanz, John. 'Hieronimo in Decimosexto: A Private-Theater
　　　　Burlesque'. *RD* n.s. 5 (1972): 89–121.
Rennert, H. A. *The Spanish Stage in the Time of Lope de Vega*. New York:
　　　　The Hispanic Society of America, 1909.
Renwick, W. L. ed. *John of Bordeaux*. MSR. Oxford, 1935.
Reynolds, George F. '*Mucedorus*, Most Popular Elizabethan Play?' In
　　　　Josephine W. Bennett, Oscar Cargill, and Vernon Hall Jr. eds.
　　　　Studies in the English Renaissance Drama. New York University
　　　　Press, 1959, pp.248–68.
Roberts, Jeanne Addison. '*The Merry Wives* Q and F: The Vagaries of
　　　　Progress'. *Shakespeare Studies* 8 (1975): 143–75.
Rose, Steven. *The Making of Memory*. London: Transworld Publishers,
　　　　1992.
Rosenberg, Bruce A. 'Oral Literature in the Middle Ages'. In John Miles
　　　　Foley ed. *Oral Traditional Literature* (*q.v.*), pp.440–51.
Ross, Bruce, M. *Remembering the Personal Past*. Oxford University Press,
　　　　1991.
Ruano de la Haza, José M. 'An Early Rehash of Lope's *Peribañez*'. *Bulletin
　　　　of the Comediantes* 35 (1983): 5–29.
Ruano de la Haza, José M. and J. E. Varey eds. *Peribañez y el Commendador
　　　　de Ocaña*. London: Tamesis Texts, 1980.
St Clare Byrne, Muriel. 'Anthony Munday's Spelling as a Literary Clue'.
　　　　Library, 4th series, 4 (1923–4): 9–23.

'Bibliographical Clues in Collaborate Plays'. *Library*, 4th series, 13
(1933): 21–48.

Sampley, Arthur M. 'The Text of Peele's *David and Bethsabe*'. *PMLA* 46
(1931): 659–71.

Sams, Eric. 'Viewpoint: Shakespeare's Text and Common Sense'. *TLS* 2
September 1983: 933–4.

'The Timing of the *Shrews*'. *N & Q* 32 (1985): 33–45.

'The Troublesome Wrangle over *King John*' *N & Q* 35 (1988): 41–4.

'Taboo or Not Taboo? The Text, Dating and Authorship of *Hamlet*,
1589–1623'. *Hamlet Studies* 10 (1988): 12–46.

'Shakespeare, or Bottom? The Myth of "Memorial Reconstruction"'.
Encounter January 1989: 41–5.

Savage, James E. 'The "Gaping Wounds" in the Text of *Philaster*'. *PQ* 28
(1949): 443–57.

Sayers, Dorothy L. ed. *Great Short Stories of Detection, Mystery, and Horror*.
Vol.1. 1928. Reprinted London: Victor Gollancz, 1947.

Schoell, Franck L. 'G. Chapman's "Commonplace Book"'. *Mod. Phil.* 17
(1919): 199–218.

Schoenbaum, Samuel. *Internal Evidence and Elizabethan Dramatic
Authorship*. London: Edward Arnold, 1966.

Shakespeare, William. (For the editions of Shakespeare's plays, see under
the appropriate editor.)

Shapiro, I. A. '*Richard II* or *Richard III* or ...?' *SQ* 9 (1958): 204–6.

'Stenography and "Bad Quartos"'. *TLS* 13 May 1960: 305.

Sharpe, Robert Boies. *The Real War of the Theatres*. Boston, MA: Heath
and Co., 1935.

Shaw, Phillip. '*Sir Thomas Wyat* and the Scenario of *Lady Jane*'. *MLQ* 13
(1952): 227–38.

Shepard, William P. 'Recent Theories of Textual Criticism'. *Mod. Phil.* 28
(1930–1): 129–41.

Sherbo, Arthur. 'Three Additions to the Canon of Dr W. W. Greg's
Writings'. *Library*, 6th series, 14 (1992): 144–5.

Sider, J. W. ed. *The Troublesome Raigne of John, King of England*. New York:
Garland, 1979.

Silk, Michael. *Homer. The Iliad*. Cambridge University Press, 1987.

Simpson, E. M. *A Study of the Prose Works of John Donne*. 2nd edition.
Oxford: Clarendon Press, 1948.

Sisson, C. J. Review of R. B. McKerrow. *Introduction to Bibliography*. *Library*, 4th series, 8 (1927–8): 478–82.

Sisson, C. J. ed. *Believe As You List*. MSR. Oxford, 1928.

Smart, John Semple. *Shakespeare: Truth and Tradition*. London: Edward Arnold, 1928.

Smidt, Kristian. *'Iniurious Impostors' and 'Richard III'*. Oslo: Norwegian Universities Press, 1964.

   'Repetition, Revision, and Editorial Greed in Shakespeare's Play Texts'. *Cahiers Elisabéthains* 34 (1988): 25–37.

Sorlien, Robert Parker ed. *The Diary of John Manningham of the Middle Temple, 1602–1603*. Hanover, NH: University Press of New England, 1976.

Sprinchorn, Evert. 'Shakespeare's Bad Quarto'. *TLS* 21 January 1994: 15; 1 April 1994: 15.

Spurgeon, Caroline F. E. *Shakespeare's Imagery and What it Tells Us*. Cambridge University Press, 1935.

Stone, P. W. K. *The Textual History of 'King Lear'*. London: Scolar Press, 1980.

Stoppard, Tom. *The Real Thing*. London: Faber and Faber, 1982.

Sutcliffe, Peter. *The Oxford University Press: An Informal History*. Oxford: Clarendon Press, 1978.

Swaen, A. E. H. ed. *James 4*. MSR. Oxford, 1921.

Tanselle, G. Thomas. 'The Life and Work of Fredson Bowers'. *SB* 46 (1993): 1–154.

Taylor, Gary. *Three Studies in the Text of 'Henry V'*. See Stanley Wells, *Modernizing Shakespeare's Spelling*.

   'The Transmission of *Pericles'*. *PBSA* 80 (1986): 193–217.

   'The Rhetoric of Textual Criticism'. *TEXT* 4 (1988): 39–57.

   Reinventing Shakespeare. 1989. London: Vintage, 1991.

Taylor, Gary and Michael Warren eds. *The Division of the Kingdoms*. Oxford: Clarendon Press, 1983.

Taylor, George Coffin. 'The Strange Case of Du Bartas in *The Taming of A Shrew'*. Part II of 'Two Notes on Shakespeare'. *PQ* 20 (1941): 373–6.

Thaler, Alwin. *'Faire Em* (and Shakespeare's Company?) in Lancashire'. *PMLA* 46 (1931): 647–58.

Thomas, Keith. 'The Meaning of Literacy in Early Modern England'. In
     G. Baumann ed. *The Written Word: Literacy in Transition*. Oxford:
     Clarendon Press, 1986, pp.97–131.

Thomas, Sidney. '*Hamlet* Q1: First Version or Bad Quarto?' In Thomas
     Clayton ed. *The 'Hamlet' First Published (Q1, 1603) (q.v.)*,
     pp.249–56.

     'The Myth of the Authorized Shakespeare Quartos'. *SQ* 27 (1976):
     186–92.

Thomson, Leslie. 'One Quarto > Two Bookkeepers > Three Texts?' Paper
     delivered to SAA annual meeting, Albuquerque, NM, 14 April
     1994.

Thorp, Willard, *The Triumph of Realism in Elizabethan Drama, 1558–1612*.
     Princeton University Press, 1928.

Thwaite, Ann. *Edmund Gosse: A Literary Landscape 1849–1928*. London:
     Secker and Warburg, 1984.

Tillyard, E. M. W. *The Muse Unchained*. London: Bowes & Bowes,
     1958.

Tomlinson, W. *Life in Northumberland During the Sixteenth Century*.
     London: Walter Scott, 1897.

Trousdale, Marion. 'Shakespeare's Oral Text'. *RD* n.s. 12 (1981): 95–115.

     'Diachronic and Synchronic: Critical Bibliography and the Acting of
     Plays'. In Bernhard Fabian and Kurt Tetzeli von Rosador eds.
     Shakespeare: Text, Language, Criticism (q.v.), pp.304–14.

     'A Second Look at Critical Bibliography and the Acting of Plays'. *SQ*
     41 (1990): 87–96.

Trussler, Simon ed. *Dr Faustus*. Swan Theatre Plays. London: Methuen,
     1989.

Turner, Robert K. ed. *Philaster*. In Fredson Bowers gen. ed. *The Dramatic
     Works in the Beaumont and Fletcher Canon*. Vol.I. Cambridge
     University Press, 1966.

     The Maid's Tragedy. In Fredson Bowers gen. ed. *The Dramatic Works in
     the Beaumont and Fletcher Canon*. Vol.II. Cambridge University
     Press, 1970.

Ure, Peter ed. *Richard 2*. London: Methuen, 1961.

Urkowitz, Steven. *Shakespeare's Revision of 'King Lear'*. Princeton
     University Press, 1980.

'Reconsidering the Relationship of Quarto and Folio Texts of *Richard III'*. *ELR* 16 (1986): 442–66.

'"Well-sayd olde Mole": Burying Three *Hamlet*s in Modern Editions'. In Georgianna Ziegler ed. *Shakespeare Study Today*. New York: AMS Press, 1986, pp.37–70.

'"If I Mistake in Those Foundations Which I Build Upon": Peter Alexander's Textual Analysis of Henry VI Parts 2 and 3'. *ELR* 18 (1988): 230–56.

'Good News about "Bad" Quartos'. In Maurice Charney ed. *"Bad" Shakespeare: Revaluations of the Shakespeare Canon*. London and Toronto: Associated University Presses, 1988, pp.189–206.

'"Five Women Eleven Ways": Changing Images of Shakespearean Characters in the Earliest Texts'. In Werner Habicht *et al.* eds. *Images of Shakespeare* (*q.v.*), pp.292–304.

'Back to Basics: Thinking about the *Hamlet* First Quarto'. In Thomas Clayton ed. *The 'Hamlet' First Published* (*q.v.*), pp.257–91.

'"Do me the kindnes to looke vpon this" and "Heere, read, read": An Invitation to the Pleasures of Textual/Sexual Di(Per)versity'. Paper presented at the SAA annual meeting, Kansas City, MO, 1992.

'"All things is hansome now": Murderers Nominated by Numbers in Variant Texts of *2 Henry VI* and *Richard III'*. In George Walton Williams ed. *Shakespeare's Speech-Headings* (*q.v.*), pp.101–20.

Vega, Lope de. *Peribáñez and the Comendador of Ocaña*. Parallel-text edition. Translated by James Lloyd. Warminster: Aris and Phillips, 1990.

Vickers, Brian. '*Hamlet* by Dogberry'. Review of Graham Holderness and Bryan Loughrey eds. *The Tragicall Historie of Hamlet Prince of Denmark*. *TLS* 24 December 1993: 5–6.

'Shakespeare's Bad Quarto'. *TLS* 4 February 1994: 15; 4 March 1994: 15; 29 July 1994: 15.

Vinaver, Eugene ed. *The Works of Thomas Malory*. Oxford: Clarendon Press, 1967.

Vincent, C. J. 'Further Repetitions in the Works of Robert Greene'. *PQ* 18 (1939): 73–7.

Walker, Alice. 'The 1622 Quarto and the First Folio Text of *Othello'*. *Shakespeare Survey* 5 (1952): 16–24.

Walker, Alice and J. D. Wilson eds. *Othello*. Cambridge University Press, 1969.

Walter, John H. ed. *Henry V*. London: Methuen, 1954.

Warren, Michael. 'Quarto and Folio *King Lear* and the Interpretation of Albany and Edgar'. In David Bevington and Jay L. Halio eds. *Shakespeare, Pattern of Excelling Nature*. Newark, NJ and London: University of Delaware Press, 1978, pp.95–107.

'*Doctor Faustus*: The Old Man and the Text'. *ELR* 11 (1981): 111–47.

'Greene's *Orlando*: W. W. Greg Furioso'. In Thomas L. Berger and Laurie Maguire eds. *Textual Formations and Reformations* (*q.v.*).

Wasson, John. 'Elizabethan and Jacobean Touring Companies'. *Theatre Notebook* 42 (1988): 51–7.

Watts, S. J. and S. J. Watts. *From Border to Middle Shire Northumberland*. Leicester, NJ: Leicester University Press, 1975.

Webster, John. 'Oral Form and Written Craft in Spenser's *Faerie Queene*'. *SEL* 16 (1976): 75–93.

Wells, Stanley, and Gary Taylor. *Modernizing Shakespeare's Spelling* with *Three Studies in the Text of 'Henry V'*. Oxford: Clarendon Press, 1979.

Wells, Stanley and Gary Taylor with John Jowett and William Montgomery. *William Shakespeare: A Textual Companion*. Oxford: Clarendon Press, 1987.

Werstine, Paul. 'Provenance and Printing History in Two Revels Editions: Review Article'. *MaRDiE* 1 (1984): 243–62.

'McKerrow's "Suggestion" and Twentieth-Century Shakespeare Textual Criticism', *RD* n.s. 19 (1988): 149–73.

'The Textual Mystery of *Hamlet*'. *SQ* 39 (1988): 1–26.

'"Foul Papers" and "Prompt-Books": Printer's Copy for Shakespeare's *Comedy of Errors*'. *SB* 41 (1988): 232–46.

'Narratives About Printed Shakespeare Texts: "Foul Papers" and "Bad" Quartos'. *SQ* 41 (1990): 65–86.

'Texts on Tour'. Paper delivered to the SAA annual meeting, Philadelphia, PA, 1990.

'Touring and the Construction of Shakespeare Textual Criticism'. In Thomas L. Berger and Laurie Maguire eds. *Textual Formations and Reformations* (*q.v.*).

White, Martin ed. *Arden of Faversham*. New Mermaids. London: Ernest Benn, 1982.

Whitworth, Charles W. ed. *Three Sixteenth-Century Comedies*. London: Ernest Benn, 1984.

Willey, Basil. *Cambridge and Other Memories 1920–1953*. London: Chatto and Windus, 1968.

Williams, George Walton ed. *Shakespeare's Speech-Headings*. New York: AMS Press, 1995, forthcoming.

Wilson, F. P. *The Plague in Shakespeare's London*. Oxford University Press, 1927.

   'Sir Walter Wilson Greg 1875–1959'. *PBA* 45 (1959): 307–34.

   Shakespeare and the New Bibliography, revised and edited by Helen Gardner. Oxford: Clarendon Press, 1970.

Wilson, F. P. with John Dover Wilson. 'Sir Edmund Kerchever Chambers 1866–1954'. *PBA* 42 (1956): 267–85.

Wilson, John Dover. 'Alfred William Pollard 1859–1944'. *PBA* 31 (1945): 257–306.

   'Shakespeare's *Richard III* and *The True Tragedy of Richard the Third*, 1594'. *SQ* 3 (1952): 299–306.

   Milestones on the Dover Road. London: Faber and Faber, 1969.

   The Manuscript of Shakespeare's 'Hamlet' and the Problems of its Transmission. 2 vols. Cambridge University Press, 1963.

Wine, M. L. ed. *Arden of Feversham*. Revels. London: Methuen, 1973.

Wright, Louis B. 'A Note on Dramatic Piracy'. *MLN* 43 (1928): 256–8.

Wright, Ronald. *Stolen Continents*. Toronto: Viking Penguin, 1992.

Yates, Frances A. *The Art of Memory*. London: Routledge & Kegan Paul, 1966.

Younghughes, S. Brigid and Harold Jenkins eds. *The Fatal Marriage*. MSR. Oxford, 1958.

Index